A HISTORY OF BLACK AND ASIAN
WRITING IN BRITAIN,
1700–2000

This is the first extended study of black and Asian writing in Britain over the last 250 years. Beginning with authors who arrived as immigrants or slaves in the mid eighteenth century, Lyn Innes includes a detailed discussion of works that were often enormously popular in their own time but are almost unknown to contemporary readers. Innes' fascinating study reveals a history of vigorous and fertile interaction between black, Asian, and white intellectuals and communities, and an enormously rich and varied literary culture which was already in existence before the post-war efflorescence of black and Asian writing. Utilizing a wealth of new archival material, Innes examines their work as part of an acceptance of and challenge to British cultural and ideological discourses. This volume offers a rich historical background for understanding contemporary British multicultural society and culture, and will be of interest to literary and cultural historians.

LYN INNES is Professor of Postcolonial Literatures at the University of Kent, Canterbury. She is the author of books on Chinua Achebe, African literature and Irish literature, and articles on African American and black British writers.

A HISTORY OF
BLACK AND ASIAN
WRITING IN BRITAIN,
1700–2000

C.L. INNES
University of Kent, Canterbury

CAMBRIDGE
UNIVERSITY PRESS

PUBLISHED BY THE PRESS SYNDICATE OF THE UNIVERSITY OF CAMBRIDGE
The Pitt Building, Trumpington Street, Cambridge CB2 1RP, United Kingdom

CAMBRIDGE UNIVERSITY PRESS
The Edinburgh Building, Cambridge, CB2 2RU, UK
40 West 20th Street, New York, NY 10011-4211, USA
477 Williamstown Road, Port Melbourne, VIC 3207, Australia
Ruiz de Alarcón 13, 28014 Madrid, Spain
Dock House, The Waterfront, Cape Town 8001, South Africa

http://www.cambridge.org

© C.L. Innes 2002

First published 2002

Printed in the United Kingdom at the University Press, Cambridge

Typeface Baskerville Monotype 11/12.5 pt   *System* LATEX 2ε   [TB]

A catalogue record for this book is available from the British Library

Library of Congress Cataloguing in Publication data

Innes, Catherine Lynette.
A history of Black and Asian writing in Britain / C.L. Innes.
p. cm.
Includes bibliographical references and index.
ISBN 0 521 64327 9 (hardback)
1. English literature – Black authors – History and criticism.   2. English literature –
Asian authors – History and criticism.   3. Blacks – Great Britain – Intellectual life.
4. Asians – Great Britain – Intellectual life.   5. Blacks in literature.
6. Asians in literature.   I. Title.
PR120.B55 I55   2002
820.9'896041 – dc21   2002025662

ISBN 0 521 64327 9 hardback

Contents

Preface and acknowledgements

In 1870 my great-grandfather travelled from Bengal to London to petition parliament for recompense for the lands taken over by the East
India Company from his family a century before. Despite considerable
support from members of parliament, especially those from Ireland, the
petition was unsuccessful. He remained in England for ten years, married the Englishwoman who became my great-grandmother, and wrote
and published a now forgotten book. After his return to India in 1880,
his two sons were sent to Dulwich College, with the requirement that
they should receive a good Muslim education. The younger son, my
grandfather, subsequently emigrated to Australia.

At school in Australia, I was intermittently and dimly troubled by the
awareness that my family's story could find no place in the British history and literature that we were taught. Only when I myself emigrated to
Britain in the 1970s did I begin to seek more consciously and actively for
a wider pattern which might make my own small piece seem less anoma-
lous. Here the work of historians such as Peter Fryer, Paul Edwards, and
Rozina Visram has proved invaluable. The attempt to follow through
the more extensive narrative of the interaction between South Asian,
black and more familiar British writers in the context of a wider cultural
and political history has been fascinating and sometimes frustrating. But
now much new work is being done by scholars such as David Dabydeen,
Anne Walmsley, Vincent Carretta, Susheila Nasta, and Sara Salih, and
although many pieces remain missing, a clearer pattern is beginning to
emerge. This book is my attempt to extend the outline and help fill in
the details.

I wish to acknowledge the generous contributions of many colleagues
and scholars, who have read and discussed sections of this study, brought
material to my notice, or have allowed me to see unpublished work in
progress. I am especially grateful to Vincent Carretta, Denise deCaires
Narain, Ian Duffield, Rod Edmond, Abdulrazak Gurnah, Stephanie

Newell, Susheila Nasta, Sara Salih, Martin Scofield, Kate Teltscher, Gillian Whitlock, and Robert Young. Their willingness to see this research as a collaborative enterprise rather than a competition is particularly encouraging in these days of ratings and league tables. Susheila's reading and commentary on the whole first draft of the book have been invaluable. I also owe a considerable debt to the many postgraduate students whose own work and discussion have informed my thinking and awareness, and who have been party to a mutual encouragement pact. In recent years, these include Pamela Albert, Emma Bainbridge, Jennifer Ballantine-Perera, Jackie Belanger, Maggie Bowers, Stephen Cowden, Paul Delaney, Delia Jarrett-Macaulay, Furrukh Khan, Eugene McNulty, Kaori Nagai, and Mark Stein. To Delia and Mark I owe an unusually large debt, for their dissertation work on Una Marson and black British fiction respectively provided conceptual, contextual, and factual material which helped inform this book. Mark has also researched and written most of the biobibliographies at the end. I also wish to acknowledge Rachel Scofield's assistance in compiling the index and proofreading the manuscript.

I am grateful to the Arts and Humanities Research Board and the School of English at the University of Kent for grants which made it possible for me to undertake the research for this book. I am also grateful to the editorial and production staff at Cambridge University Press, especially Ray Ryan, who consistently urged on the project, and Rose Bell, whose meticulous copy-editing eradicated many faults.

Sections of Chapter One have appeared in different form in *Reading the New Literatures in a Postcolonial Era*, ed. Susheila Nasta (Cambridge: Boydell and Brewer, 2000) and in *Bullán: A Journal of Irish Studies*. I am grateful to the English Association and to *Bullán* for permission to reprint these sections.

Chronological table of historical and literary events
1560–1960

HISTORICAL EVENTS		LITERARY EVENTS	
1558	Loss of Calais; death of Mary; accession of Elizabeth I		
1562	Hawkyns begins English slave trade of Africans		
1577	Drake begins his circumnavigation		
1588	Defeat of Spanish Armada	1588–92	Shakespeare's early plays including *1,2,3 Henry VI*, *Taming of the Shrew*, *Love's Labours Lost*, *Richard III*
		1590	Spenser, *Faerie Queene* (I–III); Lodge, *Rosalynde*
1600	Elizabeth I grants trading charter to East India Company		
		1601–4	Shakespeare plays including *Hamlet*, *Twelfth Night*, *Measure for Measure*
1603	Death of Elizabeth; accession of James VI as James I; union of the crowns of England and Scotland		

		1604–8	Shakespeare plays including *Othello*, *King Lear*, *Macbeth*, *Antony and Cleopatra*, *Coriolanus*
1606	Charter granted to Virginia Company		
		1611	'Authorized' version of Bible
1616	Death of Shakespeare		
1620	Pilgrim Fathers sail for America		
1625	Death of James I; accession of Charles I		
1640	Long Parliament summoned		
1649	Trial and execution of Charles I		
1649–52	Cromwell's campaigns in Ireland and Scotland		
1653	Cromwell becomes Lord Protector		
1660	Restoration of Charles II; reopening of theatres		
1665	Plague in London		
		1667	Dryden, *Annus Mirabilis*; Milton, *Paradise Lost*
1688	'Glorious Revolution'; James II flees; William III and Mary II succeed		
		1690	Locke, *Essay Concerning Human Understanding*
		1700	Congreve, *The Way of the World*
1701	War of Spanish Succession; Great Britain allied against France		

1707	Act of Union between England and Scotland		
		1712	Pope, *The Rape of the Lock*
		1719	Defoe, *Robinson Crusoe*
		1726	Swift, *Gulliver's Travels*; Thomson, *Winter*
		1728	Gay, *Beggar's Opera*; Pope, *Dunciad* (1st Version)
		1747–9	Richardson, *Clarissa*
		1749	Fielding, *Tom Jones*
		1755	Johnson, *Dictionary*
1757	Conquest of India begins under General Clive		
1759	Wolfe takes Quebec	1759	Johnson, *Rasselas*
		1759–67	Sterne, *Tristram Shandy*
1760	Death of George II; accession of George III		
1763	Peace of Paris ends Seven Years War; British gains in India and North America		
		1766	Goldsmith, *The Vicar of Wakefield*
		1768	Sterne, *A Sentimental Journey*
		1772	Gronniosaw, *Narrative*
		1775	Sheridan, *The Rivals*
1776	American Declaration of Independence	1776–88	Gibbon, *Decline and Fall of the Roman Empire*
		1779–81	Johnson, *The Lives of the Poets*
1780	Gordon Riots		
1781	British forces defeated by Americans at Yorktown		

		1782	Publication of *The Letters of Ignatius Sancho*
1783	Independence of American Colonies recognized by Peace of Paris		
		1786	Clarkson, *Essay on the Slavery and Commerce of the Human Species*
1787	Association for the Abolition of the Slave Trade founded	1787	Cugoano, *Thoughts and Sentiments on the Evil and Wicked Traffic of Slavery*
1789	French Revolution; Fall of Bastille; Declaration of the Rights of Man	1789	Blake, *Songs of Innocence*; Equiano, *The Interesting Narrative*.
		1790	Burke, *Reflections on the Revolution in France*; Blake, *The Marriage of Heaven and Hell*
1791	Toussaint L'Ouverture leads insurrection in San Domingo (Haiti)	1791	Boswell, *Life of Samuel Johnson*; Paine, *The Rights of Man* (Part 1)
		1792	Wollstonecraft, *A Vindication of the Rights of Woman*; Holcroft, *Anna St Ives*
1793	Execution of Louis XVI; Reign of Terror; Britain and France at war		
		1794	*Travels of Dean Mahomet*
1796	Bonaparte's Italian campaign		
1798	Nelson's victory at Battle of the Nile; rebellion in Ireland	1798	Wordsworth and Coleridge, *Lyrical Ballads*; Wollstonecraft, *The Wrongs of Woman*
1800	Act of Union with Ireland	1800	Edgeworth, *Castle Rackrent*
1803	Renewal of war against France		

1804	Haiti gains independence		
1805	Nelson's victory at Trafalgar		
1807	Abolition of the slave-trade in the British Empire		
1808	Peninsular War begins		
1811	Prince of Wales becomes Regent; Luddite riots	1811	Austen, *Sense and Sensibility*
		1813	Austen, *Pride and Prejudice*; Shelley, *Queen Mab*
1814	Abdication of Napoleon; restoration of Louis XVIII; Stephenson's steam locomotive		
1815	Battle of Waterloo		
1819	Peterloo massacre		
		1824	Robert Wedderburn, *The Horrors of Slavery*
1829	Catholic Emancipation Act		
		1831	*The History of Mary Prince*
		1832	Tennyson, *Poems* (dated 1833)
1833	Abolition of Slavery in British Colonies; Keble's Assize sermon	1833	Carlyle, *Sartor Resartus*
		1836	Dickens, *Sketches by 'Boz'* and the first number of *Pickwick Papers* (1836–7)
1837	Death of William IV; accession of Victoria	1837	Roper, *Escape from American Slavery*
1838	'People's Charter' published; London–Birmingham Railway opened	1838	Dickens, *Nicholas Nickleby*

1842	Chartist riots; second presentation of Charter to Parliament; Copyright Act	1842	Tennyson, *Poems*; Browning, *Dramatic Lyrics*
1846	Famine in Ireland; repeal of Corn Laws		
		1847	Tennyson, *The Princess*; Charlotte Brontë, *Jane Eyre*; Emily Brontë, *Wuthering Heights*; Anne Brontë, *Agnes Grey*; Thackeray, *Vanity Fair* (1847–8)
1851	Great Exhibition; Louis Napoleon's *coup d'état*; Fugitive Slave Act, USA	1851–2	Harriet Beecher Stowe, *Uncle Tom's Cabin.*
		1852	Dickens, *Bleak House* (1852–3)
		1853	W.G. Allen, *Colour Prejudice in America*
1854	Crimean War breaks out; Battles of Alma, Inkerman, and Balaclava (with the charge of the Light Brigade); Preston cotton spinners strike; Working Man's College opened		
		1855	Tennyson, *Maud*; Kingsley, *West-ward Ho!*; Browning, *Men and Women*; Gaskell, *North and South*; Trollope, *The Warden*; Dickens, *Little Dorrit* (1855–7); John Brown, *Slave Life in Georgia*

1857	'Indian Mutiny'	1857	Mary Seacole, *The Wonderful Adventures of Mrs Seacole*
1858	India transferred to British Crown		
		1859	Dickens, *A Tale of Two Cities*; Eliot, *Adam Bede*; Meredith, *The Ordeal of Richard Feverel*; Mill, *On Liberty*; Darwin, *The Origin of Species*; Tennyson, *The Idylls of the King* (1859–72)
		1860	William Craft, *Running a Thousand Miles for Freedom*
1861	Victor Emanuel, King of United Italy; outbreak of American Civil War, death of Prince Consort		
1863	'Cotton Famine' in Lancashire	1863	Francis Fedric, *Slave Life in Virginia and Kentucky*
1865	Suppression of Jamaican rebellion by Governor Eyre; Emancipation of slaves in American south; assassination of Lincoln	1865	Arnold, *Essays in Criticism*; Carroll, *Alice in Wonderland*
1870	Married Woman's Property Act; Franco-Prussian War; Forster's Education Act; Papal States incorporated into Kingdom of Italy; death of Dickens		
1871	Paris Commune		
		1874	Hardy, *Far From the Madding Crowd*

1876	Victoria proclaimed Empress of India	1876	Eliot, *Daniel Deronda*
		1878	Hardy, *The Return of the Native*
1880	Gladstone, Prime Minister		
1882	British occupation of Egypt	1882	Thomas Johnson, *Twenty-Eight Years a Slave*
1884	Berlin Conference and division of Africa among European powers		
1885	Congress Party founded in India		
1887	Victoria's Golden Jubilee		
		1888	Kipling, *Plain Tales from the Hills*; Ward, *Robert Elsmere*
		1889	Stanford, *From Bondage to Liberty*
1890	Parnell falls as leader of Irish Home Rule Party after being cited in the O'Shea divorce case		
		1892	Shaw, *Widowers' Houses*; Yeats, *The Countess Cathleen*
1895	X-rays discovered	1895	Wilde, *The Importance of Being Earnest* and *An Ideal Husband*; Wells, *The Time Machine*
1896	Wireless telegraphy invented	1896	Hardy, *Jude the Obscure*; Housman, *A Shropshire Lad*; Shaw, *You Never Can Tell*
1897	Victoria's Diamond Jubilee	1897	Stoker, *Dracula*
		1898	Hardy, *Wessex Poems*
		1899	Conrad, *Heart of Darkness*

1899–1902	Boer War	1900	Conrad, *Lord Jim*
1900	International Pan-African Conference in London		
1901	Death of Victoria; accession of Edward VII	1901	Kipling, *Kim*; DuBois, *The Souls of Black Folk*; Cornelia Sorabji, *Love and Life behind the Purdah*
1903	First aeroplane flight; foundation of Women's Social and Political Union		
		1905	Shaw, *Major Barbara* and *Man and Superman*; Wells, *Kipps*
		1907	Synge, *The Playboy of the Western World*; Conrad, *The Secret Agent*
		1911	Duse Mohamed Ali, *In the Land of the Pharoahs*
1914	Home Rule Bill passed by Parliament; Britain declares war on Central Powers (4 August)		
1916	First battle of the Somme; Gallipoli Campaign; Easter Rising in Dublin		
		1917	Eliot, *Prufrock and Other Observations*
1918	Second battle of the Somme; final German offensive collapses; Armistice with Germany (11 November); Franchise Act granting the vote to women over thirty		

1919	Treaty of Versailles; Amritsar Massacre; Atlantic flown		
		1920	Owen, *Poems*; Lawrence, *Women in Love*; Shaw, *Heartbreak House*; Fry, *Vision and Design*
		1922	Eliot, *The Waste Land*; Joyce, *Ulysses*; Lawrence, *Fantasia of the Unconscious*
1924	First Labour Government	1924	Forster, *A Passage to India*; O'Casey, *Juno and the Paycock*; Coward, *The Vortex*
		1925	Woolf, *Mrs Dalloway*; Gerhardie, *The Polyglots*
1926	General Strike	1926	MacDiarmid, *A Drunk Man looks at the Thistle*
		1927	Woolf, *To the Lighthouse*
		1928	Yeats, *The Tower*; Lawrence, *Lady Chatterley's Lover*, Waugh, *Decline and Fall*
1930	World economic depression		
		1935	Mulk Raj Anand, *Untouchable*; George Orwell, *Burmese Days*
1936	Death of George V; accession of Edward VIII; abdication crisis; accession of George VI; Civil War breaks out in Spain; first of the Moscow show trials	1936	C.L.R. James, *Minty Alley*
		1937	Karen Blixen, *Out of Africa*

		1938	Jomo Kenyatta, *Facing Mount Kenya*; C.L.R. James, *The Black Jacobins*; Raja Rao, *Kanthapura*
1939	End of Civil War in Spain; Russo-German pact; Germany invades Poland (September); Britain and France declare war on Germany	1939	Joyce Cary, *Mister Johnson*
		1940	Mulk Raj Anand, *Across the Black Waters*
1941	Germany invades Russia; Japanese destroy US Fleet at Pearl Harbor		
1942	Fall of Singapore; British victory in North Africa at El Alamein		
1945	Surrender of Germany; atom bombs dropped on Hiroshima and Nagasaki; Labour Government elected		
1947	Independence of India and Pakistan		
1948	The British Empire becomes the British Commonwealth; *Empire Windrush* brings 492 West Indians to Britain	1948	Desani, *All about H. Hatterr*; Greene, *The Heart of the Matter*; Fry, *The Lady's Not for Burning*
		1949	Bowen, *The Heat of the Day*; Orwell, *Nineteen Eighty-four*; Eliot, *The Cocktail Party*
1950	Labour returned at election with reduced majority	1950	Auden, *Collected Shorter Poems*; Beckett, *Molloy* (first volume of trilogy)

1951	Conservative victory at General Election; Festival of Britain		
1952	Death of George VI; accession of Elizabeth II; Kenyan war of independence ('Mau Mau War') begins		
		1954	Rattigan, *Separate Tables*; Golding, *Lord of the Flies*; Amis, *Lucky Jim*
		1955	Larkin, *The Less Deceived*; Golding, *The Inheritors*; Beckett, *Waiting for Godot* (first British performance)
1956	Egypt nationalizes Suez Canal; Britain and France intervene and are obliged to withdraw; Soviet invasion of Hungary	1956	Golding, *Pincher Martin*; Wilson, *Anglo-Saxon Attitudes*; Osborne, *Look Back in Anger*; Selvon, *The Lonely Londoners*
1957	Ghana gains Independence	1957	Hughes, *The Hawk in the Rain*; Spark, *The Comforters*; Durrell, *Justine*; Osborne, *The Entertainer*
		1958	Chinua Achebe, *Things Fall Apart*
1960	Independence gained by a number of states in the Caribbean and Africa	1960	Pinter, *The Caretaker*; Wilson Harris, *The Palace of the Peacock*; Lamming, *The Pleasures of Exile*

Illustrations

Introduction

What do they know of England who only England know?
(Rudyard Kipling, 'The English Flag', 1891)

I do not deal in happiness, I deal in meaning.
(Richard Wright, *White Man Listen*, 1957)[1]

Mais, qu'est-ce que c'est donc un noir? Et d'abord, c'est de quelle couleur?
(Jean Genet, *Les Negres*, 1958)

Kipling's line quoted above refers to men who travelled away from England in the service of empire. But it might equally refer to those British writers of African and Asian descent who travel from other islands and continents to engage with British society and culture. This is the turn that C.L.R. James gives the line when he alludes to it in the preface to his autobiographical work, *Beyond a Boundary*, asking 'What do they know of cricket who only cricket know?', and asserting, 'If the ideas originated in the West Indies it was only in England and English life that I was able to track them down and test them. To establish his own identity, Caliban, after three centuries, must himself pioneer into regions Caesar never knew.'[2] In 1984, James commented thus on the importance of the perspective contributed by Britain's black community:

Those people who are in western civilization, who have grown up in it but yet are not completely part (made to feel and themselves feeling that they are outside) have a unique insight into their society. What such persons have to say, therefore, will give a new vision, a deeper and stronger insight into both western civilization and the black people in it.[3]

James was referring to the generation of young black people born in Britain after the wave of immigration from the Caribbean following World War II and recruited by British public services and private industries to help regenerate Britain. He would have extended this category to include the many immigrants recruited from the Indian subcontinent during those years. Recent years have seen a number of events and publications celebrating that first group of West Indian immigrants on the SS *Empire Windrush* in 1948, and the multiple achievements of black British and Asian British writers and artists during the past fifty years.[4] But relatively little has been said about the black and Asian writers who preceded them, who for over 150 years prior to World War II wrote of and to British communities, contributing distinctive insights as outsiders on the inside.

This book sets out to map and explore some of that preceding history of writing by black and Asian writers who since 1750 have made a home in Britain and made their voices heard, at least for a time. It begins with Ignatius Sancho, taken as a slave at the age of two years to England, and the author of a collection of letters, the first of which is dated 1766. The main body of this study concludes with 1948, a date which can be seen as both a new beginning with that fresh influx of settlers, and also a point at which many Asian, African, and Caribbean authors and activists who had been residing in Britain before and during the war years decided to return to countries newly independent, or on the verge of becoming so. What emerges from the century and a half preceding 1948 is not so much a tradition, as little is passed on from one writer to the next, as a series of recurring preoccupations and tropes. And what also emerges, in an age when European writers increasingly sought to authenticate an ordered and stable vision of the self and society, is the explicit or implicit acceptance among black and south Asian writers in Britain of a multiple identity. Such authors found little difficulty in presenting themselves or their characters as black *and* British, or African and English, or Indian and English, or Caribbean and Scottish, or various combinations of these identities. Their works assert a sense of core humanity and selfhood at the same time as they demonstrate their flexible performance of roles, emphasizing possibility and potentiality rather than fixed definitions. Thus Olaudah Equiano presents himself as an African while he is an Englishman named after a Swedish king, and affirms his identity as a free man while he is enslaved. He is an owner of slaves while declaring antagonism to slavery; he is a trader and skilled artisan, who takes pride in serving his master well; he asserts his love for his master as he asserts his anger at being betrayed; he participates in a scheme to repatriate Africans to Sierra Leone, while remaining an Englishman; he marries an English woman. A corollary of this sense of flexible identity and dual perspective is the inventiveness the writers display, both in terms of the content of their stories, and the forms and genres which they combine or devise.

Similarly, the reading of these texts raises questions about many of the categories which have become current in contemporary critical discourse. Do labels such as 'postcolonial' or 'New Literatures in English' used to refer to the profuse creative activity which during the last fifty years has emanated from areas previously colonised by England, apply to writers such as Ignatius Sancho, Olaudah Equiano, and Sake Dean Mahomed, whose writings were first published more than 200 years ago, who identified with the English and Anglo-Irish, and were at times themselves involved in imperial enterprises? The dictated narratives of Gronniosaw, Mary Prince, and John Brown, the use and recontextualization by Equiano, Dean Mahomed and others of passages from previous writers, the mingling of travel, anthropology, and autobiography, the intersection of private and public concerns in the writing and publication of their letters and autobiographies, all complicate and subvert assumptions about genre, authenticity, and the boundaries between oral and literary composition – assumptions which for many years have been taken for granted in our literary textbooks and classrooms.

While the categories 'black' and 'south Asian' are by no means unproblematic, they serve as convenient umbrellas to cover diverse groups of writers, many of whom would not have defined themselves in such terms. Both labels are applied retrospectively to include writers of African and south Asian (Indian subcontinental and Sri Lankan) descent, even though they themselves might have accepted or insisted upon other descriptions (such as 'sable', 'Ethiopian', 'brown', British, English, Scottish, 'coloured', 'Negro', Parsi, Punjabi, Trinidadian, Sinhalese, West Indian, and so on). Although I have generally adopted the overarching terms which are current today, at times I use the terms which the writers themselves seemed to prefer. It is not my assumption that the situation of writers of south Asian birth or descent in Britain is identical to that of writers of African descent, although the distinctions have sometimes been deliberately as well as inadvertently elided. For example, Indian children and women were often brought to England and sold as slaves in the eighteenth century, and during the eighteenth and nineteenth century Indians were frequently referred to as 'negroes' or 'moors'. More recently, describing themselves as 'black' or 'black British' has been a means of affirming a political alliance on the part of writers of Asian descent with writers of African descent. A comparative study of African British and south Asian-British writers will make possible a clearer analysis of the differences as well as the similarities between them and the ways in which they have been and often continue to be read. This book will consider the changing labels and contexts with which members of the black and Asian British communities identified themselves, and will also pay attention to how they were identified by others.

Many of the writers discussed in this book as belonging to a history of British literature might be claimed also by Africa, India, the Caribbean. The criteria for inclusion is that the writer has spent a good proportion of his or her writing life in Britain, and appears to be at least in part addressing his or her work to a British audience. For most of these authors there is a double or multiple identity, which may sometimes overlap with the categories in which they are placed by reviewers and critics, and sometimes not. My contention will be that the lack of a single ethnic or national identity produces a creative tension and interaction resulting in new literary forms and new narrative and poetic techniques. Where relevant, some reference to writing in Africa, the Indian subcontinent, the Caribbean and the Americas will also be made, since such writing often provides a model or counterpoint for black and Asian writers in Britain.

The authors I have selected all resided in Britain for at least five years, many becoming permanent settlers, and the works discussed are those published in Britain and/or addressed mainly to a British audience. Thus I have not included Phyllis Wheatley or Harriet Jacobs, each of whom spent only a few months in England. I have excluded the works C.L.R. James published before he left Trinidad, as well as those written during his fifteen-year residence in the United States; nor have I made more than passing reference to Duse Mohamed Ali's autobiographical writings published in Nigeria after his departure from England in 1923. And as the main focus of this historical survey ends with 1948, I have paid relatively little attention to works published by authors such as G.V. Desani, C.L.R. James, and Mulk Raj Anand after that date. The influx of immigrants from the Caribbean, the Indian subcontinent, and East Africa in the twenty-five years following 1948, creates for black and Asian writers within Britain a significantly different kind of audience and literature, more often addressed to or incorporating a multiracial and multicultural community of readers. At the same time, the achievement of independence by India, Pakistan, and Sri Lanka, followed within the next fifteen years by the majority of most African and Caribbean states, resulted in the departure from Britain by many leading writers of the 1930s and 1940s, and a changed sense of a world and community in which the British empire ceased to exist – at least in name, and a majority of people lost their ambivalent identity as 'British subjects'.

These exclusions allow this present study to focus on those works which speak to and of a British society whose differences were seen in terms of class rather than race, often making a direct appeal to the members of that society to live up to its proclaimed ideals of freedom and justice, and noting ironically the disparity between the ways which the British describe themselves and the ways they behave. Like Richard Wright, most of these authors eschew writing of romance or happiness; rather they are concerned with the pursuit of life and liberty, and the conditions which may make happiness and individual fulfilment possible. And like Wright they choose to 'deal with meaning': the meaning of freedom; the authority of experience; the definitions of humanity; the relationship between the body, categories of the body in terms of race and gender, and the self; the distinctions between the disempowered self and potential selves; the slipperiness of language; the relationship between language and power and powerlessness. Such preoccupations may not encourage fantasy or romance, but they do often display considerable irony and humour arising from their deep sense of the absurd and the disparity between rhetoric and reality. Some of the texts can be seen as 'writing back' to pro-slavery and imperialist texts and attitudes; some might also be seen as a 'writing in', an insistence on the significance of their individual stories and voices, an assertion of existence within a larger narrative and history. The remarkable popularity of many of these narratives, which frequently went into multiple editions, demonstrates not only the effectiveness with which the stories were told, but also the power of their appeal to the 'better selves' of eighteenth- and nineteenth-century readers in Britain, in enlarging rather than merely reiterating concepts of self and community. And what emerges again and again from the mid eighteenth-century involvement of Sterne, Garrick, and Sancho, to the mid twentieth-century involvement of Eliot, Orwell, Marson, and Desani, is the sense of a community of writers and artists who sought to discard racial and cultural barriers, and disseminate an inclusive and unprovincial culture.

This study cannot and does not seek to be exhaustive. Much archival work remains to be done to uncover forgotten texts and manuscripts, and many authors who might with further research be identified as either 'black' or 'south Asian' remain undiscovered. Nor have I tried to examine every text that can be identified in these terms. My aim has been to look in some detail at a few exemplary works and authors in order to explore the preoccupations and kinds of writing which seem most representative of the periods, times, and situations they confront.

Because so many of the texts are not easily available and have long been out of print, I have quoted extensively in order to display the interest and character of the texts. In so doing, I hope to have demonstrated the need and potential for further exploration in this rich cultural history of writers and their readers.

Despite the important and invaluable histories of black and Asian peoples in Britain by scholars such as Peter Fryer and Rozina Visram,[5] relatively little is known about the individuals and communities of African and Asian descent who lived and worked in Britain, nor the conditions and cultural contexts with which they interacted. Hence, I have included in this study three contextual and historical chapters (Chapters One, Four, and Eight), to provide those who desire it with a sense of the social and cultural attitudes and the historical events which relate to a fuller understanding of the texts I discuss.

First encounters: the historical context

Although there is evidence that African soldiers came to Britain with the Roman armies in order to keep the restless natives under control, it is not until the beginnings of European imperial expansion and slave trading that they begin to make a significant appearance in literature by and about them. Peter Fryer notes the presence of a group of Africans, seized from a Portuguese slave ship, in the court of James IV of Scotland at the beginning of the sixteenth century.[1] One of these may have been the lady 'that landet furth of the last schippis' mockingly celebrated by William Dunbar in 'Of Ane Blak-Moir', of which the third stanza reads:

> Quhen schou is claid in reche apparrall,
> Schou blinkis als brycht as ane tar barrell;
> Quhen schou was born, the son tholit clippis,
> The nicht be fain faucht in hi querrell:
> My ladye with the mekle lippis.[2]

The poem perhaps refers to the 'black lady' who is featured in 'the tournament of the black lady and the black knight', an event which took place in 1507 with King James playing the role of the black knight, and which was repeated in 1508.[3]

During the same period, there are records of a black trumpeter in the court of Henry VII, who was paid 8 pence a day for his services. Some fifty years later, in 1555, a group of five Africans were brought from Ghana to England to learn English so that they could act as interpreters for English traders who had become aware of the wealth to be gained from dealing in gold, ivory and spices on the West Coast of Africa.[4] English traders and travellers brought reports which added to the mingling of factual anecdotes and fabulous legends which dated as far back as Pliny's accounts, written in the first century AD and translated as *A Summarie of the Antiquities. And Wonders of the Worlde* in 1566. Such a pot-pourri of first person narrative and myth is represented in Othello's account of the tales which won Desdemona's heart:

> Wherein I spoke of most disastrous chances,
> Of moving accidents by flood and field,
> Of hair-breadth scapes i' th'imminent deadly breach,
> Of being taken by the insolent foe
> And sold to slavery, of my redemption thence,
> And portance in my traveller's history,
> Wherein of antres vast and deserts idle,
> Rough quarries, rocks, and hills whose heads touch heaven,
> It was my hint to speak. Such was my process,
> And of the cannibals that each other eat,
> The Anthropophagi, and men whose heads
> Do grow beneath their shoulders.[5]

As the editor of *Othello* in the *Norton Shakespeare* notes, this speech and other works by Shakespeare draw on Pliny (who uses the term 'Anthropophagi'), Mandeville and Hakluyt. Presumably also the mention by Othello of his boyhood enslavement reflects current awareness of the Portuguese, Spanish, and English slave trade.

English involvement in the slave trade as a means of making a large profit began with the purchase and seizure by John Hawkyns in 1562 of some 300 Africans, whom he then sold to Spanish plantation owners in the Caribbean. Queen Elizabeth lent him a ship, *The Jesus of Lubeck*, to make a further voyage in 1564, and Hawkyns was given an official crest which showed 'a demi-Moor proper bound captive, with amulets on his arms and ears' together with a coat of arms displaying three black men shackled with slave-collars.[6] During the sixteenth century Africans, and then Asians, were brought in smaller numbers to England and Scotland as slaves, domestic servants, and prostitutes. There are records of several musicians and entertainers at the court of Elizabeth, and also of entertainments involving her courtiers wearing blackface, a custom which Ben Jonson's *Masque of Blackness* (1605) shows continuing after her death.[7] Despite her enjoyment of such entertainments, however, Elizabeth did not approve of the growing numbers of black people resident in the country. A letter sent in 1596 to the mayor of London and the mayors and sheriffs of other towns commanded that such people should be deported: 'Her Majestie understanding that there are of late divers blackmoores brought into this realme, of which kinde of people there are already here to manie... Her Majesty's pleasure therefore ys that those kinde of people should be sent forth of the lande . . .'[8] Elizabeth commissioned a Dutch merchant to arrest any black people in the land and take them to Spain or Portugal. Five years later the same merchant was again encouraged to rid the country of black people. In terms which are echoed in some of the more virulent rhetoric of the present era regarding refugees, immigrants, and asylum seekers, Elizabeth issued a second proclamation in which she declared herself

highly discontented to understand the great number of negars and Black-amoores which (as she is informed) are crept into this realm . . . who are fostered and relieved here to the great annoyance of her own liege people, that want the relief, which these people consume, as also for that the most of them are infidels, having no understanding of Christ or his Gospel.[9]

Elizabeth's proclamations are issued during the same period that English merchants were setting up systematic trading contacts with India. On New Year's Eve 1600, she granted a charter to the East India Company as the sole traders in the East and India. Twelve years later the Moghul emperor Jehangir granted the East India Company a mandate for trade in India, and during the seventeenth century trading stations or 'factories' were established in Madras, Bombay, and Calcutta. During these early years when very few white women went out to India, there was considerable interchange and some marriages between the British and the native population, despite the usual practice of separating white expatriate enclaves from the 'Black Town' where native employees lived.[10]

The next 200 years saw a rapid increase in British involvement in colonization and plantation in Ireland, North America, and the Caribbean, together with flourishing trade with India and Africa, including the slave trade. The historian Dale H. Porter reports that by 1775 merchants from London, Liverpool, and Bristol were carrying an average of 60,000 African slaves across the Atlantic each year. Not only did the slave trade itself bring large profits (a slave bought in Africa for goods worth £15 would be sold in North America or the Caribbean to English or Spanish plantation owners for between £35 and £50), but it was intertwined with other lucrative trading and manufacture. Subsidiary industries which flourished in England included shipbuilding and the manufacture of iron manacles and chains, as well as goods such as East Indian cotton and British manufactured weapons which were traded for slaves in West Africa. Ships returning from the West Indies and America were loaded with tobacco and sugar, the latter being in great demand to sweeten the coffee and tea which came from the new colonies and trading areas. Many bankers and merchants in London, Liverpool, Bristol, and other cities owned whole or part shares in the slave ships, and a substantial portion of the British economy depended on the slave trade, the West Indian plantations, and the industries which accompanied them.[11] Such dependency was openly acknowledged and encouraged by many merchants and members of parliament, for example the MP Charles Davenant in his *Discourses on the Publick Revenues*:

So great a part of our Foreign Business arising from these Colonies, they ought undoubtedly to have all due Encouragement, and to be plentifully supply'd, and at reasonable rates, with Negroes to cultivate and meliorate the Land. The labour of these Slaves, is the principal Foundation of our Riches there; upon which account we should take all probable Measures to bring them to us at easie Terms...

Slaves are the first and most necessary Material for Planting; from whence follows, That all Measures should be taken that may produce such a Plenty of them, as may be an Encouragement to the industrious Planter.[12]

Slaves were brought to England to serve the ships' captains, or given to their friends, or accompanied American and West Indian owners and their families when they visited England. The increasing presence of black people in England and Scotland is recorded in bill posters and newspapers advertising sales of slaves or offering rewards for runaway slaves. They appear also in paintings, prints, and cartoons, including many by Hogarth. David Dabydeen remarks on the variety of occupations and roles assigned to black people in the hundreds of seventeenth- and eighteenth-century paintings and prints: 'footmen, coachmen, pageboys, soldiers, sailors, musicians, actresses, prostitutes, beggars, prisoners, pimps, highway robbers, street-sellers, and other similar roles'.[13] These visual images show Indian as well as African children posed in very similar positions as pageboys and servants (see for example the paintings by Lely of *Elizabeth Countess of Dysart* and *Charlotte Fitzroy*[14]) and advertisements appear in the papers for a 'runaway Bengal Boy' (1743) and for a lost 'East-India Tawny Black' (1737).[15] As Dabydeen points out, many of these portraits and prints illustrate the degree to which black and Indian servants had become commodities, signifiers of status in a culture which displayed ostentatiously its wealth and power through the 'exotica' shipped home from the colonies and trading empires. The print, *Taste in High Life* (after Hogarth) shows a small African boy dressed in turban and plumes, as much an exotic pet as the little poodle in coat and bonnet, in a room bedecked with images and objects from China, India, France, and other worlds.

During the eighteenth century, what had been primarily a trading relationship with India, which left that country's own institutions and customs relatively unchanged, became a colonial one, with a stronger military presence. Robert Clive first contested the French participation in trade with India, and then went on to defeat the ruler of Bengal, Siraj-ud-Daula, in 1757, establishing the East India Company as the main power in Bengal. Enormous wealth was acquired by British 'nabobs' who went to India to make their fortunes, often returning with Indian servants to adorn their establishments in England. In 1773, Warren Hastings was appointed governor general of all the East India Company provinces in India, and in 1784 the British government appointed a Board of Control in London with a British administrative arm, served, except in the lowest ranks, by British and Anglo-Irish men. Many of these men took their wives with them, and these families in turn brought back maids, ayahs, and other servants they had hired in India. Warren Hastings and his wife brought back two Indian boys, aged about thirteen, as well as four maids who were later sent back to India because 'they refused to work any harder than in India and wanted to lead exactly the same life'.[16] The population of Britain also began to include many 'lascars', the sailors who were hired, or in many cases kidnapped, to serve as crew for the East India trading ships, and then abandoned, sometimes without being paid, when the ship docked in England. In 1786, a committee of relief was set up to help such destitute sailors, later widening its brief to include other destitute black people, as 'The Committee for the Relief of the Black Poor'. The committee reported that it had located 320 black people in need of relief, including 35 from the East Indies. Among those selected to settle in Sierra Leone as a place of repatriation was a twenty-nine-year-old sailor from Bengal.[17]

Estimates as to the number of black people living in Britain in the late eighteenth century vary between ten and twenty thousand. In a population of approximately three million, they were a visible minority, and their visibility was remarked upon by visitors as well as Englishmen. Philipp Thickness comments in 1788 that 'London abounds with an incredible number of these black men...in every country town, nay in almost every village are to be seen a little race of mulattoes, mischievous as monkies and infinitely more dangerous.'[18] In *The Prelude* Wordsworth looked back upon the pleasing variety of

peoples he encountered when he travelled to London from Cambridge in
1791:

> Among the crowd all specimens of man,
> Through all the colours which the sun bestows,
> And every character of form and face:
> The Swede, the Russian; from the genial south,
> The Frenchman and the Spaniard; from remote
> America, The Hunter-Indian; Moors,
> Malays, Lascars, the Tartar, the Chinese,
> And Negro Ladies in white muslin Gowns.[19]

As James Walvin points out, the increasing visibility in Britain of black
people, many of whom were slaves or former slaves, brought to the fore
the contradictions and tensions between Britain's self-identity as the
home of liberty and human rights and its role as a participant in the
slave trade and the institution of slavery: 'The society which established
the primacy of parliamentary power, and confirmed individual liberties
before the law, was equally responsible for the development of black chattel slavery.'[20] As long as slavery seemed to exist mainly in the colonies it
could more easily be ignored. But the presence in Britain and Ireland
of black men and women who had experienced slavery made possible
the powerful testimony to the humanity of Africans and the brutalities of
slavery, both of which were denied or ignored by the supporters of slavery
and its economic benefits. The issue was also highlighted in a series of
legal cases which tested the extent of the commitment of England and
Scotland to human rights and then in the fierce debate around the abolition of the slave trade which took place between 1787 and 1807. The
abolitionist movement was the biggest political mass movement which
England had ever witnessed, involving over 100 petitions and 400,000
signatories to them. It is in the context of this debate that much of the
writing by black people was first produced and read; the legal, economic,
social, cultural and literary discourses relating to slavery provide a series
of arguments and representations about the status of black people in relation to English men and women which called for an explicit or implicit
response by the first black writers and their readers.

THE ABOLITION DEBATE AND THE REPRESENTATION
OF BLACK PEOPLE

Eighteenth-century black British writers wrote and were read in a variety
of cultural and social contexts. The one that loomed most threateningly

and oppressively was the slave trade and slavery, and with it the debates for and against abolition. For many black people in Britain, slavery was not merely a past experience, but also a continuing threat. In 1749, the attorney general, Sir Philip Yorke, reaffirmed the status as mere property of people who had been purchased as slaves, even though they were now on British soil or baptized Christians, and confirmed as paramount the property rights of slave traders and plantation owners who wished to retain and return them to the West Indies or other colonies.[21] In the case of James Somerset, whose Boston master had brought him to England and when he ran away recaptured him to be shipped back to Massachusetts, Judge Mansefield in 1772 reversed the Yorke–Talbot ruling, declaring that the laws of another country could not apply in England. However, this ruling did not, and was not intended to end slavery in Britain; indeed, Mansefield expressed considerable concern about the effects of freeing 'no less than 15,000 slaves now in England' whose worth he computed at approximately £700,000.[22] For years afterwards, notices of sales and wanted notices for runaway slaves continued to appear in newspapers, coffee shops, and other public gathering places. Only in Scotland, which functioned under a different legal system, was slavery judged to be illegal in the *Knight* v *Wedderburn* case in 1778, when Joseph Knight contested his enslavement by John Wedderburn, who had purchased him in Jamaica as a boy and brought him to Scotland. It was ruled that no man or woman in the territory of Scotland could be enslaved, and that the laws of Jamaica could not apply to Scotland.

In 1788 the lucrative triangular trade between Britain, Africa, and the Americas involved more than 150 ships sailing from English ports (mainly Bristol, London, and Liverpool), with approximately one million pounds worth of goods manufactured in Britain for trade in Africa. These goods were partly sold and partly exchanged in that year for over 60,000 slaves imported from Africa, and then sold for between £30 and £40 each in the Americas. The ships then returned to Britain with cargoes of rum, tobacco, and sugar. In 1783 the view that African slaves were mere merchandise was emphasized in the case of an insurance claim brought by the owners of the ship *Zong*. A total of 130 sick slaves had been thrown overboard so that the ship's owner could claim insurance for property abandoned by necessity (the claim was that water was scarce, although the ship arrived in port with 400 gallons of water to spare). Had the slaves simply died through natural causes, the insurance could not have been claimed. The case was brought to the attention of Granville Sharp by Olaudah Equiano, and Sharp attempted to bring a charge of

mass murder against the captain and crew. The prosecution was blocked
by the solicitor general, John Lee, who asserted that the blacks were
property: 'This is a case of chattels or goods. It is really so; it is the case of
throwing over goods; for to this purpose and the purpose of insurance,
they are goods and property: whether right or wrong we have nothing to
do with.'[23] Only in 1796 did an English court rule that slaves could not be
treated simply as merchandise in a case where a Liverpool trader sought
to recover insurance for 128 Africans who had starved to death on a long
voyage.[24] The slave-trade was not abolished in England until 1807.

Even after slavery was declared illegal in England, the identity of black
people remained blurred with the correlation in most people's minds
between slavery and black skins, ironically a correlation often reinforced
by the anti-slavery crusades. Hence, the condition and background
of slavery and the discourses surrounding it were almost inevitably an
important part of the context in which black writers sought to define
their own identities, to create their own voices, and to enter into dialogue
with the community they now chose to belong to on their terms where
once they were forced to belong on others' terms.

The identification of black people with slavery was both strengthened
and contested by the growth of the empire, which entailed England's
increasingly dominant role as a ruling nation and metropolitan centre,
and her encounter with other cultures and their artefacts. Within the
growing empire, and in the context of increasing commerce and trade
from India and Africa, and the culture of consumption and commodity
goods, black and south Asian people became yet another exotic import,
a commodity which bestowed status on their owners. Thus, as noted
above, black servants, grooms, and pages were frequently portrayed in
many eighteenth-century portraits and group pictures, accompanying
their wealthy mistresses, and masters, and their animals. Such pages
were often dressed in exotic livery, featuring turbans and robes which
might have little to do with their ancestral cultures, and much more to
do with an orientalist perception of those regions. In such outfits, they
were an adornment like the ostrich and peacock feathers, the paisley
shawls, the silks, which adorned their mistresses.[25]

In literature, a series of characters were developed and reiterated
or replayed to denote the various paradigms into which black and
Indian people were inserted in order to represent varied contexts
and attitudes. Such paradigms can be seen in the construction of
Othello and Oroonoko, on the one hand, and in the figure of the black
servant or fool and Man Friday, on the other. It is interesting to note

that *Othello* was particularly popular in the eighteenth century and was performed much more frequently than Shakespeare's other plays, apart from *Hamlet* and *Macbeth*. C.B. Hogan gives a total of 265 performances of *Othello* in London between 1700 and 1750, compared with 186 for *Lear*, 163 for *Julius Caesar*, 96 for *Romeo and Juliet* (358 for *Hamlet*, 287 for *Macbeth*).[26] Also particularly popular was Thomas Southerne's dramatization of Aphra Behn's *Oroonoko*, in which – perhaps in the context of *Othello* – Oroonoko's wife becomes a white woman rather than an African. Numerous versions were presented on stage in the eighteenth century. In 1759, for example, there were three different adaptations playing in London, in one of which (by Frances Gentleman) the anti-slavery theme becomes much more prominent. Both *Othello* and *Oroonoko* present the type of the noble, highly articulate and seductive African, whose passionate nature brings him to a tragic end. It is in this paradigm that one of the first supposedly factual biographies of an African may have been read when it was first published in 1734, Thomas Bluett's *Some Memoirs of the Life of Job*, which reports some events in the life of Ayuba Suleiman Diallo. Diallo was a Muslim merchant in West Africa, who was kidnapped and enslaved in Maryland. He was rescued and ultimately freed by Bluett, brought to England, made the acquaintance of a number of English gentlemen, was ransomed by his father, and returned to Africa laden with presents from his English friends. Bluett records these details about Diallo and his country at the request of Diallo, seeking to give 'such particulars of the life and character of this African Gentleman, as I think will be most useful and entertaining', endeavouring 'to make the whole as agreeable as the nature of the subject and the limits of this pamphlet will allow'.[27]

Black people like Ignatius Sancho were perceived and perceived themselves as 'Othello-like'. His friend Stevenson tells the story of an encounter in the streets of London with a young white dandy who shouted out to him, 'Smoke Othello!' Sancho 'immediately placing himself across the path, before him, exclaimed with a thundering voice and a countenance which awed the delinquent, "Aye, Sir, such Othellos you meet with but once in a century," clapping his hand upon his goodly round paunch. "Such Iagos as you we meet with in every dirty passage. Proceed, Sir!"'[28] One of his letters refers to his shared foolishness with a number of black people, including Othello. Equiano, in a note to a letter preceding his *Narrative* and refuting the claim that his account was false, quotes Othello's final speech, 'Speak of me as I am, / Nothing extenuate, nor set down aught / In malice.'[29]

Other eighteenth-century plays and operas sometimes featured black characters. In particular Isaac Bickerstaffe's comic operas portrayed black captives and servants. The protagonist of his *Love in the City* (1767), Priscilla Tomboy, is a West Indian (white) orphan whose imperious and cruel treatment of her black servant Quasheba is contrasted with the compassionate behaviour of her English friend, Penelope. *The Padlock* (1768) features a black servant, Mungo, who is lazy and gullible, but also quick witted. Bickerstaffe gives him what purports to be African dialect. And *The Sultan* (1773), like *The Padlock*, represents themes of captivity and liberation through the figure of Roxana, a rebellious and ungovernable English slave who persuades her master to set the captive women in his harem free. The late eighteenth century also saw a strenuous output of anti-slavery poems and pamphlets, many of which were circulated in thousands as part of the campaign to abolish the slave-trade. These include William Cowper's 'The Negro's Complaint' (1788), Jamieson's 'The Sorrow's of Slavery: A Poem' (1789), and Hannah More's *Slavery: A Poem* (1788).

But attitudes towards black people, and opinions about their capacities and their humanity, differed widely within Britain and the colonies. Although Hogarth could write about the aesthetic appeal of darker skins, for all too many, a black skin was a disfigurement of the worst kind. Thus a reviewer of Hannah More's poem commented:

Black is a colour which nature abhors. The eye startles and shrinks from it when it is first presented; nothing inanimate wears this horrid gloom; and in the living world, a black skin is peculiar to animals of the most peculiar and loathsome kind.[30]

And despite the ambivalent depictions of Othello and Oroonoko as noble and learned men, many were convinced that Africans and all black people, by definition, were inferior. David Hume's footnote in his 1758 *Philosophical Essay* expresses attitudes possessed by many of his countrymen:

There was never a civilised nation of any other complexion than white, nor even any individual eminent in either action or speculation... Not to mention our colonies, there are Negroe slaves dispersed all over Europe, of which none ever discovered any symptoms of ingenuity; tho' low people without education will start up among us and distinguish themselves in every profession. In Jamaica indeed, they talk of one negroe as a man of parts and learning; but 'tis likely he is admired for very slender accomplishments, like a parrot who speaks few words plainly.[31]

CHAPTER 2

Eighteenth-century letters and narratives: Ignatius Sancho, Olaudah Equiano, and Dean Mahomed

Drawing on assertions such as Hume's regarding the inferiority of non-white peoples (and similar ones by Thomas Jefferson dismissing the achievements of Phyllis Wheatley), supporters of the slave-trade argued that Africans were subhuman, incapable of 'civilized' life, of which writing and literary creation were the most important mark, and hence suited only to manual labour and in need of firm governance by plantation owners. Abolitionists set out to counter these arguments both by an appeal to common humanity and by providing evidence of the capabilities of Africans. Africans and African Americans were placed in the position not just of arguing against the immorality of slavery *per se*, i.e. reiterating the argument made by Francis Hutcheson and Dr Johnson that slavery was against natural human justice because no human being could be regarded as mere property, but affirming that Africans were indeed human. Hence the medallion cast by Josiah Wedgwood and sold in thousands to be worn or used by supporters of the Committee for the Abolition of the Slave Trade (of which Wedgwood was one of the leading members), used as its slogan, 'Am I not a *Man* and Brother?' (my italics). But during the eighteenth-century enlightenment period, the equation between writing, civilization and humanity became established, and the question as to whether black people were capable of writing and literary creation became crucial to the debates surrounding the abolition of slavery.

Thus there is a recurring emphasis in so many early writings by Africans on these works being 'written by themselves', and many of the autobiographies are accompanied by numerous declarations and testimonials verifying their authorship (see Fig. 1). That the assumption of illiteracy should be ensured as fact was the motive and consequence of various laws in the United States and the West Indies forbidding the teaching of reading or writing to slaves. Although the legal underpinning did not exist in England, the practice of denying the acquisition of

17

1 Frontispiece to Olaudah Equiano's *Interesting Narrative* (1789).
Reproduced by permission of The British Library

literacy was enforced in this country by some masters and mistresses. Ignatius Sancho's first owners refused him access to books on the grounds that this would make him unfit to carry out his duties as a slave and servant. For this reason he ran away, and was taken in by a more liberal family, the Duke and Duchess of Montagu. Sancho was probably aware that the Duke of Montagu, when he was Governor of Jamaica, had sponsored Francis Williams and sent him to study at Cambridge in order to see what Africans might be capable of. (Williams subsequently published poems in Latin, and became a schoolmaster in Jamaica, and it is Williams that Hume refers to in the dismissive note cited at the end of my previous chapter.)

The threat perceived from the acquisition of language, and the slaves 'profit on it', is also demonstrated in Equiano's account of how he challenged the captain who was buying him as a slave. Insisting that he had not only been redeemed financially through the share of the prize money won by members of the crew during the naval battles with the French, and believing also that as a baptized Christian he was protected by English law, Equiano told his new master, Captain Doran, that his previous master could not 'sell me to him, nor to anyone else', and

besides this I have been baptized; and by the laws of the land no man has the right to sell me; and I added, that I had heard a lawyer, and others at different times, tell my master so. They both then said that those people who told me so were not my friends: but I replied – It was very extraordinary that other people did not know the law as well as they. Upon this Captain Doran said I talked too much English; and if I did not behave myself well, and be quiet, he had a method on board to make me.[1]

Although Equiano is given prominence as the founding father of writing in English by Africans, he is in fact preceded by several African authors, including Ukawsaw Gronniosaw, whose *Narrative of the Remarkable Particulars in the Life of James Albert Ukawsaw Gronniosaw, An African Prince, related by himself*, was published in 1772,[2] and Ottobah Cugoano's *Thoughts and Sentiments on the Evil of Slavery*, first published in 1787.[3] Gronniosaw's forty-nine-page *Narrative* is an account of his spiritual journey and his conversion to evangelical Christianity, retold on his behalf by a lady (later identified as the conservative evangelist and anti-slavery writer, Hannah More).[4] The preface states that

This account of the life and spiritual experience of JAMES ALBERT was taken from his own mouth, and committed to paper by the elegant pen of a young LADY of the town of LEOMINSTER, for her own private satisfaction, and without any intention at first that it should be made public. But now she has been prevail'd on to commit it to the press, as it is apprehended, this little history contains matter well worthy the notice and attention of every Christian reader. (p. iv)

The preface, by the clergyman W. Shirley, goes on to stress the evidence this narrative offers of the hand of Providence directing events which enslaved and brought Gronniosaw to Christian knowledge from 'regions of the grossest Darkness and Ignorance'. This theme is emphasised by the epigraph on the frontispiece of the *Narrative* from Isaiah xliii.16: 'I will bring the Blind by a way that they know not, I will lead them in Paths that they have not known: I will make darkness light before them and crooked things straight. These things will I do unto them and not forsake them.' The *Narrative* is presented as an example of extraordinary faith even in the most dire distress – including to 'have his wife and children perishing for want before his eyes! Yet his faith did not fail him; he put his trust in the Lord and he was delivered' (p. 11). The reader is further informed that Gronniosaw was thought to have left his native land at about fifteen, and now appears to be about sixty.

Gronniosaw portrays himself as a young boy of an indefatigably, and indeed from his family's point of view, tiresomely inquiring disposition, which leads to his dissatisfaction with his mother's teaching that sun, moon, and stars are the powers that rule the world. Together with his long description of the magnificence and munificence of the palm tree – giving shade, clothing, food and drink – his narrative might conceivably have provided the context for Blake's depiction of 'The Little Black Boy' taught 'underneath a tree' by his mother's knee about the sun where 'God does live' (pp. 8–9).

Some of these details may well have been added by Hannah More, who no doubt embellished considerably the oral account given by Gronniosaw. Or Gronniosaw himself might have included details which are reminiscent of the Bible, such as the threat of the merchants to cast him into a pit (like Joseph abandoned by his brothers). Other occurrences in the narrative recall some of the more fanciful incidents in *Oroonoko*, such as the scene in which the king who is about to behead him with his scimitar dissolves into tears and gives him over to be enslaved, or the sublime and rather surreal description of the valley of towering marble cliffs flecked with gold. Indeed, the emphasis on Gronniosaw's royal origins, and the naming of him as 'an African Prince' in the title, may well show the influence of *Oroonoko*, either from the original novel, or the various dramatic adaptations so popular in the eighteenth century. Some of the descriptions and incidents in Gronniosaw's *Narrative* become tropes in writing by subsequent black writers such as Cugoano and Equiano: the description of seeing ships as beholding 'houses with wings to them walk upon the water', the abnormality and wonder of people with white skins, although in Gronniosaw's case, we are told that the one member of his family, his beloved sister named Logwy, 'was quite white, and fair, though my father and mother were black' (pp. 8–9). Like Equiano later, Gronniosaw regards his master as a father whom he grows to love exceedingly. Most noticeably, he presents the delusion of the talking book, which recurs in the narratives of John Marrant, Ottobah Cugoano, and Olaudah Equiano in similar terms. Gronniosaw tells us:

And when I first saw him read, I was never so surprized in my life, as when I saw the book talk to my master, for I thought it did, as I observed him to look upon it, and move his lips...I opened [the book] and put my ear down close upon it, in great hopes that it would say something to me; but was very sorry, and greatly disappointed when I found it would not speak, this thought immediately presented itself to me, that every body and every thing despised me because I was black. (*Narrative*, pp. 16–17)

Although Equiano differs from Gronniosaw in his responses to the contrast between black-skinned and white-skinned people, finding the latter ugly and frightening, and commenting on the comeliness of black women, he does follow Gronniosaw's device of presenting himself as a naive and sometimes foolish lad, whose responses to 'civilization' are often laughable. Gronniosaw, or his editor, make much of his naivete, for example when he describes his amusement at finding the minister, his new master, 'talking to nobody', as he assumes he is doing when he is praying, or the incident when he rebukes his mistress for swearing, having himself been rebuked by an older black slave (Gronniosaw expresses no regret for the consequent flogging of the same elderly black slave). He is not unlike Equiano either in his desire to impress others, for he longs to return to his family not so much to be with them and to convert them, but because he 'should be wiser than all my country-folks, my grandfather, or father, or mother, or any of them' (p. 20). There are also similarities between Gronniosaw's and Equiano's accounts of their spiritual struggle and despair, their feelings of irredeemable sinfulness, before they finally find grace and salvation. Given John Bunyan to read, Gronniosaw declares, 'I found his experience similar to my own' (p. 22).

The narratives related by Gronniosaw, John Marrant,[5] and others of African birth or descent, and then edited and written down by sympathetic Christian men or women, or the poetry of Phyllis Wheatley,[6] are brought to the public in the context of Christian evangelism, and the desire to bear witness to the hand of God in reaching out, as the Reverend W. Shirley put it, even to those 'regions of the grossest Darkness and Ignorance'. Marrant's *Narrative* and Wheatley's poems were both published under the patronage of the Countess of Huntingdon, and both acknowledge their debt and reverence for her chaplain, George Whitfield. However, the writing of Quobna Ottobah Cugoano (also known as John Stuart), although drawing on the genre of the spiritual testament, is much more strongly a product of the debate over the slave trade and the abolitionist movement. The title of his first book, published in 1787, *Thoughts and Sentiments on the Evil and Wicked Traffic of the Slavery and Commerce of the Human Species*, echoes the title of one of the first and best known statements for the cause of abolition, Thomas Clarkson's, *An Essay on the Slavery and Commerce of the Human Species, particularly the African* (London, 1786). Cugoano's book is a powerful and angry polemic, basing its rhetorical appeal on philosophical, moral, religious, economic, and rational arguments, rather than personal testimony and sentiment. A number of critics have seen Cugoano as the least assimilated of the eighteenth-century African British writers. Vincent Carretta argues otherwise, placing Cugoano's work firmly in the well-established European Christian genre of the jeremiad, or political sermon, denouncing the evil of the times and warning of divine retribution.[7] Thus Cugoano warns that the slave trade must inevitably increase the national debt, corrupt the British constitution and its vaunted liberties, and bring down the wrath of God on the British unless they mend their ways.[8] He concludes his address with quotations from Jeremiah ('They have defiled my land, they have filled mine inheritance with the carcases of their detestable and abominable things') and from the Anglican liturgy, thus confirming his status as Biblical prophet and newly confirmed Christian, whose identity transcends all other identities and traditions: 'And Christianity does not require that we should be deprived of our own personal name, or the name of our ancestors; but it may very fitly add another name unto us, Christian, or one anointed.'[9] Cugoano's dual or multiple identities as African and British, as Old Testament prophet and Christian preacher, as drawing on the language of the Bible and the oral sermon, his accumulative rhetorical style and apocalyptic mode, are well illustrated in the closing paragraph of his book:

And let me now hope that you will pardon me in all that I have been thus telling you, O ye inhabitants of Great Britain! To whom I owe the greatest respect; to your king! To yourselves! And to your government! And tho' many things which I have written may seem harsh, it cannot be otherwise evaded when such horrible iniquity is transacted: and tho' to some what I have said may appear as the rattling leaves of autumn, that may soon be blown away and whirled in a vortex where few can hear and know: I must yet say, although it is not for me to determine the manner, that the voice of our complaint implies a vengeance, because of the great iniquity that you have done, and because of the cruel injustice done unto us Africans; and it ought to sound in your ears as the rolling waves around your circum-ambient shores; and if it is not hearkened unto, it may yet arise with a louder voice, as the rolling thunder, and it may yet encrease [sic] in the force of its volubility, not only to shake the leaves of the most stout in heart, but to rend the mountains before them, and to cleave in pieces the rocks under them, and to go on with fury to smite the stoutest oaks in the forest; and even to make that which is strong, and wherein you think that your strength lieth, to become as stubble, and as the fibres of rotten wood, that will do you no good, and your trust in it will become a snare and infatuation to you.[10]

Gronniosaw's *Narrative* and Cugoano's *Thoughts and Sentiments* might be seen as signposts towards Equiano's combination of personal autobiography and anti-slave-trade polemic. But the writing and publication of Equiano's narrative in 1789 is also preceded by the publication in 1782 of *The Letters of Ignatius Sancho*, a series of letters written between 1766 and 1780 to friends, family, writers, artists, and newspapers. The collection was published after his death and proved to be very popular; the first edition had nearly 1,200 subscribers (a considerable number at that period), and there were at least four more editions within the first decade. The correspondence was preceded by a brief note from their editor, a Miss Crewe who was also a recipient of several of the letters, affirming that her purpose in collecting and publishing them was 'to show that an untutored African may possess abilities equal to an European, and the still superior motive, of wishing to serve his family'.

This first and subsequent editions also included a brief biography of Sancho by Joseph Jekyll, a friend of Sancho and a member of parliament. Jekyll recounts on Sancho's behalf (his letters make only one passing mention of his childhood) his birth on a slave-ship, the death shortly afterwards of his mother, and the suicide of his father. At the age of two, Sancho was given to 'three maiden sisters' in Greenwich who believed that 'African ignorance was the only security for his obedience, and that to enlarge the mind of their slave would go near to emancipate his person'.[11] The child had been baptized 'Ignatius' when the slave ship called at Carthage; the sisters surnamed him Sancho because they thought he resembled Don Quixote's squire, Sancho Panza. From these ladies he was rescued by the Duke and Duchess of Montagu, who encouraged his reading and gave him books, and when his owners threatened to return Sancho 'to his African slavery', took him into their household, where he eventually became their butler. After he became too corpulent and gouty to continue as a servant, he was given money in 1773 to set up a small grocery shop specializing in sugar, tobacco, and other small goods. He was married to a freed West Indian woman, Anne Osborne, and had six children, whom he referred to as the 'Sanchonettes'. Jekyll offers the letters as proof 'that the perfection of the reasoning faculties does not depend on a peculiar conformation of the skull or the colour of a common integument' (p. 25). Appended to his biography of what he terms 'this extraordinary Negro' is a footnote, even longer than the biography itself, quoting the conclusions of a Professor Blumenbach whose travels and investigation of 'three negro skulls' indicate that negro mental capacities 'are not inferior to the rest of the human race' (p. 25).

Thus Sancho is presented to us as both 'extraordinary' and as 'representative'. He was also a musician, whose work has been recently collected and published, but interestingly it is the writing rather than the music which is deemed to prove his claim to equality with 'the rest of the human race'. Jekyll does not even mention it, although there are occasional references in the letters themselves to his musical compositions. Sancho dropped out of sight for almost 200 years, and only very recently have critics brought him back into vision, as part of a new interest in black British writing. (Although he was the sole black writer to be included in the nineteenth-century *Dictionary of National Biography*, he does not appear in any of the early anthologies of black writing published in America, which do include Equiano and the poet Phyllis Wheatley. In the latest *Oxford Companion to English Literature* (2000), his name appears but we are referred to a brief two-page entry on Black British Literature. The *Companion* similarly refers the reader who searches for Equiano, C.L.R. James, and Caryl Phillips to that two-page entry on Black British Literature; Naipaul, Walcott and Rushdie, however, have their own entries.)

For recent critics such as Paul Edwards, Polly Rewt, Keith Sandiford, and David Dabydeen, it is Sancho's status as a *black* writer that matters, and hence the content which relates to his colour and origins is singled out in their discussions. So the extracts in the letters which best fit into the reading back of a 'black tradition' are foregrounded: now and in his own time Sancho was brought to public attention as a consequence of his letter to Laurence Sterne, urging him to write something about the oppression of black people. Introducing himself as 'one of those whom the vulgar and illiberal call "Negurs" '(*Letters*, p. 85), and deploring the fact that not one of his favourite authors 'has drawn a tear in favor of my miserable black brethren', he goes on to inscribe himself as spokesman for the race and a predecessor of the iconic figure transcribed in Wedgwood's medallion: 'Dear Sir, think in me you behold the uplifted hands of thousands of my brother Moors' (p. 86). Sterne's warm reply was published in the collection of Sterne's letters, and is reproduced in facsimile in the special and classier edition of Sancho's letters which his son William had printed in 1802. (William was librarian for the botanist and explorer, Joseph Banks, and then became a bookseller in the premises his father had owned.)

Sterne was not only a correspondent and later a friend of Sancho's but also a model for his letter writing. Most of the letters take on characteristics of the styles and techniques which mark *Tristram Shandy* and *A Sentimental Journey* as well as Sterne's own letters. One can see this style particularly in Letters 97, 98, and 108 addressed to his friend Meheux (also addressed at times as 'Monkey') with whom he particularly enjoyed performing in the Sternian mode. Letter 97 is a letter about not writing a letter, a letter interrupted by an inkblot, and playing with puns and similes and the art of making them. Letter 98 describes with lively wit and detail a coach journey with his family, and Letter 108 juggles with stereotypes of 'blackamoors' and the false logic of discourses which categorize black people as cursed sons of Noah, discourses which are then turned upside down to celebrate the blessings Noah and his family did not enjoy.

Why should Sterne particularly appeal to Sancho as a model? One might see it merely as a similarity in temperament and a shared pleasure in the varieties and eccentricities of human behaviour. But that is simply another way of putting the question. Sterne's works constantly disrupt received genres of discourse and categories of language; the order of syntax and the stability of words are continually under question in his writing. Hence it is not surprising that he should appeal to a man who was in all ways desiring to escape the rigid categories of a society which sought to constrict so radically the possibilities for black people and to confine them as slaves, manual workers, or at best, servants and exotica. Furthermore, Sancho was a man without any knowledge of his past – his place of birth or his parents – hence he is free to inscribe himself on the blank slate, predetermined only by what he knows he will not allow himself to be defined as. Like Equiano he emerges as a man of many parts; but unlike Equiano, he does not seek a clear trajectory to his life, a beginning and an end – a project; he seeks to be as fully as possible in the present. Thus he determined to be educated, found a patron in the Duke of Montagu, was a butler, a musician, a critic of the arts, including painting, a father, a husband, a grocer, a would-be actor, a friend of Garrick, Sterne, and others, a teacher and counsellor, a gambler and a womaniser.

Moreover, Sancho embraces all topics and interests, writing on terms of equality (though carefully judged) to fellow servants, to writers, booksellers, friends, and the sons of friends. Nor does he assume that any of them should be confined by their professions: a letter to a fellow servant in the Montagu household rebukes him for not enjoying Rousseau's *Eloisa*: 'So you do not like Eloisa – you are a noddy for that – read it till you do like it. – I am glad you have seen Cymon: – that you like it – does but little credit to your taste – for every body likes it.'[12] He will quote Shakespeare, Pope, Dryden, Addison, the Bible to all alike, and is rarely patronising – except in his letters to young women. The democracy of his address relates to the multiplicity of subjects and identities – father, husband, critic, musician, political commentator, instructor – which can be contained within one letter.

He writes at length about political matters, describing the London streets during the Gordon demonstrations and riots, expressing disgust and despair over the British defeats during the American War of Independence. There are also several letters to the papers proposing ways of reducing the national debt by requiring wealthy families to send their silver to the mint, for such silver is mainly 'old and useless, kept merely for the antiquity of fashion, and the ostentatious proof of the grandeur of ancestry' (Letter 59a, pp. 123–4), improving the lives of sea men and also manning the navy, or another which jokingly suggests that the Government, in its search for 'able bodied men', should form ten companies out of the numerous hairdressers then employed in the country, and thus free English men and woman alike from wasting hours in the 'bondage' of 'French *friseurs*' (Letter 42a, pp. 92–3).

Sancho's letters to the papers (except the one just quoted) are written in formal, regulated prose, and signed Africanus. He also published his collections of music as 'an African'. Elsewhere, he frequently draws attention to and plays with his identity as an African or black man, often using derogatory terms ironically, as in the letter quoted above to Sterne. Thus he refers to himself as a 'thick-lipped son of Afric': 'As to our politics – now don't laugh at me – for everyone has a right to be a politician; so have I; and though only a poor, thick-lipped son of Afric! may be as

notable a Negro state-botcher as *****, and so on for five hundred –'
(Letter 133, p. 227). He tells his friend Meheux that he will teach him to
'wish for pleasure from Blackamoor dunderheads' (Letter 109, p. 193);
his thanks come as 'the warm ebullitions of African sensibility', and he
writes with gratitude to those 'who have charity enough to admit dark
faces into the fellowship of Christians' (Letter 66, p. 134). He sends another correspondent some 'black poetry', a satire on the court case in
which the Duchess of Kingston sued the playwright Samuel Foote for
libel (Letter 27, pp. 74–5). In writing to black correspondents, however,
he may be less ironic and playful, as in his more avuncular letter to the
young servant of the Duchess of Queensberry, Julius Soubise:

Happy, happy lad! What a fortune is thine! – Look around on almost all of
those of our unfortunate colour – superadded to ignorance, – see slavery, and
the contempt of those very wretches who roll in affluence from our labours.
Superadded to this woeful catalogue – hear the ill-bred and heart-racking abuse
of the foolish vulgar. – You, Soubise, tread as cautiously as the strictest rectitude
can guide ye – yet must you suffer from this – but armed with truth – honesty –
and conscious integrity – you will be sure of the plaudit and countenance of the
good. (Letter 14, pp. 56–7)

For his clear views on racist attitudes, one can read Sancho's rebuke to
Jack Wingrave who writes disparagingly of the 'natives' in India as deceitful and avaricious. Sancho responds by asserting that it is the Europeans
who have made them so:

The cursed avidity for wealth urged these first visitors (and all the succeeding
ones) to such acts of deception – and even wanton cruelty – that the poor
ignorant Natives soon learnt to turn the knavish and diabolical arts – which
they too soon imbibed – upon their teachers. (Letter 68, p. 138)

Sancho goes on to condemn roundly the behaviour of the English outside their own country, observing that 'your country's practice has been
uniformly wicked in the East–West-Indies – and even on the coast of
Guinea', and speaks of 'the Christians' abominable traffic for slaves'. An
earlier letter had asked Wingrave to look after two young black men who
had gone out to India; Julius Soubise, who was to set up a riding school in
Bengal, and Charles Lincoln, a West Indian musician. In a letter written
two years later he offers an ironic apology for this request, and represents
with sharp satire his 'failure' in tact for not realizing that whites could
not mingle with blacks in the Indian context:

Mark – I praise thee *sincerely*, for the *whole* and every *part* of thy *conduct*, in
regard to my two sable brethren. I was an ass, or else I might have judged,
from the national antipathy and prejudice through custom even of the Gentoos

towards their woolly-headed brethren, and the well-known dignity of my Lords
the Whites, of the impropriety of my request – I therefore not only acquit thee
honourably – but condemn myself for giving thee the trouble to explain a right
conduct. (Letter 127, p. 216)

Sancho shares with Sterne, as well as Swift whom he also admired greatly,
a mixed delight in the grotesque, often figured in images of the body as
excessive, uncontained, a source and representation of disruption, both
pleasurable and painful. Thus he refers again and again to feasting, to
food, to his corpulence, his gout, and his blackness. He sees himself
constantly from the outside, and in turn questions the outsider's vision
through the inadequacy and fallibility of the categories applied to him.
And like later writers such as Equiano, Fedric, Craft, and Desani, he
stresses his sense of a multiple identity, a self that cannot be limited by
the labels applied by others.

Nevertheless, Sancho's readers have sought to place him firmly within
one category, that of the black appeaser or 'Uncle Tom'. From the very
first publication of his letters, he has been 'framed' in 'the castle of his
skin', to use George Lamming's phrase. Sancho has been consistently
read, and we continue to read him, as a 'black' author, but what does
that mean? Readings of 'blackness' have changed over the years, and
leave a great many of Sancho's interests, attitudes, responses out of the
picture. Nor is it ever easy to read him now as his implicit reader – or
one should say, readers – might have done, for Sancho adopts numerous
voices in relation to his numerous contemporary readers, for some of
whom his colour mattered, while for others it was seemingly relatively
unimportant.

The first publication of the letters was framed not only by his editor
and correspondent, but also by a Frontispiece which identifies him as
'An African' (see Fig. 2) and is accompanied by a mezzotint of Gainsborough's portrait of Sancho, to ensure that we cannot miss the fact of his
colour. Jekyll's introduction of him as 'this extraordinary Negro' sums
up the double bind which haunted all black writers of this period and
for many years afterwards; as a Negro he was to be read as a representative of his race, as a Negro *writer*, he is read as 'extraordinary'. His
extraordinariness is in proving himself 'the equal of an European'; his
representativeness derives not only from the assumption that he speaks
for all black people, but also from his faults. – Jekyll informs us that
'freedom, riches, and leisure, naturally led a disposition of African texture
into indulgences', and goes on to cite a French writer who relates 'that in

2 Frontispiece to 1803 edition of *The Letters of Ignatius Sancho*. Reproduced by permission of The British Library

the kingdoms of Abdrah, Whydah, and Benin, a Negro will stake at play his fortune, his children, and his liberty.'[13] Later (nineteenth-century) editions of the *Letters* include the very long footnote quoting the German scientist Johann Friedrich Blumenbach's 'Observations on Bodily Conformation and Mental Capacity of the Negroes'.[14]

Given these framing apparatus, then, it is not surprising that the first reviewers of Sancho's letters all note the colour or race of the writer first, and view the content and merit of his letters in relation to that aspect. Every review published between 1782 and 1784 foregrounds Sancho's identity as a 'black of the Duke of Montague's' (sic) (*Literary Review*, August 1782) and as a Negro who writes no better than 'many other Negroes, we suppose, could, with the same advantages, have written'.[15] *The Monthly Review* (December 1783) refers to Sancho as 'this very honest and very ingenious African' and 'this amiable Black'.[16] Thomas Jefferson in his *Notes on the State of Virginia* (1787) cites both Phyllis Wheatley and Ignatius Sancho as proof of the limits of black achievement, placing them at the top of Negro attainment, but at 'the bottom of the column' if listed with their white comperes.[17] Like a number of other reviewers, Jefferson deplores the Sternian qualities in the letters – their fanciful and extravagant style, their lack of order and restraint, 'his substitution of sentiment for demonstration' – which are seen implicitly as characteristic of Sancho's racial inheritance; like his gambling, they are the indulgences to which 'a disposition of African texture' is all too prone.

Interestingly, it is a French man, the Abbé Grégoire who, in his *De la Littérature des Négres*, having summarized the life of Sancho as given by Jekyll, concentrates on his qualities as a writer, and compares him to other writers of letters such as Madame de Sevigny and Sterne. The passages he cites illustrate Sancho's style, and especially his range of tone, concerns, and sentiments, rather than his views on race or slavery. Grégoire comments on Sancho's wit, grace, and wisdom, and seeks to refute the 'severity' of Jefferson's judgement.[18] Sancho's relationship with Sterne is evidently the criteria which places him as the only British 'Negro writer' in the late nineteenth-century edition of the *Dictionary of National Biography*. Apart from that entry in the *DNB*, Sancho's name drops out of consideration for a good 150 years, till the revival of interest in earlier black writers in the 1970s, and following facsimile editions of the *Letters*, Equiano's *Narrative*, and Cugoana's *Thoughts and Sentiments*, by Paul Edwards in 1968.

So by the time attention began to turn to Sancho again, Equiano had also been rediscovered, and it is against Equiano and the tradition of the slave narrative or testament that Sancho is tested, rather than against his European contemporaries. Equiano and Cugoano more easily slotted into the category of forceful black spokesmen, most powerfully represented by Frederick Douglass and later Malcolm X. In the backwash of the 1960s and early seventies and the rhetoric of Black Power and black pride, Equiano was read as a true representative of black manhood, Sancho as an 'Uncle Tom'. Both readings were not only ahistorical, but also remarkably one-sided, ignoring a great deal of contrary evidence within the writings themselves. Nevertheless they have had a strong influence even to the present, when Norma Myer's 1996 study of blacks in Britain between 1780 and 1830 refers to Sancho as 'apologetic, complaisant' and 'self-debasing', a British form of the 'Sambo stereotype'.[19] Myers is merely reiterating James Walvin's earlier description of Sancho as 'the most obsequious of eighteenth-century blacks', just as she repeats many of the factual errors regarding Sancho's life and *Letters* to be found in Walvin's books.[20] Paul Edwards' judgement that 'Sancho's letters point clearly to his almost complete assimilation into 18th-century English society'[21] is disputed by both the black historian Folarin Shyllon and the Nigerian critic S.E. Ogude. To refute the charge of assimilation, Shyllon cites in particular Sancho's letter to Julius Soubise and his anger at 'those very wretches who roll in affluence from *our* labours' (Shyllon's emphasis).[22] Ogude, on the other hand, is more inclined to see Sancho as a man divided, suffering from the impossibility of being both black and English:

The letters show that Sancho was emotionally attached to Tory ideals although he was always conscious of his African origin. His is the sad case of what we now call the divided-self – for he was that uncomfortable phenomenon – the black Englishman. One does not realise how much the racial problem plagued a very sensitive nature like Sancho until one has read these letters.[23]

Although Ogude goes on to demonstrate the inadequacy of Jefferson's assessment, and to illustrate the richness and variety of subject and tone, the often brilliant mastery of English and the genre of the letter-writing, he also comments on what he terms 'the charming naivete' and 'passionate simplicity' of the letters. He concludes by almost endorsing the binary oppositions implied or asserted by Jekyll, Jefferson, and others:

His was a divided-self; divided between the cultural world of the decent aristocratic society of London and the dark brooding consciousness of a heritage denied of its warmth and its intense sensibility. His reading lists show how closely his intellectual life was linked to the English tradition; but his occasional urge to identify with his primitive-origins [sic] is an expression of his emotional tie with his African heritage. In a word Sancho experienced what none of his black contemporaries experienced – a tragic sense of the black predicament.[24]

In a different way, the assumption that one must choose between being 'black' or 'African' and being 'English' or 'British' underlies most discussions of Sancho, and encourages critics to place Equiano on one side of the divide and Sancho on the other. The possibility of a hybrid or multiple identity is either condemned or not contemplated, and is also undermined by the conventions of literary critical discourse which encourage sorting writers into clear categories. Thus Keith Sandiford's *Measuring the Moment*, along with Ogude's study one of the first attempts since the Abbé Grégoire's to assess and understand the contribution of early black writers, affirms Equiano as a truly 'black' writer, but like Ogude laments the 'double identity' expressed in Sancho's letters: 'what seems to emerge, then, is that as Sancho approached middle age, he felt more keenly the affliction of his double identity,... [and] found it increasingly difficult to sustain the old posture of the compliant, assimilated Black.'[25] But where Ogude saw Sancho's playfulness as 'charming naivete', Sandiford views the 'charm' not as naivete but as a deliberate masking and concealment: 'Sancho expressed this self-awareness in apologetic, complaisant terms, concealing the trenchant possibilities of his style and clothing himself in a garb of meekness and self-mockery. Thus he won that immunity which a society will typically allow an outsider whom it perceives as unthreatening to its way of life.' Sandiford contrasts Sancho with the 'more combative' temperaments of Cugoano and Equiano, both seen as writers who affirm their African identities and forcefully attack the assumptions and evils of the slave traders and owners.

These responses to Sancho have been summarized and dismissed succinctly and wittily by Sukhdev Sandhu in an essay on 'Ignatius Sancho and Laurence Sterne'. Lampooning the standard contrast between an 'Uncle Tom' Sancho and Equiano as a Malcolm X precursor, Sandhu writes:

Sancho, one infers, is an inauthentic black Englishman. How, the assumption runs, can he be 'real' if, unlike most of his fellow Negroes in the capital, he managed to escape a life of hard, maritime, plantation, or domestic drudgery by acquiring an aristocratic cicerone in the form of the Duke of Montagu? How can he have known suffering when Gainsborough's portrait shows him not only to be amply girthed, but, heaven forfend!, smiling? What chance have we of hearing the slave's primal scream when Sancho wrote so plummily, so polysyllabically? In contrast, we are often led to believe, Olaudah Equiano (whose *Interesting Narrative* was published in 1789) was the real deal: he was lean, necessarily mean, an activist who travelled the length and breadth of the United Kingdom hawking copies of his autobiography and promoting Abolitionism. In today's academic parlance, he was palpably a 'cultural worker'.[26]

Such judgements of Sancho have also been questioned by Vincent Carretta, in his notes and his introduction to his very informative edition of the *Letters*. Both Sandhu and Carretta castigate earlier ahistorical critiques and seek to place Sancho in a more complex literary, cultural, and historical perspective.

Sandhu's essays make a significant break with previous traditions of reading Sancho by allowing us to see him in different contexts. They place him in relation to Sterne, not as his black shadow, but as a writer and artist, a man of letters, who chose and adapted Sterne's techniques for reasons of temperament, philosophy, morality and aesthetics. He cites the narrator of *Tristram Shandy* regarding the moral point of Sterne's narrative technique, and refusal of linearity ('my work is digressive, and it is progressive too, – and at the same time'), and also Sterne's sermon on the Good Samaritan, praising him for his willingness to deviate from the straight line.[27] And later in the essay Sandhu tellingly quotes Sancho's letter about Phyllis Wheatley, casting a jaundiced eye on those who praised and certified her genius without releasing her from bondage: 'These great good folks – all know – and perhaps admired – nay, praised genius in bondage – and then, like the Priests and Levites in sacred writ, passed by – not one good Samaritan among them.'[28]

Sandhu and Carretta both bring in to the picture the importance of acknowledging the genre of letter writing and the rhetorical strategies which Sancho, as a self-conscious – rather than 'charmingly naive' – man of letters employed. They have pointed the way for further work which would lead to more precise identification of his strategies with regard to individual readers, the first recipients of his letters, and how these differ from reader to reader and letter to letter. Such a study would lead, I believe, to a better understanding of Sancho's writing and identity, not in terms of his relationship to a collective 'black' identity, but in terms of what Stuart Hall has called a cultural identity of 'positioning'.[29]

Although Hall's essay is directed towards the differences of positioning (between African, European, and American 'presences') of various Caribbean groups, his discussion can also be made relevant not only to the general cultural positioning of Ignatius Sancho with regard to his society and his readers then and now, but also in regard to different

readers. For whereas the writing of Cugoano and Equiano seeks to position the author more single-mindedly as an African and ex-slave addressing a generalized public audience, Sancho writes from a multiplicity of
positions to a variety of audiences, the play between author and reader
marked by differences or similarities in gender, class, status, age, and
colour. And yet, what Hall says with regard to the difference between
Martinique and Jamaica, and Martinique and France is also relevant.
He comments:

> One trivial example is the way Martinique both *is* and *is not* 'French'. It is, of
> course, a *department* of France, and this is reflected in its standard and style of
> life: Fort de France is a much richer, more 'fashionable' place than Kingston, –
> which is not only visibly poorer, but itself at a point of transition between being
> 'in fashion' in an Anglo-African and Afro-American way – for those who can
> afford to be in any sort of fashion at all. Yet, what is distinctively 'Martiniquais'
> can only be described in terms of that special and peculiar supplement which
> the black and mulatto skin adds to the 'refinement' and sophistication of a
> Parisian-derived *haute couture*; that is, a sophistication which, because it is black,
> is always transgressive.[30]

One might replace 'Martinique' with the name of Ignatius Sancho, and
'Jamaica' with that larger group of black labourers, sailors, and escaped
slaves who lived in eighteenth-century England. The Derridean notion of
the supplementary, and of meaning in relation to positioning, becomes
a useful one to allow us to move away from judging Sancho only in
relation to some imagined and static collective black identity to seeing
him as a man inventing himself, and doing so with particular flair, wit,
and compassion, at a particular moment in history.

Reading back into their historical and social context, one might see the
Letters in the spirit of the 'conversation pieces' painted and popularized
by Hogarth and other artists earlier in the century. As Jenny Uglow puts
it, 'Art that resembled conversation was both intimate and public', and
every social or group conversation involved the assuming of a persona
for the occasion. Uglow goes on to say, 'The conversation piece was civilized but informal, fanciful and new, and . . . radically different to baroque
decoration, classical solemnity, or even to the sympathetically straight-
forward portraits.'[31] My point is that the age did not demand or expect
an essential self to be revealed, nor did it use the criteria of authenticity
and sincerity – and it is as post-Romantic critics that we judge by such
criteria. Sancho's readers, many of them like him great addicts of the
theatre, would have appreciated his skill at role-playing, and his ability to

perform the right role for each occasion and each reader. His awareness of the varied letter-writing modes is made clear in his November 1777 letter to Mrs Cocksedge:

Now, whether to address – according to the distant, reserved, cold, mechanical forms of high-breeding – where polished manners, like a horse from the manege, prances fantastic – and, shackled with the rules of art – proudly despises simple nature; – or shall I, like the patient, honest, sober, long-ear'd animal – take plain nature's path – and address you according to my feelings? – My dear friend – you wanted to know the reason I had never addressed a line to you; – the plain and honest truth is, I thought writing at – was better than writing to you – that's one reason; – now a second reason is – I know my own weakness too well to encounter with your little friend – whom I fear as a critic – and envy as a writer . . . (Letter 55, p. 114)

This performing of roles was not the same as 'playing up to' or placating the white folks. An attentive reading of the letters, it seems to me, sees Sancho playfully pretending to accept certain labels and roles precisely so that his readers will reject them. The obvious example is in the famous letter to Sterne, where he identifies himself as 'one of those whom the vulgar and illiberal call "Negurs"' – thus making it impossible for Sterne or any other reader to affirm such an identification with the 'vulgar' and its connotations. But I would argue that a similar strategy runs through a great many of the letters, where the reader is placed in the position of hearing and rejecting the simple reduction of the writer to such identities as 'a blackamoor', 'a black Falstaff', an outcast from Noah's ark. It is interesting to note that the exception, where he willingly assumes and affirms the persona of an African, is in his public letters, many of which are signed 'Africanus'.

Sancho's device of offering labels and stereotypes for his readers to refuse is also part and parcel of his technique as a letter writer, a conversationalist, who actively engages with his readers, and demands their involvement. In other words he is 'writing to', rather than 'writing at' his readers. This engagement with his readers, and within the letters the frequent references to other friends and members of the family, has a further function – that of establishing a *community* of letter readers, or rather communities within communities (widening out to the readers of all the letters and readers over the centuries), within which Sancho, rather than being at the margins, is at the very centre! It is a community in part created and orchestrated by him, with its members responding to him, and finally responding to one another in relation to him.

OLAUDAH EQUIANO

Whereas Ignatius Sancho wrote as a man of many parts – a servant, a friend, a musician, a commentator on the arts, a father, a husband – who happened to be black, Olaudah Equiano's identity as an African and an ex-slave is central to the narrative persona he constructs. Sancho's letters suggest the fluidity of his identity and his relationships; Equiano presents a narrative which asserts an always already constructed personality, which cannot and will not be constrained by slavery. Equiano's *Narrative* proclaims individual achievement which reflects well on his fellow Africans; Sancho's concern is always with human relations, the maintenance of a community, a fellowship of English citizens, black and white. And for Sancho, the difference between African and English is entirely a matter of colour rather than culture, and the consequent difference perceived by some whites.

The Interesting Narrative of the Life of Olaudah Equiano, or Gustavus Vassa, the African was first published in 1789 and was read then and later chiefly as a contribution to the anti-slave-trade crusade. It was submitted to parliament as documentary evidence when the bill for the abolition of the slave-trade was being debated in 1792, and the submission included a long list of subscribers headed by the Prince of Wales, other aristocratic and wealthy patrons, and well-known supporters of the abolition movement such as Thomas Clarkson, Josiah Wedgwood, and William the son of Ignatius Sancho. This particular 1792 edition and subsequent editions also included a series of letters and testimonials indignantly refuting the claim that Equiano had not written the narrative himself and that he was not born in Africa but on the Dutch island of Santa Cruz.[32] Equiano asserts that others can testify that he spoke 'no language but that of Africa' when he first arrived in England. In so far as it was read as testimony as to the brutality and immorality, and indeed the economic impracticability of the slave-trade, the authenticity of the account was important. But in so far as it was to be read then and later as a literary work, proving that its author could be ranked among other canonized writers of his time, critics have also sought to emphasize the fictionality of his work. The questions of authenticity and value change depending on the stance of particular critics, for all of whom Equiano represents a 'first' – the originary figure. The Igbo Nigerian novelist Chinua Achebe champions him as the first Igbo writer, and finds evidence of the accuracy of his account in the place names mentioned, the use of Igbo words, the customs described, the character he expresses, and the religious attitudes.[33] Catherine Acholonu, another Igbo Nigerian critic, has further investigated the historical authenticity of Equiano's roots.[34] S.E. Ogude, a Nigerian of Yoruba origin, insists on the fictionality of Equiano's descriptions of Africa and other events, and places him in the tradition of Defoe and Swift.[35] Robert Steptoe and Houston Baker, both African American critics in university English departments, link the genre of his writing to the picaresque novel on the one hand, and to the African folk genre of the trickster tale on the other, a hybrid genre which more recent critics have seen carried on by Mark Twain as well as Ralph Ellison.

African American critics have pointed to two seminal moments in the development of a black American tradition, the slave narrative beginning with Olaudah Equiano, and the Harlem Renaissance, beginning variously with James Weldon Johnson, W.E.B. DuBois, Alain Locke, or Langston Hughes. Equiano's *Interesting Narrative* is cited as providing a blueprint for a genre which dominated writing by black Americans during the nineteenth century and continues to inform autobiographical and fictional narratives in the twentieth, including those by Frederick Douglass, Harriet Jacobs, Richard Wright, Maya Angelou, and Ralph Ellison. Critics such as Henry Louis Gates Jr, Charles T. Davis, Houston Baker and Robert Steptoe have pointed to the shared tropes and rhetorical devices in these works. All are seen to foreground a series of crucial moments: the loss or absence of an ancestral history and family, the discovery of what it means to be a slave, the discovery of book learning and the struggle to achieve it, scenes of brutality and degradation in the treatment of slaves, the importance of Christianity and the difference between true Christianity and the hypocritical Christianity of slave-traders and slave-owners, the escape to freedom in the north or in England. Many of the slave narratives are also preceded by letters and testimonials indicating that the work is indeed written by the black man or woman.

But Equiano differs from later authors of slave narratives in that he is not only the first to write such a substantial narrative, but also the first to seek to create an authentic representation of African culture and traditions. (One or two earlier writers such as Gronniosaw and Cugoano merely mention that they were born in Africa and describe the circumstances of their kidnapping, but they do not seek to describe in detail their life in Africa.) In so doing, he sets out to create both what Rushdie would later term 'an imaginary homeland', and what Benedict Anderson would term 'an imagined community'. However, that 'imagined community' becomes a flexible and changing one, both in terms of race and place. Throughout the *Narrative* he refers to 'his countrymen', signifying sometimes all Africans, and sometimes more specifically those who come from the same region and speak the same language as he did. But both the *Narrative* and the letters which precede it also lay claim to his right as a British subject, and his membership of a nation which is in its ideal form is Christian, liberal, humane, free, and proficient in the arts and sciences. (Equiano prefaces the 1792 edition of his *Narrative* with an acknowledgement of the virtues of 'a nation which, by its liberal sentiments, its humanity, the glorious freedom of its government, and its proficiency in arts and sciences, has exalted the dignity of human nature.'[36]) Much of the interest of the *Narrative* lies in its negotiation of the tension between these two homelands and his identity as an African and an Englishman, sometimes seen as a linear movement from one to the other, sometimes as an interweaving of the two or a dialectic. A further dialectic involves an implicit one with a European representation of Africa as the home of a barbaric, savage, and promiscuous society in order to justify or ameliorate the consequences of the slave-trade.

Hence Equiano begins by establishing the authenticity of his home-land from an anthropological point of view, with an account of its 'manners', customs, rituals, and economy. The 'charming fruitful vale, named Essaka'[37] where he was born is described as a kind of Eden, a world where all the women are beautiful and pure, where nature is hard-working, and where men and women alike work industriously and as a community, tilling the soil and weaving and dyeing cloth. It is appealing in its simplicity and innocence, a place where 'the natives are unacquainted with those refinements in cookery which debauch the taste' (*Narrative*, p. 35); it is also exotic in its remoteness from Europe. Essaka is depicted as a community, or nation, where the arts flourish: 'We are almost a nation of dancers, musicians and poets' (p. 34). Equiano is at pains to portray the viability, the validity, and self-sustainability of his community, which is at once local and specific and also representative of a larger African society: 'The manners and government of a people who have little com-merce with other countries are generally very simple; and the history of what passes in one family or village may serve as a specimen of the whole nation' (p. 32). Yet at the same time, the difference cannot be so great as to alienate the possibility of sympathy or empathy. Hence Equiano provides comparisons which will draw together the known and the un-known. He describes the dress of the Igbo as a 'long piece of calico; or muslin, wrapped loosely around the body, somewhat in the form of a Highland plaid' (p. 34). Musical instruments are compared to the guitar and stickado (a kind of xylophone). Doubtless, in creating this image of his homeland Equiano draws upon other sources, such as Michael Adanson's *A Voyage to Senegal, the Isle of Goree, and the River Gambia* (London, 1759), which is quoted in anti-slavery literature of the time, particularly Anthony Benezet's *Account* and in John Bicknell's poem, 'The Dying Negro', a poem cited by Equiano later in the *Narrative*. Adanson's oft-cited passage reads:

Which way soever I turned my eyes on this pleasant spot, I beheld a perfect image of pure nature: an agreeable solitude, bounded on every side by a charming landscape; the rural situation of cottages in the midst of trees; the ease and indolence of the Negroes, reclined under the shade of their spreading foliage; the simplicity of their dress and manners; the whole revived in my mind, the idea of our first parents, and I seemed to contemplate the world in its primeval state.[38]

However, although Equiano's presentation of Essaka has affinities with Adanson's presentation of African village life, there are significant differences. One is his emphasis on the lack of indolence in his society, and he goes to some lengths to detail the kind of work done by men and women, the long hours they spend, and also the fact that men and women alike serve in the militia. Nor does his representation imply 'the world in its primeval state', given the extent to which he describes the various agricultural pursuits of men and women, and the careful planning and arrangement of the housing and compounds of the village. While his stress on the industry of Africans relates to an argument which he will take up towards the end of the narrative concerning the benefits of commerce and trade with Africa, nevertheless he is also concerned to show a society that is harmonious, virtuous, and innocent of evil, hence a society which offers a vastly superior state to slavery. Such a representation serves to counter the assertions of those in favour of the slave-trade that slavery offers an improvement on what were claimed to be wholly harsh and degraded conditions in African societies.

In the face of European stereotypes of Africans as unclean, licentious, and sexually promiscuous, Equiano is also at pains to insist on the cleanliness, chastity, modesty, and strictness of laws against adultery in his native society, all to a much greater extent than in European society ('before we taste our food, we always wash our hands; indeed our cleanliness on all occasions is extreme'; 'Our women too were, in my eyes at

least, uncommonly graceful, alert, and modest to a degree of bashful-
ness; nor do I remember to have ever heard of an instance of inconti-
nence amongst them before marriage' (pp. 35 and 38)). He acknowledges
the existence of palm wine, but contrary to Amos Tutuola and Achebe
200 years later, insists that no one gets intoxicated from it. He also draws
an extended comparison between the customs and laws of the Igbo and
those of Jewish people, 'while they were in that pastoral state which is
described in Genesis' (p. 44). Here he is not only linking the unknown
with the known, but also joining in yet another debate concerning the
genealogy and humanity of Africans, by suggesting the common descent
of Europeans and Africans from Abraham, and denying also the argument that Africans are marked and condemned to be outcasts or 'hewers
of wood and carriers of water' as descendants of either Cain or Ham. Instructed by his fellow shipmate, Daniel Queen, who tells him he is a free
man, Equiano at a later point in the narrative tells how he learns about
the Bible and is struck by the similarity between the Old Testament and
his own country's laws. Here Equiano's concern to draw comparisons
between African (or Igbo) customs and the Old Testament contrasts with
Gronniosaw's absolute rejection of his native religion and customs.

Through the technique of telling his story of kidnapping from the
perspective of a child, Equiano also revises European narratives of the
encounter with Africa. His journey from the interior to the coast reverses
the Western paradigm of the explorer's journey from civilization to savagery, as he leaves behind the language and virtues of his own community
to discover African peoples living near the coast as both westernized and
lacking in the signs of civilization:

All the nations and peoples I had hitherto passed through resembled our own
in their manners, customs and language: but I came at length to a country the
inhabitants of which differed from us in all those particulars. I was very much
struck with this difference, especially when I came upon a people who did not
circumcise, and eat without washing their hands. They cooked also in iron pots,
and had European cutlasses and cross bows, which were unknown to us, and
fought with their fists among themselves. Their women were not so modest as
ours, for they eat, and drank, and slept with their men. But above all, I was
amazed to see no sacrifices or offerings among them. In some of those places
the people ornamented themselves with scars, and likewise filed their teeth very
sharp. They wanted sometimes to ornament me in the same manner, but I
would not suffer them; hoping that I might sometime be among a people who
did not thus disfigure themselves. (pp. 53–4)

From the fertile but corrupted world of coastal Africa, whose corruption
is seen not in the offering of sacrifices but the failure to do so, as well as

in the disfigurement of the body, Equiano takes us to his first astonished glimpse of the ocean and a slave-ship, awaiting its cargo:

These [the sight of the ocean and the slave ship] filled me with astonishment, which was soon converted into terror, which I am yet at a loss to describe, nor the then feelings of my mind. When I was carried on board I was immediately handled and tossed up, to see if I were sound, by some of the crew; and I was now persuaded that I had gotten into a world of bad spirits and that they were going to kill me. Their complexions too differing so much from ours, their long hair, and the language they spoke, which was very different from any I had ever heard, united to confirm in me this belief.... I asked [the black people who had brought me on board] if we were not to be eaten by those white men with horrible looks, red faces, and long hair. (p. 55)

The various editions and the revisions of the first sentences of this partic-ular passage suggest the difficulty Equiano encountered when describ-ing this episode. His first (1789) version refers to 'the astonishment, which was soon converted into terror when I was carried on board. I was immediately handled...' This is revised in the third edition to 'the aston-ishment, which was soon converted into terror, which I am yet at a loss to describe; and the then feelings of my mind when carried on board. I was immediately handled...' The version in the passage above occurs first in the fifth edition. The later attempts, as well as the revisions themselves, suggest the trauma of that moment when he first encounters Europeans.

Thus Equiano reverses the norms of colour and appearance and aesthetics assumed by Europeans in relation to Africans. The reiterated trope of cannibalism as a feature of African savagery is also turned against the white men, even including the stereotype of the large pot of human stew so beloved of Western legends and anecdotes about Africa and the South Pacific. In later sections he will emphasize the unchristian behaviour of these white men, and their extraordinarily savage behaviour to one another, for 'the white people looked and acted, as I thought, in so savage a manner; for I had never seen among any people such instances of brutal cruelty; and this not only shown towards us blacks, but also to some of the whites themselves' (p. 57). Yet another reversal occurs in the narrative when Equiano is involved in a shipwreck on a desert island, and becomes the resourceful Crusoe figure who refuses to despair, finds the resources to survive, and saves the lives of his 'white' shipmates.

Thus Equiano draws on and refashions a number of literary traditions to his own purposes; he redeploys the travel narrative to draw on the anthropological observing mode of European travellers reporting back 'home', but at the same time he resituates the European observer as the observed. There is also the narrative of conversion, the movement from sin to redemption, which again Equiano refashions, so that one has in the first section of the book a movement from innocence to experience, from paradise to hell, and in the second half of the book a second counter movement from ignorance to knowledge and salvation, both in terms of salvation from slavery and salvation from paganism. For Equiano, the second movement from ignorance to knowledge also involves the gaining of book knowledge. A third trajectory in the narrative involves his quest for community and for communication; his inability to speak the language of his captors or fellow slaves or shipmates is frequently emphasized as the source of his estrangement. Within the narrative, the community of the ship becomes a continuing image of communities which are utterly dystopian (the slave-ship), or dysfunctional (as on his first voyage to England), or where true fellowship is found, and the good of the community is dependent on the government of the captain and his treatment of the men as equals, but above all on his keeping his word.

Although the *Narrative* is presented as an intervention in a public debate, it rests its appeal on the grounds of the authentic individual and personal experience of an African 'torn away from all the tender connections that were naturally dear to the heart' and an appeal to sentiment and feeling, as the passages above illustrate.[39] In this way, he bridges the public, rational discourse of Cugoano's *Thoughts and Sentiments on the... Slavery and Commerce of the Human Species*, which in turn alludes to Thomas Clarkson's *An Essay on the Slavery and Commerce of the Human Species*, and the personal account and testimony of his spiritual conversion related by Gronniosaw and transcribed by 'an elegant lady'. As Sonia Hofkosh points out, the preface to the 1814 edition foregrounds the power of the *Narrative*'s personal appeal to the hearts and humane feelings of its readers:

Being a true relation of occurrences which had taken place, and of sufferings which he had endured, it produced a degree of humane feeling in men's minds, to excite which the most animated addresses and the most convincing reasoning would have laboured in vain.[40]

Hofkosh comments that the book proposes to present and is read as representing 'individual experience to [the readers] – both the author's and their own – creating for them an isolated, intimate space through which they can respond sympathetically to its argument. It operates from inside-out, self-referentially, narrowing its focus in order to universalise its appeal.'[41] The appeal to individual experience and sentiment, to the authority and authenticity of the personal, links Equiano with the ethos of Romanticism, and also to the individualism, the desire for self-mastery and self-autonomy, which nourishes and is nourished by capitalism. Equiano gives willingly of his labour in return for 'just' payment, and bittterly resents the injustice when the investment of his labour is refused an equitable return. And it is in keeping with this ethos that he accepts the proposition that he should purchase his own freedom, and so become his own property, unlike Frederick Douglass and Harriet Jacobs later, who resist what they see as the indignity of having to purchase their freedom. Equiano's representation of this moment of liberation, his own self-purchase, and legal manumission is eloquently conveyed:

My imagination was all rapture as I flew to the register Office; and, in this respect, like the apostle Peter, (whose deliverance from prison was so sudden and extraordinary, that he thought he was in a vision), I could scarcely believe I was awake. Heavens! Who could do justice to my feelings at this moment? Not conquering heroes themselves, in the midst of triumph – Not the tender mother who has just regained her long-lost infant, and presses it to her heart – Not the weary hungry mariner, at the sight of the desired friendly port – Not the lover, when he once more embraces his beloved mistress, after she had been ravished from his arms! – All within my breast was tumult, wildness, and delirium! My feet scarcely touched the ground, for they were winged with joy, and like Elijah, as he rose to Heaven, they 'were with lightning sped as I went on.' Everyone I met I told of my happiness, and blazed about the virtue of my amiable master and captain. (p. 136)

Thus in the description of the moment of his freedom, Equiano encapsulates all human experience, male and female, child and adult, religious, public, and private. The passage also interestingly begins and ends with religious experience, from the moment of release into this world to the moment of transport to heaven and out of this world. The invocation of these varieties of emotion and feeling is a universal one conveyed with the rhetoric and style of the sentimental novel; nevertheless, Equiano also adds a cultural supplement when he reports that his 'joy was still heightened by the blessings and prayers of the sable race, particularly the aged, to whom my heart had ever been attached with reverence' (p. 137), an attachment which (like his resumption of his African name) reiterates his continuing adherence to his native Igbo culture with its deep respect for the elders of the clan.

Unlike many subsequent slave narratives Equiano's does not end with escape or freedom. The 1845 narrative of his life by Frederick Douglass ends with his escape to the north; Harriet Jacobs concludes her *Incidents in the Life of a Slave Girl* with the words, 'Reader, my story ends not with marriage but freedom.' In extending his narrative beyond the achievement of freedom, Equiano also extends his account as travel narrative, spiritual journey, and autobiography. But he also does not wish to conclude his narrative in the West Indies, for after his numerous ventures and adventures, he has to establish himself as a member of his new home community, which is England. He tells us that despite his appeal as a freeman in his 'Georgia super-fine new cloathes' to 'some of the sable females', his 'heart was still fixed on London', and he was determined 'to see Old England once more, and surprise my old master, Capt. Pascal, who was hourly in my mind; for I still loved him, notwithstanding his usage of me...' (p. 138).

In the first, two-volume edition of *The Interesting Narrative*, Equiano gains his freedom in the final chapter of the first volume, and in that same chapter goes on to prove his worth as a free man, or perhaps his manhood, first through a violent encounter and stand-off with a slave-owner in Georgia, and then by taking command of a ship when the captain dies, so that on his successful return to Montserrat he is given the honorary title of 'Captain'. The frontispiece to the second volume shows an etching of a shipwreck, *Bahama Banks, 1767*, thus highlighting Equiano's role both as the saviour of the white crew and captain in that incident, and as the rescuer of a cargo of twenty slaves, whom the white captain wishes to prevent escaping from the hold lest they take up places on the lifeboats. Equiano intervenes and prevents him from nailing down the hatches. Thus the second volume begins by presenting Equiano in his liberated role as an equal, and indeed superior, of the white men with whom he works, and as the intermediary between those who are still enslaved and their masters. Cast away on a desert island, Equiano proves as resourceful as Robinson Crusoe in finding food and water and fashioning shelter for himself and his shipmates. Here the trope of the cannibals on the 'deserted' island is presented as an illusion. A flock of flamingoes stood on the beach and 'these, from the reflection of the sun, appeared to us, at a little distance, as large as men;...our captain swore they were cannibals.' Whereas the captain is so fearful that he wants to abandon the island, Equiano insists on approaching nearer, 'and perhaps these cannibals may take to the water' (p. 152).

But if the trials he encounters in the Americas allow Equiano to assert his manhood and also to defend his freedom, it is on his return to England that he may begin to express his full humanity. There he can learn a trade as a hairdresser, take lessons on the French horn, and attend evening school for further instruction in mathematics. When his money runs out, he takes a job on another ship, and describes his voyages to France, Turkey, Italy, Greece, and Portugal as through the eyes of a man free to enjoy the sensual and aesthetic pleasures offered by these lands and cultures. A further voyage to the West Indies offers a distanced and rather summary view of the condition of black people there: 'There was a vast number of negroes here [in Jamaica], whom I found, as usual, exceedingly imposed upon by the white people, and the slaves punished as in the other islands' (p. 171). And, 'roused by the sound of fame to seek new adventures', he joins an expedition to the North Pole in 1773, a vividly described and incident-filled journey which places him firmly as a member of the community of seamen. Throughout the brief four-page account of this adventure, he consistently uses the first person plural, 'we', 'us', 'our', rather than the first person singular 'I' which is typical of his description of earlier experiences, and where he is most frequently at odds with or distinguished from masters and crew.

The three remaining chapters of Equiano's *Narrative* focus on his spiritual search and conversion to Methodism, his entry into public life both as a leader and spokesman for the black community, and his role as a missionary. Chapter Ten seems to juxtapose and describe in considerable detail two disparate events: his futile attempts to obtain the release of a kidnapped former slave and friend, John Annis, and the depression, despair, and darkness which invade his soul in his quest for spiritual salvation. Equiano indirectly suggests that the first incident is the cause of his dark night of the soul: 'suffering much by villains in the late cause, and being much concerned about the state of my soul, these things (but particularly the latter) brought me very low', so that he decides to go to Turkey and 'never more return to England' (p. 181). Salvation and 'the glad tiding which eventually set [him] at liberty' comes when the reliance on self, his own assertion of mastery of his destination, is set aside to acknowledge himself at the disposition of God, his new 'owner' (p. 192). His conversion and new-found grace and spiritual liberty also construct him for the first time *within* the narrative as a *writer*, and he appends to this chapter a poem of twenty-eight stanzas titled, 'Miscellaneous Verses, OR Reflections on the State of my Mind during my first Convictions of the Necessity of believing the Truth, and of experiencing the inestimable Benefits of Christianity'. Two final chapters take the author and his

readers on a multitude of adventures, the failure of the mission to establish a new homeland in Sierra Leone, and a final return to his now
accepted home in England and marriage.

Unlike Equiano and the other African British writers discussed so far,
Sake Dean Mahomed,[42] the first Indian author to take up residence
in Britain, left his native land of his own free will, choosing to journey
from India to Europe and then to remain there. Born in 1759 (or possibly
earlier) in Patna, and related to the family which governed Bengal, Bihar,
and Orissa, Dean Mahomed followed in his father's footsteps as a petty
officer in the ranks of the East India Company army, before travelling
with a Protestant Anglo-Irish army officer, Captain Godfrey Evan Baker,
to Ireland, where he married an Irishwoman and remained for over
twenty years. In 1794 he published *The Travels of Dean Mahomet*, written
as a series of letters to an unnamed and fictitious friend (see Fig. 3). In
1807 he and his family left Ireland to live in England, first in London
and then in Brighton, where he gained some fame as a practitioner of
oriental medicine, patronized by wealthy and aristocratic Englishmen
and women, including the royal family. It was there he wrote *Shampooing;
or Benefits Resulting from the Use of the Indian Medicated Vapour Bath* (1822).
He died in Brighton in 1851.

Despite the differences in circumstances, and the comparative readiness of the English and Anglo-Irish to admit the humanity of Indians,
there are some similarities in the ways in which Equiano and Dean
Mahomed present themselves. The title page emphasises that the book
is 'written by himself'. Arguably this statement is more concerned with
investing the work with authenticity, and establishing its difference from
the numerous travels written by Englishmen and women such as William
Hodges (*Travels in India . . . 1780 . . . 1783*), Jemima Kindersley (*Letters from
the Island of Teneriffe . . . and the East Indies*), and John Henry Grose's *Voyage
to the East Indies*, than with asserting the author's humanity through his
ability to write. As Michael Fisher demonstrates, Dean Mahomed drew
on the writings of Grose and Kindersley, reorienting their words for
his own purposes.[43] He may also have been influenced by the success
of Equiano's *Narrative*, which Equiano promoted on a visit to Cork in
1791, and which, like Dean Mahomed's work, combines autobiography, participation in the military, and observation of scenes and peoples
in other lands. Another inspiration could be the anonymous epistolary

3 Frontispiece to Dean Mahomet's *Travels* (1794). Reproduced by permission of The British Library

novel, *Hartley House, Calcutta* (1789).[44] Yet another influence may have
been popular travel books such as Arthur Young's *A Tour in Ireland* (1780)
and Tobias Smollett's *Travels through France and Italy* (1766), which was also
written in the form of a series of letters to imaginary correspondents.

Like Equiano, Dean Mahomed commences by setting up a contrast
between his utopian native land and a more artificial and less moral
Europe. Asserting his sense of the strangeness of Ireland when he first
arrived from India, and how it contrasted with 'those *striking scenes* in
India which we are wont to survey with a kind of sublime delight', Dean
Mahomed goes on to portray the natural bounty of India and goodwill
of its inhabitants:

The people of India, in general, are peculiarly favoured by Providence in the
possession of all that can cheer the mind and allure the eye, and tho' the situation
of Eden is only traced in the Poet's creative fancy, the traveller beholds with
admiration the face of this delightful country, on which he discovers tracts that
resemble those so finely drawn by the animated pencil of Milton. You will
here behold the generous soil crowned with various plenty; the garden flowers
diffusing their fragrance on the bosom of the air; and the very bowels of the
earth enriched with inestimable mines of gold and diamonds.

    Possessed of all that is enviable in life, we are still more happy in the exercise of
benevolence and good-will to each other, devoid of every species of fraud or low
cunning. In our convivial enjoyments, we are never without our neighbours; as
it is usual for an individual, when he gives an entertainment, to invite all those of
his own profession to partake of it. That profligacy of manners too conspicuous
in other parts of the world, meets here with public indignation, and our women,
though not so accomplished as those of Europe, are still very engaging for many
virtues that exalt the sex.[45]

Despite their shared emphasis on the natural bounty of their native
lands, the generous and uncorrupted character of their inhabitants, and
the virtue of their women, these opening comments also suggest the
divergences between Equiano's and Dean Mahomed's works. Whereas
Equiano has a distinct moral and polemical purpose, and presents a
persona who speaks plainly, even naively at times, Dean Mahomed begins
by appealing to the aesthetic tastes and the curiosity of his readers. He
declares that he will 'describe the manners of [his] countrymen', who,
he proudly maintains, 'have still more of the innocence of our ancestors,
than some of the boasting philosophers of Europe'. Within the first letter
he establishes himself as a cultivated man of letters, whose allusions
to Milton and whose ready use of literary language demonstrate his
credentials as a writer, not just a witness. It is perhaps indicative of their

differences in purpose and experience that when Equiano cites Milton, it is in reference to descriptions of hell which he compares to the condition of slavery in the West Indies; Dean Mahomed cites Milton in the passage above and later in the *Travels* with reference to descriptions of Paradise, in order to evoke, and in the later citation to authorize, the natural beauty and bounty of India.

Nor does Dean Mahomed seek to recreate the narrative from the point of view of a child, except briefly when he tells of his fascination with the military and his determination to become attached to the English army. Apart from some mention of his mother's grief at losing him and 'resigning her child to the care of Europeans' (*Travels*, p. 42), the reader may easily forget that it is an eleven-year-old boy who apparently accompanies the English officers to the lavish entertainments at the Raja's palace near Patna, and observes the dancing girls 'displaying such loose and fascinating attitudes in their various dances as would warm the bosom of an Anchoret' (p. 34). Nor are we encouraged to speculate how such a young boy could have absorbed and retained so much detailed knowledge of the lay-out of military camps and officers' houses at various places, or come to know such precise details as the kind of cloth used as an undergarment by the Nawab of Bengal on ceremonial occasions and the fact that his turban contained 44 yards of fine white muslin, 'which quantity, from its exceeding fineness, could not weigh more than a pound and a half' (p. 61). Not only does Dean Mahomed erase differences of age between himself and his patron, Baker, and other Anglo-Irish or English men, he also frequently erases differences of rank, race, and culture. Once he has separated himself from his mother and allied himself with Godfrey Baker (at the beginning of Letter 3), he replaces the first person singular with a generalized 'we' when writing about army movements and events: 'Notwithstanding all her vigilance, I found means to join my new master, with whom I went early the next morning to Bankeepore, leaving my mother to lament my departure. As Bankeepore is but a few miles from Patna, we shortly arrived there, that morning' (p. 39). In Letter 4, he writes how 'we lay in Bankeepore about six months, when we received orders from Col. Leslie to march to Denapore, where we arrived in the year 1770, and found the remaining companies of the Europeans and Seapoys,[46] that were quartered here for some time before. Our camp here, consisted of eight regiments' (p. 43).

This passage is typical of those in which he writes about the army's movements. Such merging of his identity with that of the army, and particularly the English officers within it with whom he visits other officers and wealthy administrators in the East India Company, is almost total. It compares with those scenes in Equiano's *Narrative* when he is a member of the naval crews involved in the Seven Years War or later as a member of the expedition to Greenland in search of a north-west passage, although in Equiano's account there is almost always the presence of his distinctive individual experience within that collective identity.

Nevertheless, Dean Mahomed is also keen to establish his identity and credentials as a 'Mahometan' and an Indian, and a member of a superior class within India. In the first two letters, and again in Letter 11, he makes a point of mentioning that his father was related to 'the Nabobs of Moorshadabad' [Murshidabad], a relationship which might be particularly meaningful to his employers and his readers, since it was the Nawab of Bengal, Bihar, and Orissa, whose seat was in Murshidabad, who had most extensively collaborated with the East India Company and given it a mandate to govern and collect revenue in those very substantial and affluent East Indian provinces. He also devotes several letters to detailed accounts of Muslim rituals and customs, including circumcision, marriage, and burial, and sets out to correct prejudices and misunderstandings about Muslim attitudes to Mahomet and the significance of Allah. He takes pride in the culture of Muslims, describing them as 'in general, a very healthful people', bearing sickness, when it comes, 'with much composure of mind', and facing death 'with uncommon resignation and fortitude'. Although Dean Mahomed's name creates a continuing identity with the religion, and although his accounts of Muslim practices and beliefs are perhaps better informed and more favourable than for any other group, it is notable that he does not at any point speak of 'Mahometans' as 'we', and his accounts are always given as an objective, slightly distanced, observer's view. There is not much, in terms of tone, to distinguish them from his explanation of Hindu customs, castes (which he terms 'tribes'), and beliefs, although these explanations are given far less space and detailed elaboration than those pertaining to the Muslims.

Dean Mahomet's greatest enthusiasm is reserved for spectacle and for landscape. There are numerous encomiums to the grandeur and scope of Indian scenery, the fertile valleys and great rivers, the tree-lined roads 'shaded with the spreading branches of fruit-bearing trees, bending under their luscious burthens of bananas, mangoes, and tamarinds', and beneath the trees 'many cool springs and wells of the finest water in the universe' (p. 48). More often than not, such landscapes are viewed from the elevation of a grand house, owned by an official in the East India

Company. Reading the letters one is struck by the wealth and established nature of these English and Anglo-Irish officials, whose houses and estates overlooking the land they claim to govern are reminiscent of those eighteenth-century houses asserting the ascendancy of the Protestant gentry in Ireland.[47] Perhaps less reminiscent of the Protestant landlord class in Ireland is the apparent respect for the native aristocracy, and the social interaction between them, and also with and between Hindu and Muslim elite classes. But if the East India Company army general and the top officials live in considerable splendour, Dean Mahomed takes care to let us know that the palaces and entertainments of Indian princes and rulers are even more magnificent. In his second letter, for example, after his glowing description of the music and dancing laid on for the officers at the Raja's palace, he tells us that the Raja's servants then let off fireworks 'displaying, in the most astonishing variety, the forms of birds, beasts, and other animals, and far surpassing anything of the kind I ever beheld in Europe' (p. 37). In a later letter the magnificence of the Nawab of Bengal's ceremonial dress and procession is described in minute detail.

Only in the final nine letters of the thirty-eight in the volume does Dean Mahomed sometimes surface as an individual actor, with a distinctive role and perspective. Thus in Letter 30, concerning his activities when he would then have reached the age of twenty, he describes vividly the taking of Fort William, and how afterwards, 'From one of the apartments of the Imperial palace, built by Akbar, within the fort, I looked down, and beheld, as it were from the clouds, the town, four hundred feet below me: such an awful scene forms a subject for the pen of the most sublime artist (p. 113).

Here Dean Mahomed presents himself as a mature and authoritative viewer, who perceives and orders the world around him with the sensibility of an eighteenth-century European artist. In the subsequent letter, he writes not as a spectator, but as a participant with an active role, enabled by his appointment as a Subidar (or ensign) in charge of a sepoy detachment. His description of his encounter with a group of angry peasants, his struggle for survival and near drowning as he swims across the Ganges, and his rescue by other peasants, is reminiscent, in its partly self-ironic presentation, of Equiano's mode of presenting himself as not so much a hero as one who gets into scrapes, and one who owes his survival to Providence rather than traditional heroic feats. Such feats belong, in Dean Mahomed's book, to his 'superiors', both British and Indian.

Equiano had also made much of the barrier created by language, his inability to understand his captors, and his struggle to acquire English and to learn to read and write. Dean Mahomed entirely suppresses the issue of language; he does not tell us how he learned English, or whether he possessed any understanding of it when he first followed Mr Baker. We do not know how or in what language Baker ascertained that Dean Mahomed 'would like living with the Europeans', nor in what language the eleven-year-old Dean Mahomed 'told him with eager joy, how happy he could make me, by taking me with him' (p. 38), nor in what 'language of supplication' his mother entreated that he might be returned to her (p. 42). Nowhere is there any indication that the languages spoken by English administrators and traders, by Moghul rulers and other Muslims, by Hindu princes and soldiers, by the Marathas and by mountain peoples such as the Paraheas, might differ from one another, or indeed be incomprehensible from one group to the next. One effect of this erasure is the tension it creates between the conventions of literature of sensibility and the insistence on Dean Mahomed's own agency. As Kate Teltscher points out, the scene in which Dean Mahomed describes his parting with his mother and her anguished plea for his return is replete with 'the language and even the punctuation of the literature of sensibility':[48]

I would not go, I told her – I would stay in the camp; her disappointment smote my soul – she stood silent – yet I could perceive some tears succeed each other, stealing down her cheeks – my heart was wrung – at length, seeing my resolution fixed as fate, she dragged herself away, and returned home in a state of mind beyond my power to describe. Mr Baker was much affected. (p. 42)

The tears, the anguish, the 'state of mind beyond my power to describe' are all reminiscent of those scenes where mothers are parted from their children in narratives of slavery and abolitionist poems. But as Kate Teltscher also points out, Dean Mahomed is emphatic that he willingly chooses to go with Baker, and indeed has engineered the invitation by persistently placing himself in Baker's presence and seeking to attract his attention. Dean Mahomed is both seduced and seducer, both sufferer and inflicter of suffering; the reader cannot clearly find a villain or a sentimental hero in this account. This passage draws attention more powerfully than others to Dean Mahomed's conflicting allegiances as a willing collaborator in the East India Company army, and suggests the shifting positioning which runs through the whole work.

Thus although his explanations of Hindu and other local customs and beliefs are given far less space and detailed elaboration than those pertaining to the Muslims, they are nevertheless more sympathetic than accounts given by European travellers. Michael Fisher notes that Dean Mahomed draws substantially on such earlier accounts, in particular those of Jemima Kindersley and John Henry Grose, but mostly to reorient and give a more favourable gloss on particular customs condemned by them.[49] The magnificence of the Nawab of Bengal's ceremonial dress and procession is described in minute detail. So too are the Hindu and Moghul buildings of Delhi and Ayodha, and the luxurious palace and lifestyle of the Nawab Shuja-al Daula, who is, however, represented as an example of excess and decadence. One of a half-dozen extended anecdotes within the *Travels* is devoted to the fate of this Nawab, who was murdered by a princess he had kidnapped and violated, a fate which Dean Mahomed clearly regards as fitting, and an act by the princess presented, together with her subsequent suicide, as heroically virtuous in true sentimental mode: 'the violated female, with a soul, the shrine of purity, like that of the divine Lucretia,... disdaining life after the loss of honour, stabbed her brutal ravisher with a lancet, which she afterwards plunged into her own bosom, and expired' (p. 89).

Dean Mahomed's *Travels* alternate between a merging of his identity and point of view with that of the English and Anglo-Irish officers of the East India Company army, and assertion of his identity as a 'native of India', and an informant who can speak with authority not only about those of his own class and religion, but also Hindus and other groups, to correct misconceptions and prejudices perpetrated by European accounts. As an informant, he becomes one of those 'autoethnographers', who, as Mary Louise Pratt defines the term, are 'colonized subjects who undertake to represent themselves in ways that *engage with* the colonizers' own terms'.[50]

Whereas the earlier accounts of the 'pacification' or routing of Maratha and Paraheas warriors represent them as unruly and savage, in his later letters, the separate points of view become less clear, and the accounts of resistance by Indians far more ambivalent. This wavering allegiance and perspective is particularly apparent in his account of the series of encounters which result in the defeat of Raja Cheyt-singh [Chayt Singh], a ruler who had been 'either unwilling or unable' to pay the revenues demanded by Governor Hastings.[51] Not only does Dean Mahomed devote three long letters to a detailed description of the series of battles which led to the Raja's defeat, he also quotes at length the Raja's eloquent letter in his own defence, in which the Raja asserts that his rule has been an enlightened and constructive one, bringing wealth and harmony to his subjects. Dean Mahomed endorses the Raja's claims, while drawing on vague abstractions to distance himself and the actions of the East India Company from involvement in his defeat in the following words which close his account of the episode: 'Such was the happy situation of the Prince, and the philanthropy of the man, who shortly after became the sport of fortune, amidst the vicissitudes of life, and the trials of adversity' (p. 121).

Fisher speculates that Dean Mahomed's decision to leave the East India Company and travel to Ireland may have been in part a consequence of his growing difficulty in reconciling his allegiance to his country and countrymen with his allegiance to his employer. The final letter (34) preceding his announcement of that decision perhaps gives support to Fisher's suggestion. Here Dean Mahomed closes his account of further skirmishes, in which the army at times met with 'a degree of courage not to be expected in an undisciplined rabble', with a more explicit acknowledgement of the role and effects of the British occupation: 'The refractory were awed into submission by the terror of our arms; yet humanity must lament the loss of those whom wasting war had suddenly swept away.' His acknowledgement is followed by thirteen lines from a poem detailing the suffering and loss involved in war, suffering brought to innocent and guilty alike, and which can 'sweep, at once, whole Empires to the grave'. Such sentiments might well be considered appropriate by a man who has witnessed the destruction of Raja Chayt Singh's kingdom, and the disempowerment of the Mogul empire and kingdoms.

Little is known about Dean Mahomed's twenty-year residence in Cork, although his presence is noted by another 'oriental' traveller, Abu Taleb Ibn Muhammad Khan, who visited Cork in 1799.[52] In 1807 Dean Mahomed and his wife Jane moved to London, and five years later to Brighton, where he established his reputation as a medical man. Here in 1822 he published his second work, a treatise entitled *Shampooing; or Benefits Resulting from the Use of the Indian Medicated Vapour Bath, as Introduced into this Country by S.D. Mahomed*. This publication follows the genre of contemporary medical studies by including a 'scientific' explanation of various diseases, the appropriate cures, and a number of case studies, to which are appended testimonies by grateful patients. In this work, Dean Mahomed re-presents himself as born in 1749, ten years earlier than the date given in the *Travels*, and claims that he was trained as a surgeon in the East India Company army. His dual presentation of himself as drawing on both the ancient arts of Hindu medicine and the modern science of Europe is illustrated in the advertisements for the baths, as well as the portraits of himself in European and 'exotic' oriental mode. As Kate Teltscher comments, *Shampooing*, with its celebration of Dean Mahomed's skill in healing the sick and its reference to his 'introduction' of the benefits of Indian medicine, provides 'a potent counter to the familiar trope of the East as the source of the nation's infection', an image merged with the corruption associated with dissolute nabobs and East India officials, as illustrated in Thackeray's *Vanity Fair*. Thus, as Teltscher argues, Dean Mahomed becomes one of the most striking instances of the ability of some Asian and black writers to draw upon their cultural heritage and their double identity as loyal subjects and 'outsiders' to offer themselves as pathologists, able to redeem the ills which will make Britain a whole and healthy body. In this role he will be followed some five years after his death by the Jamaican medical worker, Mary Seacole, whose autobiography is discussed in Chapter Six.

CHAPTER 3

Speaking truth for freedom and justice: Robert Wedderburn and Mary Prince

The tradition of radical and Christian politics expressed by Equiano and his earlier compatriot Cugoano is continued by two members of a later generation, Robert Wedderburn (1761–1835) and William Davidson (1786–1820). Both were the sons of Scotsmen who had black mistresses in the West Indies. Davidson was the acknowledged son of the Jamaican attorney general, and was sent to Aberdeen to study mathematics. However, he left his studies to become a cabinetmaker, and settled in London, where, influenced by his reading of Thomas Paine's *The Rights of Man*, he became a member of various radical political groups. These included the Marylebone Union Reading Society and the London Corresponding Society, societies which often met in taverns to debate political pamphlets and press reports.[1] Davidson was arrested for his involvement in the Cato Street Conspiracy, a plot to blow up the British parliamentary Cabinet, in 1820, and sentenced to death. Frequently referred to as 'Black' Davidson, in contemporary reports, he identified himself rather with his Scottish ancestors, singing 'Scots wha hae wi' Wallace bled', as he was arrested.[2] Regarding the invitation by a government *agent provocateur* to join one of his 'countrymen' for a drink, the trial records report that Davidson questioned what he meant by 'countryman', and on learning that this referred to 'a man of colour', commented, 'I had no objection to going in, for though I am a man of colour, I never associated with any of them. I was very well brought up. I found them all very ignorant.'[3]

Although none of his writings survive, Davidson's eloquent defence at his trial is recorded in part in the anthology, *Black Writers in Britain, 1760–1890*, edited by Paul Edwards and David Dabydeen (1995). The complete trial record can be found in contemporary records.[4]

Robert Wedderburn, on the other hand, was responsible for a number of pamphlets and speeches which have survived in print. His brief autobiographical record, *The Horrors of Slavery*, gives a graphic and indignant account of his mother's ill-treatment by his father. His disgust and anger, as well as his sense of injustice at his own treatment, are force-fully expressed both in the text itself and in the title page, which boldly states that the author is not only 'late a Prisoner of His Majesty's Goal at Dorchester, for Conscience Sake', but also that he is the 'son of the late James Wedderburn, Esq. Of Inveresk, Slave-Dealer, by one of his Slaves in the Island of Jamaica'.[5] Suggesting that his father's 'libidinous excess' may be a consequence of his inadequate mental powers, Wedderburn describes how like many other slave-owners, his father impregnated his female slaves and sold their joint offspring:

My father ranged through his whole household for his own lewd purposes; for they being his personal property, cost nothing extra; and if any one proved with child – why, it was an acquisition which might some day fetch something in the market, like a horse or pig in Smithfield. In short, among his own slaves my father was a perfect parish bull; and his pleasure was the greater, because he at the same time increased his profit. (*Horrors of Slavery*, p. 46)

In later passages, Wedderburn underlines his contempt by inverting Bib-lical imagery and references or yoking them together with 'low' barnyard similes: his father is described as 'strutting' among his female slaves 'like Solomon in his grand seraglio, or like a bantam cock in his own dunghill'; 'slaves did increase and multiply, like Joseph's kine; and he cultivated those talents well, which God had granted so amply' (p. 47). Like many other contemporary black writers, he also draws on Shakespeare to evoke the sympathies of his readers, and in defending his mother's anger and resentment at her treatment, adapts Shylock's famous speech: 'Hath not a slave feelings? If you starve them, will they not die? If you wrong them, will they not revenge? Insulted on one hand, and degraded on the other, was it likely that my poor mother would practise the Christian virtue of humility, when her Christian master provoked her to wrath?' (p. 47).

The Horrors of Slavery, published in 1824, includes as an appendix a series of letters to the editor of *Bell's Life in London* including his half-brother's denial of any relationship, and Wedderburn's and the editor's comments. Wedderburn had twenty years earlier also published a re-ligious tract, *Truth Self-supported; or A Refutation of Certain Doctrinal Errors Generally Adopted in the Christian Church*, in which he identifies himself as 'a Creole from Jamaica'.[6] Here, like Equiano and Cugoano, he records his conversion from an earlier sinful and 'licentious' life, and his joy at receiving God's grace and conversion to Methodism. In 1817, he was at least partly responsible for the writing and editing of a small weekly titled the *Axe Laid to the Root*. But the narrative of his life, and these pamphlets, also illustrate his difference from Equiano, or his later compatriot, Mary Seacole. For whereas these writers are concerned with self-improvement, and with representing the extent of their individual achievement which often involves acceptance in English society, Wedderburn is chiefly concerned with denouncing the injustices not only of slavery, but also of a society where gross poverty and inequality is endemic. Paul Gilroy argues that the lives, and one might add the speeches and writings, of men like Wedderburn and Davidson 'offer invaluable means of seeing how thinking with and through the discourses and imagery of "race" appears in the core rather than at the fringes of English political life'.[7] Wedderburn was a follower (if one could ever apply that description to such a fiery and independent spirit) of the Jacobite Thomas Spence, who advocated the expropriation of private lands and resources for public use.[8] The *Axe Laid to the Root* (reprinted in McCalman's edition of *'The Horrors of Slavery' and Other Writings*) takes the Biblical, evangelical language of Spence and his group, but its subtitle, 'Being an Address to the Planters and Negroes of the Island of Jamaica', directs the radical politics and apocalyptic imagery beyond England to a wider context. As McCalman argues, 'the periodical's most important contribution to popular radical ideology came from its sustained attempt to integrate the prospect of slave revolution in the West Indies with that of working-class revolution in England. It thereby extended the pioneering ideas of Equiano and enriched London popular radicalism's standard anti-establishment critique which still at that time owed most of its categories to Cobbett's denunciations of "Old Corruption".'[9]

The first number of the *Axe Laid to the Root* calls on 'Africans and relatives now in bondage to Christians' to abjure the violence of 'St Domingo', but instead to show their strength and strike terror into their oppressors' hearts by a carefully planned general strike. Wedderburn speaks to them 'as the offspring of an African' and concludes by naming himself 'a West-Indian, a lover of liberty [who] would dishonour human nature if I did not shew myself a friend to the liberty of others' (pp. 81–3). In a letter to the 'Editor', Wedderburn then prophesies that Jamaica will indeed suffer the same fate as San Domingo, and goes on to declare of the future rebellious slaves, 'Their method of fighting is to be found in the scriptures, which they now are learning to read. They will slay man, woman, and child, and not spare the virgin, whose interest is connected with slavery, whether black, white or tawny' (p. 86). Further numbers of the weekly encourage the slaves of Jamaica to imagine a government devoid of class distinctions, without an aristocratic hierarchy, and a legal system whose language and practice is genuinely egalitarian. Two issues are fictionally addressed to and answered by a Miss Campbell, who is envisioned as an enlightened slave-owner, herself a descendant of the free Maroon community, and one who is persuaded to free her slaves. Her name is that of the kindly owner who purchased Wedderburn's mother, and Wedderburn even supposes her to be his half-sister. Each number also includes several songs or poems about the fate of slaves and ex-slaves. One has a chorus which begins, 'Spare a half-penny, spare a half penny,/ O spare a half, penny to a poor Negro boy [sic]' (p. 91). Another set of verses represents a version of Negro dialect in 'The Africans [sic] Complaint on Board a Slave Ship':

> Trembling, naked, wounded, sighing.
> On dis wi[n]ged house I stand,
> Dat with poor black man is flying,
> far away from his own land.
> Fearful water all aro[u]nd me!
> Strange de sight on every hand,
> Hurry, noise, and shouts confound me,
> When I look for Negro land. (p. 94)

McCalman describes the *Axe Laid to the Root* as remarkable within both its West Indian and its English contexts, and sees it best understood as 'a series of oral sermons designed to be read out to semi-literate audiences in alehouses and workshops' (Introduction to *'The Horrors of Slavery' and Other Writings*, p. 18). The imagined audiences in the West Indies create a dramatic context for the real audiences in London, and the pamphlets also employ familiar genres and language for a contemporary audience, with their mixtures of Biblical imagery, popular ballad and hymn styles, the rhetoric of evangelical sermons, political polemic, and satire and burlesque.

MARY PRINCE

Whereas Robert Wedderburn writes in his own voice, others who escaped slavery in the West Indies or southern American states and sought refuge in England, dictated their stories and had their voices mediated through those from whom they sought assistance. For such narrators, England is represented not as a nation in dire and urgent need of radical change, a nation condoning the existence and excesses of slavery, but as a community which promises liberty and justice. Rather than denounce the evils of individuals and society, the narrators appeal to the 'better selves' of Englishmen and women. *The History of Mary Prince* is thus in some ways typical of such narratives, but it is also exceptional in that it is the first such narrative told in England by a black woman.

Born a slave in Bermuda in 1788, Mary Prince ran away from her master and mistress, Mr and Mrs Wood, when they brought her to London in 1828. Alone, ill, and without resources in London, she made her way to the office of the Anti-Slavery Society in Aldermanbury, London, to seek help. Above all, she wished to return as a free woman to Antigua, to her husband, Daniel James, and other people she knew. Members of the Anti-Slavery Society sought without any success to persuade Mr Wood to let Mary Prince buy her freedom, but he was adamant in his refusal. He also tried to represent Mary as a dissolute, lazy and deceitful woman, undeserving of sympathy, and in so doing dissuaded some of those acting on her behalf from presenting her case to Parliament. A year later, having observed her conduct and being convinced 'that she was really a well-disposed and respectable woman',[10] Thomas Pringle engaged Mary Prince as a domestic servant in his household.[11] In 1830, he tried again to persuade John Wood to free her, and persuaded the governor of Antigua and various missionary friends to intervene in her favour. John Wood remained obstinate, despite the loss of any recompense for 'her value as a slave in a pecuniary point of view'.[12]

Pringle makes it clear that it was Mary Prince's own suggestion that she dictate her story and have it published, and that the defamatory letter from John Wood and his obstinate refusal to free her, encouraged him 'to accede to her wish without further delay' (p. 4). Mary dictated her history to Susannah Strickland Moodie, who was later to become known as one of Canada's earliest women authors, and who was at that time staying with Mr and Mrs Pringle.[13] In his preface, Pringle takes care to insist that the words and incidents are taken down without alteration:

It was written out fully, with all the narrator's repetitions and prolixities, and afterwards pruned into its present shape; retaining as far as was practicable, Mary's exact expressions and peculiar phraseology. No fact of importance has been omitted, and not a single circumstance or sentiment has been added. It is essentially her own, without any material alteration farther than was requisite to exclude redundancies and gross grammatical errors, so as to render it clearly intelligible. (p. 3)

Pringle's statement is corroborated by a letter from Mary Prince's scribe, Susanna Strickland, in a letter dated January 1831 to James and Emma Bird:

I have been writing Mr Pringle's black Mary's life from her own dictation and for her benefit adhering to her own simple story and language without deviating to the paths of flourish or romance. It is a pathetic little history and is now printing in the form of a pamphlet to be laid before the Houses of Parliament. Of course my name does not appear. Mr Pringle has added a very interesting appendix, and I hope the work will do much good.[14]

Susanna Strickland's identification of the narrator as 'Mr Pringle's black Mary', and her eschewal of romance and flourish are, as Gillian Whitlock suggests, a means of placing both the story-teller and the story within a particular hierarchy with regard to race, class, and genre, romance and flourish both being inappropriate to a black woman who belongs to a white gentleman.[15] Similarly, the preface and title page of this narrative emphasize its status as an authoritative truthful history rather than romance. But Strickland's letter and reference to 'black Mary' also draw attention to an issue which recurs in many narratives of the experience of slavery, the question of naming; in the various appendices and marginal notes, Mary Prince is otherwise referred to as Molly Wood, Mary Princess of Wales, Mr Wood's Molly, Mary James, and 'the woman Molly'. The issue of naming is submerged rather than explicit in Mary Prince's narrative. Mary does not speak or lay claim to a name at all, although she does make sure that we become aware of her father's name (Prince) and her husband's name (James). She also quotes her husband's referring to her as 'Molly'. The letters from pro-slavery supporters of Mr and Mrs Wood in Antigua all refer to her as 'Molly Wood' or 'the woman Molly'. According to Moira Ferguson, the earliest title for the narrative was proposed as '*The Life of Mary, Princess of Wales, a West Indian Slave*'.[16] 'Mary, Princess of Wales', was the name written into the *Charity School Spelling Book*, given her by the Reverend Curtin of the Church of England. This name, Mary told Pringle, was 'an appellation... given her by her owners'. 'It is common practice with the colonists,' Pringle adds, 'to give ridiculous names of this description to their slaves; being, in fact, one of the numberless modes of expressing the habitual contempt with which they regard the negro race. – In printing this narrative, we have retained Mary's paternal name of Prince' (p. 29, n.).

As published in 1831 (there were three editions in 1831 published in London and Edinburgh), the text as a whole presents several layers, some of which are drawn attention to by the frontispiece naming the main text as 'The History of Mary Prince', identifying her as 'A West Indian Slave' and recording that the history is 'related by herself', although there is a supplement by the (unnamed) editor. The volume also contained 'The

Narrative of Asa-Asa, A Captured African', and it is interesting to see that authorship and self-representation are not here ascribed to him. Nor is there more than a cursory attempt to convey his voice or language, and the emphasis in his tale is on slavery and kidnapping within Africa, rather than the experience of slavery under white masters and mistresses. The frontispiece for both tales contains a stanza from William Cowper's poem, 'The Negro's Complaint', in which Cowper bestows upon slaves a collective voice, speaking of patient suffering, broken hearts, and pleads that their colour should not be the reason for 'deeming our nation brutes'.

Thus Mary Prince's own story is framed by her identification as a slave and a West Indian (in contrast to Asa-Asa's identification as 'A Captured African'), and by Cowper's speaking for and representing slaves as 'patient victims' categorized and mistreated because of colour. The frontispiece is followed by Pringle's preface which emphasizes Mary Prince's own concern to speak out and tell her story and reiterates that the words and the narrative are essentially her own. The preface also explains the presence of the supplement which will contain a series of letters concerning Mary Prince's character and veracity, and Pringle's own comments on them.

Moira Ferguson, in her detailed exploration of the subtexts and contexts of Mary Prince's story, raises a number of issues for readers of the *History*. She speculates that Mary Prince may have been aware when she went to the London Anti-Slavery Society headquarters and told her story to Thomas Pringle that she would need to appeal to certain Christian assumptions and agendas if her appeal was to be effective. If so, Ferguson wonders,

how did she anticipate or set about counteracting a popular abolitionist assumption that slaves 'cannot represent themselves, they must be represented'?[17] In other words, did Mary Prince actively resist being censored or caricatured as a colonial 'other' by supporters and slave-owners alike? Was she able to encode deliberately and discreetly, customarily unnameable privations? To what extent did she acknowledge, in directing her narrative, that both sides of the slavery debate vyed [sic] for control over her? Or perhaps more likely, were her responses to abolitionists fraught with ambivalence?[18]

Both Pringle and Prince present this narrative as 'evidence'. But evidence of what? Do they share the same purpose – exactly? What evidence was the abolitionist campaign seeking, particularly with regard to the treatment of slave women? And does Mary Prince speak specifically on behalf of female slaves or on behalf of the whole slave community? In what sense does her determination to speak for herself, so that 'the good people of England might hear from a slave what a slave had suffered', suggest that the representation of slave experience by others, both abolitionists as well as pro-slavery advocates has been inadequate or deficient? And is this the same as making one's own voice heard by a particular audience?

Like later slave narratives, this one begins with the existential statement, 'I was born.' There is no genealogy, no list of ancestral forebears, no description of the geographic features or landscape – only the bare assertion of existence. Here Mary Prince's narrative contrasts with Asa-Asa's, or Equiano's and Gronniosaw's, and those of others who remember an African (and free) childhood, a place of origin to which they belong and which they can claim as their own. But, although the tone is less ironic, it is more similar to the *Narrative of the Life of Frederick Douglass* (written fifteen years later), in the baldness of its assertion. Her narrative then goes on to depict a relatively happy – and above all relatively innocent – childhood which contrasts with the brutality of later suffering experienced and witnessed, and the harsh realization of the meaning of slavery. 'I was too young to understand rightly my condition as a slave', Mary Prince declares (p. 7). But as a child she understands rightly her identity as a fellow human being – hence the irony inherent in her statement – though the irony is not so clearly underlined as in Harriet Jacobs' *Incidents in the Life of a Slave Girl*: 'I was born a slave; but never knew it till six years of happy childhood had passed away.'[19]

Prince's narrative sets up from the beginning a relationship with a 'good' and kindly mistress, Mrs Williams, and suggests a harmonious relationship with the white children, which serves to set in stark contrast the later shock of brutal and mean-minded treatment by subsequent masters and mistresses. Here she also uses the device of a child's-eye view, presenting her world without irony or commentary of later hindsight, and she tells us how she and her siblings 'used to play with Miss Betsey with as much freedom almost as if she had been our sister'. For the mature reader, however, that qualification 'almost as if' carries the weight of adult experience and knowledge, as do the preceding lines, 'I was made quite a pet of by Miss Betsey, and loved her very much. She used to lead me about by the hand, and call me her little nigger' (p. 7). The reader is left to interpret the wider resonances of this seemingly innocent childhood relationship, already imbued with the hierarchies and prejudices which will become the well-springs of her grief and anger. The language is carefully chosen to convey those already taken-for-granted relationships – Mary is a 'pet'; she is 'led' by the hand; she is claimed as '*her* little nigger'. Deprived of control over her own life, she must always be 'led'; owned by another and powerless, the power relationship is re-iterated through assertion of ownership, racial difference, the power to manipulate language, to represent others and name them (as 'nigger'). The narrative will close with an outburst against these very ingredients of the slave's condition:

They tie up slaves like hogs – moor them up like cattle, and they lick them, so as hogs, or cattle, or horses never were flogged; – and yet they come home and say, or make some good people believe, that slaves don't want to get out of slavery. But they put a cloak about the truth. It is not so. All slaves want to be free – to be free is very sweet. (p. 38)

And yet while hinting at the full and bitter understanding to come of 'her condition as a slave' these early pages also suggest the possibility of decent and equal relationships between white children and black. Fanny, the daughter of her second mistress, Mrs Pruden, regards her as a companion and pupil rather than a mere pet. The affection Mary remembers and reciprocates is conveyed in her account of their brief relationship:

Dear Miss Fanny! She was a sweet, kind young lady, and so fond of me that she wished me to learn all that she knew herself, and her method of teaching me was as follows: – Directly she had said her lessons to her grandmamma, she used to come running to me, and make me repeat them one by one after her; and in a few months I was able not only to spell my letters but to spell many small words. (pp. 8–9)

In recounting this relationship, Mary Prince not only commemorates the kindness and affection of her young friend, but also asserts her own contested potential as an equal human being (not a pet), capable of literacy, and certainly capable of more than the unremitting physical labour to which she was soon confined.

The issue of literacy becomes crucial in many other slave narratives, and interestingly, it is often through children (and sometimes women) that young slaves like Equiano, Frederick Douglass, Phyllis Wheatley (who was taught alongside her master's daughter Mary) were able to grasp the first elements of reading and writing and so negate, even if only to themselves at the time, their representation as inferior and incapable.

Later in her narrative, when she is owned by her fourth and present master and mistress, Mr and Mrs Wood, reading and writing become for Mary Prince also the means of creating a space for her own identity and self-worth. She secretly goes to classes run by the Moravian missionaries:

I did not tell my mistress about [going to the Moravian church]; for I knew that she would not give me leave to go. But I felt I *must* go. Whenever I carried the children their lunch at school, I ran round and went to hear the teachers.

The Moravian ladies (Mrs Richter, Mrs Olufsen, and Mrs Sauter) taught me to read in the class, and I got on very fast [Prince's emphasis]. (p. 29)

The achievement of literacy is both a means and a symptom of Mary Prince's determination to assert her autonomy and identity as a full human being in other ways. She becomes a convert to the Moravian church, thus abandoning the only religious allegiance permitted by her masters, the Church of England, in which she believed she would be permitted neither to become a communicant and full member, nor to marry a free man. She also meets and agrees to marry just such a free man, Daniel James, and she makes it very clear in the narrative that it was her decision, carefully considered and made on her own terms (that is, that Daniel must also become a member of her church):

When he asked me to marry him, I took time to consider the matter over with myself, and would not say yes till he went to Church with me and joined the Moravians. He was very industrious after he bought his freedom; and he hired a comfortable house, and had convenient things about him. We were joined in marriage, about Christmas 1826, in the Moravian Chapel at Spring Gardens, by the Rev. Mr Olufsen. We could not be married in the English Church. English marriage is not allowed to slaves; and no free man can marry a slave woman. (p. 30)

Such an assertion of her own autonomy enrages her owners, who assert their power of ownership in both brutal and petty ways, through flogging on the one hand and on the other by the refusal to allow Mary to enact her relationship as a wife by washing her husband's clothes. Their behaviour also underscores the powerlessness of her husband, despite his status as a freeman, as he tells Mr Wood that if he 'had known Molly was not allowed to have a husband, [he would] not have asked her to marry [him]' (p. 30). Mary tells her readers, 'It made my husband sad to see me so ill-treated.' The scene recalls an earlier one when Mary was twelve-years-old and had run away to her mother after a particularly cruel beating. Her father returns her to her then owner, with a plea that she should not be ill-treated. Once again the helplessness of the black male who cannot protect his women or children is dramatized, and once again Mary recalls the words with which the man who would be her protector seeks to preserve some sense of respect. To the modern reader, the father's words ring somewhat more bravely but perhaps less authentically than the husband's:

When we got home, my poor father said to Captain I–, 'Sir, I am sorry that my child should be forced to run away from her owner; but the treatment she has received is enough to break her heart. The sight of her wounds has nearly broke mine.–I entreat you, for the love of God, to forgive her for running away, and that you will be a kind master to her in future.' (p. 18)

The literary quality of this reported speech contrasts with her own related response – the first moment of confrontation that she narrates: 'I then took courage and said that I could stand the floggings no longer; that I was weary of my life, and therefore I had run away to my mother – but mothers could only weep and mourn over their children, they could not save them from their cruel masters – from the whip, the rope, and the cowskin.' And she tells us almost triumphantly, that he did not 'flog me that day'. He did, however, flog her almost daily for another five years (p. 18).

Her sad acknowledgement that mothers (and also fathers) could only weep and mourn, they could not save their children, brings Mary to the realization that her survival (physical and psychological) depends on her alone. While she can commemorate and pity her 'poor father' and mother in their helplessness, she can only witness their suffering, and at some deeper level acknowledge that she must help herself if she is not to be like them. That helplessness, and the terrible position of the slave mother, is vividly dramatized in an earlier memory where she recalls her mother's words when her children are all to be sold:

The black morning at length came; it was too soon for my poor mother and us. Whilst she was putting on the new osnaburgs[20] in which we were to be sold, she said in a sorrowful voice, (I shall never forget it!) 'See, I am *shrouding* my poor children; what a task for a mother!' – She then called Miss Betsey to take leave of us. 'I am going to carry my little chickens to market,' (these were her very words,) 'take your last look at them, maybe you will see them no more.' 'Oh, my poor slaves! My own slaves!' said dear Miss Betsey, 'you belong to me; and it grieves my heart to part with you.' (p. 10)

One is struck not only by the affecting use of imagery in the mother's words, but also by the insistence on recording her speech, and on the exactness of the record. The mother's vivid images of reversal, dressing her children for death rather than life, turning herself as mother into the seller rather than the nourisher and protector of her little 'chicks', also reverberate against the terms of their mistress's lament; however kindly, her relationship is seen by her as one of ownership only. They *belong* to her, and the more ordinary – almost trite – and literary expression of her sorrow ('it grieves my heart to part with you') contrasts with the poignant evocativeness of the mother's words.

The passage above, and others describing the brutal treatment of slave children, might also be read against a background of a pro-slavery discourse which frequently drew on domestic metaphors to describe slavery as a benevolent institution, in which slaves were portrayed as childlike beneficiaries of a paternalistic structure. The historian Willie Lee Rose points out the appeal of the family analogy in the nineteenth century:

Proslavery philosophers intended to suggest a benign institution that encouraged between masters and slaves the qualities so much admired in the Victorian family: cheerful obedience and gratitude on the part of the children (read slaves), and paternalistic wisdom, protection, and discipline on the part of the father (read master)... So, in the nineteenth century, the phrase 'domestic institution' came to mean slavery idealized, slavery translated into a fundamental and idealized Victorian institution, the family.[21]

Thus one of the many ways in which Prince's narrative intervenes in the debate over slavery is by insisting on the role of that so-called 'domestic institution' in violating the sacred institution of family. She vividly dramatizes the tearing apart of mothers and children, sisters and brothers, the helplessness of the natural father, the refusal of the right to marriage, the violation of conjugal bonds. And the masters and mistresses who lay claim to the roles of surrogate fathers and mothers are shown to be vicious, brutal, depraved, and depraving, callously causing injury to and neglecting those who are supposedly in their care.

As in the case of most slave narratives, Mary Prince's history is both individual and typical; she speaks and bears witness on behalf of all slaves, male and female:

– And what my eyes have seen I think it is my duty to relate; for few people in England know what slavery is. I have been a slave – I have felt what a slave feels, and I know what a slave knows; and I would have all the good people of England know it too, that they may break our chains and set us free. (p. 21)

Thus she inserts into her history the otherwise lost or suppressed stories of the two little slave boys Cyrus and Jack, whose flesh she saw 'ragged and raw with licks. – Lick – lick – they were never secure one moment from a blow, and their lives were passed in continual fear' (p. 15). She also records the torture of Daniel, when salt was rubbed into the wounds caused by flogging, and the atrocities which caused the deaths of two women slaves, Hetty and Sarah. When sent to the Turks Islands, male and female slaves alike suffered the agonies of working in the salt ponds, and male and female alike were subjected to the same vicious beatings:

Mr D– has often stripped me naked, hung me up by the wrists, and beat me with the cow-skin, with his own hand, till my body was raw with gashes. Yet there was nothing remarkable in this; for it might serve as a sample of the common usage of the slaves on that horrible island. (p. 20)

Although Mary Prince acknowledges the suffering shared by all slaves, whatever their age and gender, she also suggests particular ways in which women slaves were made to suffer under the master's power, and the consequent additional sufferings caused by the jealousy of his wife – yet another way in which the 'domestic institution' destroyed 'domesticity'. Explicit details of male sexual harassment and rape and the mistress's hatred of his victims and their children are narrated by Harriet Jacobs in *Incidents in the Life a Slave Girl*, but some similar incidents are implied in Mary Prince's narration. The description of being stripped naked by the master and beaten by him we are told 'was nothing remarkable . . . [being] . . . a sample of the common usage of the slaves on that horrible island' (p. 20). Yet there is an added indignity for a woman thus stripped naked, as the closing passages of the narrative acknowledge more openly:

Is it happiness for a driver in the field to take down his wife or sister or child, and strip them, and whip them in such a disgraceful manner? – women that have had children exposed in the open field to shame! There is no modesty or decency shown by the owner to his slaves; men, women, and children are exposed alike. (p. 38)

The approach towards being able to openly speak of the shame felt by women, their sense of outrage *as* women, is a gradual one, for the early passages suggest that these acts, or rather the feelings of sexual violation that accompany them, are unspeakable. She comments generally on the wickedness of 'buckra men' on Turks Islands ('the Buckra men there were very wicked; I saw and heard much that was very bad at that place' p. 22). But on her return to Bermuda she allows herself to speak further of her master's behaviour towards her as a female slave. And it is significant that it is the sexual harassment which provokes her to speak out, not only about unbearable suffering inflicted upon her that she complains of after her father had returned her, but to rebuke and condemn her master in scathing terms:

He had an ugly fashion of stripping himself quite naked, and ordering me then to wash him in a tub of water. This was worse to me than all the licks. Sometimes when he called me to wash him, I would not come, my eyes were so full of shame. He would then come to beat me...He struck me so severely for this that at last I defended myself, for I thought it was high time to do so. I then told him I would no longer live with him, for he was a very indecent man – very spiteful and too indecent; with no shame for his servants, no shame for his own flesh. (p. 24)

In his supplementary notes, Thomas Pringle comments that Mary Prince's 'chief faults...are, a somewhat violent and hasty temper, and a considerable share of natural pride and self-importance' (p. 55). The models of decorum promulgated for the white middle-class English female in Pringle's time appear incongruous in the context of Mary Prince's story – one might argue that her psychological and physical survival depended on the very qualities Pringle deplores, as one might infer from passages such as the one quoted above where she does defy and denounce her owners. Mary indeed takes pride in those moments when she does speak out, and it is only her 'considerable share of natural pride and self-importance' which encourages her to believe in the importance of telling her story.[22]

Yet, as Moira Ferguson suggests, the *History* reveals a number of voices and subtexts, where Mary takes on and almost parodies the discourses of those in power.[23] Ferguson takes as an example Mary Prince's acknowledgement of Mr Mortimer's advice:

Mr Mortimer tells me that he cannot open the eyes of my heart, but that I must pray to God to change my heart, and make me know the truth, and the truth will set me free.

I still live in the hope that God will find a way to give me my liberty, and give me back to my husband. I endeavour to keep down my fretting, and leave all to Him, for he knows what is good for me better than I know myself. Yet, I must confess, I find it a hard and heavy task to do so.

I am often much vexed, and feel great sorrow when I hear some people in this country say, that the slaves do not need better usage, and do not want to be free. (p. 37)

In setting apart and semi-quoting the discourse of Mr Mortimer, Mary Prince both affirms her 'hearing' of it for her Christian English readers, and, Moira Ferguson suggests, parodies it through mimicry. However, as rather more secular twentieth-century readers, we need to beware of dismissing the seriousness of Mary Prince's Christian conviction. Rather than seeing the secular meaning replacing the Christian meaning of those words, one might see them as reinforcing one another – as doubling the significance, like a harmony where the meanings intensify each other, rather than subvert. The 'quotation' includes three key terms or concepts which reverberate through the whole narrative, but which also resonate doubly in Mary's discourse although singly in Mr Mortimer's: 'heart', 'truth', and 'freedom'. Throughout her story, Mary has affirmed the truth of what she 'knows in her heart', often a truth which cannot be spoken, and which contrasts with the discourse of the master. So on being sent to Turks Islands and parted from her family, she comments, 'Oh the Buckra people who keep slaves think that black people are like cattle, without natural affection. But my heart tells me it is far otherwise'(p. 18). When Mrs Wood accuses her of being lazy and indolent, and merely pretending to be sick, Mary Prince tells us, 'I thought her very hard on me, and my heart rose up within me. However, I kept still at that time . . .' p. 32). And again, when Mr Wood curses her and refuses to let her buy her freedom, she states, 'My heart was very sore with this treatment, but I had to go on' (p. 33). In the passage immediately following her reference to Mr Mortimer's advice, she asserts the truth of the knowledge she *feels* and the authority of her own experience:

All slaves want to be free – to be free is very sweet. I will say the truth to English people who may read this history that my good friend, Miss S–, is now writing down for me. I have been a slave myself – I know what slaves feel – I can tell by myself what other slaves feel, and by what they have told me. The man that says slaves be quite happy in slavery – that they don't want to be free – that man is either ignorant or a lying person. I never heard a slave say so. (p. 38)

In this passage Mary Prince proclaims her own version of 'the truth that will set her free', and it is clear that she seeks not spiritual freedom but 'liberty' and legal freedom. Here she also asserts the truthfulness of her *speech*, and her determination to speak out – 'I will say the truth to English people', and the truth of 'what [slaves] have told me' – as against what the masters say, derived from ignorance and deceit. The final passage, which Pringle assures us 'is given as nearly as possible in Mary's precise words', dramatizes the contest of discourses – what 'they say' or 'the man says' as against what 'I say':

I am often much vexed, and feel great sorrow when I hear some people in this country say, that the slaves do not need better usage, and do not want to be free. They believe the foreign [i.e. West Indian] people, who deceive them, and say slaves are happy. I say, Not so. (p. 37)

Freedom, truth, and the power to speak it on one's own behalf, and thus speak one's own truth: these are the insistent refrains of Mary Prince's narrative, and of other later slave narratives such as those by Frederick Douglass, John Brown, and Francis Fedric. The oppositions throughout this narrative are not between black and white, as the prefacing poem by Cowper might lead the reader to expect, or even male and female, as more recent readings of Prince suggest, but between master and slave, the free and the unfree, the powerful and the powerless, liars and truthful speakers.[24] As in Douglass and Jacobs' narratives, romance is not part of the story. Mary seeks not to talk of her relationship with and courtship by her husband, but the restrictions which are imposed on that relationship by her slave status.[25] These refrains are all brought into a resounding concluding paragraph by Mary Prince:

I have been a slave myself – I know what slaves feel – I can tell by myself what other slaves feel, and by what they have told me. The man that says slaves be quite happy in slavery – that they don't want to be free – that man is either ignorant or a lying person. I never heard a slave say so. I never heard a Buckra man say so, till I heard tell of it in England . . . We don't mind hard work, if we had proper treatment, and proper wages like English servants, and proper time given us in the week to keep us from breaking the Sabbath. But they won't give it: they will have work – work – work, night and day, sick or well, till we are quite done up; and we must not speak up nor look amiss, however much we be abused. And then when we are quite done up, who cares for us, more than for a lame horse? This is slavery. I tell it, to let English people know the truth; and I hope they will never leave off to pray God, and to call loud to the great King of England, till all the poor blacks be given free, and slavery done up for evermore. (p. 38)

Against that narrative and conclusion are relegated the contesting discourses which Mary has already in advance dismissed as ignorant or lying; Pringle presents an alternative but supporting discourse, the truth of the mind in union with the truth of the heart and experience. Seeking to determine the truth partly through intuition as to motives and credibility, and largely through the tools of rational analysis, Pringle's comment below betrays the assumptions inherent in the language available to him, and his inability to hear fully Mary Prince's passionate affirmation of her humanity:

And suppose her own statement to be false, and even the whole of her conduct since she came under our observation here to be a tissue of hypocrisy; – suppose all this – and leave the negro woman as black in character as in complexion, – yet it would not affect the main facts. (p. 56)

CHAPTER 4

The imperial century

After the flurry of activities and petitions surrounding the abolition of the slave-trade, with the consequent focus on black people resident in Britain, the British seemed to lose interest in the black or Asian members of the population. Folarin Shyllon speculates that the 10,000 or more blacks recorded at the end of the eighteenth century 'married and were absorbed into the white population. Their children are now white, with no inkling of their African blood and ancestry.'[1] They were no longer seen as a special case or separate cause, but where mention is made of them, blacks and Asians are grouped among the poor and with other 'outsider' groups: Irish, Greek, Chinese. Shyllon cites a passage from Pierce Egan's *Life in London* (1821) describing a party in the East End: 'Lascars, blacks, jack tars, coal heavers, dustmen, women of colour, old and young, and a sprinkling of once fine girls...were all jigging together.'[2] There are also records of black coachmen, buskers, beggars, and political and religious radicals such as Wedderburn and Davidson. Some of these were men who had been enticed or press-ganged into the navy to serve in the Napoleonic Wars, and then demobbed without pay or pension. According to Iain McCalman, such ex-servicemen participated in most of the protests which took place in London between 1798 and 1820, and 'the West Indian mulatto or the lascar featured disproportionately in protests of this kind because the experience of being demobbed bore especially heavily on him'.[3] As mentioned previously, Wedderburn and Davidson were involved in such activities as the Cato Street Conspiracy for which Davidson was tried and executed in 1820 (he is said to have declared moments before his execution that he was 'a stranger in a strange land').[4] William Cuffay, a leading Chartist and the son of a freed slave from St Kitts, was transported along with two other black members of the movement to Van Dieman's Land in 1848. But the relatively better off African British, such as the daughter of Equiano and the children of Ignatius Sancho, do not get mentioned in contemporary writings, unless they happen to be very wealthy heiresses, like Thackeray's Rhoda Swartz, born of West Indian planter liaisons.

Nevertheless, the issue of slavery in the colonies and the Americas continued to be debated by immigrants such as Wedderburn and anti-slavery advocates such as Thomas Clarkson, William Wilberforce, and Thomas Pringle. *The History of Mary Prince* had been taken down and published in the context of the drive to abolish slavery in the British colonies, and specifically the West Indian colonies. When, in August 1833, a bill abolishing slavery in the British colonies became law, the anti-slavery movement in Britain turned its attention to other areas, including Africa, India, and North and South America.[5] The founding of the British and Foreign Anti-Slavery Society in 1839 was followed by its organization of a world convention in 1840, addressed by such well-known politicians and activists as Daniel O'Connell, Thomas Buxton, Wendell Phillips, Joseph Sturge, and the veteran abolitionist, Thomas Clarkson, as well as delegates from the Caribbean, the Americas, Africa, and the French territories. Such activities and the establishment of a journal, *The British and Foreign Anti-Slavery Reporter*, made the society the most prominent and the most broadly based of such organizations in Britain for some fifty years. Indeed the society remained in existence under various names for over 150 years. In its early years, much attention was devoted to slavery in India, which was pronounced 'virtually extinct' in 1843.

During the mid nineteenth century many men and women who had escaped from slavery in the southern states of America came to England to arouse interest and seek funds for the abolition movement in the United States. They embarked on extensive speaking tours throughout Britain and Ireland which were reported in local and national newspapers. In some cases their tours were so successful that numbers of people had to be turned away from the full to overflowing church halls and assembly rooms where they spoke. Some of these speakers remained in Britain for only a few months, others for several years. A number of them wrote of their experiences, and sold their printed accounts during their speaking tours. These accounts are written for British audiences, and set out for them not only the particularities of slavery in the southern United States, but also give dramatic stories of escape and adventure, often appealing to British preconceptions about the American wilderness.

Such speaking tours and published accounts by ex-slaves helped to fuel support for the Anti-Slavery Society, which flourished after the 1840s. During the 1840s the society focussed its attention on the sugar colonies and their employment of slave labour, on the issue of fugitive slaves who had fled north to Canada from the southern States, and on the practice in some states such as Georgia, North Carolina, Florida, and Louisiana, of 'quarantining' all coloured seamen and passengers in local gaols while the ships were in port and charging the ship's captain for their board. The refusal or neglect of some captains to pay these charges, resulted in several detainees being sold into slavery. A court action in 1850 by a coloured steward, demanding that his captain pay his wages for the period he spent in a Charleston prison, brought this practice and the existence of the Negro Seamen Acts to the attention of the British public.

By the 1850s, for most Britons the debate about slavery was equated with the debate between north and south in the United States. This focus on slavery in North America became more intense following the passage of the Fugitive Slave Act in 1851, after which escaped slaves no longer found safety in the northern states, and many journeyed on to Britain. It is in this context that Harriet Beecher Stowe toured Britain and Europe in 1852, to tremendous acclaim. Not only did thousands buy her novel, *Uncle Tom's Cabin*, but multitudes also flocked to see various dramatized versions of it. The Lord Chamberlain approved fifteen stage productions in the six months between September 1852 and February 1853.[6] While such productions may have involved some black actors, it is likely that most of them involved white actors in black face. But the appearances, lectures, and narratives of fugitive slaves who fled to Britain were almost as popular. Many of these fugitives settled in Britain and dictated or wrote their memoirs some years later, including Francis Fedric (who married an Englishwoman and ran a lodging-house in Manchester), John Brown, and William and Ellen Craft.

In the same year that Stowe's novel began publication in serial form in 1851, the Great Exhibition was held in London, celebrating Britain as the centre of empire, commerce, and trade, and featuring goods, artifacts, and peoples from all over the empire. It also attracted visitors from all parts of the globe, and helped to establish London as a metropolis that every traveller must visit, including princes, chiefs, and businessmen from India and Africa. The numbers of black visitors and immigrants were such that one Boston clergyman commented on his visit to London in 1861, 'There is no end to the colored here' (Fryer, *Staying Power*, p. 435).

The interest in peoples and artefacts from India and Africa, the popularity of *Uncle Tom's Cabin* as fiction and drama, as well as the interest in autobiographical slave narratives during this period, reveal a fascinated concern with a complex of issues to do with black and Asian people. The vehement opposition to slavery often combines with anti-American feeling and the promotion of England as a relatively civilized haven of freedom and liberty. It might be argued that the asylum given to fugitive slaves helped to palliate whatever anxieties might have been repressed as to Britain's role in the conquest of other peoples and lands. But these concerns are also 'coloured' by debates and attitudes regarding race and its significance, debates which later accrue Darwinian associations and fears of hybridity and racial mixture, and which also relate to Britain's developing imperial interests.

Jennifer DeVere Brody argues that following the 1860s American Civil War and emancipation, the racialized other is found in the colonies – in Ireland, Africa, Australia, India, and the Caribbean.[7] While it is surely the case that the concern with slavery and abolition provided a focus for much English interest in race and its relationship to social status, it is a concern which connects at a considerably earlier stage with England's colonial relationships. The Irish leader Daniel O'Connell was a prominent supporter of anti-slavery and spoke at the 1840 World Anti-Slavery Convention, making the link then, and on many other occasions, between the treatment of the Irish and the treatment of African Americans. English attitudes towards those of African and Irish descent are well illustrated in the London *Times* report on the group of Chartists arrested in 1848: 'Cuffey [sic] . . . is half a "nigger". Some of the others are Irishmen. We doubt if there are a half-dozen Englishmen in the lot.'[8] As the letters of Ignatius Sancho to Jack Wingrave demonstrate, assumptions about racial otherness and difference regarding the rulers and the ruled in India are already deeply ingrained in the eighteenth century. Against the relatively open-minded views of eighteenth-century East India Company officials and orientalists, such as Warren Hastings and William Jones (and presumably the employers and companions of Sake Dean Mahomed), the more intolerant attitudes displayed by Jack Wingrave become more prevalent in the nineteenth century.

A number of historians have named the years 1815–1914 as 'Britain's imperial century'.[9] These years witness the expansion of British administered and occupied territories, and the rapid growth of her capitalist economy dependent on expanding colonial markets and resources. In the early nineteenth century, a combination of evangelical missionary concern for reform, and utilitarian emphasis on 'progress' and prosperity as the means to releasing individual potential, led to an increasing insistence on the 'Anglicization' of Indian and other colonized peoples.

Thus the philosopher Jeremy Bentham wrote to the Bengali reformer and educationalist, Ram Mohan Roy concerning the influential historian James Mill's views:

For these many years the grand object of his [James Mill's] ambition has been to provide for British India, in the room of the abominable existing system, a good system of judicial procedure, with a judicial establishment adequate to the administration of it; and for the composition of it his reliance has all along been, and continues to be, on me.[10]

Mill's and Bentham's views are also reflected in Thomas Babington Macaulay's now famous 'Minute on Education', arguing for the need of Western education to replace Hindu, Sanskrit, Bengali, and Muslim schools and colleges in India in order to create a class of Indian 'English in taste, in opinions, in morals and in intellect'.[11]

Such views stress cultural rather than racial difference, encouraging the notion of a 'universal' humanity advancing, under British or European guidance, towards a global enlightened civilization. It is again Macaulay who succinctly expresses that assumption: 'We are free, we are civilised, to little purpose, if we grudge to any portion of the human race an equal measure of civilisation.'[12]

But assumptions about racial difference and its meaning, already a feature of the debates surrounding slavery and its abolition, become increasingly significant during the nineteenth century and the growth of the British empire, not only as a means of defining 'other' peoples, but also in defining Englishness. Thus in the late nineteenth century, Edward A. Freeman's influential six-volume history of England, *A History of the Norman Conquest* (Oxford, 1870–79) would define the essence of Englishness also in racial terms:

I will assume that what is Teutonic in us is not merely one element among others, but that it is the very life and essence of our national being; that whatever else we may have in us, whatever we have drawn from those whom we conquered or who conquered us, is no co-ordinate element, but a mere infusion into our Teutonic essence; in a word, I will assume that Englishmen are Englishmen, that we are ourselves and not some other people. I assume that, as we have had one national name, one national speech, from the beginning, ... we are an unbroken national being.[13]

Here, the assumption that racial inheritance is the crucial determinant of character, both individual and national, receives its full articulation. Englishness (however paradoxically a consequence of the Norman Conquest) is essentially Teutonic, and the same view has by this time already been demonstrated in Matthew Arnold's series of lectures on Celtic literature.[14] However, whereas Freeman stresses a homogeneity of character and culture, Arnold suggests hybridity which is both cultural and racial in the combination of (predominantly) Anglo-Saxon inheritance 'sweetened' with an admixture of Celtic. After the mid nineteenth century the belief in racial inheritance as an essential basis for character and culture is reinforced by the appropriation of Darwin's theories of evolution and distinctions between species to apply to race and to anxieties about racial mixture. Such distinctions and fears about 'miscegenation' or 'amalgamation' between races are crudely manifested in the following passage from Darwin's *The Variation of Animals and Plants under Domestication*:

The dichotomy between domestic animals and wild animals is similar to that between the civilised and the savage human societies. The wildness often shown by hybrids of domestic species had the same cause as the wickedness that characterised human half-breeds.[15]

Debates about racial origins and evolution, hierarchies of racial types, and the dangers or possible advantages of racial mixture appear in explicit and submerged form in the journals and literature of mid and later nineteenth-century Britain. Robert Young has summarized the variety of positions that could be taken and discussed their ramifications in *Colonial Desire*, where he describes the complex disagreements between those who espoused the earlier monogenist position exemplified in the abolitionist slogan, 'Am I not a man and a brother', and those who advocated various forms of the polygenist position regarding racial origin.[16]

These varying attitudes towards racial difference emerge sharply at moments of crisis, and specifically following traumatic and violent conflicts such as the 'Indian Mutiny' in 1857, the American Civil War, and the Morant Bay rebellion in Jamaica in 1865. The 1857 rebellion referred to by the British as the Indian Mutiny and by some Indian historians as the Indian War of Independence[17] was officially declared a limited mutiny of Indian 'sepoys' whose religious sensibilities had been offended by the use of pork and beef fat to grease cartridges. Disraeli dismissed this reading as trivializing the seriousness of the matter, and Karl Marx, writing as a correspondent to the *New York Daily Tribune*, saw the uprising as a response to the destruction of the local Indian economy by 'the British intruder who broke up the Indian hand-loom and destroyed the spinning wheel'.[18] While publicly dismissing the significance of the rebellion, the British government rapidly abolished the East India Company and appointed a viceroy to head the government of India. And despite Queen Victoria's 1858 proclamation disclaiming 'alike the right and the desire to impose Our convictions on any of Our subjects',[19] the earlier partial tolerance and acknowledgement of religious beliefs and practices by Hindus, Parsis, and Muslims was now seen by many as erroneous, and a more evangelical Christianizing project was advocated. The London Missionary Society urged the introduction of Christian instruction in all schools in India, arguing that the secular schools nurtured nationalism and anti-British feeling, 'pernicious errors', and 'the most demoralizing and revolutionary principles'.[20] Increasingly, missionary and newspaper reports represented 'Hindoo' and Muslim religious rituals and beliefs as idolatrous, sensual, and inducive of fatalism and passivity. Although Asians were often represented, particularly by anthropologists, as occupying a slightly higher place in the hierarchy of races than Africans, popular literature of the period and many newspaper reports also responded to the event by emphasizing more simple racial dichotomies, depicting the Indian rebels as brutish rapists lusting for the bodies of white women. As Jenny Sharpe demonstrates, the earlier civilizing mission advocated by Bentham, Mill, and Macaulay, often focussed on the abolition of *sati*, and summarized in Gayatri Spivak's words as 'White men saving brown women from brown men',[21] becomes imaged as white men saving *white* women from brown men.[22] The rhetoric of this period is exemplified in a speech for the defence of Governor Eyre by the scientist John Tyndall. Comparing Eyre's ruthless response to the Jamaicans who rioted at Morant Bay to the 'honourable and manly' conduct of British officers at Cawnpore, Tyndall endorses 'the conduct of those British officers in India who shot their wives before blowing themselves to pieces, rather than allow what they loved and honoured to fall into the hands of the Sepoys'.[23] According to Catherine Hall, 'Eyre's own "proudest recollection" of Morant Bay...was that he had saved the ladies of Jamaica.'[24] As Catherine Hall also notes, there were frequent comparisons between the 'Indian Mutiny', the 1865 Morant Bay rebellion and grossly exaggerated versions of the earlier uprisings in Haiti. Anxieties triggered by these events were also heightened by the Fenian violence in Ireland in the 1860s.

The debate over the Morant Bay rebellion and Governor Eyre's response to it engaged the mid nineteenth century's leading intellectuals and called forth opposing views with regard to race. Edward Eyre, who had previously served as Protector of Aborigines in Australia, Lieutenant-Governor in New Zealand, and Governor of the Leeward Islands, had been appointed Governor of Jamaica in 1864. It was a time of mounting unrest and disillusion on the part of the Jamaican black and coloured population, who were denied the franchise and had very limited economic opportunity. The rejection of an appeal for further land distribution led to violence at Morant Bay in 1865. Eyre sent in the army, resulting in the deaths of nearly 500 black and coloured Jamaicans. Eyre also authorized severe punishments for others who were or were thought to be involved, and ordered the execution of George William Gordon, who had acted as a spokesman and leader for the coloured middle class. A British government commission condemned Eyre's actions, and recognized that the grievances of the black population were genuine. Eyre spoke up in his own defence, and was supported by many of Britain's leading writers and intellectuals, including Dickens, Tennyson, Carlyle, Ruskin, Kingsley, Tyndall, and Murchison. British liberals and radicals critical of his actions formed an opposing Jamaica Committee which included J.S. Mill, Darwin, Huxley, Spencer, and Lyell.[25] Many of the supporters of the Jamaica Committee had been involved in abolitionist causes and assistance for freed men after the American Civil War, and also endorsed the extension of the franchise in Britain. Thus, for some Britons, anxieties about class unrest in Britain became linked to anxieties about racial and cultural conflict in the British colonies. Writing for the London Labour journal, the *Bee Hive*, Frederic Harrison commented:

This is a question far deeper than sect or colour. It does not concern Baptists, or black men, or merely the character of a public servant. I have no more liking for black men than for Baptists, and very little liking for Governor Eyre's past history ... The question is whether *legality* is to be co-extensive with the Queen's rule, or whether our vast foreign dominions are to be governed by the irresponsible will of able, absolute, and iron-willed satraps. It is on this ground alone that it so peculiarly concerns the working classes. They alone are as yet untainted by the reckless injustice with which our empire has been won and kept.[26]

As Christine Bolt demonstrates, and as the above quotation indicates, those who opposed Governor Eyre's methods were by no means free of racial prejudice.[27] Their sympathy for Jamaican or southern American Negroes assumed that such people were inferior or childlike, and therefore needed the guidance and leadership of white Britons. The debate over Governor Eyre contributed to a hardening of the virulent racism expressed earlier by Carlyle in his *Discourse on the Nigger Question*, and also discouraged the more liberal from contemplating extension of the franchise and other measures of equality to peoples whom they regarded as less progressive or innately inferior. Such views were also strengthened by the growing anthropological industry in the second half of the nineteenth century. And, as Simon Gikandi argues, liberal and conservative views alike revolved around the construction of England as a source of authority and law, defined in opposition to those who were seen to be either by nature or circumstance deprived of a rule of law.[28] Insofar as the 'imagined community' of the nation is held together by what is perceived as the nation's highest shared institution, the law, it is also defined *against* those communities or peoples which (according, for example, to Carlyle) are perceived by their very nature as negating law and morality, or (as in James Mill's case) perceived as likely to benefit from subordination to the benign authority of English law and morality. Gikandi concludes that in both cases, 'the black subject functions as the agent of what Homi Bhabha has called "a perpetual performativity," challenging the idea of the law through its real and imagined acts of insurgency and also affirming the necessity of the law and role of imperial England as the conveyor of this law'.[29]

However, the perception of these constructed racial hierarchies as either natural and unchanging or circumstantial and mutable, was not merely an abstract debate or limited in its application to the colonies. An emphasis on racial difference as natural reinforced hierarchies of class linked to colour, which in turn brought 'coloured' labourers, sailors, soldiers, and domestic servants to England (and thus further reinforced assumed links between colour and class). The more liberal view, espoused by J.S. Mill and other members of the Jamaica Committee, encouraged educational and professional development in the colonies, eventually bringing students and professionals to study and practise in British institutions. In the case of India and Africa, a number of those students and professionals were members of aristocratic families. And such events as the Great Exhibition, together with Britain's self-promotion as a centre of commerce, industry, and modernity, brought businessmen and traders as well as regional leaders, chiefs, and officials from India and Africa. The title of Rozina Visram's history of Indians in Britain, *Ayahs, Lascars, and Princes*, succinctly summarises the differing backgrounds of groups of immigrants and visitors and their motives for coming to England from the Indian subcontinent.

In the colonies, the promotion of often contradictory policies and attitudes resulted on the one hand in the offering of an educational syllabus which purportedly sought to eradicate difference, and on the other hand the setting up of rigid barriers to the advancement of colonial subjects beyond menial and clerical positions. Such barriers, and the often overt racism displayed by colonial administrators and their families, encouraged a thrust towards nationalism by those who deeply resented the gap between the promise of 'equality' and the actual refusal of it. As Gikandi points out, it was often those who most endorsed the religion and 'civilization' brought by the British, who became the most ardent opponents of British rule. Speaking of his own community in Kenya, who referred to themselves as *Athomi*, the people of the book, Gikandi notes 'how strongly they detested colonial rule, which they fought tooth and nail, often ending up in prison, and how passionately they believed in the efficacy and authority of colonial culture'.[30] Among the students and professionals who visited Britain in the latter half of the nineteenth century and in the early twentieth century were a good number whose experience in the United Kingdom and amidst colonial communities there reinforced both their opposition to British rule, and their feeling, as Gandhi famously responded when asked what he thought of Western civilization, that 'it would be a good idea'.

Many novels written during and after the mid nineteenth century betray conflicting attitudes and underlying assumptions concerning racial difference, often revealing a fascination with black bodies. Many also take difference in skin colour as a sign of innate difference in character. Thus Thackeray's 1848 novel *Vanity Fair* opens with recurring references to Sambo, the bandy-legged black footman, and features in its illustrations as well as its narrative Rhoda Swartz, 'the rich, woolly-haired mulatto from St Kitts', characterised by her emotional warmth and naivete.[31] Charles Reade's 1853 novel *Peg Woffington* includes the following passage describing the actress's black servant:

He was fed like a game-cock, and dressed like a Barbaric prince; and once, when he was sick his mistress... nursed him, and tended to him with the same white hand that plied the obnoxious whip;... but when Sir Charles's agent proposed to him certain silver coins, the ebony ape grinned till he turned half ivory, and became a spy in the house of his mistress.[32]

Here the mixture of fascination and repulsion becomes invested in both the narrator and his subject, and although the novel is set in the eighteenth century, the portrayal of the black man as childlike, apelike, and the embodiment of treachery belongs very much to the mode of mid nineteenth-century cartoons and descriptions. The obsession with skin colour, the depiction of other 'races' as apelike, and their context within

English self-construction is also seen in the letters of another novelist, Charles Kingsley, to his wife, as he toured Ireland in 1860:

But I am haunted by the human chimpanzees I saw along that hundred miles of horrible country. I don't believe they are our fault. I believe there are not only more of them than of old, but that they are happier, better, more comfortably fed and lodged under our rule than they ever were. But to see white chimpanzees is dreadful; if they were black, one would not feel it so much, but their skins, except where tanned by exposure, are as white as ours.[33]

What difference, then, does skin colour make? Such questions and anxieties are played out in the fascination with minstrel shows and 'blacking up' which was a feature of nineteenth-century English culture (and indeed earlier), and in the reviews of performances by black actors such as Ira Aldridge, who toured the United Kingdom several times between 1825 and 1860. Aldridge played Oroonoko and Othello, but he also played Lear, Macbeth, Richard III, and other major roles using white make-up and a wig. The London reviews were virulently racist, declaring not only that he was incapable of pronouncing English properly because of the shape of his lips, but also that 'it was impossible that Mr Aldridge should fully comprehend the meaning and force of even the words that he utters', and referring to him as 'the unseemly nigger'.[34] In the provinces, and in Scotland, Ireland, and Europe, however, Aldridge received high praise, played to full houses, and was loaded with honours. The significance of the contrast between his reception in London and his reception elsewhere deserves fuller investigation; it also reveals that attitudes to race in Britain were not monolithic.

In the metropolitan centre, however, the construction of Englishness in terms of imperial authority endorsed by racial difference gained strength in the late nineteenth century. Queen Victoria was declared Empress of India in 1876. Britain occupied Egypt to protect its ownership of and access to the Suez Canal in 1882. In 1884, Britain participated in the Berlin Conference, which partitioned the African continent between France, Britain, Germany, Portugal, and other European nations. Queen Victoria's Diamond Jubilee in 1897 was celebrated as a gathering of representatives from the empire, and projected as an image of imperial glory. Popular and children's literature of the late nineteenth and early twentieth century promoted the Englishman as superior hero defeating native villains and earning the respect and awe of loyal native subjects. By 1914 Britain boasted proudly that 'the sun never set on the British Empire' and in one form or another held sovereignty over Nigeria,

Ghana, Sierra Leone, the main part of Eastern and Southern Africa, the Indian subcontinent and parts of south-east Asia, many Caribbean islands, British Guyana, as well as Canada, New Zealand, and Australia. The growth and maintenance of empire was accompanied by considerable industrial development and investment, together with an increasingly competitive economic and social ethos. By 1913 sixty per cent of India's imports came from Britain and British investment in India totalled £380 million.[35] Whereas in the earlier parts of the century the debates over the abolition of the slave-trade and slavery had centred on the relative importance of morality over economics, by the end of the century crude and reductionist versions of social Darwinism and hard-nosed economic competition dismissed moral arguments and cultural relativism as sentimental and out-of-touch with contemporary scientific 'realities'. By the end of the century the capitalist ethos of laissez-faire and competitive markets had supplanted an earlier emphasis, articulated by Equiano and others, on commerce and trade as means of harmony. Despite the questions raised in the writings of Conrad, Hardy, and Gissing, about the consequences of economic imperialism, the enormous gap between the ideals used to justify it and the realities of exploitation, and despite the full-scale attack mounted in Hobson's 1902 critique of imperialism, the endorsement of England's imperialist mission prevailed. Thus H.G. Wells could write in the first volume of *Anticipations*, his three-volume socialist utopian work:

... those swarms of black, and brown, and dirty-white and yellow people, who do not come into the new needs of efficiency? Well, the world is a world, not a charitable institution, and I take it they will have to go. The whole tenor and meaning of the world, as I see it, is that they will have to go. So far as they fail to develop sane, vigorous and distinctive personalities for the great world of the future, it is their portion to die out and disappear.[36]

CHAPTER 5

Querying race, gender, and genre: nineteenth-century narratives of escape

A significant body of writing by black people in nineteenth-century Britain derives from the experiences of escaped or ex-slaves who found support and asylum in the United Kingdom. As might be expected, this body of writing has much in common with the slave narratives composed and written in the United States during the same period, but there are enough differences to make the British slave narrative after 1833 a distinct genre. Once in Britain and thus removed from the immediate threat of enslavement, the authors feel less constrained by the anxiety to tell a 'plain unvarnish'd tale' which cannot be accused of the romantic or literary flourishes abjured by Mary Prince's scribe. Although some of these narratives, such as those by John Brown and Francis Fedric, are dictated, and their scribes are anxious to insist on the authenticity of the accounts and the voices which they transcribe, they differ from earlier narratives such as Equiano's or Prince's, or those by Frederick Douglass and others in the United States, in their often self-consciously literary and dramatic quality, their occasional references to fictional texts such as *Uncle Tom's Cabin*, the elaboration of anecdotes, and the interest in bringing characters additional to the author alive. Moreover, the absence within Britain itself of communities sharply divided by colour (the colonies were a different matter), perhaps encouraged the ex-slaves themselves to have greater flexibility in questioning essentialist identities linked to race and colour. Unlike Prince, whose situation did not allow her to reiterate her story before public audiences, and unlike Equiano who apparently first wrote and then spoke in public tours about his experiences, these later narratives were initially told and retold before public audiences before they were written down. Hence the oral story-tellers had plenty of opportunity to shape and elaborate their accounts, and to judge which details and modes of telling were most effective. And whereas the narratives published in the United States often include vehement condemnations of the society they address, those addressed to a British audience almost always make much of the difference between America and Britain with regard to the latter's supposed lack of 'colour prejudice' and support for liberty. In short they seek to flatter British audiences, but also to reinforce the 'better selves' of Britons, by appealing to an imagined community of equal and freedom-loving citizens.

One of the earliest nineteenth-century narratives specifically written in Britain and for British audiences is by Moses Roper. Born in North Carolina early in the second decade of the nineteenth century, Moses Roper was the son of his master, Henry Roper, and having a mother who was a mixture of Anglo-Saxon, African, and 'Indian' ancestry, was himself near white. Seeing his likeness to the master, his mistress attempted to murder Moses with a knife and club at birth, but was prevented by his mother's mother. The mother and child were then promptly sold to a plantation owner some distance away. At the age of six, Moses was parted from his mother and sold or passed on to a series of owners. He ascribes his frequent transfers to the lightness of his skin, which he believes made him less desirable as a slave, and also caused unease and prejudice among white labourers and craftsmen with whom he might have worked. At the age of twelve or thirteen, he was sent to work in a cotton plantation, treated very harshly, and frequently flogged because, owing to his youth and inexperience, he was not able to keep up with the faster workers. The main part of the narrative is taken up with descriptions of the cruelties inflicted on him and other slaves, together with his repeated attempts to escape, involving extraordinary feats of endurance, and consequent further severe and brutal punishments. Of these one of the most cruel and humiliating involved being fastened with a 40 lb weight to a female slave for several days.

Moses Roper finally escaped by obtaining a forged pass, and then a job as a steward on a packet sailing to New York from Savannah. Seeing advertisements for him in local newspapers and fearing recapture in the north, Moses Roper sailed for England, and landed in Liverpool in November 1835. In England he was assisted by many prominent abolitionists, including Mr Scoble, the secretary of the Anti-Slavery Society, and Dr Cox, of whose church he became a member, who helped pay for him to receive an education at schools in Hackney and Wallingford and at University College, London.[1]

Roper's little 105-page tale lacks the rhetorical vigour and narrative drive of later accounts by Frederick Douglass, John Brown, and William Craft, but it has historical significance as one of the first works in this particular genre of the British slave narrative. Roper was also one of the first writers and speakers to address British audiences and to give a detailed and first-hand account of slavery in the American south. During the nine years that he lived in Britain before emigrating to Canada, he estimated that he gave 'upward of 2,000 lectures' to reform and abolitionist societies, and sold 25,000 copies in English, and another 5,000 in Welsh translation.[2] Although the narrative as a whole is somewhat rambling and repetitious, it includes some graphic descriptions of the ingeniously cruel and barbarous punishments inflicted on slaves, indicates the sexual abuse which females slaves were subject to, exposes the practice of selling the slave-owner's offspring conceived with slave-mistresses, and also underlines the hypocrisy of slave-owners who profess Christianity but deny access to Church attendance and Christian worship to their slaves. Amidst the persistent and repeated escape attempts described, there are two or three recounted in greater and more vivid detail, as for example one where running through a forest he is forced to climb a tree to evade a pack of wolves, and then is shot at by a pack of slave-hunters. He also deplores the deceptions and lies he is forced to tell in order to save himself from capture and to obtain a forged passport and set of testimonials identifying him as a free-man descended from Indian and white, noting that 'by this hasty and wicked deception, I saved myself from going to Bainbridge prison'.[3] Later writers in this genre tend to be less defensive about such deceptions, and indeed take a certain pride in their ability to outwit their oppressors.

One of the more effective episodes in Roper's book is his account of his brief reunion with his family, from whom he was parted at the age of six, and whom he rediscovers after escaping from South to North Carolina. He tells how he comes across a little girl of about six, and as their conversation progresses, gradually realizes that she is his half-sister. She takes him to their mother, who at first does not recognize him, but at last does so and, 'in an instant, we were clasped in each others' arms, amidst the ardent exchange of caresses and tears of joy' (*Escape from Slavery*, p. 33). Comparing his rediscovery of his family with the story of Joseph reunited with his brethren after being sold into slavery, Roper then tells how he was concealed by his family for a week before his dramatic recapture by a group of twelve slave-holders with pistols, and never again saw any of his family.

The fact that his family remains enslaved in America perhaps accounts for several conciliatory appeals to slave-holders and acknowledgement of those, like the 'Scotchman' William Beveridge, who treated him comparatively humanely. His preface declares that the purpose of the book is 'to expose the cruel system of slavery' and 'to convince even the hardened slave-holder' (p. xii). He declares that the events he describes will allow abolitionists and people of all persuasions to argue the case for abolition: 'Yea, even friend Breckenbridge, a gentleman known at Glasgow, will be able to possess this, and draw from it all the forcible arguments on his own side, which in his wisdom, honesty, and candour he may be able to adduce' (p. xi). And the narrative closes with a disavowal of any wish to 'degrade America in the eyes of Britons', an affirmation that he bears 'no enmity even to the slave-holders, but regret[s] their delusions', and the profound hope that 'America soon be *indeed* the land of the free' (p. 105).

ORAL AND LITERARY COLLABORATION: BLACK BRITISH AND AMERICAN SLAVES IN GEORGIA

John Brown's narrative, *Slave Life in Georgia*, first published in 1855, almost two decades later than Roper's, responds to the rather different contexts of the Fugitive Slave Act and the Negro Seamen Acts.[4] The narrative was dictated to the then secretary of the British and Foreign Anti-Slavery Society, L.A. Chamerovzow, who edited the account, and himself inserted at least two chapters.[5] Born a slave in Southampton County, Virginia, in the early nineteenth century, Brown had escaped to Canada, and then came to England in 1850, where he worked as a carpenter, and died in London in 1876, having spent almost half of his life in England.

The preface to Brown's *Narrative* aligns it with earlier narratives in its claim to authenticity, and by its reference to Othello's assertion that he tells a 'plain, unvarnished tale' (*Othello*, Act 1, Sc.3, l.90), suggests literary precedents in the very act of disclaiming any pretence to literariness:

The Editor is conscious that the following Narrative has only its truthfulness to recommend it to favourable consideration. It is nothing more than it purports to be, namely; a plain, unvarnished tale of real Slave-life, conveyed as nearly as possible in the language of the subject of it, and written under his dictation. (p. 3)

Despite this disclaimer, reminiscent of Pringle's preface to *The History of Mary Prince*, there are sections of the text which suggest the intervention of a literary consciousness. Chamerovzow was himself a novelist, the author of a number of historical romances set in or around the French Revolution, and one suspects that it is his hand and mind which fashioned the tragic story of John Glasgow, which takes up a long chapter in the text, and which differs markedly in style and tone from the more oral style of the chapters dealing with Brown's own experiences.

Chamerovzow's preface underlines another facet of the British slave narrative genre, the multiple aims of informing the 'truth' of slavery, and so helping to end it, of 'writing oneself into being' and in the process speaking for the 'race', and of producing a work which will make money for the author:

In undertaking to prepare this volume for the press, the Editor's object was two-fold, namely; to advance the anti-slavery cause by the diffusion of information; and to promote the success of the project John Brown has formed, to advance himself by his own exertions, and to set an example to others of his 'race'. (p. 4)

Brown's story as relayed to us in print does convey that sense of a voice and experience which is both individual and representative. And from the opening paragraph, he asserts the core concern of his life story, the establishment and control of his own identity and humanity in opposition to the slave identity imposed and beaten into him by a series of brutal masters. That first paragraph begins with his naming of himself, and his insistence on the significance of the name he has given himself as a free man, as opposed to the meaninglessness of the identity and names assigned to him as a slave :

My name is John Brown. How I came to take it, I will explain in due time. When in Slavery, I was called Fed. Why I was so named, I cannot tell. I never knew myself by any other name, nor always by that; for it is common for slaves to answer to any name, as it may suit the humour of the master. I do not know how old I am, but I think I may be any age between thirty-five and forty. I fancy I must be about thirty-seven or thirty-eight, as near as I can guess.[6]

This acknowledgement of the lack of knowledge, the absence of records or ground on which an identity can be taken for granted, is a feature common to many slave narratives, although none the less effective for that. So too is the vague reference to a father seen only once, but whose memory is clung to, and the loving memory of a slave mother and the sufferings she and her children incur when forcibly parted. Brown tells us that his mother's name was Nancy, but that she was called Nanny, that both his parents were slaves, and that his father's father was an 'Eboe...stolen from Africa'. He remembers his father as 'very black', but saw him only once, when he came to visit his mother, before his father was sold to a more distant owner and his mother was forced to take another husband. But the memories of his first mistress and various masters are more vivid and detailed than those of his parents, for it is day-to-day contact with them that most informs his life and his struggle for physical and psychological survival (and the two are sometimes at odds). Thus he describes his first mistress:

Our mistress Betty Moore was an old, big woman, about seventy, who wore spectacles and took snuff... She used to call us children up the big house every morning, and give us a dose of garlic and rue to keep us 'wholesome', as she said, and make us 'grow likely for market'. After swallowing our dose, she would make us run round a great sycamore tree in the yard, and if we did not run fast enough to please her, she used to make us nimbler by laying about us with a cowhide. She always carried this instrument dangling by her side, like ladies in this country wear their scissors. It was painted blue, and we used to call it the 'blue lizard'. (p. 7)

Like Mary Prince's account of the 'domestic institution', and a world in which maternal roles are perverted, Brown's portrait of Betty Moore, their mistress, tellingly shows how the herbs which might in a normal world be given to keep them 'wholesome' and healthy, are intended merely to make them marketable, and how what might from a distance look like innocent children's exercise of free spirits, running around a great sycamore tree in the yard, becomes at second glance a sadistic torture. The inversion of civilized behaviour and normality is underlined by the comparison between the whip and the domestic tools carried by English ladies ('She always carried this instrument dangling by her side, like ladies in this country wear their scissors'), thus literally bringing home to his audience of Englishwomen the corruption of domestic values embodied in slavery.

Brown's specific address and appeal to an English audience is also carried in his recurring references to the fate of John Glasgow, his mentor and friend. He tells how in one of his darkest moments he was befriended by John Glasgow, who advised him to try 'to be honest and upright, and if I could ever get to England, where he was from, and conducted myself properly, folks would respect me as much as they did a white man'(p. 24). Glasgow's words recur almost as a refrain through the rest of narrative, and Brown's reiteration of his determination to escape to England is well calculated to appeal to his British readers.

John Brown's own narrative is here interrupted by the stories of two men from Britain who both become victims of southern slavery, the black Englishman John Glasgow, and the Scotsman, John Morgan. In fact, Glasgow's story is recorded twice: once as a declaration given before a Notary Public, and added as an appendix at the end of the book, and then rewritten and inserted as Chapter Four, as part of the narrative proper. Both the statement and the chapter versions differ markedly from the oral style and language of the rest of the narrative. For while Brown's own story appears to be 'conveyed as nearly as possible in the language of the subject of it, and written under his dictation', the stories of Glasgow's life and suffering are thoroughly literary in their style and rhetorical effects. This is especially the case with the Chapter Four version, where John Brown's voice almost entirely disappears. Glasgow, we are told, was 'a native of Demerara, born of free negro parents, whose free condition he inherited, as well as their complexion [sic]' (p. 9). Employed first as a cabin-boy, he had by the age of twenty achieved the status and qualifications of an able-bodied seaman. He married a farmer's daughter from near Liverpool, 'said not to have belied the adage which is so complimentary to Lancashire, in respect of its maidens'(p. 30). Not only is the literary quality and British identity of the speaker taken for granted in such descriptions, but it becomes clearly distanced from John Brown's sense of 'us' and 'them' in the remark that the Lancashire lass had consented to take Glasgow for her partner 'in spite of his complexion and very woolly hair'.

To provide for his wife and two children, John Glasgow again took employment as a sailor with an English cargo boat sailing for Savannah. There he fell under the jurisdiction of the Georgia law which insisted on the 'quarantining' or gaoling of black seamen while the ship was in harbour. The English captain declined to pay the fees for Glasgow's release, considering them too much to pay for someone who 'was only a nigger after all', and sailed back to England without him. Thereupon, Glasgow was sold by the state of Georgia to John Brown's master, who resented his 'brave look', and 'swore he "would flog his nigger pride out of him;"' and poor John had to suffer for having the look and carriage of a free man' (p. 33). The chapter goes on to recount in horrific detail the barbarous tortures inflicted upon Glasgow, leaves him physically broken as a slave on Thomas Stevens' plantation, and ends, as does the declaration, with a plea for information about his wife and children. The chapter as a whole serves as a self-contained story which illustrates the inequities of the Negro Seamen Acts about which the British public had recently become aroused, and also appeals to British patriotism and indignation about American mistreatment of British subjects. Brown also flatters the British self-image in his affirmation of what he owes to John Glasgow: 'To John I owe a debt of gratitude, for it was he who taught me to love and to seek liberty' (p. 39). The theme of free and honest British victimized by Americans is also emphasized in Chapter Six, another self-contained story, concerning the Scotsman John Morgan, whose attempt to make a living and demonstrate the superior benefits of employing free labour as a farmer in the south result in his murder by a group of white slave-owners including John Brown's master. Morgan's wife and children are left alone and destitute.

After the pathos and heightened rhetoric of John Glasgow's story, the narrative returns to its earlier style, which allows Brown an ironic and sometimes laconic voice, heard later in writings by Mark Twain and other authors. Thus Brown reports the general celebration when his master Thomas Stevens dies: 'He was buried, any how, nobody regretting him; not even his old dog, who wagged his tail when the coffin went by his kennel' (p. 46). He describes in detail the petty thieving and deceit of his masters, and recounts with grim humour some of the experiments conducted upon him by a Dr Hamilton. One of the experiments sought to discover the best medicines for withstanding heat by placing Brown in a heated hole, covering him with blankets, and giving him various mixtures to see which would allow him to withstand the greatest heat and last longest without fainting. Brown comments with understated irony:

He found that cayenne-pepper tea accomplished this object; and a very nice thing he made of it. As soon as he got back home, he advertised that he had discovered a remedy for sun-stroke. It consisted of pills, which were to be dissolved in a dose of cayenne-pepper tea, without which, he said, the pills would not produce any effect. Nor do I see how they should have done so, for they were only made of common flour. However, he succeeded in getting them into general use, and as he asked a good price, he soon realized a large fortune. (p. 42)

Hamilton conducted other even more horrific experiments. He sought to see 'how deep my black skin went', by creating blisters on Brown's hands, legs, and feet, and raising the skin beneath. That Hamilton's obsessive curiosity about blackness (and 'how deep it went') was allied to an equal curiosity about black sexuality is implied in Brown's report that Hamilton 'also tried other experiments on me, which I cannot dwell upon' (p. 42).

Like Mary Prince also, Brown refers to other abuses which remain unspoken and unwritten about in 'polite' society, but of which the slave-community can and does speak. These include the repeated rape of a twenty-year-old black maid stolen and 'abused' by his master Finey and others. 'Our women talked about this very much, and many of them cried, and said it was a great shame' (p. 19). He describes the brutal and sadistic floggings of young slave-women, even when heavily pregnant, resulting often in miscarriages. He speaks of the complete exhaustion of slave-mothers, and the frequent occurrence of (accidental) smothering of their babies when their overworked mothers are sleeping. The truth known, spoken and unspoken by those who have experienced slavery, and the authenticity of Brown's own narrative, is on several occasions set against the lesser authenticity of white writers such as Harriet Beecher Stowe: 'Mrs Stowe has told something about Slavery. I think she must know a great deal more than she has told. I know more than I dare to tell' (p. 60). Similarly he chastens another white woman writer for telling less than the truth when he refers to claims made by the southern supporter, Mrs Tyler: 'I know better than that, and so does she' (p. 55).

The first half of Brown's narrative speaks of the unspeakable horrors of slavery, emphasising the methods by which slaves are denied any humanity and beaten into submission. It includes his account of being weighed at the age of ten like a sack of potatoes and his worth reckoned by the pound at $310, before he is sold to a trader, wrenched from his mother, and the gate is slammed in her face as she tries to say goodbye for the last time. Once torn from his family and thrust into adulthood, Brown enters a world of tricksters, in which his survival and escape depends on his learning to be a better trickster than his masters. The slave-owners cheat not only their slaves but each other; in turn, they are robbed by gangs of slave 'buccaneers', who entice or kidnap slaves from one master and sell them to another. It is a world where no one can be trusted, where forged passes are the only means of escape, where thieves and robbers offer a 'safer' survival than do 'lawful' owners, where knowledge can only be gained deviously, and can never be grounded in certainty. Brown learns to remain psychologically strong by pretending to be weak and submissive, gains information by playing the fool, and briefly escapes from his captors by pretending to be mad. Each escape is succeeded by recapture, and even more brutal floggings and punishment, including being hung from a gallows and whipped till he is unconscious, then fitted with the 'bell and horns', a 14 lb steel cap fastened with a padlock around his neck and worn night and day for three months. When describing his own sufferings, he again sets the authority of his experience against the responses of Harriet Beecher Stowe's readers:

Many people say that half of what Mrs Stowe and others have written about the punishments inflicted on slaves is untrue. I wish, for the sake of those who are now in bonds, that it were so. Unfortunately it is too true; and I believe half of what is done to them never comes to light. (pp. 75–6)

Throughout his suffering he is sustained by the memory of John Glasgow's advice: 'I was constantly dwelling on what John Glasgow had told me about freedom, and England, and becoming a man' (pp. 61–2). As with Frederick Douglass, becoming a man hardens him to grow 'defiant of my master, but I determined I would be killed in defending myself if he used me too hard'.

Brown speaks both apologetically and defensively of his own practice of deceitfulness in a system where deceit is constantly practised on slaves by their masters, although he insists that such deceit is not practised by slaves against one another. At the same time he describes in considerable detail and with some pride the ingenious and elaborate steps he took to engineer his escape. Like Huck Finn, he constructs a raft complete with a small stove, and floats down the Mississippi by night, surviving on roast potatoes and catfish. And like Huck's companion Jim, he misses the crucial landing point, and finds himself not in England (which he had assumed to exist in the vicinity of New Orleans) and a free man, but imprisoned again in the heart of slavery.

The final chapters of the narrative turn from the horrors of slavery to a gripping account of Brown's final flight to freedom, hiding and walking along the banks of the Mississippi, his many narrow escapes and near recaptures, and his adroitness at 'acting foolish' to deflect suspicion. The narration of such anecdotes about 'acting foolish', like similar ones told by Francis Fedric, might be seen as correctives to the widespread and popular 'Jim Crow' shows brought by the American 'comedian' Tim Rice, and the minstrel shows, which depicted Negroes as inherently stupid, slow, and lazy. Thus when at one point he is discovered sleeping in a hideaway, Brown gives this example of how he plays the trickster:

I was awakened by a voice, crying out – 'Hallo, old fellow! Are you asleep?'
I looked up, and remembering the advice I had received from Caesar, never to look frightened if I should be surprised by any one, I answered, without getting up:
'No, I am not asleep! I was asleep till you waked me, though.' . . .
'Which way you going?' he asked.
'I'm not going anywhere,' I replied. 'I'm sitting down.' (p. 122)

Pretending to be drunk and hungover, and claiming to come from Buffalo (as advised by a free 'coloured man' Caesar, who had also given him food and shelter), he manages to avoid capture till he finds Caesar's friend. This man gets him a free pass, and 'with that pass I assumed the name of John Brown, which I have retained ever since' (p. 125). So the climactic moment of the narrative is reached, granting the narrator the means to his freedom and a new identity which he freely chooses.

Thereafter the narrative moves from the taut drama of the escape to acknowledgement of those who helped him, and the succour and assistance given by Quaker families and guides along the 'Underground Rail-road'. The story ends with Brown's arrival in England and a brief account of his employment as a carpenter in Bristol and Lancashire: 'I worked here until I found that there is prejudice against colour in England, in some classes, as well as more generally in America' (p. 142).

Brown's agenda in telling his story has an additional strategy to his editor's. While he shares the aim of defeating slavery by bringing before the British public its cruelty and immorality, he also wishes 'to show the world that a "nigger" has quite as much will, and energy, and purpose to him, as any white man, if you only give him fair play' (p. 171). He also points out that he has contributed to the Great Exhibition and is himself an inventor.[7] And through the sale of his narrative he hopes to make enough money to buy tools and make his living as a carpenter and handyman. Brown urges a boycott of cotton from the slave-owning states, for unlike Moses Roper he cannot believe that moral persuasion will suffice to convert slave-owners from their ways. As an alternative he proposes setting up free-labour cotton plantations in the West Indies, where 'coloured people' can work together for their own benefit.

Brown's book concludes with a group of testimonials, dated between 1851 and 1854, from citizens in Cornwall, London, Glasgow, Edinburgh, and Bradford, all testifying to the author's good character and honesty. Several of them also affirm that he is a teetotaller, and that they have heard him lecture on slavery and teetotalism. The final two testimonials (from Yorkshire) offer strong support for his project to set up free-labour cotton plantations, and also comment on the effectiveness of his lectures. The Reverend Godwin of Bradford states:

J. Brown delivered a lecture at the Mechanics' Institute in this town, on Monday evening last, on which occasion I took the chair. The attendance was good; and the simplicity and common sense with which he delivered his statements and made his remarks, very strongly interested the audience. (p. 206)

BLACK LIVES, WHITE AUDIENCES: FRANCIS FEDRIC'S
TWO NARRATIVES

The process of shaping and reshaping one's story within a British context is well illustrated in the two versions of Francis Fedric's account of his experiences and escape from slavery. The first version is a short twelve-page pamphlet, published in 1859, titled *Life and Sufferings of Francis Fedric*, and the second, published four years later, a longer memoir, *Slave Life in Virginia and Kentucky*.[8]

Born in Virginia in the first decade of the nineteenth century (probably in 1804), Francis Fedric was the grandson of two Africans kidnapped from Africa. He knew both grandparents, and was taught some rudiments of the Christian religion by his grandmother, although his grandfather remained sceptical of a religion professed by slave-holders and used in order to argue the legitimacy of slavery. At about the age of fourteen he was taken by his owners to a tobacco plantation in Kentucky, where he was trained to be a house servant, winning some favour with his mistress and master as a bright and often mischievous lad. When his master died, however, he was inherited by a drunken and brutal son who sold many of the older slaves, made a habit of raping some of the younger female slaves, and flogged Francis and other slaves savagely and at whim. Francis tried to escape on several occasions, and after each attempt was caught and severely beaten. He was finally rescued by a neighbouring planter, who had given him religious instruction (against the master's will), and who assisted him to flee to Canada through the underground railway. Finding 'the Yankee prejudice against my race' existed even in Canada,[9] and following his marriage to a woman from Devonshire then residing in Toronto, he emigrated to England in 1857, and was helped to establish a lodging-house in Manchester. He had worked for an Anti-Slavery Society in Toronto, and when he came to England he continued his work as an anti-slavery speaker. One testimonial commends his public addresses as '*speaking facts* rather than prepared lectures' (author's emphasis),[10] while another comments that Fedric is 'a very effective lecturer, and is fully capable of rivetting the attention of his audience by the romantic details of his very interesting life'.[11] When his lodging-house failed as a business enterprise, he dictated his memoirs and they were sold to raise money.

Although there is some overlap between the first brief autobiograph-ical work and the second, which is almost 100 pages longer, there are significant differences in detail, tone, and effect. The first is unremit-ting in its emphasis on the tyranny and brutality experienced by slaves, and seeks to expose the ways in which 'the HORRORS OF THE SLAVE SYSTEM [sic]'[12] 'waste mind and manners, soil, and human labour' (*Life and Sufferings*, p. 3). His emphasis is on the spiritual, moral, physical, and psychological degradation encouraged by slave-holders, and he gives vivid illustrations of its effects, as in the following description of how slave-children received their food:

See the swarms of young negroes huddling together like swine in straw by night, feeding on Indian corn broth out of troughs, served up very stintingly, so as to induce such eager eating as hunger only would produce, with its consequent quarrels and disorders; the children of so many families in a gang (under the care of an old negress generally called 'Auntey') without shoes or covering for the head, their feet often in great chaps, sore and bleeding, their woolly heads sunburnt to a reddish earth-colour, presenting a sad spectacle of neglect and degradation; that creatures in such circumstances should ever become in any degree subjects of religious emotions, is a marvel. (pp. 3–4)

Whereas this short account tells of several attempts to escape and goes into considerable detail about these attempts and the dangers he endured, the later version tells of only one attempt before the final successful one, and relates more briefly his experiences of desperate hunger and encounters with poisonous snakes in the swampy area where he hides out for several weeks. The first account is well calculated to excite the interest and sympathy of English audiences in urban surroundings far from the American 'wilderness':

The whip-poor-will, a bird of that name, kept up his doleful cry in the bushes and trees, and around all night long frogs of every species croaking, and reptiles innumerable joining in wild concert, but not by their varied notes and sounds was I disturbed, the blowing snake with many others did not care to conceal themselves from my sight, their tameness was frightful to me from the first night or two. (p. 5)

He goes on to describe how snakes glide across him as he reclines, or lie on him at night, and his fear of making any movement lest he disturb and alarm the snakes. His desperate hunger, as he attempts to survive on wild berries, sometimes with dire results, is also dramatically conveyed. At one point, as he wanders in search of food, he comes across a young female slave ploughing a field and begs for bread. Despite the danger to herself if caught, she conceals in her bosom about two ounces of bread; the syntax and rhetoric with which he tells of his response when she hands him the bread effectively communicate his confusion of emotions and thoughts:

When she handed it over to me I felt how! what! I can scarcely say, I was so grateful; I have spoken of hunger, hunger was not now uppermost in my thoughts, the river, can I cross it? shall I be able after all to get away? shall I reach Canada the land of the free? Shall I, can I escape the thousand lashes? They will torment me unto death if I am caught. (p. 7)

At another point he describes, in his desperation for food, stalking a mink for almost two hours before it escapes into the water, and later in his hunger he mistakes a dog sleeping in the dark for a goose. As he flees from the barking dog, a musket shot whistles overhead, but misses him because he is bent double from weakness.

Fedric's first autobiographical reminiscence ends with a tribute to the kindness of the English towards a coloured man, 'such is the difference between this country and America', and a short poem, presumably composed by him, in praise of England as a land of liberty:

> I have escaped through countless dangers,
>   From the man who claimed my soul,
> Mind and body as his chattel,
>   Subject to his control.
> Now I have come across the British ocean,
>   Here in England is my home;
> As to those who still in bondage,
>   Brethren unto thee I come.   (p. 11)

The 1863 memoir is often more literary in style, and seeks to provide a more rounded picture of the author's character, development, and environment, while also illustrating the oppression of slavery. Whether these differences are in part accounted for by the influence of the scribe to whom Fedric dictated his story, the gentleman induced by the Reverend Lee 'to take down from his lips the memoir now given to the public',[13] can only be a matter for speculation. However, the statement in the Preface that Fedric presents 'the sunny side' of bondage reflects the reverend's distance from the experiences described rather than the overall effect of this account. What Fedric does convey are the ingenious and determined methods of resistance, and the multitude of psychological defences against the annihilation of their selfhood that the slaves employ. Whereas the first narrative begins with an emphasis on the tyranny of slave-holders and the obliteration of individual identity ('My father was a slave and worked for a tyrant master of the name of Parker; my mother was also a slave and worked for a tyrant master of the name of Parker'(*Slave Life*, p. 3), this second narrative begins by drawing attention to the stupidity of many slave-holders contrasted with the superior awareness of their slaves. Thus Fedric tells first of a mistress who was so ignorant of poultry farming that she expected each hen to lay every single day, and flogged her Negro girl for not bringing an egg for every hen. There is also the anecdote of a slave-holder who believed that the sugar brought to him must be of inferior quality because cheaper than the last lot he purchased, but was satisfied when the storekeeper sent him back the same sugar at double the price. Fedric concludes the story and its moral thus:

> The Colonel looked first at the bill, and then at the sugar. 'Aye, this is some-thing like; this is as it ought to be,' he said. I merely relate this anecdote to show what kind of persons the slave-owners, in some instances, are, and that the slaves are not always kept in subjection by a consciousness of their master's intellectual superiority, for the slaves often, behind their backs, laugh at their ab-surdities; but by a brutal system of terrorism practised upon them from their very birth. (p. 3)

In this same section, Fedric also reverses the usual representation of the slave as the victim of superstitions dispelled or played upon by the master, when he portrays Colonel R. terror-stricken by a thunder storm, and cowering in his house surrounded by the 500 slaves he has summoned in from the fields to protect him. Fedric speculates that the colonel either believed that his African slaves possessed the power to deflect the lightning, or that the colonel was privately aware that his own crimes as a slave-holder were greater than any wrongs committed by his slaves and therefore more likely to draw the wrath of God. The concern to provide an atmospheric setting for the anecdote suggests one of the ways in which this memoir strives for a more literary effect than the earlier narrative: 'The weather was warm and sultry, scarcely a breath of air stirred, and clouds of inky blackness began to rise from the distant uplands' (p. 3).[14] Fedric also takes considerable delight in narrating how as a child he played upon the terror his master and mistress had of ghosts and goblins, by producing ghostly laughter as he hid in a bush. 'The slaveholders are a very superstitious lot', he concludes (pp. 58–9).

These anecdotes illustrating the intellectual inferiority of slave-holders are followed by examples of their moral inferiority and deviousness. Whereas Fedric's grandmother tries to teach him some Christian doctrine and is a firm believer in a better world beyond, where there would be no flogging, the master summons the slave-children to inform them they have no souls: 'You are just like those cattle . . . White people only have souls' (p. 5). When his grandmother is discovered to have secretly attended a prayer meeting, she is tied to a peach tree, her back stripped: 'Her own son was then made to give her forty lashes with a thong of raw cow's-hide, her master standing over her the whole time blaspheming and threatening what he would do if her son did not lay it on' (p. 7). Throughout the narrative, Fedric reveals that the deliberate attempt by slave-holders to brutalize the slaves and make 'the utmost difference between them and the white man' (p. 8), more often results in the brutal- ization of the slave-holders and their families. In contrast to the 'natural chastity of women slaves', 'an unchaste female slave being very rarely found', Fedric asserts, despite the crowded conditions in which they are housed together with the men (p. 8), the male slave-holders indulge in brutal and multiple rape and promiscuity, while their wives and daugh- ters are titillated by witnessing and even at times participating in the sadistic flogging of naked male and female slaves. He also cites the ex- ample of a slave-holder who sold his own daughter, a quadroon, to a trader for $1,500.

In the light of such behaviour, the questions of Fedric's grandfather, portrayed as a powerful and respected man, 6'4" in height, take on greater force. 'How', he would say, 'can Jesus be just, if He will allow such oppression and wrong? Don't the slaveholders justify their conduct by the Bible itself, and say, that it tells them to do so?' (p. 11). This same grandfather at one point physically resists his master, and the young Fedric is forced to intervene to stop the fighting men seriously hurting one another.

But in addition to the dignity and authority of his grandfather's words and action, Fedric also portrays other forms of resistance and subversion. Whereas his grandfather openly questions the uses to which the Bible and Christianity are put, a slave of a younger generation may turn the Bible and its misreading against his owners. We are given the story of a slave who pretends to discover and read the following commandments from the Bible to his mistress: 'Give your slaves plenty of bread and meat, and plenty of hot biscuit in the morning, also be sure to give them three horns of whiskey a-day.' When rebuked by his mistress, he points out that she too reads into the Bible a great deal that is not there. On this Fedric affirms what have now become the received wisdom of post- colonial theory regarding 'sly civility' and 'signifying': 'Slaves are all of them full of this sly, artful, indirect way of conveying what they dare not speak out, and their humour is very often the medium of hinting whole- some truths. Is not cunning always the natural consequence of tyranny?' (p. 13).

Like Equiano and John Brown, Francis Fedric is willing to tell stories against himself, stories which expose not only his comparative innocence and foolhardiness, but also (and unlike Equiano) his willingness to deceive and employ cunning. Thus he shares with Equiano the experience of believing that he is being watched by a portrait in the room where he is working, but whereas Equiano takes pride then and later in serving his master assiduously even after he discovers his mistake, Fedric feels justified in 'going on strike': 'Thereafter, I would say to the portrait, "I's not going to work. You don't know nothing. They don't give us nothing. I's not going to work for nothing." And I did not half work, only just doing a little' (pp. 22–3). He also recounts with some enjoyment other stratagems to avoid work which he regarded as demeaning. Told to wash a dress for his mistress, he deliberately tears it, and so, despite her anger, 'was sufficiently cunning by this stratagem to escape what appeared to me the degrading womanly occupation of washing'. Similarly, and for the same reason, when commanded to do the work of a milkmaid, he persists in milking the cow from the wrong side – thus causing the cow to kick and upset the milk pail, until his mistress, in despair, takes him off the job (pp. 19–20). More than most narratives in this genre, Fedric's memoir attempts to present the voices of the plantation slaves, and to give the sense of a communal life which is profoundly influenced by the system of slavery, but not entirely demarcated by it. While they are together, the conflictual but fond relationship between parents and children survives apart from the identities as chattels that the master would like to impose, as exemplified by Fedric's anecdote of his childhood-attempt to escape a flogging (from his grandmother) for hurting another child, by pretending to be asleep. As he feigns loud snoring, the women dispute whether he is actually asleep or not: ' "He is not asleep." "But he is asleep." "He isn't asleep." "But me tell you, he be asleep." Thus the women disputed. I thought I would help myself a little, and said, "Yes, I be asleep!" I forgot. But my uncle did not forget to take me out of the straw, and to flog me well' (p. 9). Fedric also dramatizes in detail the courtship and wedding of Fanny and Jerry, two slaves, a description which does not escape some condescension, sentimentality, and mockery, but which nevertheless also affirms the genuineness of feeling between slave-couples whom all too often slave-holders will part by selling them off to different traders.

One might well see these sympathetic and almost nostalgic depictions of the slave community as a function of Fedric's distance from them in time and space, and his loss of such a community in Britain. But these representations may also be a response to the caricatures of black people prevalent in British 'Jim Crow' shows, and the exhibition of isolated black African and native American people in travelling shows.

The fullest and most intriguing representation of members of the slave community comes towards the end of Fedric's memoir in a ten-page chapter entitled 'The Negroes Party', the story of a relatively humane slave-owner, Mr Franklin, who pretends to leave his estate for a while, and then, disguised as a beggar, comes back to see how his overseer (Tom) and his overseer's wife (Sookey) behave in his absence. The chapter describes in vivid detail, with lively dialogue, how he witnesses the party they throw in his house for neighbouring slaves. He hears them discuss their masters, their plans to run away, watches them wearing their mistresses' clothes, and drinking his best liquor. Above all he watches and hears their mimicking of the master and mistress, listens to the slaves arguing over who has the best mistress or master, and the most knowledgeable, and hears particular praise for himself as a good and sensible master, praise clouded by the fear of his falling into debt and the consequent sale of his slaves: 'We couldn't be no happier if it wasn't for selling' (p. 66). In the end, the beggar is recognized, Odysseus-like, by the scar which his female slave had bathed. Mr Franklin later tells others,

that he had been to a good many theatres, but he never in his life was at one he enjoyed as much as at the Niggers' Spree. He said if some of the women had had white faces, he should have thought it was their mistresses, their manners and demeanour being exact copies of the white ladies; and Sookey told me that Mr Franklin said, 'Indeed, he never could have believed it if he had not seen it' (p. 72)

Like the narratives of John Brown and of William and Ellen Craft, this episode allows its readers, who themselves watch the complex theatre of the slave-holder watching and wondering at his slaves transformed into 'mimic men and women', to discover and understand the ways in which racial and slave roles may be understood as performances. The episode comes as an appropriate climax to a narrative which has persistently sought to undermine the assumptions which suppose a preordained hierarchy of white over black and slave-holder over slave, and at times of male over female. Here are black men and women playing white men and women in black face – yet another reversal of the minstrel performances so popular in Britain and the United States at the time ('If some of the women had had white faces, he should have thought it was their mistresses, their manners and demeanour being exact copies of the white ladies'). But not only does the scene dramatize the ways in which black women could be 'just like' and hence could be in the place of their white mistresses, it also portrays their distance, the doubling which allows them to be both inside and outside the roles they mimic, as they dissect and pass judgement on the various merits and failings of the slave-holders, and indicate their full consciousness of their own position.

Fedric turns examples of the deceitfulness of slave-holders and the superior ability of their slaves to see through their lies to flattery of his British audience. While the slave-holders tell horror stories about the British and how they 'would chop off the head of any who spoke against the government and impale it on a spike', the slaves

know better and make a joke of it... Every slave to a man has the most exalted idea of Great Britain and her possessions. Whenever we slaves have been together talking, we have always wished to be among the 'Britainers.' We looked upon them as something very superior to Americans... There was a charm about the word British which I cannot convey to any one. It meant, associated as it was in our minds with the abolition of slavery, everything which was noble and good. (pp. 100–1)

Thus his tale comes to a satisfying conclusion with his marriage to a British woman, his acceptance in Liverpool as a man among equals, and his assertion of belonging – along with all Africans (metonymically signified by his citing of a long passage from the New Testament regarding the conversion and baptism of an Ethiopian) – to the wider community of Christians.

WILLIAM AND ELLEN CRAFT: THE STORY OF AN 'INVALID' GENTLEMAN

William Craft's account of his escape to the north with his wife, *Running a Thousand Miles for Freedom*, reiterates even more insistently than Fedric the instability of categories of race and colour in relation to slavery, and the performativity of racial, gender, and slave identities. By the time they published their narrative twelve years after they fled from Georgia, William and Ellen Craft's escape had already become legendary.[15]

The tale of their ingenious and daring flight from their owners in Macon, Georgia, in 1848, with Ellen dressed as a white southern male, and her darker husband playing the role of her slave, caught the imagination of thousands on both sides of the abolitionist debate, and long before this narrative was published, had become the subject of various poems and anecdotes. We are told that the story had been recounted by abolitionists and pro-slavery people alike in fragments and in poems 'for at least a decade before the Crafts were in a position to publish their narrative'.[16] Arna Bontemps compares their story to that of Eloise and Abelard, or to a Shakespearian romance;[17] President Millard Fillmore was so infuriated by their escape and the excitement it had caused that he promised to send out the military to capture the couple.[18] Fortunately, they had by then escaped to England, where they were sponsored by Harriet Martineau, Lady Byron, and the Reverend Stephen Lushington, and given access to schooling.

The historian Benjamin Quarles notes that in 1849 William and Ellen Craft toured New England with the abolitionist speaker and escaped slave, William Wells Brown, with whom they undertook a similar tour of England and Scotland in 1851. Since their dramatic escape in 1848, their story had become 'part of the folklore of the abolitionist crusade', and people were curious to see the pair – particularly the very light-skinned Ellen – who were put on show at anti-slavery meetings, but said very little.[19] They excited great attention: 'All who see and talk with them cannot but feel a deep thrill of indignation at a system that would rob such persons of their humanity', read the report in the *Liverpool Mercury*. The crowds who came to see and hear them at a meeting arranged by the Glasgow Female Anti-Slavery Society were so great that hundreds had to be turned away. According to the reports, the Crafts, who toured Britain with William Wells Brown, were accorded 'rapturous applause', and the crowd cheered Brown's comment that while the United States 'welcomed the refugees from the banks of the Danube and Tiber, here in Glasgow 3,000 persons are assembled to welcome refugees from the banks of the Mississippi'.[20] Proceeds from the sale of a sketch of Ellen Craft dressed in her gentleman's outfit were almost sufficient to enable William Craft to buy his sister out of slavery and 'restore her to his mother'.

Thus, when the narrative was finally published twelve years after their flight from Georgia, with the sketch of Ellen, 'the fugitive slave dressed as a man', as its frontispiece (see Fig. 4), both the author and the story were well known. This accounts in part for the lack of the usual testimonials and editorial matter which preface most narratives by escaped slaves. William Craft seeks neither verification of his identity and character nor of the 'facts', and his own preface is unusual in its brevity and also in its appeal not to authenticity but to principle, citing the American Declaration of Independence as sufficient justification for their escape.[21]

4 Ellen Craft disguised as a Gentleman, from *Running a Thousand Miles for Freedom* (1860). Reproduced by permission of The British Library

Craft's narrative also differs from those of John Brown, Francis Fedric, or Mary Prince in its style and language; like Equiano's *Narrative* it is more evidently a written composition, which turns to a number of written sources and genres to establish its ground. It also differs from these earlier narratives in its explicit avoidance of details regarding physical torture and suffering. Throughout the text he cites the *principle* of slavery as the source of his opposition, and he begins by invoking Milton, not to suggest a condition of despair or a hellish or paradisal scene, but to express the foundational principle:

> God gave us only over beast, fish, fowl,
> Dominion absolute; that right we hold
> By his donation. But man over man
> He made not lord; such title to himself
> Reserving, human left from human free.
> (*Running a Thousand Miles*, p. 3)

While John Brown's narrative seeks to establish an 'authentic' oral 'voice' and to accumulate details which further verify the credibility of Brown's account of the horrors of slavery, William Craft's is a decidedly literary performance. Poems and other written texts (including Bunyan and Shakespeare, as well as Harriet Beecher Stowe) are frequently cited to endorse or compare the experiences and sentiments recounted in this narrative. But the narrative itself also displays a series of different genres and modes; a text about the performing of roles, and about the differences between appearance and actuality (including the deceptive appearances of colour and gender), this narrative really consists of several narratives – all to do with white or near-white escapes – but each told in a very different mode: journalistic, sentimental, picaresque adventure. Various passages in other modes – poetic, satiric, legal – are also interspersed. Thus, this text which describes the ways in which a series of characters 'perform' as slaves or masters, male or female, black or white, also draws attention to itself as a literary performance.

After invoking Milton and denouncing the principle of slavery in the diction of political rhetoric, Craft briefly and dramatically states his wife's genealogy and status in a bald, one sentence paragraph:

My wife's first master was her father, and her mother his slave, and the latter is still the slave of his widow. (p. 3)

There follows a long digression, written as a journalistic report and citing newspaper accounts, in which Craft illustrates the fracture in the assumed relationship between skin colour and slavery. He reports the case of Salome Muller, a young German girl who was enslaved in 1818, following her father's death, for fifteen years until she was recognized and rescued by a friend of the family in New Orleans. Thereupon, according to the newspaper report, the testimony of relatives and the proverbial midwife's recognition of specific birthmarks allowed the court to pronounce her 'free and white' (p. 5).

Following a heart-rending account of his separation from his parents and tearful parting with his fourteen-year-old sister as they are all sold to different owners, Craft embarks on a poetically embellished narrative of the sale of the mistress and five children of a white slave-owner, who had indeed treated them as a wife and children, educated the children, and left them money on his death. However, the family and the rest of the 'property' were seized by a relative, and there follows a poignant story in prose interspersed with verse telling how the mother and oldest daughter, Antoinette, die of sorrow and despair.

> O, deep was the anguish of that slave mother's heart,
> When called from her darlings for ever to part;
> The poor mourning mother of reason bereft
> Soon ended her sorrows, and sank cold in death.
>
> (p. 11)

When Antoinette, described as a paragon of beauty, Christ-like piety, and intelligence, is sold to a drunken and uneducated owner who is also her first cousin, the anguish of her brother is represented in a long narrative poem. Locked in her new owner's apartment, the fair Antoinette throws herself from the window to escape his foul advances, and her spirit leaves 'her bruised but unpolluted body' (p. 13). In a frenzy at forfeiting the girl and her monetary value, the purchaser loses himself in drink and soon dies of *delirium tremens*. But the story does not end here. Her brother and sister effect a daring escape, and in a foreshadowing of the main story, reverse the roles of master and slave by managing to remove their handcuffs, secure them on their drunken master, tie him to a tree, and, disguised as a white couple, embark on a ship to the north. Their master is so depressed and humiliated by these events that 'like Judas, he went and hanged himself' (p. 14). The story ends with Frank disguising himself as a white man to redeem his younger brother and sister (the twins), a narrative poem relating to the story, and the revelation that 'Frank and Mary's mother was my wife's own dear aunt', who had died before Frank and Mary could redeem her (p. 15).

Craft apologises at this point for diverging from the main narrative, and promises to return to it. The diversion and his apology perhaps demonstrate the difficulty Craft felt in settling upon a single mode or genre for his story. The sentimental romantic mode he employs for the tale of Frank and Mary evokes pathos and pity. It is a tale in which the hero and heroines represent a kind of single-minded nobility and integrity, a homogeneity of character and purpose, appropriate to the gallant and romantic hero of this period. Yet its motif of disguise and the deceptiveness of skin colour as well as the instability of the category 'slave' carries over to the ensuing 'main' story.

The narrative of his own escape with Ellen is told in a more factual, often slightly ironic style, and with relatively little recourse to poetic embellishment, although as they reach the relative safety of Philadelphia, Craft several times invokes Bunyan's *Pilgrim's Progress* to express their relief and hope as physical salvation and liberation are approached. Like Bunyan's Christian they are reborn, but as free man and woman rather than as Christians. The narrative is all about role-playing and role reversal, creating throughout a somewhat distanced effect between narrator, personas, and readers.

Having married 'and prayed and toiled on till December 1848', almost despairing of finding a means to escape, William at last devises a plan: 'It occurred to me that, as my wife was nearly white, I might get her to disguise herself as an invalid gentleman, and assume to be my master, while I could attend as his slave, and in that manner we might effect our escape' (p. 16). Here William and Ellen Craft gain agency not only by mimicking the roles of master and slave, wherein William masks his status as slave by *choosing* to play the role of slave, but they also reverse gender roles, whereby Ellen impersonates the patriarch and her husband takes on the domestic and submissive role of nourisher and nurse (he brings her food, and ministers to her feigned ailments). Ellen's 'femininity' is at first an obstacle, as she lacks confidence, but the denial under slavery of her identity as a woman, steels her to play her unwomanly part: she 'saw that the laws under which we lived did not recognise her to be a woman, but a mere chattel, to be bought or sold, or otherwise as her master saw fit' (pp. 16–17). Ellen then makes trousers for herself, while William purchases other pieces of the disguise bit by bit. By pretending illness and swathing her face Ellen can disguise her lack of beard, and at the same time limit her necessity to speak. Thus disguised and with dark glasses and short hair, William found that Ellen 'made a most respectable looking gentleman' (p. 19).

The narration of their decision to escape and so claim new identities seems to give William new authority as a writer. The text now shifts from its emphasis on the pathos of the slave's position, exemplified in the preceding story of Antoinette's cruel fate, to launch a scathing attack on the slave laws in the south. Craft gives a satiric account of an absurd case in which 'Victor Vagabond' and 'Judge Scalawag' between them decree the punishment of a mistress who has taught her slave to read the Bible. Nor is his denunciation limited to the south, for he also writes with scorn of the Dred Scott decision, 'the crowning act of infamous Yankee legislation', passed by a Supreme Court 'composed of nine Judge Jeffreys' declaring that no Negro could be a citizen of the United States of America, and quotes in support from a poem by Thomas Campbell:

> The while man's liberty in types
> Stands blazoned by your stars;
> But what's the meaning of your stripes?
> They mean your Negro-scars. (p. 21)

With the words, 'Come, William, it is getting late, so now let us venture upon our perilous journey', Ellen takes control of herself and the situation, and she and William 'Step out as "moonlight upon the water"' (p. 22).

From this point on, William's narrative refers to Ellen as 'my Master'. Ellen thus becomes a master, and demonstrates her mastery of her would-be masters – her fellow-travellers in the carriage – and also her mastery of language and communication. Paradoxically she controls communication by feigning deafness and illness, thus hearing and recording what she wishes to hear, and speaking only that which she wishes to speak. The highly literary command of English demonstrated in her affirmation that it is time for them to 'venture on their perilous journey' is contrasted with the 'rough' language of her white male companions as the conversation among the men in the railway carriage turns to 'the three great topics of discussion in first-class circles in Georgia, namely, Niggers, Cotton, and the Abolitionists' (p. 23). Thus, in contrast to the elegant language and appearance of Ellen as master, we are given the ugly and deformed appearance and language of a slave-dealer who offers to buy her slave. Described as a 'hard-featured, bristly-bearded, wire-haired, red-eyed monster', he asserts, following a long rant against northern abolitionists, 'These air, cap'en, my flat-footed, every day, right

and down sentiments, and as this is free country, cap'en, I don' care who
hears 'em; for I am a Southern man, every inch of me to the backbone'
(p. 25). Ellen's cool and 'proper' response to his offer to buy William is in
a markedly superior linguistic register: 'I don't wish to sell, sir; I cannot
get on well without him.' Similarly, when the captain of the steamer advises William's 'master' to 'watch his slave like a hawk when they get to
the North – too many gentlemen have lost their valuable niggers among
them d–d cut-throat abolitionists', she firmly replies that she has 'great
confidence in his fidelity' (p. 25).

Throughout the journey, as her responses indicate, Ellen is also a
master of 'double-talk', giving replies which signify a master–slave relationship to her southern male companions, but a free husband–wife
relationship to William and his present readers. Similarly when a 'well-
meaning' southerner advises 'him' against going north where 'his' slave
might be infected with abolitionist ideas, but seeking a cure for 'his'
health in Arkansas, William reports: 'My master said, he thought the air
of Philadelphia would suit his complaint best; and, not only so, he thought
he could get better advice there.'[22] Ellen deals not only in double-talk,
but also in double-hearing. Like Frederick Douglass, she discovers that
the term 'Abolitionist' signifies for her the opposite of what is intended –
'and therefore, in his opinion, [they become] not the lowest, but the very
highest, of God's creatures' (p. 295).

But while Ellen is seen to perform the roles of white, male, and master,
William also performs the role of slave. In a different way from Ellen who,
like the story of Antoinette and her family, suggests that the gap between
master and slave is a matter of chance rather than intrinsic character
or worth, William, by mimicking his role, also radically questions slave
identity; he becomes a 'counterfeit' slave, and thus destabilizes the label
applied not only to him but to all slaves. Not only does William play
the 'good and faithful slave' to his supposed master, he also enacts the
language and idiom of other slaves with whom he meets. When his
'master' stays at the best hotel in Charleston, and is treated with sympathy
and respect, William meanwhile gets into conversation with the slaves
who comment on the generous tip given by his master: ' "Your mass is
a big bug" – meaning a gentleman of distinction – "he is the greatest
gentleman dat has been dis way for dis six months." I said, "Yes, he is
some pumpkins", meaning the same as "big bug" ' (p. 300). William's
use of dialect here, and his gloss on its meaning, not only marks him as
an insider who knows the world and culture of slaves, but also as one

who can move in and out, as the dialect he assumes contrasts with his narrative style and reported speech.

The whole narrative of their journey through the south is told with considerable humour and animation, as William delights in the irony of their situation, the gap between what each of them is assumed to be and the identities that they have discarded, but which were also assumed in law and culture to be fixed and ordained. Thus he dramatizes with amusement an incident in which two young ladies are attracted to 'Mr Johnson' (the name now assumed by Ellen) and give him their shawls as pillows and attend to his comfort. 'Oh! dear me, I never felt so much for a gentleman in my life!... To use an American expression, "they fell in love with the wrong chap"' (p. 303).

Their success in carrying off the roles depends partly on the inability of white southerners to imagine their slaves as capable of anything other than the identities assigned them. Ellen displays the falseness of such fixed identities by escaping them; William displays the falseness by mimicking them, and so taking control of the role of slave. Thus the story of their escape is used to create a complex understanding of the flexible potential of those who have been categorized as 'merely' slaves, fit for nothing more. But in so doing, it radically questions other fixed categories of gender, colour, and language. The language of slave-owners and anti-abolitionists becomes exposed for its crudity, its inability to respond to nuances of speech or character, while at the same time the interplay between Ellen and William is marked by both its complexity and their reversal of roles. Here the reader becomes an insider, like Ellen and William fully aware of the irony of the situation and able to look below the surface appearances. We also become aware that the role of slave is 'performed', and yet at the same time that there is a difference between the performance of a role which is 'chosen' and the situation of the slave who has no choice, but nevertheless must still perform as if he were not capable of any other role.

The episodes in which Ellen enacts the part of a white planter are told with vivid detail; the conversations and contrivances are all savoured – as is the irony of the situation, as on the one hand she is addressed by white southerners who reprimand 'him' for treating 'his' slave too well, and on the other by abolitionists who rebuke 'him' for having a slave at all. William also recounts with considerable gusto the story of their first meal together in a hotel in the north, and the shock of the hotel owners and servants when they realize that the 'white' 'woman/man' and the black man are to eat together and stay in the same room.

THE FEAR OF 'AMALGAMATION': WILLIAM ALLEN'S
DENUNCIATION OF COLOUR PREJUDICE IN NORTH AMERICA

Although William Allen was never enslaved, his story relates to the genre
of the escape narrative both in its detailed account of how he and his
wife fled racist mobs and his designation of himself as 'a refugee from
American despotism', and also in its ironic use of this genre in the context of the supposedly free north.[23] William Allen's title, *The American
Prejudice Against Color: An Authentic Narrative, Showing how Easily the Nation
Got into an Uproar*, directs its indignation against racism in the north, and
like William Craft's narrative demonstrates the absurdities of racial clas-
sifications and attitudes in a country where many of those designated as
'Negro' had far more Anglo-Saxon or Celtic blood than African in their
veins.

William G. Allen was a Professor of Greek and German Languages,
and of Rhetoric and Belles-Lettres at New York Central College in
McGrawville, in upstate New York, according to Allen 'the only College in America that has ever called a colored man to a Professorship,
and one of the very few that receive colored and white students on terms
of perfect equality, if, indeed, they receive colored students at all'.[24]
Benjamin Quarles notes that he was, with Frederick Douglass, a participant in the Women's State Temperance Convention in Rochester
in 1852 and that 'two abolitionist weeklies carried [his] fine piece,
"Orators and Orations," an address given at Central College'.[25] Quarles cites the *Pennsylvania Freeman* (Philadelphia, October 16, 1852) as one
of these weeklies. He had earlier assisted Henry Highland Garnet as
an editor of the *National Watchman*, and in New York and Massachusetts
lectured on the 'history, literature, and destiny of the African race'. To
demonstrate the intellectual powers of African Americans he also wrote
a pamphlet titled *Wheatley, Banneker, and Norton* for distribution to his audiences.[26] At Central College he 'conceived a deep interest' in one of
the white students, Mary King, the daughter of a committed abolitionist,
and they developed a relationship 'much more significant than that of
teacher and pupil'. It was a relationship at first encouraged by Mary's
father, the Reverend Lyndon King, and her sister, but opposed by her
brothers and stepmother. However, when it was rumoured that the pair
were about to marry, a mob gathered outside the house in Fulton where
Allen was staying while giving a series of lectures, fulminating against
'amalgamation', and threatening to tar and feather both Allen and his
host, a white school-teacher who subsequently lost his position, unless

the couple were separated. If the marriage had already taken place, the mob were determined to castrate and then murder Allen by placing him in a barrel full of spiked nails. Mary King was ignominiously put on a sledge to be returned to her father's house, while Allen was rescued by a committee of citizens who 'meant no more than to save the honor of their village by preventing, if possible, bloodshed and death'. 'They were not,' Allen declares, 'men of better principles than the rabble – they were only men of better breeding' (p. 35). He describes a series of narrow escapes, amidst 'oaths and imprecations', his pursuit by the leaders of the mob to Syracuse and other towns, the deceitful attempt by one of Mary's brothers to entrap him, and the couple's eventual flight to Boston, where they were married, and to England. Apart from a four-year residence in Dublin, where Allen taught elocution, and published a second account of his experience,[27] Allen remained in England for the rest of his life, lecturing on abolition, African achievements, and working with his wife in education. He was placed as head of the Caledonia Training School which friends bought control of in Islington, London, and which became, according to the *Anti-Slavery Reporter*, 'the first instance in this country of an educational establishment being under the direction of a man of colour'.[28]

Although the introduction to the narrative declares the purpose in writing as serving the 'Anti-Slavery Cause in this country' (Britain), and although the account includes some of the features we have come to recognize in slave narratives, its project is rather different. For, as the title indicates, it is an exposure of the absurdities of colour prejudice and hypocrisy in the northern states of America, rather than the sufferings or wrongs of slavery in the south.[29] Allen's introduction deplores 'the bitterness, malignity, and cruelty, of American prejudice against color, and...its terrible power in grinding into the dust of social and political bondage, the hundreds of thousands of so-called free men and women of color of the North. This bondage', Allen goes on to claim,

is in many of its aspects, far more dreadful than that of the *bona fide* Southern Slavery, since its victims – many of them having emerged out of, and some of them never having been into, the darkness of personal slavery – have acquired a development of mind, heart, and character, not at all inferior to the foremost of their oppressors. (*American Prejudice Against Color*, pp. 1–2)

In the first part of his narrative, Allen indicates his superior status succinctly and baldly. The opening two sentences tell us that he is a 'quadroon, that is...of one-fourth African blood, and three-fourths

Anglo-Saxon', that he is a graduate of the Oneida Institute, has studied law, and was appointed a Professor of Greek and German Languages. The story of his developing romance with Mary King is told briefly in a few pages, and seeks not so much to summon up a sentimental response to their developing affection for each other, as to establish their (and especially his) integrity. The main art of the narrative is focussed on the opposition to their proposed marriage: the vacillation of the father, the hypocrisy, inconsistencies, the utter irrationality and absurdity of relatives, respectable citizens, and the 'vulgar' mob alike. The story is told vividly and with many a sharp satiric thrust. In the last section of the book, Allen widens the picture by quoting large excerpts from newspapers and letters responding to the event, almost all of which illustrate the extraordinary hysteria that the prospect of 'amalgamation' provoked. As Allen puts it, 'On the announcement of the probability of the case merely, men and women were panic-stricken, deserted their principles, and fled in every direction' (p. 105). In the village of Granby, near Fulton where the threat to tar, feather, and murder him occurred, a unanimous resolution was passed, 'That Amalgamation is no part of the Free Democracy of Granby' (p. 106). Allen condemns America by implying comparisons with various subject nations within the British empire. He speaks of the 'despotism' of American society, its denial of freedom, its barbarity, and its caste system, surpassing that which supposedly marked India's backwardness: 'Such is American Caste, – the most cruel under the sun. And such it is, notwithstanding the claims set up by the American people, that they are Heaven's Viceregents, to teach to men, and to nations as well, the legitimate ideas of Christian Democracy' (pp. 7–8).

Despite his powerful exposure of the outrageous and absurd manifestations of 'color prejudice' in America, William Allen does not quite avoid occasional manifestations of such prejudice on his own part. He pointedly identifies himself first and foremost as a quadroon, and (apart from a later passing reference to his relatively short stature) this is the only reference to his physical appearance. He remarks that 'as a class, the quadroon women of New Orleans are the most beautiful in America', having 'in general, the best blood of America in their veins' and being 'mostly white in complexion'. He is both indignant and amused when one newspaper report describes him as 'a stout, lusty, fellow, six feet and three inches tall, and as black as a pot of charcoal' (p. 58), and in an open letter to the *Syracuse Standard* angrily responds to an article in the *Oswego Daily Times* referring to him as a 'negro':

In another place in his article, he describes me as the 'negro.' This is preposterous and ridiculous. Where [sic] I a negro, I should regard it as no dishonor, since men are not responsible for their physical peculiarities, and since they are neither better nor worse on account of them. It happens in this case, however, that so far from being a negro, three-fourths of the blood which flows in my veins is as good Anglo-Saxon as that which flows in the veins of this writer in the '*Times*,' – better, I will not say, of course. (p. 72)

Not saying is, of course, a way of saying. Nevertheless it is not the 'physical peculiarities' accruing from 'negro' heritage, but the Anglo-Saxon blood which gives Allen status in his own eyes, and which should, he believes, give him status in the eyes of others. But Allen also opposed and mocked in more general terms concepts and advocacy of racial purity. He was scathing about Harriet Beecher Stowe's depiction of the 'mulatto' George Harris and her banishment of him to Liberia. Harris' concept of African nationality was, Allen asserted in a letter to Frederick Douglass, 'sheer nonsense', and he declared that Stowe should realize that 'nations worthy of the name are only produced by a fusion of races'. Despite American indignation and dismay at the mere mention of amalgamation, Allen went on to say, there was no country more characterised by interbreeding: 'Indeed, fusion of the races seems to be a trait distinctive of Americans.'[30]

Allen's book sold well in England (priced at one shilling). He and his wife toured Britain, recounting their story at many reformist venues.[31] Allen found British abolitionists respected his intelligence and learning, and treated him with less condescension than their American counterparts. According to Benjamin Quarles, Allen also wrote poetry, including the following stanza:

> Come thou, Sweet Freedom, best gift of God
> To man! Not in a storm of fire and blood
> I ask it, but still, at all events,
> and all hazards, come.[32]

The narratives discussed so far were all written during the period when slavery still existed in the southern states of America and the issue of abolition was still being debated. Thus, the chronicles written down during that time embody the concern, which also dominates earlier such narratives, to expose the horrors of slavery as well as the absurdities of the system, and to create sympathy for its victims and a determination to end such suffering and injustice. Almost all of them, therefore, appeal to and invoke the self-image of Britons as prejudice-free lovers of liberty. They also establish the humanity and intelligence of the narrators as ex-slaves and representatives of their race, and thus these later mid nineteenth-century narratives have the further purpose of responding to the literary, dramatic, and vaudeville representations or caricatures of slaves and Africans which had become so popular and widespread during this period.[33] But they are in addition intended to 'sell' as good stories of adventure and derring-do, creating humorous, sympathetic, and noble characters, both as children and grown men and women, who will appeal to readers of authors such as Dickens, Elizabeth Gaskell, and Charles Kingsley, as well as Harriet Beecher Stowe. Many of the narratives contain plots and anecdotes which had been told and retold on the public platform, performed and refashioned and elaborated in the light of audience response, in which the narrators mimic and dramatize their former selves as well as the slave-holders and their fellow slaves on the plantations in the south. Like their lectures, their written narratives were intended not only to contribute to ending slavery, but also to fund the family lives and future enterprises of the narrators as free men in Britain.

MAKING GOOD: BLACK MISSIONARIES IN BRITAIN

After 1865 and the formal abolition of slavery in the American south, narratives of slavery published in Britain place much greater emphasis on the author's personal story, and seek to demonstrate not so much a movement from bondage towards freedom as a successful striving against adversity, an example, like Booker T. Washington's, of movement 'up from slavery'. Some of these also emphasize a religious movement from relative darkness to enlightenment, which in turn may be united with a missionary zeal to spread the gospel in 'the land of their ancestors'. Thus, narratives published towards the end of the nineteenth century in some ways have more in common with those such as Equiano's and John Marrant's published 100 years earlier.

One text which seems to straddle mid and late nineteenth-century kinds of texts is Peter Stanford's episodic narrative, *From Bondage to Liberty*, first published in 1889. The preface by Stanford and introduction by the Reverend Charles Johnson offer two contrasting ways of reading the narrative, and suggest differing expectations of texts by black writers. Stanford declares that the account of his life is written 'from a sense of duty rather than as a matter of choice' to demonstrate that adversity in early life may be beneficial, and that 'if we are to win the esteem of society, acquire knowledge, or in any way advance our own interests, or the interests of our fellow-men, we must labour undeterred by difficulties or obstacles. – *Labor Omnia Vincit Improbus – Incessant pain the ends obtain'* (author's italics and translation).[34] The Reverend Charles Johnson, on the other hand, stresses the aesthetic and entertainment values of the work, comparing the humorous pathos of the opening chapters to Dickens' *David Copperfield*: 'Yet the laughter is dashed with tears, and the artistic humour only serves to throw into vivid contrast the grim struggles of the despised and orphaned lad in his desperate battle with penury and prejudice' (*From Bondage to Liberty*, p. v). Johnson goes on to endorse yet another purpose for writing and buying Stanford's book, hoping that 'the sale of this little book may assist my worthy friend in the work he has at heart, by helping to furnish him with funds and friends', and suggesting also that the book might be bought and read out of a sense of duty and reparation:

We English, who are the offspring of slave-holders and slave-dealers, owe a vast debt to the Ethiopian races, whom we have helped to degrade. The least we can do in making some amends for the shameful cruelties of our ancestors, is to treat the few Africans who visit these shores with confidence and consideration. (pp. v–vi)

Johnson appears to have been unusual in his particular sense of obligation and awareness of the privileged position gained by the English at the expense of others, and an early predecessor of those who would advocate 'saying sorry' for the wrongs done in the past. He also expresses his indignation at witnessing his friend's persecution in Birmingham, which he refers to oddly and it seems inappropriately as 'that Keblah of the oppressed'.

From Stanford's preface one is led to expect an uplifting narrative in the vein of Booker T. Washington's *Up From Slavery* published a decade later. But *From Bondage to Liberty* is both much more fragmented and much less complacently single-minded in its effect. Nor does Johnson's comparison with the pathos and sentiment of *David Copperfield* seem appropriate. One might see *Oliver Twist* as a more telling parallel, not only with regard to the story of a child taken from his parents, but particularly in relation to the episodes at the heart of the narrative, where Stanford describes in considerable detail his life as part of a gang of street urchins, led by Harry, a truly remarkable artful dodger.

Stanford's life as he reports it was certainly unusual. Born a slave in Virginia in 1859 (as he afterwards ascertained), his father and mother were separated from him and each other by sale to other plantations before he was three years old. As the Civil War ended, he was taken up by an 'Indian tribe' whose sympathetic treatment of him he ascribes to the lightness of his complexion. He tells his readers that he 'remained with them for upwards of two years, was treated as one of themselves, and was very happy the whole time of his sojourn with them' (pp. 4–5). The 'Indians' also taught him to run, swim, and fish, and to shoot with the bow and arrow. During his stay with them, Stanford learned their language, and for the benefit of his readers translates four hymns into the native American tongue he learned. One wonders why Stanford went to such lengths to demonstrate his knowledge of this native American language with four translations when one might have been adequate.[35]

At the end of the Civil War, his native American mentors left him in a wood from which he was rescued by members of the Society of Friends, taken to an institution in Boston, and then 'adopted' by an elderly Boston couple, the Stanfords, whose name became assigned to him. Peter was now about eight years old, and this is the point at which the details and characters in the narrative begin to take on a distinctive life and personality. Peter himself also comes into focus as a bright, wilful, curious, and apprehensive child, frequently beaten by his domineering mistress, whom he describes as 'the largest woman I ever saw . . . a woman of determination, quick of resolution . . . and if mental capacity could be measured by the size of the cranium, she possessed double the amount of any woman I have ever seen' (p. 6). Like Francis Fedric, the young Peter particularly resented and rebelled against what he termed his mistress' 'confused notions of the work appropriate to each sex'. Against her attempts to force him 'to discharge the duties of a girl as well as those of a boy', he rebelled 'with all the force [he] possessed' (p. 7). Following various incidents, including the fastening of fireworks to the tail of Mrs Stanford's beloved cat, and the consumption of a tin of molasses he had been sent to purchase for Mr Stanford, he was so badly beaten that he remained unconscious for many hours. Peter then ran away, hid in the coalbox of a train, and joined the 'extensive firm of "Street Walker and Co." ' (p. 29). It was thus that his group of six street urchins, aged twelve to sixteen styled themselves. They also classified themselves as 'artists' or 'timber merchants', according to whether they earned money as shoeblacks or match sellers. As the smallest member, Stanford himself was delegated to solicit food and clothes for the group. The group was led by a sixteen-year-old boy named Harry who, before he was eventually recovered by his wealthy family, taught the young Peter to read and write, recited penny novels to the rapt members of the gang, and even began to teach Peter the rudiments of algebra and Latin. Stanford portrays his younger self at this stage as a complex figure, eager for the affection and comradeship of Harry and the gang, but also subdued by them, relentlessly curious and desperate to possess learning, so much so that he finally engages in a series of fist fights with Harry in order to force him to carry on their lessons. At the same time Peter is an absurdly comical figure in his 'thunder breeches' cut down from adult trousers, boots stuffed with newspaper, and old coats with the arms cut off. Eventually, however, he becomes an 'artist', with his own box of brushes and polish, and earns enough money to afford a less comical outfit and to move from the stable in which the group lives to a rented room for them all.

Peter Stanford's desire for knowledge took him to the 'Ragged Boy's School' in New York, where he was befriended by Henry Highland Garnet and later Henry Ward Beecher. He found work at Suffield College, and after several rejections by the president and petitions on his behalf by the students was admitted on condition that he not meet in class with the white students, take no part in public ceremonies or demonstrations, and not enter the dining hall. Among the students, however, he records that his status gradually changes from 'Nigger Peter' to 'Mr Stanford' (p. 41).

At this point the narrative reminds later readers of Booker T. Washington's story – the subduing of pride in order to gain a desperately desired education, the struggle to earn his fees and the various menial jobs taken from morning to night and during vacations. The tone also becomes more staid, although rarely quite as self-regarding as Washington's. Stanford graduated from Suffield College in 1881, and with the assistance of Henry Ward Beecher and William Dodge found a place as a missionary to the coloured people in Hartford, Connecticut. Finding these people in their post-emancipation state unwilling to accept his guidance, he then sought another position and was sent to report on the condition of coloured people in 'an English colony', Canada. From there he was asked to go to England to seek assistance and plead the cause of the coloured people in Canada. Stanford arrived in England in 1883, and appears to have remained there.

Stanford's first experiences in England were far from encouraging. He arrived penniless, having being robbed on the boat. The Liverpool factory girls laughed at his Canadian outfit (fur coat, hat, and boots), calling him 'Buffalo Bill', and he was given the cold shoulder by ministers and worthies in London. For two months he wandered the streets of the capital, often hungry and fearful of eviction. He notes the presence of others of African descent, some of whom offer him assistance, but he is wary and disapproving: 'During this time I met a few coloured men, whose pursuits, however, were of a questionable character – hangers on at low theatres, dancers at cheap concert halls, and the like' (pp. 43–4). In 1885 he moved to Bradford, where he met with 'an amount of ill-feeling and mistrust which seemed incredible, but which, I believe, was in a great measure due to the past misconduct of a number of coloured men, and the bad impression they had left behind them' (p. 49). In 1889 Stanford was appointed pastor to the Baptist Church, Hope Street, Birmingham, but was

not allowed to take my position however until after a stern fight in which, through the grace of Gd and the kindness of the Rev. Chas. Joseph, and my solicitor, A.T. Carr, Esq of Birmingham, I at last came off more than a conqueror. And today, notwithstanding my birth and the colour of my skin, I am pastor in this great city of Birmingham. I have been libelled, slandered, ostracised, suspected, and opposed; but in all these troubles I have not lacked many true christian friends. (p. 54)

Like *The History of Mary Prince* and Equiano's later editions of his *Narrative*, Stanford's text is published with numerous supplements. These include testimonials to his good character, excerpts from newspaper accounts, and letters relating to the contestation of his appointment as a pastor in Birmingham. Stanford also adds a second appendix, containing two hymns and two 'tales', given 'as illustrating the religious fervour and humour of my race, and as containing profound lessons, which are worthy the attention of all thoughtful people' (p. 54). Both tales draw heavily on the use of dialect, emphasizing pronunciation rather than idiom, to convey the shrewd but heartfelt religious wisdom expressed through the speech and actions of black servants or underlings to convert their masters to more charitable and Christian ways. While the first tale presents this wisdom and goodness of heart through the 'Aunt Chloe'-like figure of 'Thanksgiving Ann', the second employs a character and an anecdote much closer to that of Stanford himself when he worked as a waiter, as narrated in the main story.

Another story of a religious convert who then becomes a minister and a missionary is told by Thomas L. Johnson, in *Twenty-Eight Years a Slave, or the Story of My Life in Three Continents*.[36] The first version of his autobiography was published in 1882, and was considerably shorter. According to the preface for the 1909 seventh edition, the earlier editions, 'of only a hundred pages', were published to raise money and interest for African missionary work, and sold 'many hundreds of copies'. This seventh edition includes commendatory letters and testimonials from that first edition – all emphasizing the religious and missionary interest rather than any other. Thus the letter from Edward Stroud Smith, dated 1882, stresses Johnson's lifelong determination to preach in his 'native land' and conveys well the combination of missionary and imperial zeal, as well as the representation of Africa, typical of many exhortations of this period:

But he is now an instrument, we believe, in the hand of Omnipotent God, to awaken the interest, and enlist the sympathy of many others, who shall carry the glorious Gospel to the dark hearths and homes of poor Africa, which seems to have borne the cross as well as the curse for so many ages. How shall we answer to the King in the day of his appearing, if we should withhold our sympathy, prayers, and money? Are *we* not responsible for the disciplining of all nations? (*Twenty-Eight Years a Slave*, p. x)

In its seventh and probably final edition in 1909, Johnson's seems to be the last of the narratives of slavery published in Britain for a British audience. Its appeal to that British audience is quite blatant, and so it seems at times is Johnson's assimilation of British attitudes towards other cultures. For Johnson, as for his contemporary, Booker T. Washington, there is a clear distinction between colour and culture, and he does not dissent from the view that civilization is by definition Christian and English in its language, doctrine, and assumptions. The narrative begins with the formula typical of many other slave narratives – the uncertainty of knowledge about his identity and place of birth:

According to information received from my mother, if the reckoning is correct, I was born 7th August, 1836, at Rock-Rayman in Virginia. I do not know the district, having been 'removed' from thence when but a child. From what I have heard my mother say about her father, it would appear he came from Africa, and was of the Guinea tribe ... My father was octoroon, that is he was one-eighth negro blood, and he was a free man. (p. 1)

Johnson recalls happy ignorance in childhood of his status as a slave, but as he sees the older children sold off, and comes to fear the white people who came to observe them, he gradually realizes 'the great difference' between white children who were free born, and black children 'who were slaves and could be sold for money' (p. 2). Like Mary Prince he emphasizes the mother's suffering at her inability to protect her children, but his image of his mother is recalled more nostalgically and more in accord with the sentimental tropes his readers would recognize, as she attempts to teach him the alphabet and their history, and as he depicts his mother's arms around him as she taught him about heaven and the Lord's prayer. His mother also teaches him that learning to read and write will be the key to his freedom. But when she attempts to have him taught by a freeman she had hired, she is punished and he is removed from her.

Johnson suggests both a childlike innocence and also a more adult questioning of racial categories and divisions when he tells his nineteenth-century readers of the slaves' idealization of Queen Victoria both as a generous supporter of freedom for black people, and therefore as herself a black woman:

It may be of interest if I mention that we had the idea on the plantation that the Queen was black, because she was so kind. Accustomed to nothing but cruelty at the hands of the white people, we had never imagined that a great ruler so kind to coloured people could be other than black; so the impression was that Queen Victoria was a coloured lady. To me she was the subject of many a dream; she often came before my mind, and filled my imagination with all manner of ideas as to the kind of person she was. I used to picture her as a black lady, amidst numerous coloured attendants, surrounded by a grandeur that exceeded all I had ever seen amongst the wealthy white people. (pp. 6–7)

Although presented as a childish and ignorant supposition, Johnson's reiteration and elaboration of his vision, shared with other slaves, of Queen Victoria as 'a coloured lady' attended by coloured servants and in all ways superior to the white people they knew, effectively subverts the assumed categories and hierarchies of race and colour in his time, while also 'demanding' the fulfilment of those dreams of humane principle and action. To be truly regal, Victoria must become her imagined black self.

Johnson's reverence for Queen Victoria is reiterated at various points in the text, as when he ascribes to her the various laws ending slavery in India and the colonies. When he finally succeeds, after extraordinary hardship, struggle, and determination, in being ordained as a minister and coming to England, he cites one of the first images which he sees in Liverpool, the famous painting of Queen Victoria handing the Bible to 'an African Prince who was on his knees receiving it'. Johnson recounts the story that this prince

had come to England to find out what was the secret of England's Greatness; when the Queen gave him the Bible, and said, 'This is the secret of England's Greatness'. From that day in September, 1876, this statement has again and again confirmed, in my mind, that the secret of England's greatness is the Bible, God's message to this sin-cursed world. (p. 25)

A black-and-white photograph of the picture is placed immediately before the opening page of the narrative of his life, and so acts as the vision
towards which the whole narrative leads, a vision of participation in
England's greatness, and which grows out of those early mentions of the
idealization by the slave community of Queen Victoria and her court.
In a sense, Johnson implicitly presents himself as a parallel both to the
African prince who comes to England to discover 'the secret of its greatness', and as identified with England (symbolized by Victoria) as the one
who will give the Bible to Africans.[37]

For Johnson identifies both with the British self-image of benevolent
enlightener of the heathen, and indeed with the sense of assured superiority to those heathen Africans: 'Nineteenth century ENGLAND has shown
to the world that she is the champion of distressed humanity [author's
capitals]' (p. 82). His other lasting memory on his arrival in Liverpool
is of the children in the Jackson Ragged School singing the following
words:

> I was not born a little slave to labour in the sun,
>   Wishing I was but in my grave, and all my labour done;
> I was not born as thousands are where God was never known,
>   And taught to pray a useless prayer to BLOCKS OF WOOD
>   AND
> STONE [author's capitals].   (p. 88)

Johnson lamented that he 'could not join in with this great company of
happy English children, for I was born a little slave, and had laboured
in the sun'. The song marks his difference in terms of freedom and
origin rather than colour; it also marks the 'good fortune' and sense of
superiority instilled in even the poorest of English children, for whom
slaves and Africans – the heathen – represent the less fortunate, and
whose identity is formulated in terms of whom they are not – those
unfortunate 'others'.

But before he can become 'Englished', Johnson must recognize the
extent of his ignorance and unenlightenment, portrayed in particular
through his fragile grasp of the English language and English learning.
As an example of 'all [his] darkness', he cites his ignorance of the word
'Antipodes', and his indignant response to the explanation of its meaning: 'My "intelligence" felt quite offended, and I enquired in a rather
peremptory way if the Professor intended to suggest that people on the
other side of the globe hung on like flies' (p. 107). Here as in earlier
passages, Johnson presents himself in specific detail in the figure of the

fool. While he is a slave, it is a role he plays deliberately in order to trick
the master and his children into teaching him to read and write. In the
first episode, like Frederick Douglass, he determines to become literate
when he hears of his master's reasons for disapproving it. But his use of
dialect to fool the master contrasts with Douglass' silent determination
and so also contrasts with the self that Douglass constructs in his narrative. One anecdote tells of a slave named Burney who forged a pass
and tried to escape. His master tells Johnson of the consequences of this
behaviour:

'All this', said he, 'Burney's brought upon himself because he knew how to write'.
'Lor's o'er me', I said, 'is dat so?' He answered very gravely, 'Yes, that is so'.
When I got by myself, I said, 'If dat is so, I am going to learn how to write, and
if I can get to Boston, I know I can get to Canada.' (p. 12)

Similarly, he tells how he learns to spell by playing on his young master's
vanity:

At night, when the young master would be getting his lessons, I used to choose
some word I wanted to know how to spell, and say, 'Master, I'll bet you can't
spell "looking-glass."' He would at once spell it. I would exclaim, 'Lor's o'er
me, you can spell nice.' Then I would go out and spell the word over and over
again. (p. 13)

If asked why he wanted to know, he would answer that he wanted to see
'how far you are'. He would also get the boy to read to him, and flatter
him into reading it twice so that he could gain the information (p. 13).

Once he is free, however, he becomes an involuntary fool, striving
to use polysyllabic words and grandiloquently sounding phrases that he
does not fully understand in order to sound impressive. Just as then his
use of such words in sermons and speeches produced the opposite effect
to the one desired, so here his earnest pursuit of understanding and
mastery of the language, results in hearty laughter among his class. The
overall effect in this text is an odd and ambiguous one, evoking at times
an image of Johnson which seems uncomfortably close to minstrel-show
stereotypes, and yet at the same time demonstrating in the language of
his narration his ability to 'rise above' them. A long ten-page section of
the narrative is interrupted to cite examples of 'Negro achievements',
quoting from reports of speeches by visiting speakers such as B. Johnson,
giving statistics on the rapid gains in 'Negro literacy', or citing Paul
Laurence Dunbar as examples of literary achievement.

In 1876 Johnson and his wife, Henrietta, sailed for England to study
there before going as Baptist missionaries to Africa. Although his first

impressions of Colorado (where he had his first experience as a preacher) and Africa provide detailed descriptions of the landscape, the wild life, the embryonic towns and cities, he provides no descriptions of English landscapes or peculiarities. His first encounters with England stress its difference from America, as a centre of civilization, Christianity, and brotherhood. He asserts that he was received everywhere, among all classes of people, as 'a man, a Brother, and a Christian, and made to feel perfectly happy'.

Whereas Britain is depicted as entirely an urban environment, without any sense of a rural world existing outside of London or Manchester, and whereas his experience there is one of warm friendship and intense learning, Africa is represented as a picturesque landscape of trees, rivers, and native huts, featuring at a distance 'tall Mandingoes, Joloffs, and natives of other tribes in their native dress' (p. 129). Johnson rarely deviates from received English representations of Africa and Africans as primitive barbarians, engaging in 'unspeakable rites', including human sacrifice and cannibalism. Yet these accounts of mass human sacrifices and wicked practices by the Ashanti and the Dahomey and the 'cannibals' of Bonny are interpolated with passages which praise the thriving and beautiful cities of Freetown or Monrovia or Lagos, details of the fertile and bountiful natural resources of the African areas he visits. He has particular praise for Liberia, the country colonized and governed by freed slaves. Johnson tells us, without a hint of reservation, 'There were 30,000 freed slaves and their descendants, and 2,000,000 natives subject to their control, and all under this elevating code of laws' (p. 129). In this section of the book, the emphasis moves from autobiography and the account of his own personal story, to travel narrative and anthropological observation, catering to the curiosity of his British audience about 'exotic' Africa. Where his own experience is recounted, it takes up the ingredients of adventure story, and the familiar features of European encounters with Africa – his voyage up the river, besieged by hostile tribes waving machetes, the bouts of fever, the beliefs in witchcraft, the awe and fear of the natives at seeing a match struck and catch fire, the gratitude of 'good' natives. For Johnson as for Conrad's Marlowe, Africa is 'truly [one of] the dark places of the earth' and 'the undisputed territory of the devil'. Yet after listing a series of African horrors – worship of serpents and crocodiles, or of lakes and rivers, the selling and eating of human flesh – Johnson adds, 'But I saw nothing of this at Bakundu' (p. 129).

Johnson's narrative presents us with his achievement in becoming the perfect embodiment of Englishness, whose brown skin and racial inheritance supposedly will also make him the perfect ambassador to the 'uncivilized' peoples of Africa. Given his belief that it is his racial inheritance which will allow him and other African Americans to endure the climate and its ravages better than Europeans can, it is a tragic irony that his wife died within a few months of reaching West Africa, and he himself soon after became too ill to remain there.

During the nineteenth century, the lectures and writings of African Americans who sought asylum and fulfilment in Britain found a receptive audience. In their desire to find a community which was less absolute in its divisions of colour and gender, and in which biological inheritance did not predetermine status, these authors constructed an imaginary community of free and equal citizens. Such constructions flattered their audiences, and also reinforced the British self-image as the most civilized and humane of nations contested by the growing power and claims of the United States. It is ironic that this British self-image was a recurring motif in the justification of its continuing role as an imperial centre, a role which simultaneously bolstered the very racial divisions which the fugitive slaves subverted through their narratives. But their works also drew upon and mingled in new and sometimes subversive ways oral and literary genres, sentimental and realist modes, standard and varied spoken forms of the English language. Their hybrid works bring together journalistic reporting, adventure stories, satire, verse, and fictional techniques to reveal a physical and mental world in which the body becomes a commodity, a source of racial and sexual aggression, a focus of identity, and yet a means of refusing and denying its commodification. For these reasons, the British slave narratives interrogate the core assumptions and conventions of much Victorian writing and self-construction.

CHAPTER 6

Travellers and reformers: Mary Seacole and B.M. Malabari

During the latter half of the nineteenth century, Britain hosted an in-creasing number of visitors from the colonies who came out of curiosity, or to seek education or further knowledge or work, or to contribute their own knowledge and learning to various British enterprises. Many of them stayed in Britain for several years, or divided their residence between Britain and their other home country; many of them also recorded their impressions, both favourable and unfavourable, for the benefit of their British readers. Such visitors included Mary Seacole, from Jamaica, John Ocansey from Ghana, and from India, Pandita Ramabai, Cornelia Sorabji, and Behramji Malabari. While Ramabai and Sorabji came to study medicine and law respectively, Seacole and Malabari came as established professionals, Seacole as a medical worker, and Malabari as a poet, journalist, and reformer. Ocansey, like John Eldred Taylor later, came to England to sort out business arrangements, and published an account of his visit in 1881.[1] This chapter will concentrate mainly on Mary Seacole's autobiographical text before ending with a briefer dis-cussion of Malabari's 1893 account of his sojourn in Britain, *The Indian Eye on English Life*.[2] I have allocated Chapter Seven to a full-scale dis-cussion of Cornelia Sorabji's extensive autobiographical, fictional, and other prose writings, together with an account of the three novels and two biographies written by her sister, Alice Sorabji Pennell.

Mary Seacole's account of her *Wonderful Adventures... in Many Lands* was first published in 1857,[3] a year after her return from nursing and cater-ing in the Crimea, and quickly went into a second edition. Dedicated by Mary Seacole to Major-General Lord Rokeby, K.C.B. 'by his lordship's most grateful and humble servant, Mary Seacole', and accompanied by a portrait of the author in plumed bonnet and sober dress gazing unflinchingly at the reader, it conveys from the very beginning her dom-inant self-representation as a practical woman whose chief satisfaction lies in putting her considerable skills to the service of the British armed

5 Frontispiece and illustration from Mary Seacole's *Wonderful Adventures* (1857).
Reproduced by permission of The British Library

forces (see Fig. 5). This representation is reinforced by the introduction
by the London *Times* war correspondent, W.H. Russell, who contrasts
Mary Seacole with Anna Comnena, a woman who some seven centuries
previously had written about her experience running a large hospital in
Constantinople:

She is no Anna Comnena, who presents us with a verbose history, but a plain
truth-speaking woman, who has lived an adventurous life amidst scenes which
have never yet found an historian among the actors on the stage where they
passed.[4]

Russell goes on to note the 'uniqueness' of this work in literature. He
praises Seacole's courage, her charity, her character, and her patriotic
services to England:

If singleness of heart, true charity and Christian works; if trials and sufferings,
dangers and perils, encountered boldly by a helpless woman on her errand of

mercy in the camp and battle-field, can excite sympathy or move curiosity, Mary Seacole will have many friends and many readers.

Like those earlier immigrants, Robert Wedderburn and William Davidson, Mary Seacole is keenly aware of her dual Scots and Jamaican 'Creole' inheritance, and takes considerable pride in both. Although she also expresses ambivalent attitudes towards the latter, she nevertheless identifies herself firmly in these terms: 'I am a Creole, and have good Scotch blood coursing in my veins' (*Wonderful Adventures*, p. 55). Born in 1805 in Kingston, Jamaica, and christened Mary Jane Grant, Mary Seacole tells us her mother was a free Creole woman, a healer and a boarding-house keeper, while her father was a Scotsman and an army officer. To her paternal inheritance, Mary Seacole assigns her fondness for army life and her interest in war, as well as an energy 'not always found in Creole life' (p. 55). Having devoted nearly one-and-a-half pages to her Scottish ancestry and its benefits, Mary Seacole only briefly mentions her mother, to whose inheritance she attributes her skills in medicine, for her mother was, 'like many of the Creole women, an admirable doctress' (p. 56). Despite the cursory reference to her mother or other relatives, apart from her brother, it is this 'inherited' skill in medicine that Seacole particularly emphasizes, and frequently affirms her superiority to European doctors and scientists in her understanding of the causes and cures for particular diseases. Thus when she encounters and treats an outbreak of cholera in Cruces, she comments, 'I believe that the faculty have not yet come to the conclusion that the cholera is contagious, and I am not presumptions enough to forestal them; but *my people* have always considered it to be so [my emphasis]' (p. 76).

Her knowledge and skill is acknowledged in New Granada and Jamaica, when she alone is able to treat and cure cholera and yellow fever. But in England all her attempts to put her gifts and understanding to the service of the British are dismissed with barely disguised contempt or indifference. She is particularly stung by the 'brush off' she receives from the woman who coordinated the recruitment of nurses to assist Florence Nightingale in the Crimea, Elizabeth Herbert, wife of the Secretary for War. Although here and elsewhere she disclaims feelings of resentment, she makes it clear that she realizes that it is her colour that prevents them from taking her seriously:

Many a long hour did I wait in his [Sidney Herbert's] great hall, while scores passed in and out; many of them looking curiously at me. The flunkeys, noble creatures! marvelled exceedingly at the yellow women whom no excuses could get rid of, nor impertinence dismay, and showed me very clearly that they resented my persisting in remaining there in mute appeal from their sovereign will. At last I gave that up, after a message from Mrs H. that the full complement of nurses had been secured, and that my offer could not be entertained. Once again, I tried, and had an interview this time with one of Miss Nightingale's companions. She gave me the same reply, and I read in her face the fact, that had there been a vacancy, I should not have been chosen to fill it. (p. 125)

Mary Seacole cannot forebear comparing her own reception with that of Florence Nightingale's, and the support and encouragement received by the latter when she determined to serve the 'sons' of England. Amidst a chapter full of commendations and letters of praise from soldiers and officers she ministered to, she cites the poem later published by *Punch*, 'who allowed my poor name to appear in the pages which had welcomed Miss Nightingale home': 'And – be the right man in the right place who can – / The right woman was Dame Seacole.' She adds triumphantly,

Reader, now that we have come to the end of this chapter, I can say what I have been all anxiety to tell you from the beginning. Please look back to Chapter 8 [the chapter which describes her vain attempts to join Nightingale's nurses], and see how hard the right woman had to struggle to convey herself to the right place. (pp. 174–5)

The Wonderful Adventures of Mrs Seacole in Many Lands might be seen as structured around three separate 'home-comings' to England, culminating in her return and ready welcome after the Crimean War. In the first chapter of the narrative, the author writes of her longing to travel to England, and how she was 'never weary of tracing on an old map the route to England; and never followed with my gaze the stately ships homeward bound without longing to be in them, and see the blue hills of Jamaica fade into the distance' (p. 57). But when she does get the opportunity to travel to England at about the age of seventeen, the only memory she records is of the mockery she and her cousin encountered:

I shall never forget my first impressions of London. Of course, I am not going to bore the reader with them; but they are as vivid now as though the year 18– (I had very nearly let my age slip then) had not been long ago numbered with the past. Strangely enough, some of the most vivid of my recollections are the efforts of the London street-boys to poke fun at my and my companion's complexion. I am only a little brown – a few shades duskier than the brunettes whom you all admire so much; but my companion was very dark, and a fair (if I can apply the term to her) subject for their rude wit. She was hot-tempered, poor thing! and as there were no policemen to awe the boys and turn our servants' heads in those days, our progress through the London streets was sometimes a rather chequered one. (p. 58)

Interestingly, this is the only comment she makes about her first visit to London – the one thing she believes worth recollecting for her readers, and which still rankles. The passage also exemplifies her complex response to her own colour and ancestry and perceptions of it. She is anxious to emphasize her lighter complexion in comparison to her darker companion, and she plays to her readers by sharing with them a jokey pun at the expense of her companion as she notes that she was 'a fair subject... for their rude wit'.

Throughout the autobiography, Seacole refers to herself as a 'yellow woman', although she cites others (including *Punch* magazine) who refer to her as 'brown' or 'berry brown'. She frequently plays on that doubleness of vision – seeing herself through the eyes of others as exotic and alien, sometimes with weary irony, and sometimes with amusement. In Jamaica, New Granada, and the Panama, her colour is comparatively invisible, except to the despised 'Yankees' whom Mary Seacole, like the refugees discussed in the previous chapter, contrasts unfavourably with her ideal of an England where all are treated as free and equal. In these countries she identifies to a greater extent with the population of African descent, consisting of many escaped or freed slaves whose spirit and intelligence she compares with what she views as a cowardly and demoralized indigenous population and 'superstitious' Spanish Catholics.

Seacole is particularly scathing in her response to the North Americans, whom she portrays as unremittingly vulgar, lawless, and prejudiced. According to her they are 'always uncomfortable in the company of coloured people, and very often show this feeling in stronger ways than sour looks and rude words'. She affirms her pride in her relationship, manifested in the 'few shades of brown upon my skin' to those whom the English 'once held enslaved, and whose bodies America still owns' (p. 67). One of the highlights of her autobiography is her report of a speech by one such American and her response to him. Representing with a dash each pause made to turn in his mouth a quid of chewing tobacco, Mary Seacole records his toast to her thus:

'Well, gentlemen, I expect you'll all support me in a drinking of this toast that I du –. Aunty Seacole, gentlemen; I give you, Aunty Seacole –.... Well, gentlemen, I expect there are only tu things we're vexed for –; and the first is, that she ain't one of us –, a citizen of the Great United States –; and the other is, gentlemen, that Providence made her a yaller woman. I calculate, gentlemen –, you're all as vexed as I am that she's not wholly white –, but I du reckon on your rejoicing with me that she's so many shades removed from being entirely black –; and I guess if we could bleach her by any means we would –, and thus make her acceptable in any company as she deserves to be –. Gentlemen, I give you Aunty Seacole!' (pp. 97–8)

Mary Seacole's response was short, sharp, and eloquent. Like Ellen Craft, her use of the 'Queen's English' and her balanced, grammatical sentences, contrast tellingly with the broken sentences and 'non-standard' English of her would-be redeemer. It is noteworthy that her own speech, and that of other Jamaicans and African Americans is always represented in standard English, although the style of her narrative is often closer to oral speech than literary sentences and diction. But 'Yankees' and later the Irish and sometimes Cockneys are given a non-standard idiom which allows Seacole herself to be seen as a member of a literate professional and English class. Thus, after disassociating herself from the speaker's views regarding her complexion, she tells him and his audience:

'If it had been as dark as any nigger's, I should have been just as happy and as useful, and as much respected by those whose respect I value; and as to his offer of bleaching me, I should, even if it were practicable, decline it without any thanks. As to the society which the process might gain me admission into, all I can say is that, judging from the specimens I have met here and elsewhere, I don't think that I shall lose much by being excluded from it. So, gentlemen, I drink to you and the general reformation of American manners.' (p. 98)

Having escaped the dubious company of such Americans, and the rough and lawless masculine world of the Panama gold-rush, Seacole is dismayed to find that racial prejudice among the British professional and upper classes may be an even greater barrier to her fulfilling her dream of service. And having determined to fund her journey to the Crimea herself by setting up a catering firm with Mr Day, a Jamaican relative of her former husband, she is not amused to hear that the firm of Seacole and Day has been dubbed 'Day and Martin', after a firm of blacking manufacturers (p. 127). Sightseeing in Constantinople on her way to Balaclava, she finds that she has become the sight to be seen, the most ordinary and yet the most exotic amidst other exotica. Her presence, as an 'unprotected Creole woman' surprises the 'cunning-eyed Greeks', raises the eyebrows of the 'grave English', causes the 'vivacious French' to contort their shoulders, and wakes the 'sleepy-eyed Turks' (p. 132).

Amidst the soldiers and in the hospitals, however, she is recognized and welcomed as one who truly belongs – here at last she is at home. Or rather, to begin with, she is amongst those to whom she provided 'home' comforts and mothering in Jamaica, for those who recognize her are members of the regiments formerly stationed in Kingston. But gradually, she becomes nurse and 'mother' to all England's sons in the Crimea, and indeed she represents herself as a kind of 'Mother England' as she explains her keen desire to serve in the Crimea: 'If I could feel happy binding up the wounds of quarrelsome Americans and treacherous Spaniards, what delight should I not experience if I could be useful to my own "sons," suffering for a cause it was so glorious to fight and bleed for!' (p. 122). As the war proceeds, and as she ministers to the bored and lonely as well as the wounded and diseased, officers and ordinary soldiers alike, Seacole increasingly is acknowledged as 'Mother Seacole'. Further, she becomes a representative of English womanhood, somewhat to her amusement, as she comments how the Russians in Tchernaya were 'very much delighted ... to see an English woman', and wonders whether 'they thought they all had my complexion' (p. 223). Her soldier comrades at one point even pretend to the Russians that she is Queen Victoria, paying her 'the most absurd reverence' (p. 225). Given her acceptance and indeed her central role as nurse and nourisher in the Crimea, it is perhaps not surprising that peace and the return to England at first bring feelings of regret and alienation. Amidst so many who look forward to 'the delights of home and the joy of seeing once more the old familiar faces', her fellow-feeling lies more with those who are indifferent, those who 'as well as I, clearly had no home to go to' (p. 226). And yet, for Seacole the return to England does prove to be a home-coming. The contrast could not be more marked between the mockery or indifference she records on her previous two visits, and her sense of being 'at home' on this, her final return:

For wherever I go I am sure to meet some smiling face; every step I take in the crowded London streets may bring me in contact with some friend, forgotten by me, perhaps, but who soon reminds me of our old life before Sebastopol ...

Where, indeed, do I not find friends? In omnibuses, in river steamboats, in places of public amusement, in quiet streets and courts, when taking short-cuts I lose my way oft-times, spring up old familiar faces to remind me of the months spent on Spring Hill. (pp. 232–3)

Paradoxically, the very sign of her alienness in those earlier encounters, becomes the sign of her familiarity, the signal for recognition, celebrated in the rather banal jingle published in *Punch* which she herself cites with some pride:

> That berry-brown face, with a kind heart's trace
>   Impressed in each wrinkle sly,
> Was a sight to behold, through the snow-clouds rolled
>   Across that iron sky.   (p. 235)[5]

Although Seacole begins by asserting the significance of her healing skills, and makes these her claim for cultural and personal distinction, her final acceptance in England is at times closer to the characterization of Aunt Chloe in *Uncle Tom's Cabin*, than either Florence Nightingale or Madame Curie.[6] The autobiography traces her complex and often ambivalent attempt to assert and define a role on her own terms, often in the face of and contrary to contemporary views and discourses of 'race' and gender. Following her account of her grief following her husband's death, she takes care to both affirm her feminine charms and insist that the decision to depart from the usual feminine role is a matter of choice rather than necessity:

And here I may take the opportunity of explaining that it was from a confidence in my own powers, and not at all from necessity, that I remained an unprotected female. Indeed, I do not mind confessing to my reader, in a friendly confidential way, that one of the hardest struggles of my life in Kingston was to resist the pressing candidates for the late Mr Seacole's shoes. (p. 61)

As Gillian Whitlock points out, Mary Seacole asserts her identity not only in terms of her dual cultural/racial inheritance, but also in terms of a 'creolization' of gender roles; she is both a doctor and a nurse, a business entrepreneur and a housekeeper/cook.[7] She studied with doctors in Jamaica as she helped treat cholera and yellow fever patients; she also single-handedly and entirely on her own initiative performed a post mortem on an infant that had died of cholera in Cruces, so that she could understand better the causes and consequences of the disease. The passage in which she describes this confessedly transgressive act is both defiant and defensive. She portrays herself as at the same time a determined scientist in the pursuit of objective knowledge, and a sympathetic mother figure, cradling the dead infant in her arms. Public and domestic gender roles are also united in her setting up of the significantly named 'British Hotel' in Cruces (in contrast to the 'Independent Hotel' set up by her brother!), a predecessor of the 'British Hotel' on Spring Hill in the Crimea, which allows her to create a microcosm of the British imperial ideal, 'a regime of domestic order, cleanliness and propriety is put into place amidst chaos, where law, order, and appropriate gendered and sexual behaviour is non-existent'.[8] Mary Seacole creates an identity which represents her as a woman who comes into her own in what Mary Louise Pratt has termed 'contact zones', areas where different cultures interact, and, as Gillian Whitlock says, 'raw social spaces where chaos and disorder prevail, where boundaries and appropriate behaviour are not in place'.[9]

At the same time, Mary Seacole is anxious to distinguish herself from and thoroughly disapproves of women whose *appearance* signals the crossing of gender boundaries, as she condemns visitors such as Lola Montez and European women who dress in men's clothing, such as George Sands, disparaging 'those French lady writers who desire to enjoy the privileges of man, with the irresponsibility of the other sex, [who] would have been delighted with the disciples who were carrying their principles into practice in the streets of Las Cruces' (pp. 122–3). She herself frequently mentions her womanly dress, including the pastel-blue dress and bonnet which gets caked in red mud as she crosses the Panama isthmus to Gatun, and the yellow crinoline she wears as a sightseer in Constantinople. Similarly, she expresses a 'feminine' coyness about her age at the very beginning of her narrative, and in the passage concerning her first visit to England quoted earlier. Her insistence that her 'judicious decisiveness' is the quality which allows her to become a *heroine*, and does not disqualify her as a woman, also, however, qualifies her as a true Englishwoman. And just as she is keen to disassociate herself from Europeans such as George Sands, or the Spaniards and Amerindians, her autobiography reiterates her truly English contempt for all who 'belong to other nations'. Thus, the very first paragraph ends with a double-edged disclaimer which characteristically allows her to invoke the praise of others, while expressing her claim to an identity which is not to be confused with other 'others': 'Some people, indeed, have called me quite a female Ulysses. I believe they intended it as a compliment; but from my experience of the Greeks, I do not consider it a very flattering one' (p. 56). A later passage, as she describes her travels to South America, expresses her distrust of porters and lawyers she encountered there, the former 'possessing my luggage with the same avidity which distinguishes their brethren of the pier of Calais or the quays of Pera' (p. 68). Throughout the autobiography, Mary Seacole plays to the prejudices of her English readers, and thus aligns herself with them, in her contempt for Greeks, Turks, most Frenchmen, and her conviction that the English alone are courageous, decent, and trustworthy. As a writer, she aligns herself at one point with English traditions of travel writing with a reference to Sterne in which she compares the oaths of a Spanish 'padrone' to Corporal Trim in *Tristram Shandy*. Her anti-American feeling is also vehement and in tune with English views of Americans as vulgar, crude, and arrogant, and indeed, her one rather subdued criticism of the English is to suggest that they might share the colour prejudice associated with Americans.

Mary Poovey has written about the ways in which the Crimean War allowed women such as Florence Nightingale to bring together two kinds of mid-century narratives, 'a domestic narrative of maternal nurturing and self-sacrifice, and a military narrative of individual assertion and will'.[10] Seacole's narrative belongs in this context, and in the context of a public thirst for news and narratives of the Crimean War, but hers is both more complex and tonally more varied in its negotiation of the roles she performs as a specifically Creole representative of 'Mother England', bringing distinctive cultural skills and knowledge as well as a Creole 'supplement' as a nurturer and cook to the service of her 'sons'.

Mary Seacole at one point declares that she sought to be a Crimean '*heroine* [author's italics]' (p. 123). Her claim to be a heroine, and yet not an ordinary or conventional one in the mode of Florence Nightingale, is endorsed by the *Times* correspondent W.H. Russell, who emphasizes both that her book is 'unique in literature' and records scenes 'which have never yet found a historian among the actors on the stage on which they passed' (p. 49). In addition to her vivid record of some of those scenes – among the gold-seekers in the Panama area, the boats and mule trains which took her there, the battlefields in the Crimea – one of the merits of her autobiography, and a characteristic she shares with many earlier black writers, is her sense of self-irony, and her willingness to portray herself in a far from heroic light. In the very first chapter she reveals how she offered to pay the cook on her Jamaica-bound ship, which had caught fire, £2 to lash her to a hen-coop should the ship be about to sink. The descriptions of her mud-stained clothing and devices to remain respectable in the undomesticated natural and social surroundings of New Granada, at the same time illustrate her indomitable determination and allow the reader to smile, along with the narrator, at this rather bedraggled 'heroine'. One is reminded of Equiano's ironic self-depiction on his runaway horse, although Mary Seacole never allows herself to be seen as gullible or innocent, and only rarely as vulnerable (after her husband's death, and when she is refused a place among Florence Nightingale's band of nurses).[11] Her often vivid descriptions of the chaotic conditions on the goldfields, the extraordinary meals and lack of manners, the mixture of men and women there, show her sharp observing eye, her skill with language, and also her sense of what will appeal to her English readers.

Mary Seacole's *Wonderful Adventures* was commended to its readers by the *Illustrated London News* in July 1857[12], where a Grand Military Festival was also announced to raise funds for the now bankrupt Mrs Seacole. The festival, held over four nights at the Grand Surrey Gardens, played to capacity crowds of over 10,000 each evening, but due to mismanagement failed to raise more than a couple of hundred pounds for Mary Seacole. The book, however, proved to be very popular, and quickly went into a second edition. It appealed to a popular interest in the events and personalities of the Crimean War, as well as all those who were aware of Mrs Seacole's work, for she had indeed succeeded in becoming a 'Crimean heroine'. Her fame and the goodwill felt towards her are recorded by the report of the Grand Military Festival in the London *Times*:

Nothing could have been more triumphantly successful . . . Notwithstanding that the charge for admission was quintupled, there was an immense concourse in the hall, and it need scarcely be said that the audience was of a character more 'exclusive' than is customary at transpontine musical performances . . . Mrs Seacole sat in state in front of the centre gallery, supported by Lord Rokeby on one side, by Lord George Paget on the other, and surrounded by members of her committee. Few names were more familiar to members of the public during the late war than that of Mrs Seacole . . . At the end of both the first and second parts, the name of Mrs Seacole was shouted by a thousand voices. The genial old lady rose from her place and smiled benignantly on the assembled multitude, amid a tremendous and continued cheering. Never did woman seem happier, and never was heart and kindly greeting bestowed upon a worthier object.[13]

Mary Seacole was awarded the Crimea Medal, normally awarded only to those who had done distinguished service in battle, and other medals. The bust of her sculpted by Queen Victoria's nephew, Count Gleichen, shows four medals pinned to her chest.[14] Ten years after this first benefit, *Punch* again promoted a fundraising effort on behalf of Mrs Seacole and supported by Queen Victoria, indicating that she was still held in considerable esteem.[15] She seems to have prospered thereafter, owning houses in London and Kingston, and leaving an estate of over £2,600 to her sister Louisa, other relatives, and various charities, a considerable amount for that period.[16]

Nevertheless, Mary Seacole's fame was all too soon eclipsed, and within two decades Florence Nightingale alone was associated with the Crimean War as a heroine and nurse. The reasons for this eclipse are multiple, including Florence Nightingale's own continued writing and commentary on medical care and conditions in England and abroad (including India). Nightingale and her biographers also promoted an image very different from Seacole's. Mary Poovey refers to Harriet Martineau's 'obituary' upon the rumour that Nightingale was dying in 1856 in the Crimea, where Martineau in addition to praising Nightingale for effecting 'two great things; – a mighty reform in the care of the sick, and an opening for her sex into the region of serious business, in proportion to their ability to maintain a place in it', also commends her 'gentle voice', her 'teaching' of her little Russian prisoner, and her angelic image as the Russian prisoner claims that when he dies he 'shall go to Miss Nightingale'.[17]

Poovey argues that Nightingale represented herself as a servant, a domestic woman, rather than one who possessed medical knowledge equal to that of the male doctors; at the same time she also presented herself as a detached and efficient administrator, akin to a military leader:

These two versions of Florence Nightingale most obviously consolidated two narratives about patriotic service that were culturally available at mid-century – a domestic narrative of maternal nurturing and self-sacrifice and a military narrative of individual assertion and will. The heroine of the first narrative was typically self-effacing, gentle, and kind; her contribution was to fit others to serve; her territory was the home. The hero of the military narrative, by contrast, was characteristically resolute, fearless, and strong-willed; his service often entailed excursions into alien territory, the endurance of great physical hardships, and the accomplishment of hitherto unimagined deeds.[18]

Seacole fitted the second narrative, of the enterprising and efficient adventurer/administrator in battle and in foreign arenas, but she rejected a role in the first, or at least on the terms outlined by Poovey or projected by Nightingale, refusing to be either self-effacing or subservient. She also contested Nightingale's belief that diseases were self-generating, insisting rather on the effects of contagion, and searching for external causes and cures, rather than Nightingale's method of rest and ventilation. And she sees her knowledge and powers as equivalent to those of 'the faculty', the male doctors and scientists. Moreover, while Nightingale's biographies and self-writings efface her body, reinforcing her representation as angelic and disembodied, Seacole frequently draws attention to her physical being – her clothing, her skin, her face, her stoutness, her colourful dress and appearance, as well as the food and wine she supplies and herself enjoys. Thus, although she is at times anxious to portray herself as properly female, she eschews the 'feminine' angel-in-the-house ideal which Nightingale and her biographers endorsed. Seacole might well be seen as supporting what Alice Walker and other twentieth-century African American women would refer to as a 'womanist' identity, rather than a 'feminist' one.

Seacole also differs from Nightingale in her attitudes to class. Nightingale reveals an implicit and sometimes explicit distrust of the lower orders. Thus she declares that moral order in military hospitals is higher than in civil hospitals, but once discipline is relaxed 'there remains of the soldier a being with as much or more of the brute than the man'.[19] In contrast, Seacole comments frequently on how respectful and 'civil' even the most lowly of the soldiers are, at least those who are British. For Seacole the category of brutish men is confined to Yankees or foreigners. As Simon Gikandi comments, Seacole's *Wonderful Adventures* may be read as 'the affirmation of the "free colored's" entitlement to an English identity',[20] an entitlement which nevertheless has to be constantly emphasized and reiterated in the face of recent and continuing oppositions within the metropolis between white English and coloured colonial subjects, as well as free English and 'African' slaves. Seacole is also able to use her position as a 'distinctive' English subject of hybrid ancestry, however, to affirm her chosen persona as a woman adventurer and entrepreneur, a motherly nurturer and a doctor, and thus to evade the restrictions of the feminized English nurse or disembodied angel in the house.

While Seacole asserted her identity as a loyal British patriot, determined to serve the 'sons' of England, Behramji Malabari insisted both on his loyalty to the Queen and on his detachment from a British identity, while seeking to serve 'the daughters of India'. Where Mary Seacole related most closely to the officers and soldiers, and to other men in the outposts of empire, Malabari spoke on behalf of women in India, and focussed much of his description of England on English women. *The Indian Eye on English Life*, the title of his book describing his encounter with England, makes clear that his perspective is distinctively Indian, and indeed, declares him as not merely *an* observer, but as a representative Indian who can speak for his country and culture as a whole. And whereas for Seacole the differences she deals with are mainly to do with colour and racial prejudice, for Malabari the essential differences are matters of culture. From a Parsi family in Bombay, Malabari had been educated in mission schools in India, and established a reputation as a poet and journalist. Among his first publications were a long sequence of poems in Gujarati and a collection in English titled *The Indian Muse in English Garb*.[21] This collection, a skilled series of verses in the metres and forms and language prevalent among Romantic and early Victorian poets, with some very competent satires in Augustan mode, was dedicated to the English reformer Mary Carpenter (who visited Bombay in 1875), and copies were also sent to Florence Nightingale, Tennyson, Lord Shaftesbury, Max Muller, and other luminaries. Max Muller advised Malabari to seek to express his 'truest Indian thoughts' in the English language, rather than seek to 'be' English, asserting that 'It is in the verses where you feel and speak like a true Indian that you seem to me to speak most like a true poet'.[22] (Malabari went on to translate Muller's Hibbert Lectures on the 'Origin and Growth of Religion as Illustrated by the Religions of India' into the vernacular Indian languages and then disseminate them throughout the subcontinent.) However, Malabari's reputation both in India and England was particularly attached to his publications condemning 'child marriages', for not only had he published a series of articles in Indian newspapers, he had also published in 1887 a report titled *Infant Marriage and Enforced Widowhood in India: Being a Collection of Opinions For and Against Received by B.M. Malabari from Representative Hindu Gentlemen and Officials and Other Authorities*.[23]

It was his concern for reform of Hindu marriage customs that brought Malabari to England in 1890 in search of support for his crusade, and a similar concern underlay much of the writing by his fellow Parsi reformer and writer, Cornelia Sorabji. But whereas Sorabji wrote as a Christian and an Indian, Malabari wrote rather as an Indian who claimed authority through a rereading (he claimed a correct reading) of the Vedic texts and their pronouncements concerning women and marriage. Malabari recognized his marginality as a Parsi, although this did not in his view limit his authority as a spokesman on behalf of Indian women, and he compared his situation to that of the early nineteenth-century abolitionists who were outside the culture of African and Caribbean slaves and their owners.[24] Furthermore, he claimed to speak not only on behalf of Indian women, particularly widows, but '*as the widow*' (my italics).[25]

Malabari brought with him for distribution in England a pamphlet titled *An Appeal from the Daughters of India*, written by him and published at his own expense.[26] Once in England, he set out to understand and 'map' London, by walking the streets, and observing and encountering the city's inhabitants. As Antoinette Burton points out, his resulting text, *The Indian Eye on English Life*, both extends and responds to a series of texts published in the 1890s, such as William Booth's *In Darkest England and the Way Out* and Margaret Harkness' *In Darkest London*, texts which seek to 'differentiate the East from the West End of London', mapping London itself as a colonial space and 'the East End in particular as a site of colonial diaspora'.[27]

Offering his book to the British public as written by 'a stranger in blood, in creed, and in language', Malabari presents himself as a representative of a much older civilization astonished by the rawness, crudeness, lack of refinement, and energy of this 'new civilization'. Like some earlier writers (including Equiano and Melville), he takes the ship on which he sails to England, ironically named *The Imperator*, as metonymic of the global society he belongs to, with its English and German officers and passengers, and its lascar sailors. Here the recurring issue of language and communication is first raised, as Malabari expresses his irritation at the English refusal to learn the languages of others, and their dismissal of 'Babu English'. 'I should like to know how many Englishmen speak Bengali half so well as Bengalis speak English', he comments. Malabari then goes on in the subsequent chapters to display his own mastery not only of standard English, but also a variety of English idioms and dialects, with ample dialogue from a Scottish maidservant, various English policemen, cab drivers, landladies, and businessmen, and including a bravura scene with numerous voices and examples of patter from an East End Cockney market.

But these voices are heard and attended to mainly towards the end of his travelogue. The first impressions of London are of meaningless noise and bustle, of people rushing everywhere, too breathless to talk. In particular he is shocked by the women pushing their way through the crowds, or sitting next to men, their bodies pressing against his, in the omnibus or train. The city strikes him as dull, monotonous, and grey, but also terribly fragile, 'perforated from end to end' by underground networks of trains and tunnels. He is appalled by the newspapers 'reeking with realistic sensationalism', the materialism, and lack of concern for community and family, the extremes of wealth and dire poverty seen in the contrasts between robustly confident and well-dressed middle and upper class matrons, and the pale, exhausted, often emaciated girls who toil in the factories. He finds London dirty and unhygienic, the houses cramped and airless. In short, it is a picture of London and Western society which invokes many of the tropes used in missionary and

European travel writings to describe India and Africa. Indeed, he deliberately draws on the language of such writings, obsessed with peoples who supposedly worship idols and fetishes, to summarize his Indian perspective on English life:

People live in a whirlwind of excitement, making and unmaking their idols almost every day. They seem to be consumed by a mania for novelty; everything new serves to keep up the fever of excitement. Today they will set up a fetish, anything absurd, fantastic, grotesque, and worship it with breathless enthusiasm...In a word, the English seem to be as fickle as their weather. Flit about poor butterflies of a brief season, and drink your fill of the poisoned nectar you so madly crave.[28]

Malabari visited London on three occasions, and although he believed that it was especially in the interests of Indian women that British sovereignty over India should continue for some time, he remained ambivalent about English society and its values. He admired the English literary tradition, but deplored the lack of refinement in English manners and speech; he was attracted by the freedom and confidence manifested in the behaviour of middle- and upper-class English women, but was highly critical of what he saw as their selfish neglect of children and family; he hated the English weather, the endless conversations about it, its effects, as he believed, on the fickle English character, but he admired the luxuriant green parks and countryside it yielded; he deprecated the materialism and individualism, but could not help giving due respect to the material achievements they produced. His closing lines as he leaves London place him as a sympathetic but deliberately distanced observer between both worlds:

And now farewell to London, dirty little pool of life, that has grown and expanded into an ocean – the biggest, the muddiest, and yet the healthiest of this iron age...The noise and bustle – the everlasting clang of feet, the whistling of engines and smoking of chimneys – are music to my ear, but it is a music which, like my native tom-tom, I should prefer hearing at a safe distance.[29]

CHAPTER 7

Connecting cultures: Cornelia and Alice Sorabji

One of the many 'colonials' who came to study in Britain in the late nineteenth century was Cornelia Sorabji. Her early residences in England overlapped with the visits of Malabari, and she must have been aware of him and his writings. One may speculate that she both responded to and resisted Malabari's claim to speak on behalf of the 'daughters of India', and in later life she too became their spokeswoman, writing evocatively and working to represent Indian women in purdah and improve the lot of female Indian children.

Born in Nasik, India in 1866, the daughter of the Reverend Sorabji Kasedji, a Christian convert of Parsi descent, Cornelia and her six sisters and one brother were given an 'English' upbringing, but also encouraged to understand Indian culture and customs. On the first page of her autobiographical *India Calling* she disowns Ram Mohun Roy's 'Anglophobia', affirms 'Macaulay's famous minute about the English Language and the World of our new Civilization',[1] and comments on the change wrought by the example of English wives of missionaries and civilians who had set up schools for girls. When the University of Bombay was established in 1857, her father had helped secure a resolution that women should be equally admissible. She compares the Parsi community favourably with other religious groups in India, and also with the British:

They have, like the British, helped the development of trade, and being, as a community, rich, prosperous, and generous, have been responsible for many public benefactions in the cities where they live; giving the lead, indeed, in these directions to native Indians themselves. We have lived in isolation, but in real friendship and understanding with all races and communities in India... Parsees have no social customs to which the West would take exception – unless, indeed the disposal of the dead – exposure to a swoop of birds in a Tower of Silence – be counted as one such.[2]

Paradoxically, Cornelia Sorabji casts her father's courageous conversion to Christianity in the tradition of the deep religious conviction which led the Parsi community to journey from Persia. Unlike many other writers discussed in this volume, she is able and desirous to place herself firmly within a family tradition and inheritance, celebrating both her mother and father for their courage, intelligence and communal spirit.[3] Above all, Sorabji emphasizes her dual (or triple) inheritance and education, Parsi, Indian, and English:

We were told tales of our ancestors in Persia, and our forebears and immediate family in the Parsee community in India. We were made proud of that community; but from our earliest days we were taught to call ourselves Indians, and to love and be proud of the country of our adoption: while the history of our Parents made us love also the people and country to which George Valentine and Cornelia Ford belonged.[4]

Sorabji goes on to point out that her parents' conception of a united Indian community, bringing together religions, languages, and cultures, foreshadowed, fifty years before its time, 'Political India'.[5] Her father, a committed Christian and a missionary, also wrote books on Parsi tradition and history. Her memoir of her sister, Susie Sorabji, subtitled 'Christian-Parsee Educationist of Western India'[6] promotes both in its title and its praise for her sister's work, advocacy of a hybrid identity and affirmation of all beliefs, as her sister supervised three schools for Parsi, Muslim, and Hindu children (two of them founded by her mother). Here and in her memoir of her parents, as well as in her own autobiography, Cornelia Sorabji portrays a childhood community exemplifying tolerance and respect for all religions, customs, and races. With regard to nationalist movements, however, her politics were in many ways conservative, and while in England during 'the thrilling days of the Irish Home Rule Controversy', she declared herself 'a staunch Unionist' (*India Calling*, p. 37).

Cornelia Sorabji determined at an early age to fight for the rights of women confined to purdah. She obtained a first class degree from the Deccan College in Poona (the first woman to be admitted to the college), and when denied because of her sex a government scholarship to study in England, taught English literature at the all-male Gujerat College in Ahmedabad, and saved enough money to go to Somerville Hall, Oxford, enrolling in 1889 for a Bachelor's degree in civil law – the first woman of any race or nationality to do so. There she also received financial assistance from a 'substitute scholarship' funded by influential sympathizers in England such as Lord and Lady Hobhouse and Florence Nightingale, and was befriended by the Master of Balliol,

Benjamin Jowett. Through Jowett and her other connections she and her
brother Richard (who was a student at Balliol College) met an array of
distinguished intellectuals and politicians, including Gladstone, Asquith,
and Balfour (who encouraged her to read *The Real Charlotte* by Somerville
and Ross if she wished to know 'all that is material about Ireland'
(p. 38)). She was frequently invited to stay with Mr and Mrs Max Muller
(whom Malabari also knew), and records meetings with J.A. Froude, Mrs
Humphrey Ward, Lady Carlyle, the Tennysons, and the Toynbees. She
was also presented to Queen Victoria, who sent a message suggesting that
'one of her [Sorabji's] "pretty colours" (not white) would be permitted'.
Sorabji obliged by wearing an 'azalea' (pinkish-yellow) sari (p. 44). On
later stays in England she met other luminaries. Holman Hunt began
a portrait of her in her sari, but his increasing blindness prevented him
from completing it (p. 44). She was asked to write an 'Indian play' for
George Alexander, with a major role for Mrs Patrick Campbell. Sorabji
adapted an ancient Sanskrit play, which she was then asked to put into
blank verse. When she read the play to Mrs Campbell, the actress regretted that her role was not the most important one, and asked for changes.
'Do change it,' Sorabji reports her as saying. 'I long to play in Indian
draperies. Do I not remind you of an Indian dream?' To which, when
pressed, Sorabji replied that Mrs Campbell reminded her of a snake,
because of her sinuous movements, a reply which apparently pleased
the actress (p. 47). Sorabji declined to make the changes, however. Nor
would she compromise when a friend sent the play to George Bernard
Shaw; he was keen to see it produced, but suggested introducing a modern scene, 'the incident of the Ninth Lancers and the Durbar'. Offended
by Shaw's suggestion, which she saw as a joke on his part, Sorabji cast
the play aside (p. 48).

Being the only woman law student at Oxford required singular
strength of will and tolerance on Sorabji's part. She was at first refused
permission to read law, until the Warden of Somerville intervened on
her behalf. Of one of her tutors she wrote to her family that she wished
'he would treat me like a man and not make gallant speeches about
my "intellect" and "quickness of perception"'. The same tutor openly
wondered whether he was not 'wasting her time when he [was] coach-
ing her'.[7] She was told she would not be able to sit the examinations
with the other candidates 'because the London Examiner for the B.C.L.
Examiner refuses to examine a woman' (p. 28). Sorabji insisted on her
right to be examined in the same way as the other candidates, and a
special decree was passed by the university permitting her to do so.[8] She

passed her examinations in 1892, but was not formally admitted to the degree until after 1919, when women were finally allowed to become barristers. Nor was she permitted to take the solicitor's examinations, although she joined the solicitors Lee and Pemberton at Lincoln's Inn to obtain professional training, where elderly ladies wondered audibly whether she was 'a New Woman' or whether the sari-wearing Sorabji might be an even newer species (p. 35). Although Sorabji is careful to acknowledge the hospitality and generosity of many Englishmen and women, she does not refrain from portraying, at times with some amusement or irony, the prejudiced assumptions which she encountered as a woman and as an Indian:

Dear old ladies were always trying to convert me ... the heathen at their gates. And they would talk to one very loudly in pidgin-English – 'Calcutta Come?' 'Bombay Come?' Only once did I try to undeceive a proselytizing old lady. She regarded me reproachfully, 'But you *look* so very heathen!' (p. 52, original emphasis)

She also tells the story of Mrs J.R. Green, widow of the Oxford historian, who invited her to tea 'to meet some "African Chiefs" whom she had picked up somewhere' in order to encourage their women 'to adopt your dress'. And she closes the account of her first stay in England with the anecdote of an English clergyman who comes to see her in Chelsea:

He advanced with both hands outstretched.
'It's so good to see you,' he said. 'So like Home!'
I'd never seen the man before, and said:
'Do you know India?'
'No.'
'Or my People?'
'No! But it's *so* like Home to see you. I've been working among the Coolies in South Africa!' (p. 53)

Sorabji returned to India in 1894 to work on behalf of '*purdah nasheen*' (women living in seclusion), although she continued to make frequent extended visits to England for the next thirty years. On one such visit in 1922 she was able formally to accept her degree and become a member of Lincoln's Inn. She was appointed to the special post of advocate for women in Bengal, Bihar, and Orissa, and there observed changes in India from the vantage points both of Indian women and the British administrators and viceroys, whom she knew and commented on freely. She regretted the partition of Bengal, and also regretted Gandhi's growing emphasis on what she perceived as 'anti-Britishness' as distinct from an emphasis on self-help for Indians. Her sympathies were with Gokhale rather than Gandhi.[9]

Her monograph on *The Purdahnashin* provides a handbook for English women (and perhaps Indians) who wish to assist those in purdah.[10] The book is dedicated to 'Her Excellency Lady Chelmsford, At whose suggestion this little monograph was put together', and contains a foreword by the Countess of Minto, which pronounces that

> it must be many years before the cult and science of zenana will be ready to emancipate itself outside its own world... Until these orthodox masses are gently guided towards the goal of knowledge, until the homes from which the boys come are different, and until the mothers are enlightened, the English-speaking India [sic] cannot reap the full benefit of their advanced schemes for education.[11]

While Sorabji herself does not dismiss the value of 'enlightenment', she is nevertheless careful to stress that only those who 'are convinced that there is something to learn about Purdahnashins and something to learn from Purdahnashins' can benefit from reading the monograph.[12] Purdahnashin workers should first steep themselves in Eastern texts, the traditional ones for the ideals imbibed by Indian women, and then study Hinduism 'as it now is' to understand the significance of religion and religious ceremonies in day-to-day life, and to acknowledge Hindu etiquette. Furthermore, Sorabji insists, 'knowledge of the vernacular is absolutely indispensable. "Kitchen" Hindustani will not do.'[13] Like Malabari she establishes herself as an authority on earlier Hindu history and culture, and refers to these to authorize her support for a more liberal view of women's roles and talents. She notes that in earlier times women in India 'took their part in the counsels of their country and of their households', were educated in traditional scriptures and learning, respected for their learning, and led their armies in the field.[14] Now, she declares,

> the Indian woman has come to think of herself only as a child-bearer. She must realize that a woman has also other uses and functions in the world. She needs to forget herself as being of a different sex from a man, before she is thrust out into a world of men and women. And nothing but education can do this.[15]

Sorabji proposes a programme for gradual education and instilling in women the desire to be taught, but such a programme would discourage imitation of the West as far as possible in the orthodox Hindu home in dress or otherwise, and encourage the revival of old designs for embroideries, jewelry, furniture, etc.[16]

Cornelia Sorabji retired from active work in India in 1929 and settled in England, where she remained until her death in 1954. Between 1901 and 1934 she published at least thirteen books and pamphlets, including autobiography, biography, short stories, and drama. She was also an organizer and editor for an anthology entitled *Queen Mary's Book of India* (Harrap, 1943), sold to raise funds for Indian troops wounded in the war.[17] Most of the books and short stories were published in Britain, and address a British audience; many were written while she was resident in England. Her first book, *Love and Life behind the Purdah*, published in 1901, is a collection of eleven short stories and anecdotes, including three stories which had previously appeared in the journal *Nineteenth Century and After* and another which had been first published in *Macmillan's Magazine*.[18] The collection is dedicated to 'MH and the Fragrance of English memories', and prefaced with an 'Introductory Note' by the Marchioness of Dufferin and Ava, and a 'Letter to the Author' from Lord Hobhouse. In her commendatory introduction the marchioness vacillates between admiration on the one hand for Cornelia Sorabji's prowess and strength of character which enabled her to 'pass the examinations which, in the case of a male student, would qualify him to practise at the Indian bar', and on the other hand for the attractiveness with which the author portrays 'the tender, faithful, meek, and lowly character of the Indian woman'.[19] Likewise she admires the peace and seclusion of the lives spent in purdah, and 'the way in which the virtues of patience, charity, self-forgetfulness, and devotion to duty, flourish in this silent and secluded world', while also hoping that with 'the march of Christianity and civilisation' women will no longer have to endure such 'trials peculiar to the lives of Indian women'.[20] While the marchioness reads the stories as realistic fictions, charming and attractive, with an appealing cast of characters, Lord Hobhouse responds to them as documentary evidence for the need to mitigate customs affecting women's rights in India (rights which he also advocates for women in Britain), and an extension of Sorabji's battles on the legal front.

The first and longest story in the collection, 'The Pestilence at Noonday', almost literally pronounces a plague on all their houses! Its heroine Sita has, like Sorabji herself, been encouraged to read and write, to study foreign languages and traditional lore. Her husband has been gone for nine years when a plague strikes the region, while Sita seeks to find a means of survival other than an arranged second marriage in order to provide food for her son and her father. The story displays ignorance, 'prejudice', and superstition on the part of its Indians, played upon by a

demagogic and shallow young nationalist; it also portrays the sheer cal-
lousness of a British trader. Moreover, the British trader has borrowed
large sums of money from Sita's father and merely laughs when asked
to pay it back, although the family is in desperate straits. On the other
hand, the British government official and his wife and the British medical teams are seen as enlightened and concerned to 'save' unwilling
and ignorant Indians from the consequences of the plague. Sita and her
father and older generation of Indians are portrayed sympathetically as
principled and decent members of their family and community, although
misguided in their adherence to tradition and their mistrust of the British.
Readers are given just enough information to realize that Sita's name
recalls the legendary Sita who sacrificed herself for her husband even
though he had caused her destruction, and thus this story which ends
with the tragic deaths of mother, child, and father, has allegorical resonances, suggesting the tragedy of a nation which has been exploited and
impoverished by unscrupulous colonizers or Trinculos. But India's plight
is also seen to be the consequence of the actions of a younger generation, young men who either desert their country or resort to self-serving
and misguided nationalism which prevents its citizens from being guided
by the wisdom of Prospero. This narrative was originally published in
the cultural/political journal *Nineteenth Century and After* with the rather
less literary title 'An Indian Plague Story', a title which emphasizes the
sociological and realist aspects of the story over the tragic tale of the
abandoned wife, son, and father.[21]

Most of the stories feature a young heroine whose education by a
father or husband makes her unlike the other women in the *zenana* (the
women's quarters), and often the focus of their envy and spite. In many
cases she is finally abandoned by her husband in favour of an arranged
political or financial union, or dies giving birth to a longed-for male
heir. Almost all of the women are victims of rigid social customs which
lead to tragic consequences: one takes the place of her twin sister as a
sati on the funeral pyre of the sister's husband and rejects the offer of a
young English administrator to rescue her; another, a Parsi woman, dies
because of the ritual flogging which her husband must inflict because
she has been 'contaminated' by holding in her arms her dead baby;
another (based on an actual case recounted in *India Calling*) is robbed of
her considerable wealth and cast out of the palace into poverty because
of the jealousy and intrigues of her son and his wives. Yet another heroic
woman protagonist, distrusted and cursed by other women because of
her childlessness, pretends death so that her husband can freely marry a
younger and more fertile woman who can bear him a son.

Sorabji's evident sympathy for these women, almost always beautiful and dutiful, often a paradoxical mixture of unusual learning, precocious intelligence, and childlike psychological and material dependence, suggests that they express to some extent her own feelings of alienation and rejection as an educated, unmarried, and childless woman in India. But while such heroines, however much endowed with courage and dignity, belong to the mode of sentimental fiction, and dwell in the realm of pathos, the characters and worlds surrounding them often belong to more robust and realist modes. The communities of women are characterized by lively, often spiteful chatter, and preoccupations with appearance, jewelry, and fads (one wealthy woman purchases 100 concertinas, another as many harmoniums) which contrast with the more generous and intellectual inclinations of the heroines. Their speech in turn is contrasted with the voices of English women, confident, direct, down to earth, casting a cold eye on life and death, and often missing or rejecting the subtle nuances of Indian social structures or the eloquence, but also the romantic 'exoticism', of Indian tradition and dialogue. Thus 'The Pestilence at Noonday' moves from the sheltered and aesthetic surroundings of a once wealthy Indian establishment where father-in-law and daughter converse in almost Biblical cadences, to a the hustle and disorder of the township streets, to the assured and ordered world of an English encampment:

'There is really nothing more luxurious than tent-life in India!' It was an Englishwoman who spoke her thoughts aloud and she spoke in a brisk, cheery voice. She seemed about forty years or thereabouts; the eyes were small and round and kindly, and the sunburnt face beamed health and benevolence.[22]

Published in the same year as Rudyard Kipling's *Kim*, and at a time when fiction about India by writers such as Flora Annie Steel, G.A. Henty, Bithia Mae Croker, F.W. Bain, and Thomas Anstey Guthrie was widely read, Sorabji's collection of stories reveals an awareness of the literary contexts in which India was so often presented.[23] At times her portrayal of Indian women as beautiful and tragic victims does not seem far removed from representations in some British fiction. All too often they find themselves caught in a losing conflict between tradition and modernity (defined as British custom and understanding), and in one story, 'Love and Death', an Indian woman educated in England and trained as a doctor reverts to stereotypical colonialist fictional type, when she cannot resist joining the group of 'savage' fire-walkers she is watching: 'Then there is a sudden, quick, convulsive sob – for, carried past all self-control, the doctor-girl has joined the band of seven vestal virgins.

The word is given, and there they are, the white-robed seven, treading the flames'(*Love and Life*, p. 99). But while the other fire-walkers survive, the Western-educated 'doctor-girl' is severely burned and dies in her own hospital. The ending of the story is ambivalent: the priest believes she was 'tainted with infidel observances'; her fiancé's father declares that his 'experiment' in educating his son's betrothed was a mistake and declares an end to all reform; the son who had likewise been trained as a doctor and grown to love and respect his fiancee, 'thought otherwise' (pp. 100–1).[24]

While at times reiterating particular tropes and representations found in Anglo-Indian fiction of the period, Cornelia Sorabji also allows us to question such representations and shows how the tables might be turned. The two British men in 'Pestilence at Noonday' are introduced as men 'who might have served, at an imperial exhibition of human beings, as typical of the Anglo-Indian', the codes and routines of officialdom and rule having 'robbed their faces of much individuality. They were no longer John Caldecott and Henry Symonds – they were the trusted commissioner and the successful tea-planter' (*Love and Life*, p. 22). But the second Anglo-Indian exhibit, the feckless British trader, Henry Symonds, turns out to be not only a character given to 'brainless extravagances', but also one described as allowing 'an entire severance between wit and sentiment' and possessing 'a curiously sensual and selfish aestheticism'. Moreover, we discover that he had even 'written a stray novel or two'. One might well see an implicit analogy between his insensitive exploitation of a generous and trusting Indian patriarch and the exploitation by Anglo-Indian writers of India and its people for an English audience. Mrs Caldecott's description of Sita's father-in-law suggests such Anglo-Indian depictions when she is described as looking up from her writing-table and saying, 'I was quite forgetting... that there is a queer old man waiting in the office-tent, to see the planter sahib. He is a most picturesque creature, with a certain quiet dignity in his face and bearing' (p. 25). And, a little later, when John Caldecott watches Henry Symonds contemptuously tearing up the bond he had given that same 'picturesque creature' some years before, Caldecott draws on other familiar representations and suggests that the whole scene would make a good play:

'Hallo, Symonds! What's the row? Is the wife's prince a badmaash?'
'Oh no! He's only a creditor claiming ten thousand rupees, *and more* – that's all! That's the bond!' and he pointed to the torn fragments in the waste-paper basket.

Caldecott shook his head unbelievingly. 'You were always an actor, Symonds,' he said, 'and that was really a fine scene. Put it into your next play: it will be a variation on the immortal Shylock.' (pp. 26–7)

For Symonds, Caldecott, and his wife, Indians belong mainly to the aesthetic and literary realm; they are 'picturesque creatures', 'princes' or 'villains' (badmaash), and they are the background against whom the British enact the main roles. The comparison of Sita's father-in-law to Shylock is telling: on the one hand, no comparison could be more inaccurate, while on the other the comparison seems appropriate for Caldecott because both Shylock and the Indian are 'foreigners' whose shared alien status obscures their profound differences.

Sorabji adopts a variety of narrative voices and techniques for her stories, including in one case ('Behind the Purdah') the persona and language of an English doctor, Rebecca Yeastman, who tells part of the story in letters 'home' to a woman student friend. In fact, this story is told through a series of frames. It begins with a detached and ironic presentation to a generalized reader of a visitor's impressions of a dilapidated palace wall and buildings:

A straggling building with a spiked gateway, sadly out of repair and needing manipulation in the opening, as it led through a bare courtyard to a portico that did its best to be imposing –, such was your introduction to the royalty of Balsingh Rai, of an Indian principality. And if indeed the iron and mortar had failed to impress you, there was always the chance that the ill-dressed, ill-drilled guard would excite what was lacking in sentiment. (*Love and Life*, p. 139)

Having panned over the desultory courtiers, and a group of tailors sewing 'some cheap Manchester print', this unsentimental camera eye then focusses in on the figure of Dr Rebecca Yeastman (the name suggests her brusquely unfeminine character) 'through whose sun-spectacles we have been looking' (p. 141). The brisk and business-like jangle of her bracelets is evoked, and there is a far from kind description of her walk:

For so self-possessed, brisk a person, her walk was a surprise; 'twas rather like a camel's – head protruding, steps long and halting – but it did, nevertheless, suggests dogged steadfastness of purpose; and she was a thoroughly good creature, every faculty of her: of that you were certain. (p. 143)

Sorabji's style here effectively conveys shifting perspectives between the Englishwoman and those who observe her, shifts and ambiguities which subtly include the reader as both outsider voyeur and insider observed and observer. The sun-glasses worn by the English doctor also suggest a flawed vision, one that filters out varying shades of light. A few pages on, the observer finds herself observed, as she begins a dismissive inventory of the room where she waits ('Plush and broken crockery') and suddenly becomes aware of 'the steady scrutiny of a pair of black eyes'. Led through labyrinthine corridors in which she soon loses her bearings, Dr Yeastman at last finds herself in the room of her patient, where she is blinded not by the sun but the dark. She fails to realize that she is being used not to cure the patient but to put her scientific knowledge about poisons to the service of the intrigues of those who wish to get rid of the prince's mother, who is then accused of poisoning the Rani and cast out of the palace.

In the second section of the story the scene moves to London, where again the light is grey and obscure, where, in a room filled with European artefacts and prints and with William Morris wallpaper, an English woman reads Rebecca Yeastman's letter, 'and you – you creep behind her and read over her shoulder' (p. 152). The letter, written in the language of a brisk, cheerful, and very literate English woman, narrates the consequences of her investigations into the poison, refuses to feel regret about her intervention ('Why should I prick my fingers with the thorns other people gather?'), and in anthropological mode goes on to describe local customs and entertainments which she has been invited to observe by the Raja. One of the entertainments, which she roughly transcribes, is a skit about an English magistrate administering British justice:

A florid Englishman (the mask was really good), sits at a camp-table, holding his migratory court upon a criminal charged with murdering his wife. As he does not yet know the language, he works through an interpreter.
Magistrate. How old was your wife?
Criminal. Ten years.
Interpreter (fearing that the minority of the victim might heighten the heinousness of the crime, to a civilised mind). He says, sir, she was an old woman of some sixty-five years. (p. 155)

Thus Cornelia Sorabji in this story assumes the mask of a white woman doctor, and observes her (and her white female reader) observing a performance of a drama in which an Indian actor puts on the mask of a white magistrate. Issues of language, modes of discourse, interpretation and misinterpretation are also brought to the foreground, along with metaphors of light and shade, sight, blindness, and insight. In contrast to the rigid and inflexible, perhaps two-dimensional, attitudes and observations of the monolingual Rebecca Yeastman (or of the English characters in 'Pestilence at Noonday'), the Indian characters, and above all the author herself, are seen to be capable of speaking in a number of languages and voices, and of performing many roles, both 'English' and Indian. Race and culture are shown to be a matter of performance rather than biology, and Sorabji herself is the most triumphant performer of all, a mistress of all languages. Performances can also be used to deceive and manipulate others, however, as is shown in both this story and 'Pestilence at Noonday' (not only in the scene where Henry Symonds tears up the bond, but also in an episode where Sita pretends compliance with the British medical team in order to lead them away from her sick child and hidden father-in-law). But there is also the suggestion in other stories, notably 'Love and Death' where the Indian woman doctor regresses to the 'savage' customs of her native hill-people, that 'race' is a deeper and more essential identity than culture and that women are more vulnerable to such regression to biological identity than men, for the male Indian doctor remains aloof.

Sorabji draws on a variety of narrative techniques and voices for her stories. 'Urmi' begins by evoking the grey streets of London contrasted not only with the colour and variety of Indian landscapes but also with the richness of Indian history and culture, which includes the monuments and social structures set up by the Muslim Akbar, as well as the healing powers of the Hindu god Krishna and the poetry of the fourth-century Sanskrit poet Kalidasa. Some are told as if an oral anecdote by a local member of the community, some by an English-speaking Indian, some by an Englishman or woman, and some in a voice which suggests a learned or aristocratic speaker of Hindi. 'Love and Death' opens with the following exclamation in what the reader would take to be the most typically English of male voices: 'I tell you Stewart, it's playing the very deuce with a man's life to treat him as I have been treated!' (*Love and Life*, p. 87). His companion replies in similar voice, and it is only after two pages into the story that we learn that the first speaker is a 'foreigner', an Indian sent at the age of seven (as Kipling was) to be educated in England. 'Pestilence at Noonday' begins with a more archaic or elevated form of speech, the voices of an aristocratic Indian wife and her husband:

'But you will forget me, my lord.'
'Yes! 'Tis not unlikely,' was the response. 'I shall have many things to interest me: knowledge to acquire, the world to sample, a name to make.' (*Love and Life*, p. 3)

This conversation between husband and wife in turn contrasts with the more formal and stately speech of a member of the older generation, Sita's father-in-law: 'Nay, mother of Rama!', he said. 'I would speak with thee. Give to the care of the trusty Mukti this thy son, and come thou with me to the lotus pond' (p. 15).

Similar forms of speech and diction are used by Kipling and other Anglo-Indian writers (Such as Flora Annie Steel) to convey the language used by 'traditional' Indian speakers. Compare, for instance, the following conversation between Kim and the Lama:

'Have I failed to oversee thy comforts, Holy One?'
'A blessing on thee.' The Lama inclined his solemn head. 'I have known many men in my so long life, and disciples not a few. But to none among men, if so be thou art woman-born, has my heart gone out as it has to thee – thoughtful, wise, and courteous; but something of a small imp.'[25]

Sorabji's stories were first published in the same media as works by Kipling, Steel and others, and so it is unlikely that she was not aware of these writers, or they of her. 'Behind the Purdah,' perhaps the most self-conscious of Sorabji's stories with regard to the complexities of Indian–English relationships and representations, first appeared in *Macmillan's Magazine*, a journal which also published numerous stories and poems by Kipling, sketches and stories by Steel, essays on the 'Sikh soldier' and the 'Goorkha [sic] Soldier' by Major Pearse, as well as essays on colonial Australia, on Shakespeare, Fanny Burney, and the Irish.[26] Among the contributions to the magazine in the earlier part of the decade, when Sorabji was resident in London, are a number of poems by Kipling, but published under the pseudonym of 'Yussuf'. These include the now famous 'Ballad of East and West', and others such as 'The Ballad of the Last Suttee', and the 'Ballad of the King's Jest'.[27] Thus Kipling assumes an Oriental mask through which to represent his northern Indian characters, as Sorabji would later adopt an English mask to represent Indian and English characters.

Among the contributions to *Macmillan's Magazine* are an essay by G.A. Levett-Yeats on 'My Indian Garden' and a rather melodramatic story by Flora Ann Steel about the narrator's gardener, 'Heera Nund'. One of Sorabji's sketches in her collection, *Sun-Babies*, published in 1904, might well be seen as a response to such pieces, as indeed the collection as a whole might be read as a counterpart to *Kim*.[28] Dedicated to 'Her of the West because she Understands', *Sun-Babies* contains seven vivid and affectionate sketches of Indian children and a folk-tale about the monkey kingdom. The opening story, 'His Master's Slave', tells of an Indian orphan boy not unlike Kim in his precocious wisdom about the ways of the world and in his self-sufficiency. Like Kim, he can be 'thoughtful, wise, and courteous; but something of an imp'. He wins the affections of his master and mistress, quickly raises his status, and thoroughly enjoys lording it over the other disgruntled and bemused servants in the household. 'The Chota Chaudikar' describes the son of the watchman (the Chaudikar), who delights in assisting with the gardening, and can barely wait each morning to show his mistress new insects, new birds, and new plants. Where Sorabji excels is in her ability to convey the extraordinariness of these ordinary characters and their worlds, and her work thus contrasts with the distanced and laboured descriptions of Levett-Yeats, or the mingled melodrama and contempt which characterize Steel's stories. And while Steel can never refrain from noting the colour of her Indian characters – her gardener, Heera Nund, has 'bandy, hairy brown legs', and a 'fat, remarkably black baby'– Sorabji rarely draws attention to skin colour; her attention is focussed on character and expression. The notable exception is the final piece in this collection, 'The Feast of Lights', which portrays an albino girl 'as uncanny as an albino Jap-puppy with pink eyes and a "skinned" look about its coat'.[29] The girl's 'freakish' colour is matched by the high-pitched voice she puts on to emulate an 'English' style of singing, and her obsession with pleasing 'the handsome ones', the English soldiers. The song she sings or screeches ('Daisy, Daisy'), her behaviour, her appearance, all contrast with the dignity and deeply rooted respect for spiritual traditions and attitudes, the 'at-home-ness', of the other children and especially the girl children portrayed in the remainder of the volume. This story, placed significantly at the end of the volume, suggests Sorabji's dismay at Indian attempts to mimic Englishness, resulting in a travesty of the West's most superficial and banal aspects rather than a deeper and more dignified blending of East and West.

A similar dignity and respect for tradition characterizes the women Sorabji describes in her third collection, *Between the Twilights*.[30] Published in 1908, this series of 'studies of Indian women by one of themselves', as the collection is subtitled, consists of fourteen legends, tales, and sketches of individual women. One essay, 'Portraits of Some Indian Women', had been published previously in the journal, the *Nineteenth Century and After*, and is perhaps more clearly oriented than some of the other studies to- wards explaining to British readers 'the whole idea of marriage in the East' which 'may seem irrational to the alien'.[31] Although pitying the plight of the Indian wife, the 'Portraits' are distanced ones, sharing the supposed alienation of her readers, and, except when they are grand-mothers, presenting Indian wives as wholly submissive, helpless, and held in small respect by their spouses. She argues that such a subordinate role was not sanctioned by the Vedas or early history, and concludes that 'the time when the nation could be served by a grovelling womankind – if ever such time there was – is past'.[32] Speaking of new attitudes towards Hindu windows, and their opportunities to serve the community, Sorabji ends her series of 'Portraits' with an uncannily prophetic forecast, given the role of Indira Gandhi some seventy years later: 'What a redemption of that curse of the widowed, what a revenge on Time, if the widow herself take the foremost place in this regeneration of Indian womanhood!'[33]

Other essays in this collection are more meditative in style, taking their tone from the significance of the title, where the short period between the twilights, between the setting of the sun and the appearance of the first stars, is described by Sorabji as a period for silence and reflection, and an hour of enchantment, when the mysterious and other-worldly come into their own. The title also refers to the subjects of her studies, the women of the *zenana*, who 'float elusive in the half-light between two civilizations, sad by reason of something lost, sad by reason of the more that may come to be rejected here-after.'[34] What may be lost is evoked in the stories of gods and goddesses told by the women, their reverent fulfilment of marriage and mourning rituals, as well as daily worship, their interpretations (often very different from the men's) of the legends and legendary figures, such as Kali and Devi, who serve as models and warnings.

Sorabji's interest in preserving and sharing Indian cultural heritages is also demonstrated in the collection of *Indian Tales* she published in 1916.[35] Illustrated by Warwick Goble, the collection includes simplified versions for children to read or hear of traditional Indian legends from the Mahabharata and Ramayana (such as the story of the legendary Drau-padi), and of former rulers – 'Baber the Tiger', 'Sher Khan', 'Humayan'. One might read these tales as in part an attempt to rescue the names es-teemed in Indian culture and history from their trivialization in Kipling's *Jungle Book*. This publication marks the beginning of a series of more elab-orately illustrated and 'aestheticized' books produced in England and for British readers in the 1920s and 1930s. A second volume titled *Sun-Babies* is lavishly illustrated with water-colour studies of Indian women and children, in which the faces are abstract and expressionless against a de-tailed background of Indian landscape, carpets, or fabrics.[36] The cover illustration is of a soulful young Indian boy in a red cap, and the book is dedicated to 'Geoffrey, Killed in action in France, 26th March, 1918', whom the author apostrophizes as a young Englishman she had known as a loved and loving small child. Referring to an Indian lad who delights in being pronounced by an English visitor a 'good fellow', she makes it clear that this is a book for English readers: 'So here he is – our common goodfellow – gravely crossing to the English bank of the river, in the paddle-boat built for us by the publisher.'[37] The ten brief stories lack the narrative and descriptive detail of the 1904 volume of the same title, like the illustrations conveying charm rather than the vitality and complexity of those earlier studies. But there is some humour and irony, as in the final story about a dog named Wanglo, a dog whose birthplace is unknown, but 'he was blue-blooded and a British subject – and that ought to be enough for you'.[38]

Sorabji's one published dramatic work first appeared in the *Nineteenth Century and After*, and was then published as a separate text, *Gold Mohur Time: 'To Remember'*.[39] A note explains that the title is taken from the Gold Mohur tree, introduced to India from Madagascar, and that inside the flower one can see filaments in the shape of a peacock. Hence the name was probably originally 'Gul Mohur' – peacock flower – but has been corrupted to 'Gold Mohur'. As the note suggests, the play is a poetic allegory with dance and pageant about transplantation and translation. Set in Bengal, it places on the stage two main characters, an elderly mystic who reflects on the changing manifestations and beauty of the Gold Mohur trees, and his grand-daughter, born in Persia, who seeks to nourish roses (Persian rather than English) in her garden. The grandfather shakes his head at the girl who 'seeks to grow her transplanted flower in our so different soil' and laments her refusal to 'open her eyes to see that, though the earth breath in our heat time kills her roses, it brings to perfection our gorgeous gold mohur trees'.[40] The mystic then poses the central question of the drama: 'What is best for this beloved country of ours? Who shall best serve it – the transplanted ones or the children of our own Earth Mother?' The Persian roses and grand-daughter remind us that the question refers not only to transplanted British, but also to the Moghul and Parsi cultures which predate the British influence.

Sayida (his grand-daughter) reminds him that he himself has declared, 'They are all Indians, if their feet are planted in our soil, and if they live from day to day by us, or if they serve us.'[41] In Act 3 of the play, the old mystic is seen on his death-bed, giving Sayida a packet of verses which she opens and reads in the final Act of the play. These verses, presumably composed by Sorabji herself, bring an enigmatic message, mingling the language and wisdom of East and West. This seems to have been Cornelia Sorabji's last published creative work, although it is later followed by two autobiographical books, and it conveys the double and sometimes paradoxical commitment that underlies all of her work to representing the validity of Indian culture while also questioning it.

Cornelia Sorabji's youngest sister Alice trained as a doctor, married an English missionary doctor, Theodore Leighton Pennell, and not long after his death in 1912, moved to England, where she died nearly forty years later. She is the author of three novels, and also wrote a biography of her husband.[42] Pennell dismayed more conservative fellow missionaries by wearing Pathan dress and, presumably, by marrying an Indian wife. He and Alice Sorabji first met in Bahawalpur in 1906, where she was a doctor at the Zenana Hospital.[43] The biography focusses closely on Pennell's rather unorthodox activities, emphasizing his success as an evangelist and medical healer and the affection and esteem he received from the Afghans and Indians he worked with. Occasionally there are discreet glimpses of Alice herself (although she does not identify herself explicitly), working beside him and travelling as a comrade in a marriage which lasted just three- and-a-half- years until Pennell's illness and early death of septic poisoning a few days before the birth of their son. The biography also contains extensive extracts from Pennell's diaries.

The 1914 full biography was followed a year later by a glossy, shorter and simplified version, *A Hero of the Afghan Frontier*, 'retold for boys and girls'.[44] This work is advertised in a series of missionary biographies published by Seeley including *Judson, the Hero of Burma*, and *On Trail and Rapid by Dogsled and Canoe: The Story of Bishop Bompas's Life among the Red Indians and Esquimo*. But the context in which this book is promoted, and the intermingling of Christian and imperial ideologies, is also emphasized by a comment on the title page, which notes that 'A distinguished officer said of Pennell, "The presence of Pennell on the Frontier is equal to that of two British regiments".' A maturer and more solemn version of Kipling's Kim, Pennell dressed in Indian clothing also participates in the defence of the North-West Frontier by seeking to pacify the natives and win them over to the British side. The biography is written in short uncomplicated sentences, and supplies simplified information about the peoples of the Frontier. Thus the boys (and perhaps some girls) are told that 'the Pathan is never happy except when he is fighting'[45] and that 'As he is a very wild kind of man his fighting is not always on civilised lines.'

Moreover, Pennell declares, although they have 'many good qualities', 'the Pathans are all brought up with the idea that stealing is quite a splendid profession, and killing their enemies only a part of a man's business'. And lest the boy and girl readers are not sufficiently clear about how to judge these people, Alice Pennell lets them know that 'the Pathans are bigoted Mohammedans, and their Mullahs (or priests) teach them that if they kill a Christian, they are sure to go to Paradise'.[46]

Alice Pennell's first novel, *Children of the Border* [47] is based on an amalgamation of several anecdotes recorded in the biographies, including the story of a couple who journey with their ten-year-old daughter over the mountain passes seeking medical help for the mother, and another tale of a Pathan warrior whose gangrenous leg must be amputated.[48] Advertised by the publishers as 'an exceptionally true and vivid novel. A fine story introducing a collection of characters well chosen to display frontier life in its various aspects',[49] the novel is dedicated to Theodore Pennell, and introduced with a foreword by Field-Marshal Sir William R. Birdwood praising the book for 'being able to trace...something of the influence exercised by her husband on the Frontier'. Declaring the novel a vivid portrayal of Pathan life, the field-marshal recommends that readers also turn to Dr (i.e. Theodore) Pennell's *Among the Wild Tribes of the Afghan Frontier*.[50]

Despite these announcements which affirm its anthropological and historical veracity, the novel is both more complex and more highly romantic than the biographies might lead us to expect. Islamic beliefs and rituals are presented with relative sympathy as integral to the life of the Frontier villagers, opening and closing the novel with the invocation, '*Allahu Akbar! Allahu Akbar*'. All the main characters, male and female, are outstandingly handsome, courageous, and loyal, and the language they speak places them in the mode of archaic, romantic epic. Thus, the ailing wife of the clan leader, Mani Khan, when asked if she has the strength to make the long and arduous journey over the mountains to visit the 'Feringhi' healer, responds: 'If thou art there, king among men, I have strength for all things, thou and the light of our eyes – Margalara, the Little Pearl.'[51] And local colour is painted in vivid detail, complete with swaying camels, layers of ethnic clothing, sounds and scenery of mountain passes, rushing streams, pine forests, and ever-wary armed sentries on the watch for tribal enemies.

But what at first seems merely an isolated and exotic world untouched by the West, soon begins to include more complex and wide-ranging currents. The village patriarch is keenly aware not only of the deadly

feuds between local clans (referred to as tribes), but also 'the bigger business of fighting the British Raj on the east and south, and the Amir
of Afghanistan on the north-west'.[52] The men discuss events affecting
Islam the world over, the discontent in India, and the probable action of
Turkey, Egypt, and Afghanistan – 'for these were questions of burning
moment and meant everything to these men'. In passing, we are made
aware of a munitions trade involving Germany 'and even Englistan',
which furnishes both the internecine warfare and the resistance to British
armies, and there is reference to strong secret networks bringing com-
munications, news, arms, and merchandise. There is talk of a united
movement involving 'Mohammedans of Afghanistan and even India' as
well as Egypt and Turkey, while we also learn that many of the workers
in a clandestine rifle factory are ex-soldiers from the British Indian army,
who have joined up long enough to learn 'the art of war, so as to contend
successfully against the British when the time arises'.[53]

Against this system of warlike values and structures, we are introduced
to 'the Feringhi doctor' whose behaviour and attitudes clearly mirror
those of Theodore Pennell, the man worth 'two British regiments' on
the Frontier. Of this doctor, Mani Khan, the patriarch declares, and his
companion replies:

'But now we go to India to seek that *Feringhi* of whom men tell such wondrous
tales. He treats our people as though they were his own, and heals all manner
of diseases. Yet men tell me, though he is a man and comely, he knows not the
use of a rifle, and teaches, forsooth, of forgiveness in place of revenge.'
'I know him indeed, and he is, as thou sayest, a man, but probably like most
blasphemers, he is mad, else he would use his manhood to some purpose, and
have a good tale of lives to his credit.'[54]

Also set against the masculine ethos embraced by men and women
alike in the Frontier societies, is Mani Khan's tenderness to his wife and
his delight in his daughter, whom he eventually allows to become a leader
of the village, sitting in judgement on disputes. The daughter, Margalara
(Little Pearl) is portrayed as a truly romantic heroine, beautiful, intelligent, loving, and a child of nature. In her innocence and affinity to nature
(as well as her name) she has some kinship with Nathaniel Hawthorne's
Pearl in *The Scarlet Letter*, while like Pearl's mother she defies the rigid
mores of her society by responding to her instincts and emotions.

Alice Pennell frequently implies a clear contrast between the 'children
of the border' (the title is telling), portrayed as noble savages, and the
'civilized' Westerners like the doctor and English officers. But at times

such oppositions are undercut by other episodes, and in particular the memorable description of Margalara's husband Zaman Khan's experiences as a soldier after he responds to 'the Angrez' call for soldiers 'to go over the black water, to fight for them against another *Feringhi* tribe'.[55] This is an early and rare acknowledgement in fiction about World War I of the significant role played by soldiers from the Indian subcontinent, and also a moving portrayal of the bleakness and trauma of the experience. Zaman Khan's bravery in battle is emphasized as he and his Afghan friend Bahaddur fight alongside Sikhs, Britons, Panjabis, and Mahrattas 'against a foe of whom they knew but little, and for a cause that was not their own'.[56] This episode in the novel foreshadows and compares with Mulk Raj Anand's later novel about Indian soldiers on the Western Front, *Across the Black Waters*.

Perhaps less persuasive or typical of the experience of Indian soldiers, is the description of Zaman Khan's visit to England, where he is awarded medals for bravery, greeted by the King, tours Windsor Castle, and is befriended by an English major. Eventually he returns rather reluctantly to Afghanistan, to die nobly in a clan battle. The novel ends with a long elegaic lament by Margalara, reminiscent of the laments from the Irish oral tradition by Ellen O'Leary for her husband and by Deidre for the sons of Usna.

The publicity for Alice Pennell's second novel, *The Begum's Son*, described the author as

one of those rare beings, a native of India who is also a competent and attractive writer of English. She has the ability to tell a fine story and to ensure that it is true, for her knowledge of the life and the peoples of our Empire in the East is great. In this story she treats of the conditions of the ruling class in India and shows how influential may be the mother at Court. Incidentally she touches upon questions of Imperial concern, such as the desirableness of educating Eastern youths in western lands.

The opening chapter of this novel sets India's present history in the context of a history of invasions and powerful rulers, beginning with Alexander the Great. But the focus of the novel is on the court intrigues which threaten the succession and indeed the life of the rightful inheritor of a princely throne, intrigues successfully resisted and evaded by the young prince's courageous and noble mother. Her son Sher Dil is sent to a school run by an enlightened Englishman, John Renfrew, who insists on a curriculum which includes Urdu, Persian, and the study of the Koran, as well as English texts. Covering the first quarter of the twentieth century, the novel makes passing comment on the independence movement and other events during this period in the Indian subcontinent. It includes a largely pro-British view of the Amritsar 'affair' in 1919, referring to seditious groups, 'malcontents, professing to hate everything British', who nevertheless 'did not scruple to use the train and telegraph, nor did they refrain from using English, the one tongue which men from distant parts of the country had in common'.[57] In the omniscient narrator's view the 'inevitable swift punishment' which followed the violence of the Amritsar demonstrations fell mainly on the innocent, while the perpetrators behind 'the whole foolish, useless, suicidal business' escaped and hid.[58] Pennell also belittles Afghan sympathy for Indian independence, remarking that to the Afghans the cry 'to throw off "the Yoke of the Foreign Oppressor" seemed as good a cry as any', while 'the irony of a still more or less primitive country helping Indians to secure freedom did not strike any of the "patriots"'.[59] Although the author is dismissive of the Sikhs and Afhgans, she does, however, indicate some respect for Gandhi, noting that 'the great Leader of the moment was preaching "No Resistance" and "No Violence," and this did not fit with the feelings and the purpose of the impatient mob'.[60]

The novel ends, however, with a scene of reconciliation and celebration, as the protagonist Sher Dil marries a spirited, enlightened but not too modern Muslim girl, and the marriage is celebrated at a tea-party given by the Begum and attended by John Renfrew and his wife, and by the friends Sher Dil had made while serving in the British army. And so E.M. Forster's 'not yet' which ends *A Passage to India*, and his depiction of an enlightened Englishman, based on his own experience as a tutor and secretary to an aristocratic Indian family, is revised four years later in Alice Pennell's novel to suggest greater optimism about the meeting of cultures and reconciliation of British and Indian peoples.

While Alice Pennell's first two novels might be categorized as historical romances, her third, *Doorways of the East*,[61] is more in the genre of a realist Bildungsroman, following the educational, moral, and political development of Ram Ditta, a Punjabi, from childhood to middle-age. Ram Ditta's growing consciousness and changing attitudes towards religious and political encounters in England and India are paralleled by and contrasted with the changes which take place in his wife, Kamala. This third novel also differs from the others in that it is centrally concerned with questions of identity, the meaning of being 'Indian' in a changing world, but also the meaning of Englishness, and varying perspectives. Ram Ditta and others move between and among varied identities and positions, sometimes in reaction to the reactions of others (such as the Indian students at Cambridge or the Englishmen in India). The novel is also interesting and amusing in its portrayal of the differences between English and American responses to Indians, and within those contexts, differing male and female responses. Throughout the novel, Pennell often assumes the discourses of race and class and empire, and at the same time questions those discourses.

Structurally, the discourses of empire and colonialism are tied into the two ancestral figures who frame the novel, Ram Ditta's great-grandmother Mathaji, who fiercely holds to Indian tradition and custom, particularly with regard to her insistence on an arranged marriage for Ram Ditta, and the barely disguised figure of Theodore Pennell, as the 'Doctor Sahib', the ideal Englishman who brings both Western medical technology and Christianity to India. This patriarchal figure is respected, one might say idolized, by Mathaji and the whole family, whose sons defer to his ideals, and persuade Mathaji and the women to do likewise. As Mathaji's son declares, 'The Doctor Sahib was my "Guru;" you know, Mathaji, you yourself count him among the holy ones...he is still my beloved Master, and I will keep all the rules he ever made!'[62] Throughout the novel, the figure of the great doctor remains always in the background as an ideal of Englishness and Christianity, contrasted with and respected by the great-grandmother, and her ideals and traditions. (At a later point, the author will comment that Gandhi and his ideals are Christian rather than Indian, deriving from the pacificism and communal ideals of missionaries such as Pennell, rather than Indian ethics.)[63] This gendered structure, in which Indian traditions and ideals are represented by a woman, and English ideals as a man, is reinforced at various points in the novel, and most clearly in the following conversation between Ram Ditta and a Muslim businessman with a revolutionary past, Akbar Hussein, now mellowed in his views and domiciled in the United States:

'It is, to my mind, absurd to talk of friendship or enmity between England and India, as we do' [Hussein declares]. 'An autocratic man looks upon his wife as his possession, but she is his wife, even if she has no glory but that which is a reflection of his own. And if she has a fortune, she is all the more prized by him. Well, India is the wife with a fortune...'

'But it is no crime for a man to value his wife more highly for what she brings him,' said Ram Ditta. (*Doorways of the East*, p. 133)

Throughout the novel, the parallel between marriage and imperial relationships is reinforced by the foregrounding of a plot which centres on the relationship between Ram Ditta and the wife found for him by his father to conform with his beloved great-grandmother's dying wish. The comparisons between filial independence and national independence, the freedom to choose for oneself, the role of the husband in asserting his independence, and the tragic fate of the wife who asserts her own independence and that of all Indian women, creates a series of interesting, sometimes overdetermined, and often complex tensions.

While Ram Ditta struggles to find a balanced view, which allows him to accept the benefits of Western education, technology (he is an engineer), and morality, Kamala reacts *against* the West and also against the constrictions placed upon Indian women. Ram Ditta's moral and educational quest is not an easy one: he faces loneliness and crude racism at his English school where he finds the words 'native', 'Nigger' and 'Blackie' called after him or scrawled on his desk, his books, his maps (p. 25). But the love and self-confidence given him by his great-grandmother allow him to shrug off such epithets, and indeed to feel himself superior to English boys 'of the mentality of those who could hurl such ridiculous epithets at him, that a difference in anything so material as a shade of skin was not a sign of inferiority'. Later, when he is an engineer in India, he is able to look upon arrogant 'lower middle class "box-walla"' English civil servants in the same light. Nevertheless, on his first return to India, he finds Indian customs and traditions strange and 'uncivilised', while at Cambridge he finds himself alienated from other Indian students who find themselves forced, because excluded from other social activities, into a kind of ghetto which blurs distinctions between Hindus, Punjabis, Muslims, and other groups. Ram was 'not at home with the men with whom he was supposed to have most in common. He did not speak or understand any of their languages, nor did he share their anti-British views. And they considered him "too English" to be received into their midst.' On the other hand, those English students who did seek him out irritated him by their self-consciously 'noble' airs; all too often they seemed patronising, tactless, or cranks (p. 93). Ram is saved from his bitter isolation by his science tutor, and particularly by the friendship of his tutor's mother, Mrs Foster. The name perhaps echoes that of the author E.M. Forster, while Ram also contests Forster's conclusion in *A Passage to India* that friendship was not yet possible, with his own conclusion that personal friendship between people of different races (and with people like Mrs Foster) is 'the only solution of this question' (p. 100).

Nevertheless, it is only by returning to India that Ram becomes aware of its variety, its cultural values, and complex politics, very little of which is acknowledged in England. Yet, his attitudes continue to lack balance as we are told that his experiences at Cambridge and alienation from the English students at Cambridge have made him treasure the old traditions and customs: 'To hell with British attitudes ... ; he could now see clearly, and he saw Mathaji as the ideal Mother' (p. 161).

But 'the ideal Mother' is contrasted with Ram Ditta's real mother, Devi, who is roundly criticized by Ram's eminently sensible sister Shanti for her neglect of the family and the contrast between her actions and her words. Instead of giving her husband and children the love and care they crave, Devi in her role as 'Woman Leader' is 'always off making speeches and chairing meetings!' In Shanti's view (and Shanti often appears to speak with the voice of the author), this mother is to be condemned for her 'selfishness' in sacrificing others to her own aims and ambitions (p. 55).

It is particularly ironic, therefore, and the author heavily underscores the irony and the tragedy, that in his desire to become a family man and in so doing to sacrifice himself to the wishes of his 'ideal Mother', Ram Ditta marries a young woman who will seek above all to emulate Devi, and make her name as a leading spokeswoman for women's causes and for Indian independence. Pennell is merciless in her portrayal of this young woman who dreams of being a 'Woman Leader, one whose name would be on everyone's lips, one who would be spoken of by the Women's associations and leagues throughout India as a goddess' (p. 176).[64] Invited to speak at a women's conference Kamala 'blossoms out as an orator, with the gift of the gab that was peculiar to her country, as it was to many other Oriental countries, as well as to Ireland' (p. 254).[65] But her ready acceptance and the fame of other Indian women speakers are, in the author's view, also a consequence of the ignorance of Western audiences who patronizingly applaud whatever Indian women leaders tell them and lack the knowledge to question their sweeping generalizations.[66] (Given the activities of her own mother, and the fame achieved by her sister, Cornelia, one cannot help wondering whether there is some personal animus lurking behind the reiterated condemnations of Devi and Kamala.) In contrast, Shanty, the good sister and wife, also works for women's causes, but discreetly, never neglecting her family, and always shunning publicity.

In England, however, Kamala falls in with extremist groups, heavily coloured with 'the red tint', we are informed, and her ambition turns to working for Indian independence rather than 'just' the independence of women. Back in India, she is caught up in the increasingly violent demonstrations and boycotts organized by Gandhi's less disciplined followers. Unlike the author, and her hero Ram Ditta, Kamala and her kind are unwilling to admit that the bitterly condemned British were responsible not only for 'the language which allowed them to unite', but even for 'the very ideas that they were at the moment spreading, ideas of freedom of speech, enfranchisement, which had been given them' (pp. 263–4). The conclusion of the novel dramatizes the author's view of the self-destructiveness of 'extremist' and 'terrorist' activities increasingly embraced by Indian activists. Kamala is killed by a bomb intended to assassinate a 'distinguished guest' at an academic convocation at the university where her husband teaches. Six months after her death, we are told in the final two sentences of the novel that a grieving Ram Ditta discovers that Kamala herself had written 'a pamphlet on bomb-throwing as a justifiable means of securing independence. . . . It was the pamphlet found on the bomb-thrower when he was caught a week after her death. . .' (p. 364; ellipses as in the original).

Although from a marginal Indian community themselves, neither Cornelia nor Alice Sorabji hesitated to take on the authority to represent other communities within India, and they both respond to the views, attitudes, and characterizations offered by the most popular Anglo-Indian fiction writers of their time, including Kipling and Forster. They shared an acceptance of many Christian and Western ideals, but the fiction and other writings by the two sisters offer contrasting attitudes towards Indian identities and the role of Indian women in their own communities. Alice Sorabji in many ways endorses the exoticized view of the 'noble' and 'manly' North-West Frontier 'primitives' much admired and written about by Englishmen (such as Kipling), and also shares official British disapproval of aggressive independence movements and aggressive spokeswomen for women's rights. Cornelia Sorabji, on the other hand, presents an often more complex, ambivalent, and hybrid picture of Indian women and Indian culture, and certainly of English men and women who speak for or about it.

CHAPTER 8

Ending empire

This Empire is a coloured Empire. Most of its subjects – a vast majority of its subjects – are colored people. And more and more the streets of London are showing this fact. I seldom step into its streets without meeting a half-dozen East Indians, a Chinaman, a Japanese or a Malay, and here and there a Negro. There must be thousands of people of color in this city... One senses continually the darker world.

(W.E.B. DuBois, August 1911)[1]

In the early decades of the twentieth century London was the heart and controlling centre of an empire which laid claim to an enormous proportion of the world's territories in and around the African, Indian, Asian, American, and Australasian continents.[2] But its very role as the metropolitan heart of empire also ensured that it would become the heart of resistance to empire. It brought together intellectuals and professionals from diverse parts of the world, who came to study in Britain's universities, as well as businessmen who aspired to greater control of economic affairs and resented trade restrictions set up to favour the British in their own countries. Discrimination against Africans, Afro-Caribbeans, and Indians who qualified as doctors and lawyers in England but were then barred from practising in the hospitals and law courts led to the formation of organizations which would resist such discrimination and publicize the extension of such behaviour by British representatives and clerks in the colonies. These organizations in turn formed links with black and Asian workers in Britain (many of them seamen brought to England as crew on merchant ships and then abandoned). Additionally, a number of Indian immigrants sought election to the British parliament where they could speak on behalf of Home Rule. In this cause, they often formed a united front with Irish parliamentarians such as Charles Stuart Parnell and Frank Hugh O'Donnell. African leaders also found common cause with Irish nationalists, and saw Irish cultural activities as models to be emulated. Thus the Ghanaian (Gold Coast) lawyer, political leader, and author J.E. Casely Hayford, founder of the Gold Coast Aborigines' Society, wrote in his 1911 study, *Ethiopia Unbound*:

I should like to see *Ethiopian Leagues* formed throughout the United States in much the same way as the *Gaelic League* in Ireland for the purpose of studying Fanti, Yoruba, Hausa, or other standard African languages, in daily use. The idea may seem extraordinary on the first view, but if you are inclined to regard it thus, I can only point to the examples of Ireland and Denmark, who have found the vehicle of national language much the safest and most natural way of national conservancy and evolution.[3]

Among the Indian immigrants who combined representation of English, Irish, and Indian subjects and causes was Dadabhai Naoroji, son of a Parsi priest, who came to England in 1855 to help set up the first Indian business house in Britain. He was also appointed Professor of Gujerati at University College, London. He opposed discrimination in the Indian civil service, and was president of the London Indian Society which he helped to found in 1865. Naoroji became known to a wider British audience following the general elections in 1886, when after Naoroji had unsuccessfully stood for Holborn, the prime minister, Lord Salisbury declared that

however great the progress of mankind has been, and however far we have progressed in overcoming prejudices, I doubt whether we have yet got to that point of view where a British constituency will take a black man to represent them...at all events he was a man of another race who was very unlikely to represent an English community.[4]

Much of the liberal British press criticized Lord Salisbury for expressing such views, some indeed pointing out that Naoroji, a Parsi, was in fact lighter-skinned than Salisbury. It was argued that discrimination in terms of skin colour was retrograde and likely to encourage the feeling of Indian and other nationalists that they could not depend on the British to support their progress and emancipation. But many newspapers endorsed Salisbury's views, asserting the incongruity of electing a man from a 'conquered country' or a 'Baboo from Bombay' incapable of understanding the 'delicate' and intricate traditions of the House of Commons. A letter to the *Times* from Sir Lepel Griffin, chairman of the East India Association and former chief secretary in the Punjab, demonstrates the complex of racial prejudice and attitudes which was sadly typical of many members of the English establishment:

An alien in race, in custom, in religion, destitute of local sympathy or local knowledge, no more unsuitable representative could be imagined or suggested. As for the people of India, Mr Naoroji no more represents them than a Polish Jew settled in Whitechapel represents the people of England. He is a Parsee, a member of a small foreign colony, probably Semitic in origin, settled in the west of India. The Parsees are the Jews of India, intelligent, industrious, wealthy... But they are quite as much aliens to the people of India as the English rulers can possibly be.[5]

Although Naoroji stood as a Liberal candidate, some Liberals were also lukewarm in their support, and there was a suggestion that Naoroji might be more easily electable in Scotland. There were several attempts to have his selection as a candidate in Central Finsbury reconsidered and alternative candidates were nominated. However, Salisbury's attack strengthened Liberal backing, which was shored up further by the assurance from former Indian Viceroy Lord Ripon that Naoroji would be 'a most valuable MP' and a true spokesman for the interests of the Indian people.[6] Naoroji was eventually elected in 1892. His success was regarded with distrust and scepticism by many English papers, and one took consolation that at least Naoroji was not a 'Bengali Baboo'. The *Scottish Leader*, however, congratulated the people of Finsbury for being 'free from the stupid and illiberal prejudice of colour'.[7]

Naoroji served in the House of Commons until 1895 when he stood for re-election but was defeated in the general rout of the Liberal party. Both inside and outside parliament he espoused causes such as the trades unions, women's franchise, and Irish home rule. He was a consistent and eloquent spokesman for Indian independence and against colonial malpractice. Like many other black and Asian intellectuals and activists before and after him, he appealed to British claims to represent liberty and democracy, and the title of his book, *Poverty and Un-British Rule*, published in 1901, is indicative of that appeal.[8] Here Naoroji developed the argument made in a number of speeches that unlike the Moghuls, the British neither promoted Indian industry nor employed Indians. Instead Indians were forced to pay taxes to support an exorbitantly expensive British administration and army, and their agriculture and trade were distorted for the benefit of the British economy. He claimed that £30–£40 million was extracted from India annually, and that British rule brought increased poverty and famine.

Elected president of the Indian National Congress three times (in 1886, 1893, and 1906), Naoroji was influential in shaping its economic ideology and in insisting on the link between capitalism, exploitation of the working class, and economic exploitation in the empire. He attended the International Socialist Congress in Amsterdam, and appealed to the working men of the whole world to join with the working-classes of India to end British rule.[9] After over fifty years in England, he returned to India in 1907, where he died in 1917.

Naoroji was the most prominent of a number of South Asians who sought to enter politics in Britain in the late nineteenth and early twentieth century. Another Parsi from Bombay, Mancherjee M. Bhownaggree, came to study law in London in 1881, settled permanently in England from 1891, and in 1895 stood as a Tory and won Bethnal Green Northeast. Bhownaggree wrote a history of the East India Company and translated into Gujerati Queen Victoria's *Leaves from the Journal of Our Life in the Highlands*. Rozina Visram suggests that Bhownaggree was selected as a candidate by the Tories in order to counter Naoroji's nationalist views in parliament and to denounce the 'agitators' who tried 'to sow discontent with the British rule'.[10] He insisted on the benefits of British rule, and supported the 'union' of Britain and India. And so whereas Naoroji, as a Parsi, was denounced as an alien unrepresentative of either Indians or British, Bhownaggree, also a Parsi of similar background but very different ideology, was promoted as a true spokesman for India and for British imperial interests. He was re-elected in 1900, and his support for British rule in India won him the satiric title among Indian National Congress partisans of Mr 'Bow-and-agree'.[11] However, he did on occasion join with Naoroji to condemn the treatment of indentured Indian workers in South Africa and the West Indies, and was also a vocal supporter of women's rights in India and Britain.[12] Another supporter of British rule, because he believed it to be in the interests of Indian Muslims, was Syed Ameer Ali, founder of the National Muhammadan Association in India and later of the London branch of the All-India Muslim League. He was a regular contributor to journals and newspapers on Islamic affairs and his views were treated with considerable respect. The *Times* obituary on his death in 1928 declared that he represented all that was best in East and West and that his writings gave him 'a permanent place in the English literature as an interpreter of Islamic Code, antiquity and history on the lines of progressive thought'.[13]

Relatively conservative spokesmen such as Ameer Ali and Bhownaggree were opposed by a younger and much more radical generation of students who came from India to study in England, and who were based in India House in London. It is this changing climate that Alice Sorabji Pennell replicates and regrets in her third and final novel, *Doorways of the*

East. This more radical generation included Shyamaji Krishnavarma, founder of India House, who came to London from Orissa in 1897. Krishnavarma founded the Indian Home Rule Society in 1905, and edited the *Indian Sociologist*, a penny weekly, to express the society's views.[14] Students such as Vinayak Savarkar at India House helped organize demonstrations and meetings, such as the annual Martyrs' Day meetings commemorating what they termed the 1857 'Great Indian National Rising', and which the British referred to as the 'Indian Mutiny'. Savarkar translated the autobiography of the Italian nationalist Mazzini, and drew on his rhetoric with reference to freedom for India; he also wrote a book, *The War of Independence, 1857*. The students declared their sympathy with Irish, Turkish, and Egyptian nationalists, and urged Sikh and other Indian soldiers to help overthrow the British. They studied and published information on bomb-making, and took lessons in the use of firearms.[15] In 1909, Madan Lal Dhingra, a young activist associated with India House, assassinated Sir William Curzon Wyllie, a civil servant whose task was to keep a watch on the activities of Indian students in Britain. Dhingra was hanged at Pentonville in August 1909. His statement was suppressed by the authorities, but another copy was found and given to David Garnett who succeeded in persuading the *Daily News* to publish it on the morning of his execution. The statement read in part:

I attempted to shed English blood as a humble revenge for the inhuman hangings and deportations of patriotic Indian youths . . . I believe that a nation held down by a foreign bayonet is in a perpetual state of war. Since open battle is rendered impossible to a disarmed race I attacked by surprise . . . As a Hindoo I felt that wrong to my country is an insult to God.[16]

Following these events, India House was closed down, and, after an unsuccessful rescue attempt by Indian and Irish nationalists, Savarkar was deported and imprisoned for ten years. In Ireland, posters of Dhingra celebrated him as a martyr in the cause of national freedom.

During this period, a number of Indian politicians visited England to speak on behalf of India. Among the more 'moderate' spokesmen was Gopal Krishna Gokhale, representing the Indian National Congress, and speaking on various occasions to the National Liberal Club and the Fabian Society about Britain's duty to India, and the need for equal treatment of Indians. Support came from the Labour party for more radical speakers such as Bipin Chandra Pal and Bal Gangadhar Talik. Keir Hardie had been guided by Tilak on a visit to Poona, and Hardie in turn invited him to speak to working class and trades union congresses in Britain in 1918–19. While in England, Tilak also got to know George Bernard Shaw, Sidney Webb, and Ramsay MacDonald, who advocated Indian independence.

Students from Africa and the Caribbean also used London as a base for resistance to British imperialism. When the Trinidadian Sylvester Williams came to London to study law in 1897, he founded the African Association, whose aim was to encourage a 'feeling of unity and to facilitate friendly intercourse among Africans in general', as well as to appeal to British and colonial governments to redress the wrongs suffered by their African subjects.[17] Williams was also one of the main organizers of the first Pan-African conference, held in London in 1900, and editor of the short-lived journal, *Pan African*.[18] Williams had studied in the United States before coming to England, and no doubt there had become aware of leaders such as W.E.B. DuBois and Booker T. Washington. His belief that peoples of African descent must unite to further their interests presumably was also influenced by the writings of the eminent writer and defender of the African race, Edmund Wilmot Blyden, born in St Thomas, and then Liberian commissioner and envoy to Britain. Blyden's emphasis on the 'African Personality' as complementary to the European intellect prefigured later aspects of 'negritude', and differed from the views of another eminent African, the surgeon James Africanus Beale Horton, from Sierra Leone. The author of seven books, Horton called for independence for West African peoples, asserted their intellectual equality with Europeans, and proposed the foundation of a West African university, which would also educate women.[19] A spokesman and writer on behalf of Africans who appealed, in the tradition of the abolitionists, to evangelical Christians, was Celestine Edwards.[20] He published a short biography of Bishop Walter Hawkins, a former slave, and was editor of two religious magazines, *Lux*, from 1892 till 1894, and *Fraternity*, from 1893 till 1894. The latter magazine was the journal of the Society for the Recognition of the Brotherhood of Man, and was particularly strong in its opposition to racism.[21]

It was Sylvester Williams' African Association, however, which first brought together in London members of the African diaspora, including black men and women from Antigua, South Africa, Sierra Leone, the Gold Coast, Trinidad, and the United States. The organization of the Pan-African conference was begun in 1898 with the specific aim of addressing 'the treatment of native races under European and American rule' and particularly South Africa, West Africa, the West Indies, and the United States.[22] It was given financial support by Dadabhai Naoroji, whose work on behalf of Asian people may have 'inspired Williams to seek to do the same for his own people'.[23] The conference, with thirty-seven delegates and a number of observers, was held in Westminster Town Hall in July 1900, the first time ever, Williams declared, that 'black people had assailed London with a conference'.[24] The conference was addressed by, among others, Bishop Walters, president of the National Afro-American Council, Mrs Anna J. Cooper, a Latin teacher from Washington, Benito Sylvain, the Haitian aide-de-camp to the Ethiopian Emperor, Sylvester Williams, and W.E.B. DuBois. These speakers, together with the Reverend Henry D. Brown (from Canada) formed a new Pan-African Association whose primary aim was 'to secure Africans throughout the world true civil and political rights', and signed the conference 'Address to the Nations of the World', which declared that 'the problem of the Twentieth Century is the problem of the colour-line' and demanded that 'the cloak of Christian missionary enterprise' should no longer be allowed 'to hide the ruthless exploitation and political downfall of less developed nations'.[25] The conference also sent a petition to Queen Victoria decrying the forced labour, pass systems, and segregation inflicted upon black men, women, and children in Rhodesia and South Africa. Among the members of the newly formed Pan-African Association in London were the composer Samuel Coleridge-Taylor, John Richard Archer, future President of the African Progress Union and England's first black mayor (Battersea),[26] and Jane Cobden Unwin, wife of the publisher T. Fisher Unwin.

John Richard Archer's address to the African Progress Union at its inauguration in 1918 reflects the growing militancy of colonized peoples, especially following World War I, during which Britain had commandeered the services of millions of Indian, African, and West Indian soldiers and labourers. Where the first Pan-African conference and parliamentary spokesmen such as Naoroji spoke in terms of reform and appeals for recognition and equality, Archer and later activists were more likely to speak of rights and demands. Thus Archer told a cheering audience:

The people in this country are sadly ignorant with reference to the darker races, and our object is to show them that we have given up the idea of becoming hewers of wood and drawers of water, that we claim our rightful place within this Empire. That if we are good enough to be brought to fight the wars of the country, we are good enough to receive the benefits of the country. One of the objects of this association is to demand – not ask, demand; it will be 'demand' all the time that I am your President. I am not asking for anything, I am out demanding.[27]

Archer took part in the first International Pan-African Conference organized by W.E.B. DuBois in Paris in 1919, and subsequently in the series of Pan-African conferences held in the early 1920s jointly in London, Lisbon, and Brussels.

Earlier nationalist movements and the 1900 Pan-African Conference had been led by and reflected the concerns of a relatively small and privileged group of students, intellectuals, and businessmen. The war brought to Britain the presence and consciousness of more numerous and less privileged groups of black and Asian sailors, labourers, and soldiers. After years of discrimination and exploitation, black men were welcomed into the merchant navy, and encouraged to work in munitions and chemical factories. African, West Indian, and Indian troops fought in Europe and the African continent against the Germans, and their courage was acknowledged publicly in the British press and through the award of medals and decorations. Thousands died on the battlefront, or as the result of wounds and disease, and many were sent to British hospitals for treatment. Peter Fryer estimates that there were approximately 20,000 black and Asian people in Britain by the end of the war.[28] Many were housed in separate or segregated hostels, such as those provided for Indian soldiers in Sussex.

Following the end of the war and the demobilization of troops, black people whose labour had been in demand found themselves shunted aside and resented. Crippled black soldiers recuperating in a Liverpool military hospital were attacked by white soldiers (and defended by others); there were race riots in Tyneside and Cardiff directed against Arab, Somali, and Chinese residents in 1919; 120 black workers were sacked from a Liverpool sugar refinery in the spring of 1919 because white employees refused to work alongside them. Racial attacks and tension became more widespread. A West Indian was lynched by a white mob in Liverpool, and a police report noted that in June 1919 organized gangs of between 2,000 and 10,000 white men wandered the streets of Liverpool 'savagely attacking, beating, and stabbing every negro they could find',[29] and wrecking and burning houses occupied by black people. In Liverpool and Cardiff much of the hysteria, often encouraged by local newspapers, was directed against relationships between black men and white women.[30] There were racial attacks also in London, and national as well as local newspapers published letters advocating the repatriation of black people. In response to the prejudice against black men mixing with or marrying white women, the prominent journalist and editor of the *African Times and Orient Review*, Duse Mohamed Ali, himself married to a white English woman, had published a scathing essay in the *New Age* and later an article in his own journal pointing out the lack of concern regarding the exploitative behaviour of white men towards black women in South Africa and other countries.[31] A letter from Sir Ralph Williams in 1919 received a sharp response in the *Times* five days later from Felix Hercules, who also remarked on the hypocrisy of those who ignored the seduction of young black girls in South Africa and the West Indies by white men, attacked Sir Ralph for inciting racial violence, which 'can only have one ultimate result, the downfall of the British Empire', and went on to conclude:

If Sir Ralph Williams thinks that the problem can be solved by sending every black or coloured unit forthwith back to his own country, then we should be compelled to see that every white man is sent back to England from Africa and from the West India islands in order that the honour of our sisters and our daughters there should be kept intact.[32]

As a founder-member of the African Progress Union, and editor of the *African Telegraph*,[33] Hercules campaigned vigorously for the rights and due compensation for Britain's black community. Like many other black people within and outside of Britain, he was outraged when black troops were prevented from taking part in the 1919 London Peace March, and saw a clear connection between the government's behaviour towards its coloured community within Britain and its policy regarding the colonies. Far from rewarding African, West Indian, and Indian soldiers, sailors, and workmen for their whole-hearted participation in the war effort on behalf of Britain, Hercules maintained, the government gave nothing but insult and injury. According to Hercules, the implicit command of 'get back to your kennel, you damned dog of a nigger!', and the 'supineness of the Imperial Government during the race riots [drove] home the fact that they approve of them, that they are in line with Imperial policy'.[34]

The global social unrest which followed World War I, including the revolution in Russia, the uprising and continued war against the British in Ireland, the demonstrations and massacre in Amritsar, the race riots in the United States, fed the fears of the British government as well as the bitterness and militancy of 'coloured' peoples in the colonies and in Britain. For many, socialism seemed the most adequate long-term response to imperialism and the capitalism which was believed to be its driving force. In the next decades, many of the most influential political thinkers and anti-imperialists were to be Marxists. Those who spent some time in Britain (and in some cases almost a lifetime) included Claude McKay, Shapurji Saklatvala, George Padmore, C.L.R. James, Kwame Nkrumah, Jomo Kenyatta, Paul Robeson, Ras Makonnen, and

Claudia Jones.[35] Their objectives – to end British rule over African, West Indian, and Asian territories – were supported at various times not only by anti-imperialists such as J.A. Hobson, whose 1902 study *Imperialism* had vigorously demonstrated the hollowness of the economic, political, and moral arguments used to justify British colonialism, but also by left-wing activists and intellectuals such as Sylvia Pankhurst, Nancy Cunard, Victor Gollanz, Fenner Brockway, Sidney and Beatrice Webb, George Bernard Shaw, George Lansbury, and Keir Hardie.

The late 1920s and the 1930s saw the development of numerous or-ganizations within Britain to further the interests of black and Asian people in Britain and in the colonial territories. These included the West African Students Union (WASU), organized by Lapido Solanke in 1925, the League of Coloured Peoples, founded by Harold Moody in 1931, the Negro Association in Manchester, the Coloured Peoples' Association in Edinburgh, the United Committee of Coloured and Colonial People's Association in Cardiff, the African Union based at Glasgow University, and the International African Service Bureau. These groups came to-gether or worked in concert on various causes, but perhaps the chief one which united them prior to World War II was Mussolini's invasion of Ethiopia in 1936, and the failure of the British government to support Ethiopia's appeal to the League of Nations. In response to this event, and the British continuation of oil sales to Italy, C.L.R. James wrote in *The Keys* (the relatively moderate journal of the League of Coloured Peoples):

Africans and people of African descent, especially those who have been poi-soned by British Imperialist education, needed a lesson. They have got it. Every succeeding day shows exactly the real motives which move imperialism in its contact with Africa, shows the incredible savagery and duplicity of European Imperialism in its quest for markets and raw materials. Let the lesson sink in deep.[36]

With C.L.R. James as chairman, Amy Ashwood Garvey as treasurer, and Jomo Kenyatta as secretary, the International African Friends of Abyssinia was formed in order to speak out and organize support on behalf of Ethiopia. It organized a reception for Haile Selassie when he came to London in 1936, and lobbied MPs on his behalf. This committee was later to be replaced by the IASB, the International African Service Bureau, with many of the same members but a wider brief embracing the rights of all those of African descent.

If World War I and the lack of acknowledgement and reward for Indian, African, and West Indian contributions to the war effort resulted in disillusionment with the possibilities of constitutional reform leading to self-government, World War II increased the urgency of demands for independence. By 1942 it had already been acknowledged that Indian self-government could not long be warded off. In West Africa and the West Indies, trade unionists and other radical activists were making strong demands. It was in this context that the IASB joined with a number of other organizations inside and outside Britain to form the Pan-African Federation and to hold in Manchester the influential 1945 Pan-African Congress. Manchester was the base for the Guyanan restaurant owner and activist, Ras Makonnen, and had also become known as a city in which 'the coloured proletariat in Britain...had made a name for...fighting various areas of discrimination'.[37] The Manchester Pan-African Congress was designed to address not only international issues but also 'increasing discrimination in Britain', and to dramatize the intrinsic connections between empire and British industrial wealth. Makonnen wrote:

You could say that we coloured people had a right there, because of the age-old connections between cotton, slavery and the building up of cities in England ...Manchester gave us an important opportunity to express and expose the contradictions, the fallacies and the pretensions that were at the very heart of empire.[38]

The conference was designed to follow the World Federation of Trades Unions Congress held in Paris in September 1945, and the Anti-Colonial Peoples Conference held in London in June, which had brought together groups from India, Ceylon, Burma, Africa, and the West Indies. Thus it sought to align working-class and 'third world' issues on both a local and international scale. Delegates included Kenyatta, Nkrumah, Hastings Banda, and DuBois. There were also delegations from the Federation of Indian Organizations in Britain, WASU, and the Somali Society. Thus the Manchester conference involved a large number of those who were to form the political leadership in British Africa and many other newly independent nations in the 1950s and 1960s. There were also delegations from trades unions and political parties throughout the African and West Indian colonies.

The first day of the conference was devoted to 'The Colour Problem in Britain', a problem exacerbated by the British government's tacit agreement to collaborate with the United States military's desire to maintain segregation between black American servicemen and white servicemen and women. Discussion at the conference denounced discrimination in employment and by the legal system, and raised the problem of the unwanted babies of black American servicemen. A resolution was carried demanding that discrimination on account of race, creed, or colour be made a criminal offence.[39] The conference also approved a militant statement demanding freedom, democracy, and social betterment for the colonies, condemning 'the monopoly of capital and the rule of private wealth and industry for private profit alone', and calling on 'the educated Colonials' to join with workers and farmers in organizing strikes and boycotts in the battle against imperialism.[40]

Britain's imperial connections, her role as a cultural as well as a political centre, along with the trauma of World War I, also stimulated significant changes in the artistic forms and sensibilities which developed during the first decades of the twentieth century. As Henry Louis Gates has pointed out, Modernism was a 'mulatto movement'. Many people are aware of the impact of African art on European artists such as Derain and Picasso, and the popularity of jazz with many serious musicians as well as in the dance halls of Europe. But modernist writers also sought models from outside Europe, as can be noted with regard to the fascination of Ezra Pound and Yeats for Chinese and Japanese poetry and drama, the references to Indian subjects and imagery in the poetry of Yeats and T.S. Eliot, Eliot's use of jazz rhythms and African American references, and in the United States as well as Europe, writing by white authors about 'Negro' subjects. Much of Conrad's work questions the assumptions about racial or cultural superiority which justified European imperialism, and to a lesser extent one could argue that Kipling reveals a certain schizophrenia in his attitudes towards rulers and ruled and their cultures, as does Leonard Woolf in his fiction and letters about Sri Lanka. Arguably, modernist art and writing is in some ways a consequence of the growing awareness of alternate cultures and alternate modes of perceiving the world and expressing these perceptions. The coming together of some of the most gifted and articulate representatives of countries and cultures throughout the empire produced not only the double consciousness of which DuBois spoke, but the awareness at least of a multiple consciousness, and the readiness to question the assumptions, traditions, doctrines of the English ruling culture as well as native cultures. At the same time, the growing nationalist aspirations of colonized peoples stimulated cultural nationalism and a celebration of indigenous art forms and aesthetics. The Harlem Renaissance provides one influential example of such cultural nationalism, which increased awareness of and interest in African art. In India, Vivekananda and others promoted a Pan-Asian cultural aesthetic and philosophy, which was seen to challenge and complement European values.

Indian writers and intellectuals such as Sarojini Naidu and her younger brother Harindranath Chatterji were members of the 'Monday Evening' group which met with Yeats, Pound, and others to discuss literature and ideas in London between 1910 and 1914. When Rabindranath Tagore visited England in 1912, Yeats and Pound enthusiastically promoted him as a poet who, according to Yeats, represented 'one of the great events in [his] artist [sic] life'.[41] Yeats helped with the translations and wrote an introduction for Tagore's *Gitanjali*, published by Macmillan in 1912. Pound's preface to the six Tagore poems published in *Poetry London* in December 1912, compared the discovery of Tagore's poetry to the great moments of the Renaissance, when artists discovered the Greeks.[42] That sense of divided or double consciousness which the encounter with other cultures stirred is conveyed in Yeats's introduction to *Gitanjali*, where he writes that Tagore's poems 'stirred my blood as nothing has for years...We are moved...because we have met our own image, as though we had walked in Rossetti's willow wood or heard, perhaps for the first time in literature, our voice as in a dream.'[43] And the double consciousness becomes mingled with a doubleness – perhaps duplicity – of motivation when Yeats advocated Tagore's election to the Royal Society of Literature as a 'a piece of wise imperialism', for 'I believe if we pay him honour it will be understood as that we honour India also for he is its most famous man today.' Similarly, Pound noted in *Poetry London* that 'world-fellowship is nearer for the visit of Rabindranath Tagore to London'.[44]

The 1930s and 1940s saw an increasing presence in the major British cities, and especially London, of intellectuals from the colonies, and many of them played a key part in British intellectual and cultural life. They included C.L.R. James from Trinidad, who came in the first instance to assist the cricketer Learie Constantine in the writing of his autobiography; also from Trinidad came George Padmore, James' boyhood friend, fellow Pan-Africanist, and author of numerous books and articles on imperialism, Pan-Africanism, Communism, and Ghana. Una Marson, poet, playwright, and activist from Jamaica, worked for the BBC in London, and founded and produced the programme which was eventually to become *Caribbean Voices*, providing an outlet for writers such as V.S. Naipaul, Andrew Salkey, Samuel Selvon, and George Lamming. Other writers and intellectuals who worked for the BBC included G.V. Desani, author of the extraordinary avant-garde novel, *All About H. Hatterr*, and

Attia Hosain, the novelist, who presented a women's programme on the BBC's Eastern Service in the late 1940s. As noted in the previous chapter, Cornelia Sorabji, an Indian writer of fiction and drama, a lawyer and campaigner for women's rights, settled in England after 1929 until her death in 1954. Her sister Alice, author of three novels, also settled in England after her missionary husband's death in 1912. Thurairajah Tambimuttu from the then colony of Ceylon, became editor of *Poetry London*, and was himself a poet. Krishna Menon, a lawyer from Malabar in south India, who lived in London from 1924 till 1944, edited for Bodley Head between 1932 and 1935 the Twentieth Century Library, a series which included J.A. Hobson's *Democracy*, Winifred Holtby's *Women*, Naomi Mitchison's *The Home*, and J.H. Driberg's *The Black Races*. He also edited a series for the publishers Selwyn and Blount. In 1935 Allen Lane founded Penguin books, and asked Menon to found and become editor of a companion series, Pelican Books, a series which was to be non-fiction, serious in content, and with an educational bias. The first book in the series was George Bernard Shaw's *Intelligent Woman's Guide to Socialism, Capitalism, Sovietism, and Fascism*, for which edition Shaw especially wrote the section on Fascism.[45] Other works brought out in the early Pelican series were Roger Fry's *Vision and Design*, J.B.S. Haldane's *The Inequality of Man*, H.G. Wells' *A Short History of the World*.

Menon was also an untiring campaigner for Indian independence, and in 1928 became secretary of the Commonwealth of India League, for which he sought and obtained the support of such distinguished men and women as Bertrand Russell, Harold Laski, Stafford Cripps, and Ellen Wilkinson. The league's parliamentary committee included at one time some 100 MPs. Following Indian independence he was appointed India's High Commissioner in London. He was also a hard-working Labour councillor for Ward 4 in St Pancras, where, among other things, he organized the travelling library and the Camden Festival.

The year 1948 brought a new generation of immigrants and settlers, as well as renewed violence against the established black community. In Liverpool rioting broke out when black seamen and members of the approximately 5,000-strong black community there were attacked verbally by members of the National Union of Seamen, and physically assaulted by white crowds and policemen.[46] Two months earlier, the SS *Empire Windrush* brought 492 West Indians to England, recruited by the British government to fill empty jobs in transport, health services, factories, and the postal service. Other West Indians gradually followed, and by 1958 over 125,000 people had emigrated to Britain over the previous ten years. During the same period about 55,000 rural workers from India and Pakistan were encouraged to come to work in England's industrial cities. All of them, under the 1948 Nationality Act, passed in the year that the British Empire became the British Commonwealth, were British citizens, granted UK citizenship as citizens of Britain's colonies and former colonies. Many were skilled and non-manual workers, and many were to become distinguished authors, for example the poet and winner of the Queen's Medal, James Berry, who came over in 1948 on the second ship from Jamaica, the *Orbita*. The post-World War II years also brought numerous students, journalists, and professionals from the West Indies, Africa, India, Pakistan, and Sri Lanka, some of whom stayed in England for many years or settled there permanently. Among those who came from the Caribbean were Samuel Selvon, V.S. Naipaul, Beryl Gilroy, Andrew Salkey, Kamau Brathwaite, Michael Anthony, Stuart Hall, and George Lamming.[47]

Although there was official encouragement and welcome from the government and in some of the media for these workers called upon to help reconstruct post-war Britain, hostility and discrimination in housing and employment were commonly experienced. White trade unionists frequently demanded quotas or refused to work with black and Asian people. In 1958, such hostility and racism erupted in the Nottingham and Notting Hill riots. These and reactions to them were stoked by sensationalist reporting in the media,[48] and in turn led to demands that immigration restrictions should be imposed. A bill restricting immigration to those who had employment vouchers was passed in 1962, even though all those in the newly and about to be independent colonies were legally citizens of the UK, and in 1965 a second bill imposed strict limits on the number of vouchers that could be issued. Thus, in the years when externally there seemed to be recognition of the right to equality and democracy as numerous ex-colonies acquired independence, internally, racism and discrimination seemed to be gaining ground and appeared to be given state sanction. These were the circumstances in which a new generation of British-born children of black and Asian citizens would grow up.

CHAPTER 9

Duse Mohamed Ali, anti-imperial journals, and black and Asian publishing

The first half of the twentieth century saw not only the growth of a community of students, professionals, activists, and businessmen in England, but also the growth of newspapers and journals which helped to establish the real and imagined communities which linked those groups within Britain and to their ancestral countries, or to a wider community of colonized and oppressed black and Asian peoples. One of the most significant of these journals was the *African Times and Orient Review* (later renamed the *Africa and Orient Review*), edited by the Egyptian actor, writer, businessman, and entrepreneur, Duse Mohamed Ali.

Born Mohamed Ali in Alexandria in November 1866 (later taking the name Duse Mohamed in honour of one of his guardians), Duse Mohamed Ali was the son of an Egyptian army officer and his Sudanese wife. In autobiographical accounts, he reported that he had had to leave Egypt as a child during the Nationalist Rising of 1881–2, and had lost contact with his family. He states in *In the Land of the Pharaohs* that he was educated in Britain from 1876, and had resided there from 1884. Apart from trips to the United States and the Caribbean, he lived in Britain until 1923, earning his living mainly through work with travelling theatres and his writing.[1] In addition to his best-known work, *In the Land of the Pharaohs*, he wrote a history, a novel, playlets, a musical comedy script, a full-length autobiography, and many journalistic pieces.[2] Drawing on Duse Mohamed's own autobiographical writing, as well as contemporary official records and letters, Ian Duffield gives a fascinating account of Duse Mohamed's early years as a member of various theatrical troupes and as a journalist, an account which both reinforces and revises views of the cultural milieu of the decades ending the nineteenth and beginning the twentieth century.[3]

In 1883, Duse Mohamed sought work as an actor at the suggestion of a friend who had seen him as Morocco in *The Merchant of Venice* and found a small walk-on part, probably as a black slave, in the Roman drama,

Claudian, a play performed by the company of Wilson Barrett, a leading actor-manager at the time.[4] The company went to the United States with *Claudian*, and Duse Mohamed afterwards undertook his own tour, billed as 'The Young Egyptian Wonder reciter of Shakespeare'.[5] On his return to England, he joined a company managed by Sarah Thorne, playing in Brighton, Margate, and Ramsgate, and later took the role of Nubian slave in *Hypatia* at the Theatre Royal, Haymarket. He also played in pantomime at the Theatre Royal, Drury Lane. Other larger parts came to him in smaller northern companies, with whom he probably played the role of Uncle Tom in the perennially popular *Uncle Tom's Cabin*, and the cruel lecherous Muslim, Nana Sahib, in *Jessie Brown: Or the Relief of Lucknow*, by Dion Boucicault. He also had a part in Boucicault's *The Octoroon*,[6] and played Osman Digma, a stereotypically cruel, treacherous, and lustful Arab, in a tour of *On Active Service*, a melodrama by Herbert Leonard. In the late 1890s he himself wrote a one-act play, *The Jew's Revenge*, heavily indebted to scenes in parts of *Hypatia*, but set in Egypt. Duse Mohamed played the part of the crafty and vengeful Jew, Josephus, a performance described as 'powerful and impressive'.[7] He received favourable notices also for his performance as 'the man vulture' in *Because I Love You*, where his 'dusky countenance' was perceived as 'heightening the effect of a weird and "creepy" impersonation'.[8] Other roles included in 1901 that of a murderous and hypocritical Muslim Arab slave-dealer, the abductor of a beautiful white woman, in Maurice Goldberg's *Secrets —: Or The Cross and the Crescent*. In a scenario characteristic of the popular fiction and drama of the time, the heroine is rescued by a noble British naval lieutenant, who urges his followers to clear the deck of 'these black swabs' and rejoices in seeing 'the black skunks' run.[9]

As Ian Duffield points out, Duse Mohamed found himself mainly confined to stereotyped and often demeaning roles as black slaves, despicable Muslims, and background figures. Such roles may well have deepened his consciousness of the endemic prejudice and misrepresentation of coloured peoples, whether African or oriental, and encouraged him later to write a history which foregrounded the perspective and roles of Egyptian participants, and also to emphasize the common cause of African and Asian peoples in his journal, the *African Times and Orient Review*. On the other hand, his involvement in the theatrical world allowed him to encounter such figures as Oscar Wilde (in 1893) and Edward, Prince of Wales. He was to write about both encounters later.

Duse Mohamed Ali's theatrical career, including as he later related, the production of another of his own plays, *A Cleopatra Night*, was interspersed with other ways of making a living. He worked on the Liverpool docks and in various manual jobs. But from the last decade of the nineteenth century and throughout the rest of his life until his death in Lagos in 1945, journalism became an increasingly important occupation, and it is as a journalist and editor that his reputation deserves attention.

His early writings describe the lives of the 'down and out' in Liverpool and London, with critical reports of the Salvation Army doss-houses and what he terms their 'ricebowl Christianity'. He reported on debates at the House of Commons, and there met and became friendly with the Irish MP, Frank Hugh O'Donnell, an ardent defender of nationalist rights in Ireland, India, and Egypt. He also met the first 'coloured MP' elected to the House of Commons, Dadabhai Naoroji, and records long discussions with him, as well as a meeting in 1892 at a play about the Indian Mutiny, *The Round Tower*.[10] As a freelance journalist in Hull at the beginning of the century, he contributed romantic stories, historical and autobiographical sketches, and a 286 line ode, 'Hull's Coronation Ode', to the *Hull Lady*.[11] Written in blank verse, 'Hull's Coronation Ode' includes praise for William Wilberforce as one of Hull's foremost heroes, and reminds readers of Britain's 'stain that smirched the proud escutcheon, / Of England's vainly boasted liberty'.[12] This journal also includes advertisements for Duse Mohamed Ali's services as a teacher of elocution and a presenter of drawing-room recitals. He founded the Hull Shakespeare Society, which performed costumed Shakespeare recitals.

In the second half of the first decade of the twentieth century, Duse Mohamed Ali can be located in London, occasionally finding roles on stage, and also participating in various theatre tours. At the 1908 Franco-British exhibition in London, he was billed as 'the Great Egyptian Actor-Author', and dressed in Egyptian costume to give lectures on the finding of Moses in a piece entitled *Pharaoh's Daughter*. Reviewers commented both on his national dress and appearance and the excellence of his English. As Ian Duffield comments, this episode displays the divided identity imposed upon him: 'the more "British" he became, the more to the British, he seemed a bizarre stranger'.[13] Duse Mohamed also established himself as a literary agent, and undertook the writing and staging of a musical comedy, *The Lily of Bermuda*, by Ernest Trimingham, a coloured Bermudan. The musical proved to be a financial disaster, and apparently also an artistic one.[14]

Between 1909 and 1911, Duse Mohamed Ali developed his skill and his reputation as a journalist, writing a series of articles for the *New*

Age, edited at that time by A.R. Orage.[15] Under Orage's editorship, this journal (financed in part by George Bernard Shaw) published an eclectic collection of political and artistic contributions, including works by H.G. Wells, Ezra Pound, George Bernard Shaw, and Cecil Chesterton. Its mixture of literary, cultural, and political contributions, and its critical response to British imperialism and racism, provided a model for Duse Mohamed when he went on to edit his own journal.

Duse Mohamed's first contribution to the *New Age*, 'White Women and Coloured Men. The Other Side of the Picture', is a provocative and acerbic response to an article in the *London Opinion* by G. Hamilton McGuiness, who deplored marital and other sexual relationships between white women and 'half-civilized' oriental men, especially Asian students. In reply, Duse Mohamed pointedly referred to the hypocrisy of whites who set up and frequent brothels in Eastern seaports, and asserted that far from being 'half-civilized', Egypt and the 'middle east' were the cradle of what is deemed Western civilization. This latter assertion was to become a significant part of the argument in his book, *In the Land of the Pharaohs*, and other articles published as he was writing it. The technique of reversing the perspective of British readers is employed more fully in a series of five pieces, published between February and April 1909, titled 'Western Civilisation through Eastern Spectacles' which may owe something of its technique and observations to Behramji Malabari's *The Indian Eye on English Life* (discussed in Chapter Six). In this series, Duse Mohamed adopts the persona of an un-Anglicized Egyptian, for whom all things British are something new and strange, and often absurd or grotesque. He contrasts the lives of wealthy, indolent women with those of poor working women in factories, sympathizes with the suffragettes, asserts that British justice unjustly favours the rich, and comments on the contrast between the indifference of missionaries to the evils in their home country while they deplore the moral failures of other races. Like Sake Dean Mohomed and other predecessors, he expresses his views in the format of a series of letters addressed to a group unfamiliar with the country he is writing about. But whereas Sake Dean Mahomed uses a very English literary style, Duse Mohamed adopts a kind of stage-Arab, as in the following passage:

So shall I feel that my work is done and the great prophet, whom Allah protect, may gaze upon me from afar with eyes sweetened with the honey of approval, and lips wreathed in garlanded smiles, whose essence shall exceed the Attar and the Spices in their surpassing odour.[16]

On a visit to England in 1910, Theodore Roosevelt gave a speech endorsing British involvement in Egypt, and impressing the need of a 'firm hand' as the only way to deal with 'uncivilized peoples, and especially with fanatical peoples'. Roosevelt went on to argue that 'civilized nations' should collaborate in 'conquering for civilization savage lands' and in 'subduing wild man and wild nature'. Infuriated by this representation of Egypt, Duse Mohamed Ali persuaded A.R. Orage to let him publish a refutation, which appeared in the *New Age*, which in the same issue published an article supporting Roosevelt's views. Duse Mohamed compared the Egyptian nationalists with the Irish, the Boers, the Japanese, and also the Americans, who found violence a necessary means in their independence struggles. The essay produced a continuing debate and series of letters in the *New Age*. Orage encouraged Duse Mohamed Ali to write a book on the subject, a history of Egypt, and helped him find a publisher, Stanley Paul. Duse also published an article along similar lines in *T.P.'s Magazine*,[17] a journal proclaimed by its editor, T.P. Connor, as 'a forum where everybody of every country, of every school, will be allowed to have his say ... The Western and the Oriental, the orthodox and the heterodox, the rebel and the stout advocate of existing things, all will have these pages for their free platform.'[18] Duse Mohamed Ali's two final contributions to these magazines, 'Quo Vadis' in the *New Age* and 'The Coloured Man in Art and Letters' in *T.P.'s Magazine* are interesting for their breadth of reference, their Pan-Africanist vision, and wide reading.[19] In 'The Coloured Man in Art and Letters', he writes of Booker T. Washington and W.E.B. DuBois as important complementary figures concerned with material and cultural progress for those of African descent. Edward Blyden, Frederick Douglass, J.J. Thomas (the author of *Froudacity*), and the Dominican intellectual A.J. Celistina-Edwards are also cited as significant contributors to political and cultural thought.

But it was his book on Egypt, *In the Land of the Pharaohs*, that put Duse Mohamed Ali on the national and international map. It addresses a British audience, and draws widely on black writers such as those referred to above. In the tradition established by Equiano for those who speak on behalf of an oppressed group, Duse Mohamed begins by establishing his authenticity and credentials. The frontispiece features a photograph of the author in a fez, thus clearly identifying Duse Mohamed as an Egyptian and as a black man. In his introductory pages, Duse Mohamed acknowledges the existence of many 'histories' of Egypt, and denounces their common lack of impartiality, accompanied by the increasing misrepresentation of Egypt in the English press, all prejudicial to home rule. He insists:

That I am qualified to deal adequately with the period under consideration, there need be little doubt. In the first place, I am a native Egyptian with a full knowledge of the aims of my fellow-countrymen, and consequently in sympathy with their sufferings – socially and politically. In the second-place, not only was I in the city of Alexandria during its bombardment, but the fact that my father was an officer in the Egyptian army and an ardent supporter of Ahmed Arabi – laying down his life gladly for the cause of Egyptian independence in the trenches of Tel-el-Kebir – gave me ample opportunities not only of coming into contact with many of the leaders of Egyptian reform, but of obtaining a first-hand knowledge of their views; a knowledge not imparted to any European then resident in Egypt, excepting of course Mr Wilfred Blunt and Sir William Gregory, and I believe Dr John Ninet.[20]

Having established that he can represent Egypt's cause 'as one having authority' (*Land of the Pharaohs*, p. 2), Duse Mohamed proceeds to denounce Orientalism in terms that will be reiterated by Edward Saïd over sixty years later. Declaring that contrary to the accusations 'of the usual "Oriental incapacity"' Arabi Pasha and his men were of 'unquestionable ability' and had already outlined the reforms later introduced by Lord Cromer, Duse Mohamed asserts, 'Colour prejudice is at the root of most of the "Oriental incapacity" which bulks so largely in English literature' (pp. 2–3). Whereas Anglo-Saxon educational achievement is accounted erudition, he notes, Oriental educational attainments are indiscriminately labelled 'educational veneer', or 'a veneer of Western culture'; and 'this applies not only to Orientals, but to all the coloured races of the world' (pp. 3–4). For Duse Mohamed the existence of elaborate Indian temples and buildings and complex religions in India and the East clearly refute claims of 'Oriental inferiority', and he points to the Alhambra Palace in Granada as exemplifying Islam's positive attitude towards life, in contrast to Christianity, especially Protestantism, which he sees as negative. Both as a journalist and a political commentator, Duse Mohamed thus belongs more in the tradition of Cugoano and Wedderburn than the more conciliatory mode of Mary Seacole or Cornelia Sorabji. Nevertheless he concludes his introduction by declaring, as do Equiano, Mary Prince, and later abolitionist writers, that it is because he believes 'the people of Great Britain to be, not only a freedom-loving race, but possessed of a genuine desire to see other nations as free as themselves', that he is 'emboldened to pen these pages' (p. 5).[21]

The book proves to be a scathing attack on British involvement in Egypt and the arrogance of British leaders, written with vigour and forceful but cutting sarcasm. Thus he describes in an appropriately long and swelling sentence, the inflated pretensions of Disraeli and his government entering upon the 1878 treaty which Duse Mohamed views as a bartering of their honour 'to cover up a political act of double-dealing and disgrace':

Preceded by paeans of Press adulation and theatrical display that might have done credit to the most exacting of Eastern potentates, the Rt Honourable Benjamin Disraeli, Earl of Beaconsfield and the Most Noble Marquis of Salisbury went forth in the summer of 1878 as befitted her Britannic Majesty's plenipotentiaries, on their triumphal progress towards the city of Berlin, where at that famous conference of the 13 June they were to determine the fate of European Turkey, and of the Christian subjects of His Sublime Majesty the Sultan. (p. 28)

In the Land of the Pharaohs offers in its approximately 300 pages a very detailed account of British and European involvement in Egypt in the latter part of nineteenth century, with an exposure of various intrigues, misunderstandings, and misrepresentations. Duse Mohamed affirms his intent to foreground a historical narrative that has been marginalized, and to write a counter-history when he presents his version of the Fashoda incident, an incident which Sir Reginald Wingate referred to as '"a nightmare which is better forgotten," and Lord Cromer, in his history, dismisses the subject with a footnote' (p. 243). In response to this attempted suppression of a 'nightmare' event in Egyptian history, Duse Mohamed resurrects and reinstates it as a crucial event in the history of Egyptian nationalism:

For my part I have given it prominence, partly because of its being the key to the *aggressive* Nationalist agitation that followed, and also because of the unjust accusations of disloyalty brought against the Egyptian officers; and, finally, by reason of its effect upon native opinion with regard to the subsequent intentions of Great Britain in Egypt. (p. 243)

Duse Mohamed not only retells Egyptian history 'from the inside', but also denounces Western justifications for their imperial mission, insisting that the claim to be involved in a civilizing enterprise is a mere disguise for materialist interests. His condemnation of British materialism echoes that of Yeats and other Irish intellectuals, and will be reiterated in later years by African and Caribbean intellectuals and leaders such as Césaire and Senghor:

Thus England, in the multiplication of her conquests, whereby trade is advanced, plutocrats wax rich and opulent, and in the interests of 'civilisation' and 'Christianisation' of primitive races, and races that are not primitive, who are held in tutelage and subjection 'for their moral welfare', so that there might be diamond princes and cotton kings, and other grades of a most ignoble band of financial aristocrats, only paving the path of materialism with the agonised groans of human subjugation, at the end of which lies her utter dissolution. (pp. 215–16)

Duse Mohamed's powerfully expressed political arguments and moral indignation are interspersed by contemptuous but humorous caricatures of 'arrogant, self-seeking' Englishmen in the Egyptian civil service. He represents them as of two types: the one a young aristocrat with no training or equipment, the other a 'nondescript' who works his way up by fawning. The latter he names 'Mr Swellibus', who goes out and meets those 'in his class who malign the climate, the native, and everything in "beastly Egypt, don't you know"' (p. 219). Mr Swellibus has a 'nigger' to look after his togs and clean his boots, he settles in the European quarter with servants for himself and his wife, and acquires a lifestyle far more luxurious than anything that would have been possible for him back in England. Thus, Duse Mohamed claims, it is in the interest of Mr Swellibus to keep Egyptians uneducated, unable to progress and fill his place. He responds to claims that 'Egyptians are not ripe for self-government' by declaring that 'no more were the people of England ripe for Lord John Russell's Bill' extending the franchise, a bill opposed by the Tories of the time. The book concludes by prophesying the end of a British empire, weakened internally by the growing opposition of oppressed subject races and externally by the growing strength of Japan.

Clearly addressed to a British audience, and proclaiming the author's credentials as a spokesman for the Egyptian nationalist, *In the Land of the Pharaohs* was widely and sympathetically reviewed in Britain as well as India and the United States (an American edition was brought out in 1911). Although Duse Mohamed's reception in Britain was somewhat dented by revelations that large sections of the book were plagiarized, this does not seem to have affected the high esteem with which he continued to be held in the United States and Africa.[22] The shadow cast on his reputation in Britain, and the favourable reception he received in the United States and elsewhere, may well have encouraged Duse Mohamed Ali to set up his own journal addressed to an international and non-European audience as well as to sympathizers in Britain, the *African Times and Orient Review*.

In 1911 the Universal Races Congress was held in London, attended by intellectuals and political activists from all over the world. The executive council of the congress passed a resolution advocating the establishment of '"a journal of Comparative Civilisation" for the discussion of burning social and economic questions of the day from the standpoints of the different national civilisations, ideals, and values'.[23] Certainly this resolution, which Duse Mohamed Ali refers to in the first issue of the *African Times and Orient Review*, was an important inspiration for the journal he set up, and the cover design by Walter Crane (an angel of peace, Concordia, holding hands with Africa and Asia) was a modified version of the congress insignia. Moreover, many of the journal's subscribers had been participants in the congress, and thus provided him with an international readership. However, it was a Sierra Leonean businessman, John Eldred Taylor, who provided the finance. Taylor wished to set up a commercial journal to promote trade and investment between the coast of West Africa and Europe, but he agreed to allow Duse Mohamed to combine commerce with culture and politics as the journal's brief, and established him as editor, director, and manager, with an office at 158 Fleet Street. Despite changing management and support (after the first issue, Taylor was ousted by a group of other West African businessmen and professionals, including J. Casely Hayford), and the financial collapse of the company in 1914, Duse Mohamed Ali managed to keep the journal going, sometimes sporadically, for almost nine years. In its final emanation, from January till December 1920, it was retitled the *Africa and Orient Review*.[24]

The first issue, which appeared in July 1912, announced itself 'A monthly journal devoted to the Interests of the coloured Races of the World', and listed 'Politics, Literature, Art, Commerce' as the areas it would address. The editorial cites the 'recent Universal Races Congress, convened in the Metropolis of the Anglo-Saxon world' as having 'clearly demonstrated that there was ample need for a Pan-Oriental Pan-African journal at the seat of the British Empire, which would lay the aims, desires and intentions of the Black, brown, and Yellow races – within and without the Empire – at the throne of Caesar'.[25] The editorial goes on to argue that 'an understanding of the views and cultures of these peoples, so consistently distorted and garbled in the British press, would bring love and admiration', for 'we as natives and loyal subjects of the British Empire, hold too high an opinion of Anglo-Saxon chivalry to believe other than that African and Oriental wrongs have but to be made manifest in order that they may be righted'. And it concludes that the aim of the journal is no less than the achievement of 'universal brotherhood between White, Yellow, Brown, and Black under the protecting folds of the Grand Old Flag'.[26] On the second page of this first issue the editor's range of sympathies and reading is indicated by his call for contributions from the 'young and budding Sun Yet Sens, the Mustapha Kamils, the Blydens, the Conrad Reeveses, the embryo Frederick Douglasses, and Paul Laurence Dunbars'. The African and Oriental wrongs made manifest include a critical report of the Canadian government's refusal to allow visas to the spouse and children of Sikhs studying there, and a graphic and caustic account of the public flogging of two northern Nigerian clerks in Zaria for their failure to prostrate themselves before a minor British official. This story made a strong impact in Britain and elsewhere, and in the process attracted the support for the journal and its editor of a group of prominent West African professionals and businessmen, including J. Casely Hayford, Dr Quartey-Papafio, and E.J.P. Brown from the Gold Coast, all three of whom were members of the Gold Coast Aborigines Rights Protection Society.[27]

To attract written contributions and subscribers, Duse wrote to various prominent intellectuals and leaders asking them to comment on whether a 'newspaper operated by coloured people' would be appreciated by the British public, and whether it would 'promote goodwill between Orient and Occident'. He received and published replies, many of them rather brief and evasive, from Booker T. Washington, the Countess of Warwick, Annie Besant, Sir Sydney Olivier (Governor of Jamaica), Hugh Massingham (editor of the *Nation*), A.R. Orage, and Samuel Coleridge-Taylor, the distinguished British musician of Sierra Leonean descent. Duse was not much impressed by the terse response from W.E.B. DuBois, 'I think it would be a good thing if a review like yours could be supported in London, but I do not see how it could possibly pay.'[28] In Duse's view such a comment was 'disappointing and pointless'.

In addition to these reports and a full-page advertisement and citations from glowing reviews for *In the Land of the Pharaohs* and also for a second book by Duse Mohamed, *The King that Was*,[29] this inaugural issue includes a report on 'The Negro Conference at Tuskegee' with photographs of the assembled delegates,[30] as well as an account of the 'First Universal Races Congress', held at the University of London, 26–29 July 1911. There is an article on 'The Race Problems of Hawaii' by James A. Rath, and the first of a series of short essays on Morocco by Charles Rosher (a white journalist who dressed in Moroccan attire). Apart from a poem, 'If I were King', by Joan Vanderbilt, much of the rest of this inaugural

issue is made up of Duse Mohamed Ali's own compositions, including
a witty satirical poem, 'Poor Pompey's Plea to Caesar', the first of a series of 'national poems' in ottava rima published under the pseudonym
'Delta'.[31] He wrote many of the book reviews, mainly of books on Africa,
Morocco, and the situation of the American Negro, including a novel
by Frances Grierson on slavery, *The Valley of the Shadows*, which Duse
Mohamed considered superior to *Uncle Tom's Cabin* and more likely to
endure. Under the nom-de-plume 'the Stage Stallite' he reviewed theatrical events, and there is a critical review of Henry Beerbohm Tree's
Othello, objecting that the custom of playing Othello as 'a cocoa-coloured
Arab' and the 'gradual white-washing' of Othello in British and American productions runs against the language of the text.[32] Additionally,
Duse Mohamed penned a regular feature titled 'A Monthly Round in
London Town' which casts an ironic eye upon such events as lectures on
missionary activities, on alcoholism in Nigeria, and on 'The Black Peril'
in South Africa – attacks by black youths on 'unprotected white women
and girls'. While censuring such attacks, Duse Mohamed also points out
the lack of reporting of the many more frequent attacks on black women
by white men.[33]

This first issue sets the pattern for those that appeared during the
next two years of the *African Times and Orient Review's* life. Subsequent
numbers include contributions from Marcus Garvey, who worked as a
messenger boy for the *Review* in 1912 and 1913,[34] Booker T. Washington
(a lengthy piece on Tuskegee Institute, with pictures of the buildings),
Casely Hayford on the Gold Coast Land Tenure and Forest Bill, 1911
(with an enormous pull-out photograph of chiefs and dignitaries assembled to protest against the bill), Manuel Garcia on 'The Truth about
Cuba', and the Indian journalist and activist Sundara Raja on atrocities
in Persia, and the role of Russia and England. There are essays on Abdul
Baha, leader of the Bahai movement, on West African marriage customs,
on lynchings of Negroes in the United States (accompanied by grim photographs), and on European and US economic pressure on Japan and
its effects on cultural and racial relations. These diverse political essays
are interspersed with trade advertisements for such enterprises as the
Uganda Railway situated in 'British East Africa: the Land of Superior
Settlers',[35] and cultural reviews and contributions. Duse Mohamed Ali
himself wrote a long appreciation of the eminent black British musician
Samuel Coleridge-Taylor, accompanied by an obituary, a full-page photograph, and a facsimile of his letter to the editor written three days
before his death.[36] There are dialect poems such as Charles D. Clem's

'Fetch Dat Slippah Heah',[37] a parody of Kipling's verse titled 'If Kipling were a Negro',[38] and poems by Sarojini Naidu, the Indian poet and future politician who was in London during those years and a member of Yeats' 'Monday Evening Circle'. An article on Ira Aldridge, whom Duse Mohamed refers to as 'the African Roscius',[39] is preceded in an earlier number by a review of his daughter Luranah's recital in London on 7 June 1913, accompanied by her sister Ina.

Christmas 1912 saw a lavishly illustrated bumper Christmas issue, featuring two short stories by Duse Mohamed Ali, 'Katebet the Priestess' and 'Abdul' published under his own name, as well as a series of vignettes titled 'British Museum Types' under the pseudonym 'Delta'. Of the two stories, 'Katebet the Priestess' is perhaps the most interesting for its setting in Egypt and its use of a strident Cockney dialect to represent an ill-informed pair of English tourists unimpressed by Egyptian mummies in a museum. As they pause before the remains of Katebet, 'rescued from oblivion to be exposed to the vulgar gaze and yet more vulgar jest of the thoughtless multitude, ticketed like some felon with the number 6665', the following dialogue takes place:

> 'Sai, Bill! wot price the bloke's toe-rags?'
> 'Don't be silly, Emma; it ain't a bloke, it's a lady.'[40]

But while Emma remains oblivious and insensitive, the story takes an intriguing turn when Bill (who is an apprentice to a bookbinder) becomes possessed and hears the priestess speak and tell her story. As a consequence of hearing this story, Bill is transformed, and becomes aware of a much wider world and philosophy than he has hitherto inhabited. The story thus demonstrates that Arnoldian optimism expressed in the inaugural issue's editorial, that 'an understanding of the views and cultures of these peoples, so consistently distorted and garbled in the British press, [will] bring love and admiration'.

In 1914, the journal's financial difficulties became insuperable and it ceased publication until 1917. Duse Mohamed later claimed that the unwillingness of banks or printers to give him credit was largely due to pressure exercised by Sir William Lever, the soap manufacturer, following the publication in the *Review* of a satiric cartoon and report exposing Lever's exploitation of African workers and farmers and fraudulent activities in West Africa.[41]

But Duse Mohamed could not be suppressed, and the *Review* reappeared, somewhat intermittently, in 1917 and 1918. These later issues feature many poems and political articles by the Ghanaian Kobina Sekyi.

The nature and love lyrics by Sekyi form a contrast to his acute political analyses and reports, some of which are critical of the Garveyite and Booker T. Washington views (supported by Duse Mohamed) on commercial self-help as the best hope for African and Asian progress. There are also strong nationalist essays from Sundara Raja concerning the destruction of Indian cottage industries by the imposition of British trade rules, and from Shaikh M.H. Kidwai denouncing moderate Indian leaders and British policies.[42] At the same time, Duse as editor proclaims his support for the British empire 'to the last drop of blood and to the last penny in the coffers'.[43] These later volumes continue to feature contributions from W.F. Hutchinson, a Ghanaian who had lived in England for some time, as the journal's war correspondent, reporting on the role of coloured troops both on the battle front and in the factories supplying materials and weapons for the war effort.[44] Hutchinson was later to become the journal's deputy editor while Duse Mohamed Ali was travelling to West Africa in 1920. The October 1918 number includes an 'Open letter to Sir Arthur Conan Doyle' responding to his assertion that it is 'unthinkable' that the African colonies 'should be returned to the detriment of the Natives'. The letter argues that their not being returned to self-government' would be even more – and has long been – to the detriment of the natives.

After a hiatus in 1919, the journal was relaunched as the *Africa and Orient Review*, with an Egyptian number in January 1920, and a sphinx featured on its newly designed cover. Its aspirations to a diverse and inclusive readership are indicated on its cover, which announces, 'If you are a Cabinet Minister / If you are a Thinker / If you are a Writer / If you are a Politician / If you are a Publicist – *The Africa and Orient Review* is of necessity to you.' The ten issues published during 1920 contained the same diverse political and cultural mixture as the earlier version of the journal, but also included a regular autobiographical series titled 'Vis-a-Vis', in which Duse Mohamed Ali related his 'impressions of Important and other Personages' he had met. The first account is of his encounter with King Edward ('Good old Teddy!') at the Savoy theatre in the eighties. Introduced by D'Oyley Carte to the then Prince of Wales as Mohamed, 'a young friend of Sullivan's from Egypt', the Prince asked jokingly whether he was 'the son of one of Arabi Pasha's rebels'.[45] Duse Mohamed replied that his father had died fighting for Egypt's liberty, and the Prince spoke of his admiration for those ready to die for their convictions, whether those convictions were right or wrong. While the Prince and Duse Mohamed clearly differed on this matter, the latter asserts that the Prince was a true gentleman, who belonged to 'the good old days when a man of breeding was respected in England – and there was no "colour bar"'. Such respect for the 'darker peoples' of the empire and their religions and cultures, Duse Mohamed ascribes to the insistence of Queen Victoria. Like earlier writers such as William Allen, Thomas Johnson, and Mary Seacole, he views later manifestations of colour prejudice as the consequence of American influences, and 'the invasion of a herd of cheap Americans who subsequently came to teach the Briton not only how to make money quickly, but also how to ruin the Empire with greater expedition by classifying all men of colour as "niggers"'.[46]

Other 'Personages' commented on in the 'Vis-a-Vis' series were Oscar Wilde (of whom Duse Mohamed disapproved), Dadabhai Naoroji (celebrated as England's first coloured MP and spokesman for Indian Home Rule), Cecil Chesterton, Sir William Conrad Reeve, and Frank Hugh O'Donnell (the Irish nationalist MP who also supported Indian and Egyptian nationalists). The accounts are narrated in an informal colloquial style, with a mixture of self-deprecation and self-aggrandizement, and sometimes allow a humorous anecdote, as when a foreign diplomat falls asleep in front of the ever loquacious O'Donnell. They reveal something of Duse Mohamed's own sense of status in these later years, while also revealing his earlier more diffident self, and they evoke a world in which colour was perhaps less of a bar than class when it came to social and cultural mingling. However, Duse Mohamed's comparatively rosy view of those late Victorian decades must be qualified by the experiences which are not recounted in the *Africa and Orient Review*, but which are allowed to resurface in his later autobiographical series published after he had emigrated to Nigeria in the *Comet*), when he is writing for a specifically Nigerian rather than a British audience.[47]

Duse Mohamed continued his journalistic career in Nigeria, where he published numerous articles, became managing editor of the Lagos *Times* and (briefly and concurrently) the *Daily Telegraph*, and from 1933 until his death in 1945, the *Comet* (later the *Daily Comet*). Since these articles and enterprises were addressed to a West African audience mainly, I have not included them in this discussion.

Duse Mohamed Ali cannot be deemed either an outstanding writer or a profound thinker. He is not averse to clichés and there are many inconsistencies in his arguments. Nevertheless he is a fascinating figure whose life and work demonstrate his times, and the varied ways in which white and black Britons interacted during almost four decades when the empire was at its height. Duse Mohamed grasped what opportunities he could, and the founding and maintenance of the *African Times and Orient Review* and its successor was a significant achievement, giving expression to the views and aspirations of many major and minor participants in the development of nationalist, Pan-African and Pan-Asian thought. His journal spoke up for the civil rights of all peoples, while his insistence that Africa and the Orient should form a broad resistance to British prejudice and imperialist aims went far beyond the Pan-Africanism that characterized American and Caribbean movements of the time, and it is only in more recent years that collaboration between members of 'the Third World' has become accepted as a *sine qua non*. Moreover the journal achieved a remarkably wide readership, reaching out to almost all areas of the British empire, the Americas and beyond. Among the places which had agents for the *African Times and Orient Review* were West Africa, South Africa, New York, Louisville, Memphis, Los Angeles, the West Indies, Canada, Australia, New Zealand, Cairo, Tokyo, Calcutta, Lahore, Kuala Lumpur, and Colombo.[48]

LATER ANTI-IMPERIAL JOURNALS

While the first half of his career suggests that Duse Mohamed Ali was not unlike many of his predecessors and contemporaries in seeking to work within and speak to a majority Anglo-Saxon and Anglo-Celtic society, his founding and editing of the *African Times and Orient Review* suggests a changing focus. Now his writing is addressed just as much to an audience outside as well as inside the United Kingdom, and he appeals directly to Britain's coloured population for support and contributions. This change to a multiple rather than a single audience inside and outside Britain becomes characteristic of a series of journals and newspapers based in Britain in subsequent years. Just as the African businessmen and politicians who supported the *African Times and Orient Review* saw the usefulness of setting up a journal in the heart of the empire, and manipulating the English cultural scene and its tools to express their own aspirations, so too a number of other Caribbean, African, and south Asian intellectuals and activists engaged in similar strategies.

One such journal was the *Islamic Review*, to which Duse Mohamed Ali contributed a series of essays on Islamic thought and culture and which was advertised in the first and subsequent issues of the *African Times and Orient Review*. An earlier and far less conservative journal was the *Indian Sociologist*, a penny monthly, edited by Shyamaji Krishnavarma, a lawyer educated at Balliol College, who settled in England in 1897. As noted in a previous chapter, he was the founder of India House, a hostel for Indian students in London, and the India Home Rule Society. The *Indian Sociologist*, published more or less regularly from 1 January 1905 till July 1914, was fiercely anti-imperialist, and sought to remind the British public that 'they can never succeed in being a nation of freemen and lovers of freedom so long as they continue to send members of the dominant classes to exercise despotism in Britain's name upon the various conquered races that constitute Britain's military power'.[49] An admirer of Herbert Spencer, Krishnavarma adopted one of his statements as the paper's motto: 'Every man is free to do that which he wills, provided he infringes not the equal freedom of any other man.'[50] He advocated the necessity of resisting aggression, and believed physical force would be necessary to eject the British from India, declaring that 'the only methods which can bring the English government to its senses are the Russian methods'.[51]

A similar ideology was later expressed through the pages of the *International Negro Workers' Review*, which first appeared in 'hectographed' form in the late 1920s, and then as a monthly journal as *The Negro Worker*. Although published in Hamburg, then Copenhagen, and finally Paris, it was an English-language journal, mainly concerned with conditions in British Africa and the African diaspora, and made up of a high proportion of articles by London-based intellectuals such as George Padmore, I.T.A. Wallace Johnson, and Arnold Ward.[52] These authors, along with other Marxists, also contributed to the *African Sentinel* and *International African Opinion*, both of which appeared in the 1930s. Additionally *International African Opinion* in the late 1930s published essays by many others, including Jomo Kenyatta, Nancy Cunard, and T. Ras Makonnen.

Contemporaneously with the *Negro Worker*, appeared an ideologically more eclectic journal, *WASU*, the voice of the West African Students' Union, whose first issue appeared in March 1926. Although primarily an acronym for the union, founded in London in 1925, the title simultaneously referred to a Yoruba word meaning 'to preach', a Ghanaian term for 'self-help', and an Igbo word meaning 'to speak first in one's own interest'.[53] Contributions largely reflected the concerns of students from West Africa, and placed considerable emphasis on Yoruba culture and law, but there were also contributions from the distinguished African American scholar, Alain Locke,[54] and in a 1935 issue an article from Paul Robeson titled, 'I Want Negro Culture.'[55]

The 1930s also saw Marcus Garvey resident in London and editing his journal, *The Black Man*. This journal consisted largely of Garvey's own writings, frequently attacking other black leaders such as his old enemy DuBois, and ignoring groups in London such as WASU. However, *The Black Man* did at times publish interesting contributions from others such as the Guyanan short-story writer, Eric Walrond, who settled in England in 1932. His essays published in Garvey's journal include 'The Negro Before the World', 'The Negro in the Armies of Europe', 'A Fugitive from Dixie', 'On England', and 'The Negro in London'.[56] In this second quarter of the century, the strong African American influence tended to emphasize a Pan-Africanist approach, to the benefit of nationalist movements in Africa and the African diaspora, but also at times to the detriment of the vision of Oriental and African unity earlier embraced by Duse Mohamed Ali.

One exception was a more broad-based and middle-class periodical, *The Keys*, the journal of the League of Coloured Peoples in London, which although mainly concerned with issues affecting peoples of African descent, also addressed discrimination against Asian people in Britain and the colonies. The League of Coloured Peoples had been founded by the Jamaican-born physician Harold Moody in 1931 to form a united resistance to racial prejudice and discrimination.[57] *The Keys* appeared four times a year, and was edited by such eminent intellectuals as W. Arthur Lewis, Una Marson, and Peter Blackman while they were resident in London. Each issue of the journal printed the aims of the League:

To promote and protect the Social, Educational, Economic, and Political interests of its members; to interest members in the Welfare of Coloured peoples in all parts of the World; to improve relations between the Races; to cooperate and affiliate with organizations sympathetic to coloured people.[58]

Although frequently criticized for its moderate stance and 'elitism', *The Keys* and its later manifestation, *The League of Coloured Peoples' Newsletter*, consistently exposed and attacked many scandalous cases of discrimination and injustice, both in Britain and abroad. It led the fight to seek justice for coloured seamen in Cardiff in 1935, it was outspoken in defence of Haile Selassie and Ethiopia following Mussolini's attack in 1935, and it was highly critical of British policy in the West Indies. Contributors included intellectuals as diverse as C.L.R. James and Alistair Cooke, and the journal maintained a high standard throughout its life from 1931 until 1939.[59] Its successor, *The League of Coloured Peoples' Newsletter* appeared as a small monthly pamphlet throughout the 1940s. Less impressive in format than *The Keys*, the *Newsletter* nevertheless continued to publish essays from such distinguished contributors as Paul Robeson, Learie Constantine, George Padmore, W. Arthur Lewis, and Eric Williams.[60]

In October 1945 the fifth Pan-African Conference was held in Manchester and was one of the events which stimulated a new monthly publication, *Pan-Africa*, managed and edited by T. Ras Makonnen, an immigrant and successful restauranteur from Guyana. The editorial board included George Padmore, the South African journalist and novelist Peter Abrahams, and Dinah Stock, an English sociologist who had assisted Jomo Kenyatta in the writing of *Facing Mount Kenya*. *Pan-Africa* described itself as a journal of African life, history and thought, and incorporated not only Anglophone Africa and the African diaspora in the Americas, but also Francophone and Lusophone Africans. It was a substantial journal, but produced only eleven issues during 1947 before its banning by colonial governments and harassment of subscribers forced it to close down. Contributors included W.E.B. DuBois, Langston Hughes, and Rayford W. Logan.[61]

These varied journals and news sheets were significant for providing a voice and a sense of community for black and Asian people in Britain, as well as a means of dialogue between the metropolis and the 'outposts' of the empire. Moreover, their publication and promotion of works by African American scholars, poets, and writers created a milieu and model for intellectuals of Caribbean, African, and Asian descent who had settled in Britain and whose writings will be discussed in greater detail in the following chapter.

CHAPTER 10

Subaltern voices and the construction of a global vision

Writing in 1984, C.L.R. James looked forward to a generation of black people born and educated in Britain, 'intimately related to British people', but never completely part of the British environment because of their colour. He went on to assert: 'Now that is not a negative statement. Some of the finest writers on western civilisation, Dr W.E.B. DuBois and Richard Wright, have written from that perspective.'[1]

Among some of those finest writers one might also include C.L.R. James, who is in many ways the foremost example of a generation who came in the 1930s and 1940s to Britain from the colonies to seek wider opportunities for knowledge and the fulfilment of their considerable potential. Like DuBois, he was thoroughly immersed in the major literary, philosophical, and historical writings produced in the West; like DuBois he wrote in a number of genres – fiction, history, political philosophy and commentary, history, the essay, and in James's case, drama; like DuBois also, he invented new combinations of these genres in order to express the multiple experience and consciousness of black people who are both a part of and apart from 'western civilisation'.

Cyril Lionel Robert James was born in Trinidad in 1901, came to Britain in 1932, and except for fifteen years in the United States (from 1938 till 1953) and four years in the West Indies (from 1958 till 1962), made his home there until his death in 1989. In an autobiographical essay James categorically affirms that 'the origins of [his] thoughts are to be found in Western European literature, Western European history, and Western European thought'.[2] He claims further that his generation was influenced by 'the tenets of Matthew Arnold', seeking to bring 'sweetness and light' to the people. As a young man in Trinidad, he personally subscribed to over a dozen leading English, French, and American newspapers and magazines, and he read all the great authors he could in the local library. James insists that he was not exceptional in his reading, which he shared with his boyhood friend George Padmore, and it compared in its range with the reading of another Caribbean contemporary, the Martiniquan poet Aimé Césaire; all three of them were to become Marxists. But as he explains in this essay and in his autobiography, *Beyond a Boundary*, being black in the West Indies in the 1930s meant that in order to progress and to widen one's opportunities, he had to go abroad. And he places the leading Caribbean writers in the same category as Conrad, Eliot, Yeats, Joyce – all foreigners and the most important writers of this century. All of them are 'men who know the language and can take part in the civilisation, but are not part of it, who are outsiders and looking at it from the outside'. In his view the 'only English writer who can stand up is D.H. Lawrence – and he couldn't live in England at all'.[3]

James had made his living in the 1920s in Trinidad as a school-teacher and as a reporter on cricket, a game he himself played regularly. With writers such as Albert Gomes, Ralph de Boissière, and Alfred Mendes, he also helped to found two literary journals, *Trinidad* (1929–30) and *The Beacon* (1931–3), where his earliest short stories and essays were published.

In 1932, the leading cricketer Learie Constantine invited James to join him in Lancashire and help write his autobiography. It was a period of industrial unrest and radical activity among the factory workers in Nelson, Lancashire, where Constantine lived. There James completed work on a short biography of Captain André Cipriani, a French Creole mayor of Port of Spain, who had been outspoken in his criticism of the colonial government.[4] The opening paragraphs of this political biography establish a style and voice which will be typical of James' later writings, a voice which is direct, precise, and sure of its position; a style which is plain, suggests speech rather than literary syntax, but handles crescendo, cadence, and balance with powerful effect, as in the following sentences:

During the last eighteen years, [Cipriani] has been engaged in a series of struggles against the bad manners, the injustice, the tyranny, and the treachery of Crown Colony Government. This book will give a plain and documented account of these struggles. The movement seeks a change in the constitution. The remedy to be applied must be constitutional.[5]

A condensed version of *The Life of Captain Cipriani* was published a year later by Leonard and Virginia Woolf's Hogarth Press under the title, *The Case for West Indian Self-Government*. In that same year, James became a regular reporter on cricket for the *Manchester Guardian*. Indeed, the six years James spent in England before his departure for the United States in 1938 were extraordinarily productive. In 1936 he published his one novel,

Minty Alley. He studied the works of Trotsky, Marx, Engels, and Lenin, became an active member of the International Labour Party and one of its leading spokesmen, wrote his study of the Communist International, *World Revolution*, organised the International African Friends of Ethiopia (later to become the International African Service Bureau – the IASB) to oppose Italian aggression, and wrote the play, *Toussaint L'Ouverture*. This play was staged in March 1936 at the Westminster Theatre in London with Paul Robeson in the main role and James himself in a smaller part. It had grown out of material he was working on for his important historical study, *The Black Jacobins*, and a more general *History of Negro Revolt*, both published in 1938. During these years he also edited the IASB journal, *International African Opinion*, and, in 1937 and 1938, the Marxist Trotskyist paper, *Fight* (later renamed *Workers' Fight*).

Biographer, historian, political theorist, activist, public speaker, dramatist, novelist, sports writer, essayist, literary critic: at first glance one might consider James so disparate in his output that it is impossible to find a central core. But such diversity is not exceptional in black and south Asian writing, as the work of DuBois, Wright and Baldwin in North America demonstrates, and in Britain the writings and activities of Cornelia Sorabji, Duse Mohamed Ali, Mulk Raj Anand, and, later, Stuart Hall. For C.L.R. James, as for some of his predecessors and contemporaries, the varied writings and lectures were tied to a shared and urgent concern to give a voice and presence to the people ignored or dismissed in the historical and literary works in the European canon. Thus *Minty Alley* rejects a late nineteenth-century or Georgian poetic aesthetic which eschews social comment to focus on neither the world of the 'big house' in the Caribbean, nor that of the rural landscape and peasantry, nor the growing interest in folklore and folk forms.[6] And while his contemporaries and fellow-members of the *Beacon* group in Trinidad, Albert Gomes and Alfred Mendes, advocated a literature which broke away from 'self-indulgent primitivism',[7] or enslavement to British traditions, and sought to depict the lives of the poor and 'barrack yard' life, their works suffer from a rather distanced and sociological view of the characters they portray. *Minty Alley* is a vivid and often disturbing representation of a household in the slum district of Port of Spain, based in part on James' own observations when he rented lodgings in a similar house. But unlike many other novelists of this period who adopt socialist realist precepts and underline a political moral or programme, James allows the world he portrays to live and speak within its own terms, manifestly confused and incoherent as they may be.

James effectively deals with the problem of the distance between the author (as well as his readers) and his characters by making this part of his literary subject. The people and events are all seen through the often bemused point of view of Haynes, a twenty-year-old assistant in the town's only bookshop, who takes a rented room in a ramshackle boarding-house in the poorer area of the city. Indeed, James emphasizes the limitations and incompleteness of Haynes' vision through recurring images of his peering and listening through cracks in his wall, over-hearing snatches of conversation, puzzling about the meaning of the partial scenes and arguments he has glimpsed. This device draws in the reader, who seeks to interpret and piece together those fragments, while also accentuating the naivete of Haynes and the barriers between the bookish world in which his fiercely protective mother and her servant have nurtured him and the much more jagged and fluid world which the boarding-house dwellers inhabit.

As in many later Caribbean and black British novels, the house serves as a metaphor for society, encompassing various gradations of colour, ethnicity, and class. Haynes observes variations of colour with detailed precision, and the foregrounding of such observations tells the reader much about the attention paid to degrees of colour in Caribbean society, as well as the links between colour, class, and social status. On first meeting Mrs Rouse, the owner of the house, he notes that she is plump but shapely, and that 'her face was a smooth light-brown with a fine aquiline nose and well-cut firm lips. The strain of white ancestry responsible for the nose was not recent, for her hair was coarse and essentially negroid'(*Minty Alley*, p. 29). Her niece, Maisie, he remarks is 'not as light in colour as the aunt', but nevertheless 'smooth-skinned and brown'. On his first morning in the house, he observes two young black men working in the kitchen, a 'long, bony black girl', and then 'a little boy, nearly white', and 'wonders at the presence of so fair a skin among all those dark people' (p. 32). Soon after this he meets the landlord, Mr Benoit, whose 'very dark skin and curly hair showed traces of Indian blood', and Philomen the Indian servant, who is 'fat, and brown and pleasant-looking' (p. 33). And finally, the household is aroused to excitement and a flurry of activity by the arrival of the little boy's mother, spoken of always as 'the Nurse', 'a short, thin, fair woman in nurse's uniform' (p. 33). Together, the nurse's profession and colour give her a kind of status and glamour within the household enhanced by her bringing of luxury gifts (liquor and cake), her display of relative economic superiority, and her determination to send her son to an exclusive private school for which she pays two dollars a month.

But while the nurse brings order and communal life to the household, for which she is a focus of discussion and a source of recognition, she also brings disturbance to Haynes' world, and revelations of sexuality, tension, and violence underlying the surface order and glamour of her microcosm. Lying on his bed and peering through a crack in the wall, Haynes the voyeur observes first the servant girl being kissed by Benoit, and then Benoit embracing the nurse. Excited by these passionate exchanges, Haynes suddenly acknowledges his own sexual interest:

To read about these things in books was one thing, to hear and see them another. And Haynes, though passionately interested in women and always reading about them, had never since he had grown up kissed or been kissed by a woman who was not related to him . . . And here now he had been pitch-forked into the heart of the eternal triangle. (p. 37)

That last phrase, his reading of what he has observed in such overdramatized and cliched terms as 'pitch-forked into the heart of the eternal triangle', reveals that Haynes is still caught within the framework and discourse of his literary world. A little later his identity as voyeur rather than participant is emphasized as he sits 'waiting to see the household set about its daily tasks', feeling that 'the stage was set for a terrific human drama' (p. 38).

But the human drama is more than he can handle – and he is forced to become an unwilling and ineffective participant in one of the most disturbing scenes in the novel, the nurse's savage beating of her child, a scene which shocks the reader out of a complaisant view of the household, and works as a prelude to our understanding of the tensions and desperation which underlie so much of that world where economic survival is a continual struggle. When the boy is first struck (for playfully asking Maisie for a kiss), he runs naked to Haynes for protection: 'He was stark naked and his whole body heaved. All over his skin the cane had raised red weals of flesh, one almost continuous from the left shoulder across the chest almost down to the navel' (p. 43). The nurse makes it clear that the longer he stays away the longer the beating that awaits him, sits calmly with the cane by her side, and cruelly taunts the child when he pleads for pardon:

'Mammy! Mammy! Beg Pardon!' sneered the nurse, and showed her teeth in a smile for the first time. She shook the cane playfully at him. 'Doggie! Doggie! Look bone!' she said. (p. 45)

As he listens to the boy's screams and 'the thud of the cane on the little body', Haynes is filled with distress and shame at his failure to intervene.

Like the rest of the people in the household, he accepts the cruel beating as terrible but unavoidable. The event is deplored by all, and yet witnessed as if yet another drama. Nevertheless, when the nurse comes to attend to his hurt foot that same evening and on a daily basis thereafter, Haynes accepts her ministrations and says not a word about the beating.

The reader shares with Haynes a fascination with the passion, volatility, complexity, and suffering played out in the household. There is plenty of drama, indeed melodrama, to be staged. And yet Haynes is reluctant to see himself as a player, although the reader – and indeed the other characters – are much more aware of the role he plays as a prize lodger, a man of books who could be a counsellor, a wise listener. As such he fails to take upon himself the authority his education and status give him; he desires to remain an onlooker, and in that sense might be seen representative of the educated lower-middle class in Trinidad, who accept the status their education gives them, but not its responsibilities. He neither seeks to analyze and understand the reasons for the incoherence of the lives led by the poor, nor can he respond adequately to their passion. The potential and hunger for a fuller, richer life is dramatized particularly by Maisie, the wilful, lively, witty young niece of Mrs Rouse, who is attracted to Haynes by his world of books, music, culture, and eventually seduces him. Rather like Pegeen in Synge's *Playboy of the Western World*, she 'makes a man' of this rather timid and unassertive outsider who represents the richer and fuller world she yearns for, although in the end it is Maisie who leaves the narrow but vibrant world of the backyard and emigrates to America. Like Synge also, James makes his characters live through the power and vitality of their speech, while at the same time presenting the harsh economic reality of their daily lives.[8] Part of James' achievement in this, his only novel, arises from his willingness to refrain from authorial explanation and intrusion. As Kenneth Ramchand points out, the partial vision which comes through Haynes' perspective and protected youth 'limits his ability to guess, the characters retain autonomy as familiar but not fully known beings. Each has a mysterious life of his own.'[9] And as Ramchand also remarks, *Minty Alley* allows the reader to comprehend 'the mutually impoverishing alienation of the educated West Indian from the people'.

In the same year that *Minty Alley* was published, James wrote the play *Toussaint L'Ouverture*,[10] which the management of the Westminster Theatre agreed to stage if he could persuade Paul Robeson to play the lead role. This he did. James writes amusingly about the rehearsals for the play, when Robeson would firmly suggest major cuts in the long and rather static speeches James had composed.[11] Although Robeson's performance was praised, the play itself received ambivalent notices. Charles Darwin, critic for the *Times*, found the play interesting and informative, but rather static and wooden in its dialogue, while Ivor Brown, writing for the *Observer*, wished that the dialogue was less prosaic and more poetic. Both critics, however, applauded the portrayal of Toussaint L'Ouverture, as a character of powerful intelligence, acting through 'reasoned determination' rather than the 'whining' or 'hysterically defiant tone' that Darwin had expected in a play about slavery![12]

The expectations about the play, and the desire for a more 'poetic' form and language might well have been encouraged by Eugene O'Neill's *The Emperor Jones*, which played to considerable acclaim – again with Paul Robeson in the lead – in London in 1928. O'Neill's play is not explicitly about Toussaint L'Ouverture, but it is about a 'Negro' who becomes lord of a West Indian island, and the comparison could not be missed. However, rather than emphasizing the black leader's 'reasoned determination' it enacts his reversion to hysteria and 'savagery', and the gradual casting off of his regal clothes images his apparently inevitable reversion to the primitive once the veneer of civilization is cast off. One can speculate that the portrayal of Toussaint by both James and Robeson intentionally counters the assumptions inherent in O'Neill's representation of the black man who dares to equate himself with a white ruler. Possibly also, the figure of Marcus Garvey, whose New York parades featured him in the costume of an imperial viceroy, hovers in the background.

Reading the play now, one wonders if the cool reception was also a consequence of its formal as well as its political radicalism. The series of opening scenes are almost cinematic in their conception, several freeze frames of slaves singing a revolutionary song in patois as they dig, interspersed with other fragmentary scenes depicting four slaves dressing the hair of a white lady who smiles at her reflection in the mirror as two of the slaves are beaten, a slave whipped for stealing a chicken which is then commandeered by his owner, snatches of political talk by white plantation owners set against snatches of political talk by slaves. Each of these brief 'snapshots' is illuminated in different ways – the slaves in silhouette against a night sky, the domestic scenes more brightly lit. Act 1 opens with the Madame Bullet, mistress of the plantation where Toussaint L'Ouverture is a slave, singing Mozart's aria 'Vendetta ti cheggio' from *Don Giovanni*, and quickly opens out the multiple significations of the aria as we become aware of the master's interest in Madame Bullet's mulatto servant, Marie-Jean, who is also desired by the vengeful Dessalines. These early sections of the play might well have provided the illustrations for Frantz Fanon's studies of the psychology of 'the wretched of the earth' who seek to take the master's place.

Although primarily a 'political play', *Toussaint L'Ouverture* is concerned to present the full complexity and humanity of its main protagonist and the other characters, black and white. It is also unusual at this stage in the attempt to recover and revision black history, both in its openness about the existence of slavery and hierarchical structures in Africa, and in its willingness to acknowledge the role played by women in the San Domingo Revolution. James also gives detailed attention to the complex interrelationship between political pressures and cultural attitudes, in which pragmatism generally overrides racism, and sometimes reinforces it. There is much wry humour in the play, as when Toussaint and Maitland, the British general, are heard dictating dispatches which are identical in wording but opposite in their intended outcome respectively to the French and British ministers for foreign affairs. And there is also much bitter irony, as in the scene which demonstrates that Toussaint has put far too much faith in Napoleon Bonaparte's willingness to recognize him as an official, and has failed to understand that Napoleon will dismiss him as 'an impertinent black'.[13]

In the penultimate scene of the play, Dessalines' wife reads him a passage from Racine's *Iphigenie*. Of the language and subject of the play, Dessalines comments: 'Well, that suits them in France. In France they write plays. But listen, listen. That is San Domingo. We can't write plays about voodoo.'[14] C.L.R. James has, of course, written a play about San Domingo, a play which includes scenes of voodoo, and two years later was to publish a major historical work on the revolution that the black people of San Domingo planned, fought and achieved.

James' historical study, *The Black Jacobins: Toussaint L'Ouverture and the San Domingo Revolution*[15] documents many of the details dramatized in the play. But whereas the play focusses chiefly on the man, and the agency of the black masses and Toussaint's immediate circle, the history is much more concerned with the interconnection between events in France and Europe and events in San Domingo. Paul Buhle describes the book as 'an extraordinary synthesis of novelistic narrative and meticulous factual reconstruction',[16] but although the narrative drive is strong, the emphasis is on the economic, political, and social forces which created a situation in which men of exceptional intelligence and ability such as Toussaint, Dessalines, Moise, and others could seize the opportunity to end slavery and establish an independent black state. As James wrote, 'Men make their own history, and the black Jacobins of San Domingo were to make history which would alter the fate of millions of men and shift the economic currents of three continents. But if they could seize opportunity, they could not create it.'[17]

The Black Jacobins is a remarkable work of scholarship based on detailed documentation from eighteenth- and nineteenth-century French sources; it is also a work much ahead of its time. It revises British and European histories of abolition by insisting on the importance of economic forces and world capitalism, rather than philanthropy and altruism, as the crucial elements bringing about reform. James scathingly declares, 'A venal race of scholars, profiteering panders to national vanity, have conspired to obscure the truth about abolition'.[18] He marshals evidence to demonstrate that Wilberforce was merely a tool of mercantile interests in Britain, and that it is the loss of the American colonies and rivalry with the French and their prosperity derived from the slave colony of San Domingo that changes British attitudes between 1783 and 1807. This argument was to have a powerful influence on later historians such as Eric Williams and Walter Rodney. He is one of the first historians to insist on the agency of the black slaves and freemen, together with the mulattoes, in freeing themselves, and he links this to the agency of the masses, affirming that conditions in San Domingo and the sugar plantations made the black slaves a more developed and organized proletariat than any in Europe at that time. And in emphasizing the agency of black men, their abilities as political and revolutionary leaders, he also points a moral for the time. As Robert Young comments, James rewrote history, 'not so much to retrieve a lost African culture, as in the case of Diop, but rather to retrieve a subaltern history of black resistance, and, subsequently, to put Africa at the centre of contemporary history'.[19] Writing, as we should remember, in 1938, James himself comments:

Of the men who were to lead their brothers to freedom, none of them as far as we know was yet active. Dessalines, already 40, worked as a slave for his black master. Christophe listened to the talk in the hotel where he worked, but had no constructive ideas. Toussaint alone read his Raynal. 'A courageous chief only is wanted'. He said afterwards that, from the time the troubles began he felt that he was destined for great things. Exactly what, however, he did not know; he and his brother slaves only watched their masters destroy one another, as Africans watched them in 1914–1918, and will watch them again before long.[20]

Paul Buhle notes the influence of Trotsky's *The Russian Revolution*, which James praised as one of the greatest works of history ever produced, but also contrasts Trotsky's emphasis on the backwardness of Russia with

James's emphasis on the modernity of San Domingo. And one of James's major achievements is his interweaving of European and 'black' history, rather than their separation in terms of national or racial categories, through his insistence on class as the most important basis for understanding historical change. Referring to Toussaint's misplaced trust in the French authorities, James wrote:

It was in method, and not in principle, that Toussaint failed. The race question is subsidiary to the class question in politics, and to think of imperialism in terms of race is disastrous. But to neglect the racial factor as merely incidental [is] an error only less grave than to make it fundamental.[21]

In November 1938, James left England for America where he had been invited to undertake an extensive tour to speak on the imminent war in Europe and the socialist response to it. In April 1939 he visited Trotsky in Mexico, and journeying back through the southern states of America, witnessed a kind of racial discrimination far more comprehensive than any he had experienced in the West Indies or Britain. The fifteen years he spent in America allowed him to develop and formulate his ideas about class and race, his rejection of what he defined as state capitalism in Russia, his growing disassociation from Trotsky, and his understanding of American culture and its influence. In 1952 he was interned on Ellis Island for allegedly 'anti-American' activities (fellow internees included Claudia Jones and Elizabeth Gurley Flynn). During his internment he wrote *Mariners, Renegades, and Castaways*, an exploration of American culture which uses Melville's *Moby Dick* as its starting point.[22]

Expelled from the United States, James returned to post-war England in 1953, and became a regular cricket reporter for the *Manchester Guardian*. During the next decade he combined his reporting on cricket, visits to the West Indies and Ghana, political involvement in the West Indies, with a serious study of the game and its cultural, social, and political contexts in the Caribbean. This study culminated in *Beyond a Boundary*, a book which brings together a number of genres in a new way to create a work which is at once autobiography, cultural history, sports commentary, and political and social analysis.[23] In his brief preface to the book, James puts it differently: 'This book is neither cricket reminiscence nor autobiography. It poses the question: *What do they know of cricket who cricket only know?* To answer involves ideas as well as facts.'[24] He goes on to assert a series of connections which might summarize all of his writings, and could indeed be relevant to many of the writers discussed in this study:

If the ideas originated in the West Indies it was only in England and in English life and history that I was able to track them down and test them. To establish his own identity, Caliban, after three centuries, must himself pioneer into regions Caesar never knew.[25]

For the extraordinary range, intellectual power and originality of his writings, C.L.R. James stands above other black and Asian writers in England in the 1930s and 1940s. But he does not stand apart. The work and presence of Jomo Kenyatta and George Padmore, among others, have been referred to in Chapter Eight. Kenyatta lived and studied in Britain for fifteen years, from 1931 until 1946, and in the same year that James published *The Black Jacobins*, published his seminal study of Gikuyu culture, *Facing Mount Kenya*.[26] His study sets out to challenge the image of the Gikuyu promulgated by 'those "professional friends of the African" who are prepared to maintain their friendship for eternity as a sacred duty, provided only that the African will continue to play the part of an ignorant savage so that they can monopolise the office of interpreting his mind and speaking for him'.[27] Like Chinua Achebe some twenty years later, his mission is to show 'that African peoples did not hear of culture for the first time from Europeans'.[28] And like C.L.R. James, he does not hesitate to warn Europeans of the consequences of their monopoly both of African land and the discourse which represents Africans to others:

But the African is not blind. He can recognise these pretenders to philanthropy, and in various parts of the continent he is waking up to the realisation that a running river cannot be damned forever without breaking its bounds. His power of expression has been hampered, but it is breaking through, and will very soon sweep away the patronage and repression which surround him.[29]

In addition to James and Padmore there were other writers from the West Indies who helped create a political and cultural context in which 'Caliban' might 'establish his own identity'. In the same year that James arrived in England, a young woman from Jamaica, four years his junior, also made the journey from the West Indies to London. She was Una Marson, the daughter of a Baptist parson, like James an avid reader of English and American literature, and like James also a respectful admirer and critic of the academic education, with its thorough study of modern and classical literature, she had received at her elite secondary school modelled on an English public school.[30] Like James, she had become involved in setting up and editing a magazine, in her case a magazine which not only strove to encourage a local literary and artistic culture but also to express feminist views. *Cosmopolitan* was the first journal in Jamaica to be published and edited by a woman, and Una Marson affirmed in this monthly magazine, 'This is the age of woman: What man has done, women may do.'[31] She also wrote and published articles on Jamaican and Kingston local politics, poverty, the need for technical education, the plight of small independent farmers, and on Marcus Garvey, whom she viewed as a man whose message – if not his methods – should be taken seriously.[32] While still in her early twenties in Kingston, she had written and produced the play, *At What a Price*, and published two volumes of poetry, *Tropic Reveries* and *Heights and Depths*.[33]

Marson used the small profits from her play to travel to England, arriving in July 1932, and found lodgings in the house of Harold Moody, founder of the League of Coloured Peoples.[34] She became an active member of the league and, unable to find paid work as a secretary, took on the role of secretary to the league and in 1934 became editor of *The Keys*, the league's journal. In 1933 she had staged at the YMCA, as a league activity, her play *At What a Price*. The play, portraying the 'coming of age' of Ruth, a country girl who goes to work as a stenographer in Kingston, is seduced by her boss, and returns home pregnant, was well-received by the *Manchester Guardian* critic and also by *West Africa*, whose reviewer described it as 'a delightful Jamaican comedy' and a 'capital rendering of middleclass life'. In particular, critics in Jamaica and London praised the scenes dramatizing the humour and light-heartedness of the young women working in the office, and her intelligent and telling use of 'local colour'.[35] The play was also performed at the La Scala theatre in central London with a diverse all-black cast, making it the first black colonial production in the West End. Again, the reviews were favourable.[36]

As editor of *The Keys* and a frequent spokeswoman for the League of Coloured Peoples, Una Marson came into contact with international debates about the situation and future of peoples of African descent, with African students, activists and spokemen for their countries, as well as Indian nationalist movements. She was aware of the work of James and Padmore and Paul Robeson, but strongly opposed their Marxist ideologies, being rather an admirer of Booker T. Washington. As Rhondha Cobham comments in naming Una Marson as a 'foremother' of black British women writers, Marson's experience in England gave her a 'new awareness of herself as a black woman', which grew out of both a defensive reaction to British racial stereotyping and prejudice, but also her 'affirmation of racial and cultural solidarity with other Caribbean and African peoples among whom she worked in England'.[37] The poetry she wrote during this period reflects that wider exposure, with an increasing

A History of Black and Asian Writing in Britain

emphasis on 'black' themes, on race pride, and rejection of assimilation to white attitudes and aesthetics. She wrote several poems which parody and revise canonic English poems, such as Blake's 'Little Black Boy', Yeats' 'Lake Isle of Innisfree', and Kipling's 'If'. A number of her poems reflect and challenge the stereotyping she encountered as a Jamaican woman in London, as in these lines from 'Little Brown Girl':

> Little Brown Girl,
> How is it that you speak
> English as though it belonged
> To you?[38]

and from 'Black Burden':

> I must not laugh too much,
> They say black people can only laugh
> I must not weep too much,
> They say black folk weep always.[39]

Like the African American poet Langston Hughes, she begins to draw on folk forms and rhythms, and to use the cadences and idioms of colloquial speech, as in her poem 'Kinky-haired Blues':

> Now I's gwine press me hair
> And bleach me skin.
> I's gwine press me hair
> And bleach me skin.
> What won't a gal do
> Some kind a man to win.[40]

In poems like these, Marson is one of the earliest black women poets to address the issues of a white aesthetic which is absorbed by black men when it comes to standards of female beauty, an aesthetic which is at least implicitly questioned by the woman speaker. Like Langston Hughes and James Weldon Johnson also, she celebrates the language and spirit of black church worship, although her worshippers are women, and she particularly exalts the joyful loudness of their voices:

> Join de chorus,
> We feeling it flowing o'er us –
> You is no chile of satan
> So get de spirit
> And shout – sister – shout –
> Hallelujah – Amen –
> Shout – Sister – Shout![41]

The language here hovers uneasily at times between African American and English poetic idioms ('We feel it flowing o'er us' belonging to the latter), but the Harlem Renaissance models allow Marson to move away from her earlier rigid adherence to traditional English literary forms, and to adapt new forms and idioms. Thus she does begin to use Jamaican patois in poems such as 'Quashie Comes to London' and 'Foreign', both of which adopt the persona and voice of a Jamaican man. Perhaps her most successful poem in Jamaican patois is 'The Stone Breakers', cast as a dialogue between two women breaking stones for road-building:

> 'Liza me chile, I's really tired
> But wha fe do – me mus' brok de stone
> Dough me han' dem hat me –
> And de sun it blin' me –
> Well – de good Lard knows
> All about we sorrows'.

> 'But whey fe do, Cousin Mary,
> Me had fe buy frack fe de pickney dem,
> Ebry day dem hab fe feed,
> Dem wortless pupa tan roun' de bar
> A trow dice all de day –
> De groun' is dat dry,
> Not a ting will grow –
> massy Lard, dis life is hard.[42]

During her first stay in London, she also wrote a light-hearted play, *London Calling*, which, according to Delia Jarrett-Macauley, reflects 'her experiences of colonial students in London'.[43] Her most impressive and original play, *Pocomania*, written after her return to Jamaica, makes powerful and effective use of patois as well as drawing on the religious culture of marginalized black groups in Jamaica.

In London Marson became involved with various women's movements, speaking at the Women's International League Conference on 'Africa: Peace and Freedom' in 1934, and attending meetings of the British Commonwealth League, which sought to encourage women's groups in Commonwealth countries and to 'raise the status of women of the less forward races'![44] On one occasion, speaking on 'Bars to Careers', she shared a platform with Winifred Holtby, a writer whom she admired for her feminist and anti-colonial stance, and with whom she subsequently talked and corresponded.[45] Marson also represented Jamaica at the 1935 congress in Turkey of the International Alliance of Women for Suffrage and Equal Citizenship. Of her vigorously applauded speech to the assembled delegates from over thirty countries, attacking racism in the colonies, in North America, and 'even in London', the *Manchester Guardian* reported that this 'negro woman of African origin from the former slave world of Jamaica, brought a new note into the assembly and astonished them by the vigour of her intellect and by her feminist optimism'.[46] In the light of that reporter's astonishment, it is perhaps Marson's optimism that should surprise us. Her success there led to an invitation to work as a 'collaborateur' for the League of Nations in Geneva, a temporary post, which was followed by her work as secretary to the Abyssinian Legation in London, and her commitment to the cause of Abyssinia and Haile Selassie. She accompanied Haile Selassie as his personal secretary to the League of Nations where he pleaded for support, and was devastated by the failure of his mission and the indifference of the Western powers, including Britain. Marson returned to Jamaica in September 1936.

Two years later, Una Marson was encouraged to return to England to give evidence to the Moyne Commission's inquiry into conditions in Jamaica following the series of strikes and labour uprisings which unsettled the colonial government and resulted in several deaths and many injuries when the police fired into the crowds of strikers. In London, she began some freelance work for the BBC, which led eventually to her appointment as a full-time programme assistant coordinating broadcasts under the title, *Calling the West Indies*. Originally designed as a programme to enable British-based West Indian servicemen to contact family and friends in the Caribbean, Una Marson soon gave it a cultural agenda, drawing on West Indian writers and artists in Britain at that time.[47] When she returned to Jamaica in 1946, the programme had become a literary one, broadcasting, often for the first time, fiction and poetry by authors in the West Indies as well as Britain. On Marson's departure, Henry Swanzy, an Irishman, became the producer, and the programme, which Marson had renamed *Caribbean Voices* in 1943, continued under his direction for a further eight years.

The new title, *Caribbean Voices*, derived in part from a BBC feature edited by George Orwell, called *Voice*. Orwell's intention was to expose younger poets 'handicapped by the paper shortage and whose work isn't as well known as it ought to be', and often involving readings by the poets themselves.[48] Marson took part in the fourth programme, where she referred to the work of the Harlem Renaissance poets, James Weldon Johnson, Countee Cullen, and Paul Laurence Dunbar, and also read her own 'Banjo Boy', a poem which shows the influence of Cullen, and perhaps Claude McKay. She also took part in a later programme,

featuring T.S. Eliot, Mulk Raj Anand, and other writers of English and
Asian origin. Her own regular BBC series involved the work of writers in
the Caribbean, visiting writers from the West Indies and elsewhere, and
also British-born writers such as L.A.G. Strong, and Stella Mead. Strong
wrote the preface to Una Marson's fourth collection of poems, *Towards
the Stars*, published by the University of London Press in 1945. The first
of her books which was not self-published, this collection contains many
poems from her earlier collections, but nearly half of the poems here
reflect the bleakness of much of her experience in England during the
war years. Thus she writes in 'Frozen Winter 1941':

> The heart of humanity is frozen.
> It is too cold for Poets to sing.[49]

And in 'Black Burden':

> I am black
> And so must be
> More clever than white folks
> More wise than white folks
> More discreet than white folks
> More courageous than white folks
> I am black
> And I have got to travel
> Even further than white folks
> For time moves on.[50]

The collection received a brief notice in the *Times Literary Supplement*, but
it is perhaps more an indication of the reviewers' preconceptions than
the nature of Marson's poetry that the longer reviews were in education
and charity oriented magazines. Thus the reviewer for *Teachers' World and
Schoolmistress* declared the collection 'splendid stuff' with some poems 'as
primitive as the island of Jamaica on which the authoress was born'.[51]
She was also compared to W.H. Davies, whose collected poems had
been published in 1943.

In view of the foreword by her supporter, L.A.G. Strong, such reviews
are not altogether surprising. Strong remarks that Marson's poems

have a quality which is rare in the modern world. Do you by any chance remember the scene in *Porgy* where a negro [sic] in the courtyard of a tenement
began rhythmically to hammer a box, and in a few seconds dozens more had
begun to clap their hands and sing to the rhythm of his strokes? To say of a poet
that his work is artless is a doubtful compliment; but there is a spontaneity, a joy
of living, which when it is married to simple and musical words can give, now
and then, something which only the greatest artists achieve consciously.[52]

Strong goes on to affirm that Marson's verses have all the spontaneity of the scene in *Porgy*, and compares her also with the Irish poet, Padraic Colum, 'the favourite poet of cottagers and farm labourers in his own country'.[53]

Strong's foreword illustrates the difficulty faced by black authors in escaping from the imposed stereotypes and preconceptions which prevented even (and perhaps especially) their well-wishers from viewing their works clearly. Far from being endowed with 'spontaneity', Marson's lyrics in this particular collection are notable for their adherence to the conventions familar to readers of the English Georgian poets. The first section of this small collection is made up of 'Poems of Nature', in which nature is recognizably English in its habitual images of primroses, lambs, and April flowers. The one poem which questions these conventions, in part by referring to Browning's well-known 'Home Thoughts from Abroad' and reversing its rejection of sunny climes and 'the gaudy melon-flower', is the final poem in this section, 'Home Thoughts in June', with memories of the Poinciana trees blossoming in Jamaica.

The third and final grouping in this volume, 'Poems from Life', brings together some of the poems about black experience published in *The Moth and the Star*, although it omits many of those which expressed most forcefully and creatively the oppressiveness of racism, both intended and involuntary, in London. Those that are included are typically the balder statements which one would have supposed difficult to represent as either spontaneous or joyous, such as 'Black Burden' or 'Politeness', which refers back to Blake's well-known poem:

> They tell us
> That our skin is black
> But our hearts are white.
> We tell them
> That their skin is white
> But their hearts are black.[54]

Other poems in this final section reflect her experiences as a member of the International Women's Movement ('To the I.A.W.S.E.C.') celebrating the courage of women in England and throughout the world, and project a vision of racial harmony. Thus the penultimate poem in the collection and one of the last to be written by Marson, speaks of a struggle for racial equality which she will play her part in but without the expectation of seeing it achieved in her lifetime.[55]

Una Marson left England in 1945 for a tour of the West Indies. The trip was extremely successful but exhausting, and on her return to the BBC she suffered a nervous breakdown, as she explained in a letter to George Orwell two years later: 'I suppose that the last you heard of me was that I had returned to London from my hectic West Indies tour, had a nervous breakdown, and had to return to Jamaica for rest and recovery.'[56] But after two years, Marson became a driving spirit in Jamaican literary and political activities again, as an organizer of literary events, publications, and as a journalist and critic. When she returned briefly to London in 1964, following her attendance as a delegate to a seminar on 'Social and Cultural Integration in Urban Areas' in Haifa, Israel, she found the city much changed. Some of the people she had known as budding writers or actors back in Jamaica, Barbados, Trinidad and Guyana, such as Andrew Salkey, George Lamming, Vera Murphy, Vivian Virtue, and Jan Carew, now formed part of a thriving social and cultural West Indian community in London, many of whom had been influenced by and profited from *Caribbean Voices*. Marson interviewed Salkey on radio while she was in London, before taking a job in Israel in January 1965. But high blood pressure and illness forced her to return to Jamaica again, where in May 1965 she died of a heart attack.

A photograph taken in 1942 as a record of the BBC monthly radio programme *Voice* shows Una Marson seated in the centre, flanked on either side by T.S. Eliot and the Indian novelist Mulk Raj Anand. Others in the picture include M.J. Tambimuttu, editor of *Poetry London*, George Orwell, the Indian writer Nayayana Menon, and William Empson. There remains to be written what could prove to be a fascinating history of the involvement of writers from the Indian subcontinent, Sri Lanka, Africa, and the Caribbean in the formulation of an international British-based culture which was then disseminated to various countries by the BBC World Service. Each of the figures in this photograph played an important role in a variety of World Service programmes, reading from their own work, selecting from the work of others, encouraging a sense of a community of writers within Britain and beyond. In addition to Una Marson, Mulk Raj Anand and M.J. Tambimuttu, those who contributed significantly to the BBC World Service cultural programmes during the late 1930s and the 1940s included G.V. Desani, Attia Hosain, Pearl Connor, and Ronald Moody. *Caribbean Voices* continued until 1958, having provided an outlet, financial support, and guidance for writers such as Samuel Selvon, Michael Anthony, Andrew Salkey, Stuart Hall,

Ian McDonald, V.S. Naipaul, Kamau Brathwaite, and John Figueroa. V.S. Naipaul succeeded Henry Swanzy as editor and presenter in 1954, and he was succeeded in turn in 1956 by the Guyanan novelist Edgar Mittelholzer.[57]

Mulk Raj Anand is probably the best known of the many south Asian writers who lived and worked in England during the war years. Born in Peshawar in 1905, he came to England in 1925 as a postgraduate student in Philosophy, and in 1929 gained his doctorate from the University of London for a dissertation on Locke, Berkeley, Hume, and Russell. Except for brief visits to India and Europe (including involvement in the Spanish Civil War as a member of the International Brigade), Anand remained in England for twenty years and in 1938 married the actress Kathleen Van Gelder. Like Cornelia Sorabji, he found his English professors kind and hospitable, but imbued with 'an unrelieved Kiplingism, and…the doctrine of "trusteeship"', or at best, as in the case of Bonamy Dobree, 'a static liberalism'.[58] Despite the existence of 'a few men of liberalizing tendency who had definitely repudiated sectarianism and the Nationalist-Imperialist idea [such as] Leonard Woolf, H.N. Brailsford, Lowes Dickinson, E.M. Forster', Anand found that all too many writers and intellectuals in England in the twenties and thirties were unable to embrace equal right of citizenship to Africans and Indians.[59] As a student with fellow activists in the 1920s and early 1930s he read Gandhi's *Young India* and 'followed his thoughts on national freedom as our main food, day and night, while we worked in Krishna Menon's India League Office in the Strand'.[60] His experience of the 1926 General Strike, his reading of Marx and involvement with trade union intellectuals and activists, together with a brief sojourn in 1932 on Gandhi's Sabarmati Ashram, led to a deep commitment to socialism and humanism as the keystones of his vision. Back in England after working with Gandhi, he completed his first novel, *Untouchable* (signed off as written in 'Simla – ss *Viceroy of India* – Bloomsbury', and dated 1933). He tells how he showed the first draft of this novel to Gandhi, who 'cut a hundred and fifty pages out of the two hundred of my stream-of-consciousness prose *a la* Joyce', saying, 'You know an untouchable boy wouldn't talk in those long sentences. He wouldn't talk at all – he has no mouth.'[61]

This first novel, a short and vividly detailed account of a day in the life of a member of the untouchable caste, a sweeper and latrine cleaner, was sent to and rejected by nineteen publishers until, according to Anand, it was accepted by Laurence Wishart conditionally upon the inclusion of a preface by E.M. Forster. Forster's endorsement, according to Anand, was required to 'protect the book against being called "dirty" because it dealt with dung'.[62] This preface, included with the first 1935 publication of the novel, does indeed insist that *Untouchable* is 'indescribably clean', having 'gone straight to the heart of its subject and purified it'.[63] Forster remarks additionally that the novel could only have been written by an Indian who is also an outsider, who mingles insight with the detachment and depth that comes through his study of philosophy.

Having described in detail the everyday life of a young sweeper named Bakha, the indignity and deprivation he and his sister suffer because of their outcaste status, his protagonist's own acceptance of his inferiority mingled with stifled resentment, Anand's novel offers three possible resolutions to that suffering. The first is proffered by a Christian missionary, whose limited understanding of the vernacular and vagueness, as Bakha sees it, about the identity of Jesus, make him unpersuasive. The second and more powerful promise of change comes from a speech by Mahatma Gandhi, declaring that 'untouchability must end' and demanding that 'all public wells, temples, roads, schools, sanatoriums, must be declared open to the Untouchables'.[64] Responding wholeheartedly to Gandhi's call, Bakha is then startled by a duo who together, perhaps, provide an almost caricatured image of Anand himself, seeking a way of bringing together Western modernity and Indian sensibility. One is a young man just come from '*Vilayat*' (England), dressed in an English suit, yellow gloves, white spats, and wearing a monocle, who loudly denounces Gandhi's '*swadeshi* and spinning wheel' as belonging to the fourth century BC, while 'We live in the twentieth. I have read Rousseau, Hobbes, Bentham and John Stuart Mill.'[65] The other is a young poet, Iqbal Nath Sarsar, perhaps modelled on Muhammad Iqbal whom Anand admired and had already written about,[66] who insists on Gandhi's greatness and importance as a liberator, on the richness of Indian culture, and the need also to accept and use for their own ends, 'the machine', 'machines which can remove dung without anyone having to handle it' and so remove the profession of sweepers and their 'untouchability'. The novel ends with Bakha resolving to tell others about Gandhi's message, and also to 'find the poet some day and ask him about his machine'.[67]

All six of Anand's novels written in the thirties and early forties focus on the lives of Indians who are the victims of an oppressive social and economic system, and all might be classified as socialist realist in mode.[68] Anand had helped found the All-India Progressive Writers' Union in London in 1935, and was instrumental in formulating its manifesto. The founding of the union is recalled thus by a fellow member of the group,

Sajjad Zaheer, who was later to become the secretary-general of the
Communist Party of Pakistan:

I have had the good fortune of having known Mulk...since 1930, when we
were both young and in our twenties and were students in England. During
the last years of my stay in England, in 1935, Anand and I, together with a few
other young Indians, founded the Indian Progressive Writers' Movement. This
was the seed from which developed the great progressive Writers' Movement,
spreading to almost all the great languages of India, blessed and supported by
such eminent figures as Tagore and Premchand.[69]

The Manifesto called upon Indian writers to record change, assist
progress, and introduce 'scientific rationalism in literature'. The association declared that its aim was 'to rescue literature from the conservative
classes – to bring the arts into closest touch with the people', and to
promote a literature which dealt with 'the basic problems of existence
today – the problems of hunger and poverty, social backwardness and
political subjection'.[70] Such criteria are fully met by Anand's second and
third novels, *The Coolie* and *Two Leaves and a Bud*, which represent the sufferings of landless peasants in India, exploited as factory workers or as
tea-plantation workers respectively, and in conflict with factory and plantation owners. These two novels, despite their tragic endings, also suggest
the possibility of change through a united proletariat. Both were banned
in India by the British government, and the second was also banned in
Britain to allay 'the resentment of tea plantation owners and magnates'.[71]

Anand's fourth novel, *The Village*, begins a trilogy focussing on the life
of Lal Singh, a Punjabi peasant. The second novel in this trilogy, *Across the
Black Waters*, published in 1940, is a vivid and convincing portrayal of the
experience of Indian regiments on the European front, and according to
the critic M.K. Naik, deserves to be set beside Remarque's *All Quiet on the
Western Front* and Crane's *The Red Badge of Courage* for the honesty and compassion with which it presents the experience of the ordinary soldier.[72]
In almost all ways the novel forms a striking contrast with Sake Dean
Mahomed's account of his service with the British and Irish in the East
India Company army. Although both protagonists join the army to seek
adventure and glamour, and both are the sons of men who have served
with the British military forces, Lal Singh's experience is one of utter
confusion and disorientation. The novel opens as the troop ships reach
Marseilles, whereupon Lal Singh and his companions are hailed by
incomprehensible shouts, commands, greetings, and signals. Anand conveys vividly the cacophony of meaningless sounds which assail Lal as they

disembark, his vagueness and incomprehension of the differences between French and English attitudes and geographies, his romantic vision
of the England he thinks he is going to visit ('He was going to Vilayat after
all, England, the glamorous land of his dreams, where the sahibs came
from, where people wore coats and pantaloons and led active, fashion-
able lives – even, so it was said, the peasants and the poor sahibs').[73] What
he does experience is numbing cold and hunger in the muddy trenches,
a series of long dreary days and sleepless nights, punctuated occasionally
by air-raids, sniper fire and shrapnel, and futile assaults on enemy
(German) positions, and also a growing and intense comradeship and
dependence upon the dwindling community of his fellow sepoys. Anand
represents the consciousness and speech of these men as thoroughly
immersed in Indian cultural references and perspectives, their memories
and dreams embracing familiar and religious figures from home, a
cultural world intensified rather than adulterated or altered by their
contact with European soldiers and civilians, who continue to regard
them as welcome allies but also as exotics to be watched and sketched.
Thus when at the end of the novel Lal Singh is captured and taken
prisoner of war by a German he feels only the same fatalism with which
he experienced the manoeuvres and actions ordered by the French and
British commanders. He is simply at the mercy of yet another European.

Anand returned to India in 1945 after the war. His novels following
independence take a more psychological and individualistic turn, as in
the semi-autobiographical sequence beginning with *Seven Summers* (1951)
and *The Private Life of an Indian Prince* (1953). Ironically, perhaps, these
later works have more in common with E.M. Forster's exploration of human psychology and relationships between individuals, a preoccupation
which Anand had earlier evaluated as a limitation in Forster's *A Passage
to India*:

And it is well known that all he was interested in was personal relationships
between human beings. He is very suspicious of, if he does not actually despise,
a political attitude in art . . . he has been forced by events now and then to take
a political attitude, but I must respect his premises and judge him according to
his own theory, which is 'only connect'.
   The theory does not, however, exclude social criticism, or even politics in
a broad sense; it only means that Mr Forster was deeply concerned with the
psychological . . . Thus he had very little to say, but he said it very well.[74]

While a number of Indian critics have judged Anand's early novels as
flawed because of their 'propagandising' project, critics in England were

more generous in their responses, comparing him to Dickens and Balzac. The *London Mercury* reviewer declared *The Coolie* 'a rare example of the manner in which material that lends itself to propaganda can be so treated as to produce a pure effect of art...in simply telling the story and drawing the picture, it moves us as no didactic work could'.[75] V.S. Pritchett remarked of the same novel that it displayed 'a humane sensibility of the first order' with none of the 'crudity of thought' so prevalent in 'politically-conscious novels', and C. Day Lewis commended Anand for being 'no melodramatic doctrinaire'.[76] The Australian writer and critic Jack Lindsay particularly praised Anand's contribution to the potential of the European novel as well as to Indian fiction. Speaking of the Lal Singh trilogy, Lindsay wrote:

In the trilogy Anand has validly extended the method with which he began *The Untouchable* [sic]. He has rediscovered the Indian epical tale in terms of the contemporary struggle...[fusing] the methods of Chatterjee, Tagore, Prem Chand and the methods which Anand has learned from his study of the European novels. The result is one long experience in adapting Indian folk elements to Western eyes and the European elements to Indian eyes. In stabilizing and extending the Indian novel, Anand is also adding to the tradition of the Indian novel.[77]

Anand may be seen in the context of other thirties writers of the period, such as C.L.R. James, although it is mainly North American writers such as Steinbeck and Wright, or 'colonial writers' such as Katherine Susannah Pritchard and Christina Stead, who incorporate a socialist vision in their fiction. The British and Irish insiders who were strongly influenced by Marxism during this period seem to have been poets and dramatists, such as Shaw, O'Casey, Auden, Hugh McDiarmid, and C. Day Lewis. And alongside these, the dominant poetic traditions represented by Hardy and Eliot prevailed. Writing about this period, Anand comments on the impact of the rise of fascism, 'the quintessence of capitalism', which had begun to encroach on the elementary liberties of human beings in Europe, and how this directed writers to consider their responsibilities as citizens. And so he found among younger European writers a shared concern and artistic vision:

If the response of the older European writers to these and kindred problems was limited, there was ample confirmation in the thinking aloud of the younger writers like Aragon, Malraux, Auden, Spender, Day Lewis and others that the questions they were asking themselves were more or less similar to ours in India, and irrespective of race and colour, we shared similar concepts and aspired towards kindred objectives...All of us were united, wherever we were, with thousands of others in the faith that we could defend world heritage from the attacks of the fascists of Germany, Italy, and Japan, as well as the reactionaries of our own countries, and help to build a new healthy civilisation on the reserves of enormous potential power for good of human beings; that we could help to achieve political and economic freedom for all and change our environment and ourselves in the process of this struggle. It is quite true that a few writers like Mr Eliot were convinced of the essential sinfulness of man and stepped aside, but even they, in their curious way, preferred democracy to fascism . . . In England, where I was most of this time, the younger intelligentsia were at last awakening. I tried then, with other writers, to face up to the crisis before us, the great all-enveloping crisis which had not only to do with Hitler and Mussolini, but with the British Imperialists, the orthodox churches, and all the decaying spiritual and cultural values, with life itself, in view of the choice for progress or utter destruction.[78]

Other south Asian writers in England at this time judged Eliot and Forster more favourably. The Sri Lankan poet and editor, M.J. Tambimuttu embraced a poetics which acknowledges its debt to T.S. Eliot, while the Indian writer G.V. Desani, like Anand also a philosopher and a contributor to BBC programmes during the war, departs entirely and flamboyantly from that socialist-realist tradition in a manner comparable perhaps to his contemporary, the Irish writer Flann O'Brien, and his successor Salman Rushdie. Tambimuttu edited a collection of essays reflecting on and honouring Eliot's work, and himself contributed a gently parodic poem in Eliot's honour. Speaking after Tambimuttu's death of his limitations and achievements, Mulk Raj Anand commented on the failure of his (Tambimuttu's) generation to understand 'the need to participate in the struggle of the people to to evolve a sharing society'.[79] Tambimuttu's achievement, in Anand's view, was to 'rescue creativeness in the face of war and destruction' bringing together those 'who believed in creativity and sought wholeness'. It was this belief and quest which made Eliot so important to Tambimuttu.[80]

As editor of the magazine *Poetry London*, published sometimes more regularly than others from 1939 until 1951, Tambimuttu exercised a significant influence on the development of poetry during those years. Although Tambimuttu's own editorials and essays called for the restoration of the romantic and lyric traditions in poetry, and celebrated the role of poetry in 'descending to the roots of life', and reuniting the unconscious, spiritual and emotional worlds with the everyday,[81] *Poetry London* incorporated a truly catholic and cosmopolitan approach, publishing work not only by Louis MacNeice, George Barker, Anne Ridler,

Lawrence Durrell, and Kathleen Raine, but also by Garcia Lorca, Pablo Neruda, Paul Eluard, and (on the occasion of Gandhi's death) a translation of a Gujerati poem. There were essays by such diverse critics as George Orwell and Kathleen Raine (including their opposing views on Eliot and a series of responses by readers on those views). The magazine also featured covers and illustrations by Henry Moore, Graham Sutherland, Tanguy, Miro, and Fahr-el-Nissa Zeid.

Tambimuttu's anthology of poems written between September 1939 and early 1942, *Poetry in Wartime*,[82] draws mainly on poems published in *Poetry London*, and seeks to introduce younger poets to a wider public. Thus he includes not only single contributions by established authors such as Auden, Empson, C. Day Lewis, MacNeice, and Spender, all specifically reflecting on aspects of the war, but also four or five poems each from then relatively unknown poets such as Vernon Watkins, Anne Ridler, Kathleen Raine, Alun Lewis, Lawrence Durrell, and Nicholas Moore, some of whose poems respond not only to war, but also to childbirth, christenings, lovers, and natural landscapes.

Tambimuttu himself wrote and published a long sequence of poems titled *Out of This War*.[83] The preface to the sequence is autobiographical, telling how 'with the suns of twenty-five summers in [his] fist' he travelled from 'a seaweed-dangled house in a tropic sea' and 'bit the narrow stone of a London alley'.[84] He depicts Sri Lanka, the world he leaves behind, as an ancient, sensuous, but static world, which he escapes to experience its opposite:

> That's why I stretched a rope across the ocean,
> Became the tight-rope walker of my dreams.
> Searched for antipodeal experience, to round
> The small circumference of a sesame-seed.[85]

The second of the poems in this sequence of six offers meditations on the causes of violence and evil, drawing upon the wisdom of the Buddha. It is followed by a powerful evocation of the suspense and terror of an air-raid:

> The time is harvested and hung
> Dying, that brings love and growth showing its fingers.
> This is the time of bombs and white nightmare
> Soaking red through faces. This is time that lingers
> To touch the brain with madness. Does it care, O does it care
> If the slow bells of desolation are rung
> Over the dead land...[86]

From concentration on that precise and contemporary moment of the air-raid, in poems II and III, the sequence moves to a long recapitulation of mankind's history of violence, warfare, rape, and counter-violence:

> Under the lee of the great European rock,
> We rape and are not satisfied.
> But the Other One lurking behind – the wicked *voyeur*,
> Rattles his glad sabres and grows bloody-eyed.[87]

The final poem is a long commemoration of Dunkirk, lamenting the 'yellow-haired heroes' who died there, and wonders whether they died still believing in 'the dead word:'

> Old gestures and phrases bent you before their whips;
> Did you believe them, or did the doubt fell
> You, like France, even before you fell.[88]

and ends with a moving and eloquent elegy:

> But their eyes are shut to the exploding night;
> The heart falls away in the weathered dust.
> The evil has tunnelled to the bone
> Of our gold days, to disasters blown.
> We have no hands to hold, no eyes to weep;
> And as the sweeping rain adds clod to heap
> We add the minutes to a dead season,
> The season of Nought and hibernation. (p. 23)

That stanza illustrates both the virtues and limitations of Tambimuttu's poetry. Often he can combine concrete imagery, sensation, and thought into a powerful cumulative set of images and complex ideas. His use of enjambement and cadence is masterful, and many verses have a sonority and rhetorical force which add to their power. But all too often a sequence of fine lines is damaged by one that is pretentious or banal.

Out of This War, in its preoccupation with time past and time present, and in some of its phrases and cadences, manifests the influence of T.S. Eliot. Tambimuttu acknowledges Eliot's friendship and encouragement in the foreword to a poem written for Eliot on his sixtieth birthday, published as *Natarajah*, but originally titled 'Mr Eliot's Circus', perhaps in its visiting of Eliot's themes and symbols and putting them through different and rather 'exotic' paces, recalling Yeats' use of this trope in his 'The Circus Animals Desertion'. *Natarajah* reads as a pastiche, and at times a parody, of a variety of Eliot's works, and it is difficult to know how to read it.[89] Tambimuttu himself describes the poem as a birthday garland, which incorporates bits of Eliot's lines and some of his 'moods and weathers', and likens his practice to that of his grandfather, S. Tambimuttu, who 'wove what he assimilated from poets of his acquaintance into birthday-mats for them', a practice which was common in Sanskrit India and Tamil Nadu.[90] But whereas Eliot might be said to weave elements and borrowings from Sanskrit and other cultures into a European work, expressive of a European consciousness, Tambimuttu's project seems in part to 'orientalize' Eliot. Thus Natarajah gives the poem its title, naming the aspect of Shiva as Lord of the Dance, whose cosmic dance creates and preserves all things in the universe. The images and voices in the poem including 'The lyre-bird's dancing, Cleopatra's smile', recreate an array of 'other' worlds, sought, desired, and exploited by European imperialists:

> The minah calls out of the palm frond, the girls through the lattice;
> Marble bodies brown in the straight light.
> Oranges, oranges loved by the kings of England,
> Sesamum oil in kerosene tins and citronella,
> Copra for mills and figs for the girls of Kandy.
> 'The company was floated on ten thousand,
> Now the profits are soaring to a million.'[91]

The second section of this poem parodies and turns 'The Journey of the Magi' into a reverse journey of European explorers moving towards and through the tropics. Their 'hardships' and the passing exotica are described in detail and in the same worldly wise voices as Eliot's Magi are given, only to reach a very different revelation, the huge, semi-legendary, poisonous upas-tree, a journey and revelation which pick up Eliot's allusions to *The Heart of Darkness*.

Tambimuttu hoped that the poem would amuse Eliot, and no doubt it did, but the overall aim of this garland, or pastiche, or 'birthday-mat', whether it should be seen as tribute or commentary, is difficult to discern. Perhaps, echoing the term used by G.V. Desani to categorize his hybrid and parodic work of fiction, we can simply call it a 'gesture'.

In 1947 Aubrey Menen published his first novel, *The Prevalence of Witches*, a work which gestures in many directions.[92] Born in London in 1912, the son of an Indian businessman and his Irish wife, Aubrey Menen worked as a drama critic, stage director, and in radio, before becoming an education officer in India. Drawing on this experience and narrated by an education officer sent to the very and voluntarily 'backward' Indian province of 'Limbo', *The Prevalence of Witches* takes broad aim at a number of targets. Balanced not very finely between a satire of British Raj and a portrayal of recalcitrant and 'trickster' subjects, the novel is at times reminiscent of Joyce Cary's African novels, Conrad's *Lord Jim*, or Evelyn Waugh's *Black Mischief*. What makes the novel intriguing is its sequential unsettling of the reader as what appears to be the object of comedy constantly turns out to be the means for turning the tables. The 'natives' of Limbo at first are portrayed as uncomprehending, superstitious people, in thrall to witch doctors and the witches they devoutly believe in. By the end of the novel they appear to be far less 'silly' than their would-be rulers and educators, for whom they pretend ignorance. In a scene reminiscent of the one described earlier in Cornelia Sorabji's 'Behind the Purdah', they perform a play which mimics perfectly the behaviour and gestures of the watching governor of the province. Their reluctance to send their children to school and failure to see its usefulness seems justified when the Governor of the province, referred to throughout as the 'King of Limbo', decides first to limit their reading entirely to Victorian newspapers and texts, and then, when he finds them making excellent copies of realistic illustrations and photographs, insists that they should be taught how to do proper 'primitive' drawing. The Governor himself shows them how to do it, and envisions a nice little trade in primitive artefacts. Here the satire on modernism and the European celebration and manipulation of primitivism as an artistic mode and a commodity is effective. The novel also features a fake Oxford-educated Swami, an Indian judge who subscribes to the Rationalist Society and eschews all forms of spiritualism, and a character who acts as a kind of guru to his Oxford comrades, Bayard Leavis, a man who asks questions in order to allow himself to answer them at length, and who 'was clearly determined to talk of the reaction of a cultivated man to a savage country'.[93] Described as a man whose career begins with the publication of a poem by T.S. Eliot, Bayard Leavis's kinship to Frank Raymond Leavis seems to be brandished before the reader. But he moves from modernist to post-modernist critic at the end of the novel when he proposes to provide Limbo with an invented history, which includes the eccentric Governor who has been at the centre of the novel we have just read:

'Now what is needed is for us to give a past history to Limbo. I have been thinking it over. I have been making some notes. Of course, I shall need to do more research before they are complete. I must now tell you of the first and rather eccentric King of the Limbodians that I have invented...'[94]

Aubrey Menen returned to England in 1947 and then took up residence in Italy until 1981, when he moved to India for the last eight years of his life. He published two autobiographical works, several travel books, and nine novels, including in 1957 *The Abode of Love*, a novel about a harem in nineteenth-century England, which obliquely subverts the Victorian orientalist obsession with the '*zenana*' or 'harem' in India and the Middle East.

A gesture, is how G.V. Desani defined his experimental novel-length work of prose fiction, *All About H. Hatterr*, a work received with delight, fascination, and some bemusement when it was first published in 1948.[95] Desani was born in Nairobi in 1909, the child of immigrant parents from the Punjab, but when he was four his family moved to Sind (now in Pakistan). He visited England for two years from 1926 till 1928, working as a film actor, and returned again in 1939, remaining there for thirteen years, during which he worked as a broadcast journalist and lectured widely. His introduction makes a point of declaring that *All About H. Hatterr* was written in London during the war years. Desani left London in 1952 to study and practise Mantrayoga in India.

With reference to *All About H. Hatterr*, T.S. Eliot commented, 'In all my experience, I have not met with anything like it.' At first, and even second and third glance, many readers may say the same, although further consideration of comparisons might bring to mind Sterne's *Tristram Shandy* and Dickens' *Pickwick Papers*. Later critics have compared Desani to James Joyce, while Salman Rushdie has seen Desani's work as a predecessor to his own. The epigraph to the work jokily sets up the problem of category with a warning to readers:

Warning!
    'Melodramatic gestures against public security are a common form of self-expression in the East.......' (*Anglo-Indian writer*)
    Indian middle-man (to author): Sir if you do not identify your composition a novel, how then do we itemise it? Sir, the rank and file is entitled to know.
    Author (to Indian middle-man): Sir, I identify it a *gesture*. Sir, the rank and file is entitled to know.

When the middle-man declares there is no market for gestures but there is an immediate market for novels, and that he is a literary agent, not a free agent, the author agrees to have his work categorized as a novel.[96] The warning is followed by a preface which plays with questions of authorship ('There are two of us writing this book. A fellow called H. Hatterr and I'), issues of truth and fiction whereby the author admits his propensity for telling lies ('Life seemed so many clashes and contests, sorry! And, well, Invention helps!'), and especially questions of publishing and readership, as he is rejected in turn by a typist, a psychiatrist, a 'Book-keeper', a 'Cashier', an 'Allied Soldier' (these three forming a 'Gallup poll' sample of 'mass reaction'), a writing school, by Betty Bloomsbohemia ('the Virtuosa with knobs-on'), and finally by the critic Pius Prigg Pilliwinks.

As the 'warning' implies, a gesture is subversive of 'public security', a form of self-expression, a response to life, a jest also which refuses pre-defined categories, and seeks to derail goods travelling on straight lines, straight lines and categories which are then mimicked and caricatured in the subsequent brief dialogue, where repetition and the demands of the unfree market also force the author to assume the category of novelist, while at the same time throwing into questions the definitions and expectations of that genre.

Desani questions other categories and conventions, particularly with regard to assumptions about character. H. Hatterr declares himself from the beginning a hybrid character, 'biologically fifty-fifty of the species', an 'Indian' who is the orphaned (or one might say hi-jacked) child of a Malaysian woman and a European sailor, taken from his mother and 'colonised' by a Scottish missionary. At the age of fourteen he fled the restrictions of the missionary's care, in search of his mother and his 'lebensraum', taking with him an English dictionary, the school stereoscope complete with 500 slides of European scenes (his 'second love after [his] mother'). Even the 'style-name' he assumes suggests his hybridity and the signalling of his character as gesture and performance as both a merchant of Indianness, and one who assumes the missionary educator's pretentious and ill-fitting costume:

I assumed the style-name H. Hatterr ('H' for the nom de plume '*Hindustaani-walla*', and '*Hatterr*', the nom de plume inspired by Rev. the Head's too-large-for-him-hat), and by and by (autobiographical I, which see), I went completely Indian to *an extent few pure non-Indian blood sahib fellers have done* [author's italics].[97]

But as the above quotation suggests, hybridity is not just a matter of racial mixture, it also refers to the mingling of cultural traditions and conventions, and Desani's fiction is a gesture towards and against such traditions. In a later section, signalled earlier in the book so that we do not fail to recognize its significance, Hatterr is instructed in the conventions of Englishness, by a Sheikh who has assumed the trappings bestowed upon him by 'Eaten' (Eton), 'Arrow', and the '*Ell See See*' (LCC), and who can tell Hatterr (in his present name of Baw Saw) of the magic rituals of

Burns night, where ladies do the *Neezup*, the 'burrasahibs' call for *Kon-yak! Konyak!*, and all join in the singing of *Oldlongsigh*. He assures Hatterr that he has only to wear the appropriate necktie, that mystic symbol revered by the English, to become a burrasahib. Hatterr's 'mutual introduction' to his interlocutors, to the English, to the English literary tradition, begins with a mock Shakespearian dialogue between 'the figure of a feller', a ghostly figure of Shakespeare carrying a folio, and Hatterr, a Hamlet substitute, who questions his own being. The concluding pages of the first edition of the novel, according to Desani, 'show him as Faustus-Caspar'.[98] In between, Hatterr alludes to a multitude of English and European writers, including Sheridan, Shelley, Keats, as well as Latin and Sanskrit texts. The mock ending (for there follows in subsequent editions a supposed commentary), invokes a demotic multilingual European world, both alluding to and replacing the literary European and Sanskrit chants which end T.S. Eliot's *The Waste Land*. But the cheerfully stoic tone of the ending and the character of Hatterr, ever curious and indefatigable, the outsider who refuses to be a victim, is more reminiscent of Joyce's Leopold and Molly Bloom than Eliot's alienated characters:

I carry on.

Meanwhile, and regardless, I am putting questions to fellers: *and* regardless of the unanswerable *What is Truth?* (And, regardless, *too*, of whatever the word *Truth* is the *Translation* of!)

Maybe, damne, all humans – the Shem, Ham, and Japheth – just like you say, come from one branched-off source: our grand-dad chimpanzee, our gorilla grandma, and the orang-patriarch. O.K. and granted. But sans sense, primates, and progeny of puny primates! Why bite one another *now*, though your ancestors might have?

Parlyvoo la France, chums?
Repondez s'il vous plait! *man hunting man!*
Ach, mein Gott! Are human beings fools or what?
In the interim . . . while I wait, and you tell, *mach's nach, aber mach's besser, viz.*, Carry on, boys, and continue like hell!

Desani's protagonist, like Joyce's Bloom, asserts in the face of all opposition (the preceding pages have detailed a fracas with a Mr Punchum) and in the face of a world torn by war and violence in India as well as Europe, an insistence on human brotherhood, and an affirmation of life against hatred and death. Just as Joyce dated *Ulysses* 1914–18, as an act of creation during the destruction of World War I, Desani explicitly declares that his work is the product of 'the warring years'. Published in

1948, it opposes the violence and death which so horrifically dominated both World War II and the partition of the Indian subcontinent. Like Joyce also he opposes to the monolithic and linear vision of nationalists on each side, his multifaceted, stereoscopic, and non-linear vision. Thus his work is not only a gesture in the face of narrow nationalism and racism which results in war, but also in the face of novelists such as Anand and Raja Rao, whose characters are defined by their Indianness, and/or their status as victims of history and class.

English and American critics responded to Hatterr's exuberant and anarchic humour, the often fantastic and surreal world, the brilliant parodies, the playful inventiveness of his language and imagination, with delight and amusement. But Desani's comments suggest that they saw Hatterr as a specifically Indian phenomenon, and therefore funny. In his statement accompanying the publication of his poetic drama *Hali*, Desani makes no mention of Hatterr's Indian context or background, but insists that Hatterr is 'a portrait of man (Homo Sapiens *vulgaris*). If you will write down H. Hatterr's fears, desires, appetites, hopes (not his experiences), you will find that he is no longer the odd fellow he seemed at first', and that 'H. Hatterr and you' are fundamentally alike. Hatterr, he claims, has 'the characteristic pandemonium of a crowd. He is the popular mind expressing itself: at its best, at its worst, now bawdy, then vulgar, but important: because he's *us*.'[99] Desani in this statement also makes clear the distance between himself and his creation, for whose speech, language and punctuation he had to undergo (as Joyce did for Molly Bloom)

a disciplined process of 'unlearning'; every idea, thought, name, noun, adjective, expletive, must undergo a metempsychosis; and there must be a seal and a stamp on his 'untutored' punctuation too. I now know that a certain consequence of my fidelity to the canons of my craft was a verdict that I was '*terribly funny*'.[100]

And he gives notice of a new H. Hatterr, 'This time, little ones, "a prophet"; not "the clown".'

The poetic play, *Hali*, published in 1950, does portray 'a prophet', a representation of Indianness as far removed from Hatterr as possible.[101] It receives the somewhat puzzled endorsement of both T.S. Eliot and E.M. Forster in their very brief statements prefacing the work. A mystical and mythic play, in poetic prose, *Hali* presents 'the passion' of its protagonist, and his vision of Good and Evil. Its mode is tragic rather than comic, its language measured and elegaic, rather than inventive and playful. It seems intended to emphasize the distance between Desani and Hatterr, and to present another equally significant facet of the author's mind and talent.

However, it has been *All About H. Hatterr*, that has made both the most immediate and the most lasting impact on later readers and writers. Most notably, one can see its acknowledged influence in Salman Rushdie's episodic, inventive, and hybrid works, not only in the imaginative exuberance of his characters and narrators, but also even in small details such as the estrangement of names, misheard, misspelled, or mispronounced, such as Hatterr's 'ell see see' and Rushdie's 'Ellowen Deeowen' (L-O-N-D-O-N). There is a moment in Rushdie's *Satanic Verses* when the figure of Ignatius Sancho appears; the spirit of Sancho, and his friend and comic writer, Sterne, also inhabit Desani's 'gestural' novel. Like Sancho and Sterne and later Rushdie, Desani eschews the 'narrow one-dimensionality of the straight line'.[102]

CHAPTER II

Epilogue

The 1950s witnessed the end of one era and the beginning of new kinds of writing by black and Asian writers who settled in Britain. Not only did the post-war demand for labour bring economic migrants in large numbers, an influx inaugurated by the arrival of the SS *Empire Windrush* from the Caribbean in 1948, but also it had become clear that the expatriate professional and administrative classes in the former empire would be replaced by indigenous persons. These came to the United Kingdom in increasingly large numbers to acquire the British professional training and higher education often required for an appointment in their home countries. Many of these stayed on and became well-known writers. Among those who came to write, study, and work in Britain in the first two decades following World War II and then remained there were the poet Dom Moraes (from Bombay), novelist and short story writer Attia Hosain (from Lucknow), novelist Kamala Markandaya (from Bangalore), poet Ketaki Kushari Dyson (from Bengal), historian and travel writer Nirad Chaudhuri (from east Bengal), novelist and journalist Furrukh Dhondy (from Poona, India), novelist Salman Rushdie (from Bombay), fiction and travel writers V.S. Naipaul and his younger brother Shiva Naipaul (from Trinidad), novelist Sam Selvon (also from Trinidad), poets James Berry and Andrew Salkey, who was also a novelist, (from Jamaica), novelists Wilson Harris and Edgar Mittleholzer (from Guyana), novelists Buchi Emecheta (from Nigeria), Lauretta Ngcobo (from South Africa), and Abdulrazak Gurnah from Zanzibar. Ngcobo and Gurnah came to England as political refugees, as did many writers of Asian descent from East Africa in the late 1960s. The list is by no means exhaustive, but rather is indicative of the multifarious places and cultures from which these writers came.

Both the size and diversity of this influx of writers and other workers produced a significant shift in black British writing. Although black and south Asian authors before the 1950s often spoke on behalf of an alternative group, they spoke as individual representatives and primarily addressed a white British audience. Moreover, the culture and community they represented mostly lived elsewhere – in Africa, the Indian subcontinent, the Caribbean, or the southern states of America. Now authors increasingly spoke of and to a black and south Asian community *within* Britain. And whereas earlier authors such as Equiano, Francis Fedric, and Cornelia Sorabji sought to *recreate* a community distant in time and place, this new group of immigrant authors were often seeking to *create* their community here and now in Britain. It is in this role as a creator of community that Samuel Selvon's writing is particularly innovative and significant. *The Lonely Londoners*, published in 1956,[1] assembles a cast of West Indian and African men seeking companionship and support in the face of a bleak, impoverished and unfriendly white London. Through their stories (or 'ballads') and through the voice of the narrator, Moses, this diverse group of Jamaicans, Trinidadians, and Africans comes into being as a gathering of people who find their identity less through their different places of origin than through their mutual presence in London. This new group identity is expressed through the language of the narrator, a subtle blend of Trinidadian and other West Indian idioms and inflections with standard English. Selvon also published a number of novels and short stories set in his native Trinidad, but in 1975 produced in *Moses Ascending* a sharply satiric sequel to *The Lonely Londoners*.

But as in the earlier part of the twentieth century, the presence of a black and Asian community in the metropolitan centre also helped to create a new sense of community and shared aims between representatives of the colonial cultures in Britain and 'back home'. Mingling with the increasing numbers of temporary and permanent immigrants from all parts of what was now named 'the British Commonwealth', were many students and professional writers such as Edward (Kamau) Brathwaite and George Lamming (from Barbados), Wole Soyinka and John Pepper Clark (from Nigeria), and Ngugi wa Thiong'o (from Kenya). It was in Britain that writers such as Ngugi encountered writings by the Francophone Caribbean author, Frantz Fanon, and George Lamming's powerful and innovative novel, *In the Castle of My Skin*,[2] and his eloquent and influential essays on cultural politics, *The Pleasures of Exile*,[3] all of which were to have a profound influence on Ngugi's career as an educator and writer.

George Lamming was one of the key speakers at the first two Caribbean Artists Movement (CAM) conferences, held at the University of Kent, Canterbury in 1967 and 1968. The conferences grew out of a series of smaller group meetings which began in January 1967, and featured monthly readings and discussions of work by Caribbean, African, and African American writers and artists. Kamau Brathwaite was a regular participant, as were the poet and publisher John LaRose, novelist and sociologist Orlando Patterson, and poet and novelist Andrew Salkey. Others who frequently attended or spoke at the meetings and conferences included C.L.R. James, James Berry, Kenneth Ramchand, and Wilson Harris.[4] Both the interaction between artists from different Caribbean islands, and the discussions and formulations concerning the objectives of a meaningful Caribbean art, were to have a continuing influence on art and cultural politics produced in the Caribbean itself once writers such as Brathwaite and Lamming had returned there. In Britain and in the Caribbean, it had the consequence of questioning the centrality of the English canon, and of creating alternative foci and lines of communication and response. As in the earlier part of the century, journals such as *The West Indian Gazette*, edited by Claudia Jones, and the CAM *Newsletter* and its successor in the Caribbean, *Savacou*, became important outlets for the publication of black British and Caribbean writers. Publishing houses such as John LaRose's New Beacon Press and Eric and Jessica Huntley's Bogle L'Ouverture Press came into existence and have continued to publish important new works and collections by black British and Caribbean writers.

The CAM group debated and sought to redefine the language, forms, and content of a Caribbean and black British writing appropriate to a community which had also redefined its audience. In Britain CAM writers and artists were becoming aware of innovative fiction and poetry drawing on oral and folk traditions, jazz structures, and spoken idioms, published by African and African American writers such as Chinua Achebe, Langston Hughes, and Ralph Ellison, as well as Hispanic and Francophone Caribbean writers such as Léon Damas, Nicolas Guillén, and Aimé Césaire. Encouraged by their creative brilliance and success, Brathwaite, Lamming, Selvon, and others fashioned a language which recalled the voices and idioms and rhythms of everyday Caribbean life and culture. For Brathwaite this involved specifically rejecting in his poetry the iambic pentameter line characteristic of the English poetic tradition, and drawing on calypso, blues, and African drum rhythms. Brathwaite, James Berry and Samuel Selvon also drew on oral and folk traditions, as had Una Marson earlier, to make Caribbean voices heard within the English literary tradition. Berry's series of 'Lucy' poems, in the form of letters from a Jamaican woman settled in London and writing back to a friend in her former home, vividly evoke the contrasts in place and culture through the voice of a Jamaican Londoner.[5] Berry's poems, like Brathwaite's, were most effective when performed by the poet and heard by audiences – first at CAM meetings, and later much more widely throughout England. Such poems, and works by a subsequent generation of poets such as John Agard and Grace Nichols from Guyana, and Linton Kwesi Johnson from Jamaica, both celebrated and authenticated the presence of Caribbean-inflected voices, and hence bodies, in Britain. Through the performance of their poetry to multicultural audiences within the United Kingdom, these poets created and reinforced a sense of communal identity and established a hybrid oral/literary tradition different from but affiliated to the pre-existing English literary tradition. Or rather, in their speaking directly to and of groups rather than individuals, one might see their work as giving new life and new directions to an older oral/literary tradition characterized by Chaucer's *Canterbury Tales* and the drama of Shakespeare.

The aims and aesthetics embraced by some members of CAM did not appeal to all writers who had emigrated from the West Indies or Africa or the Indian subcontinent. V.S. Naipaul was never a member of CAM, and his fiction, unlike Selvon's, maintained a clear distinction between the standard English of the narrative persona, and the Trinidadian voices of his characters. Despite the sympathetic fictionalizing of his father's story in the most Dickensian of his novels, *A House for Mr Biswas* (published 1961), West Indian critics such as George Lamming and Wilson Harris saw Naipaul's early fiction as cruelly satiric and disdainful of the Caribbean community, while Harris argued that Naipaul's adherence to what Harris saw as the traditional genre of the 'novel of manners' reinforced static and unchanging views of a people and a society desperately in need of growth and change, particularly as the new West Indian nation states came into independent being.[6] Although reservations have frequently been expressed by Caribbean and other 'Third World' writers and critics, such as Chinua Achebe, Naipaul's reputation within Britain has continued to grow, resulting in the award of the Booker Prize in 1971, a knighthood in 1990, the David Cohen Prize recognizing 'a lifetime's achievement by a living British writer' in 1992, and the Nobel Prize for Literature in 2001.

Notwithstanding their differences and disagreements, Naipaul in his early fiction shares with other immigrant writers a preoccupation with the search for accommodation in both the literal and the metaphorical sense. That search is suggested by the title of *A House for Mr Biswas*, in which at one point the protagonist expresses a kind of existential terror at the thought of remaining alone, isolated, and unaccommodated. *The Mimic Men* (1967) regards with disdain and sharp scrutiny the disjunction between European architectural, political, and cultural structures and traditions, and those of the newly independent peoples and places in the Caribbean. Its narrator, an exiled political leader, traces his life and search for order through a series of bleak lodgings and hotel rooms in London, as well as ramshackle or pretentious villas in the Caribbean, finally affirming his existence as a permanent lodger or guest, a man without rootedness. There is a difference, and not only in class, between Naipaul's inhabitants of isolated attic rooms, and Selvon's narrator and friends who come together in the basement rented by Moses. But, as Susheila Nasta has pointed out, there is also an affinity in their sense of transience, the discovery that the myth of finding a home and motherland, a tradition to which they could lay claim, was a barren one. For Naipaul's protagonist, Ralph Singh, the magic of the past is powerless, the city remains colourless and two-dimensional.[7] Moses and his black London compatriots invoke with a certain awe legendary names such as Piccadilly Circus and Trafalgar Square, but even after many years, London remains both theirs and not theirs.

The generation of writers who came to England in the 1950s and 1960s were typically male and single, and often believed themselves to be transient. Twenty years later, a new generation of authors, male and female, write out of the experience of being located in Britain, many of them either born in the United Kingdom or arriving as young children. Their fiction often focusses on the attempt to make a home in Britain, and frequently the protagonists are women, seeking to hold their families together and establish some sense of permanence. Buchi Emecheta's *Second Class Citizen* (1974), David Simon's *Railton Blues* (1983), Caryl Phillips' *The Final Passage* (1985), Ravinda Randhawa's *A Wicked Old Woman* (1987), Abdulrazak Gurnah's *Dottie* (1990), and Farhana Sheikh's *The Red Box* (1991), all explore with varying degrees of complexity and ambivalence the meaning and consequences for young Caribbean, African, and Asian women, their husbands, siblings, and children, of living in a British community which is reluctant to accommodate them. The 1980s also saw the emergence of many women writers and supportive groups such as the Asian Women Writers' Collective (including Ravinder Randhawa and Ruksana Ahmed), and the Caribbean Women Writers group. Much of their early work was featured in anthologies specifically devoted to writing by black and/or Asian women, and often reinforcing a rather homogenized sense of the situation and writing of immigrant women in Britain. Such collective identities were useful in establishing the presence of black and Asian women writers in Britain, expressing a sense of empowerment through collaboration, and often addressing specific grievances against their male counterparts. They were, however, temporary, and many of the women anthologized in those early years have gone on to create powerfully individual visions and, indeed, to influence male writers to give greater attention to women characters.

Writers such as Randhawa, Gurnah, Phillips, Rushdie, and, more recently on film and television as well as in fiction, Hanif Kureishi and Meera Syal, also play satirically and ironically with the stereotyped identities within and against which those of Asian and African descent in Britain find themselves living. Kureishi's novel, later translated to film, *The Buddha of Suburbia*, wittily satirizes both the English liberals and the immigrant Asians who trade in ethnicity. John Agard, who arrived in England from Guyana in 1977, performs his sardonic poem 'Stereotype' with straw hat, beach shirt, and accompanying trappings denoting popular images of the Caribbean. Such texts and performances recall and reiterate the understanding expressed through the works of black writers, such as Sancho, Fedric, Brown, and Craft in the previous century, that race and ethnicity are constructed identities, which may be performed differently within different contexts and for different audiences.

While many writers explore a new sense and consequence of location and identity in Britain, these and others also continue to a marked degree the tradition of travel writing which was such a feature of eighteenth- and nineteenth-century texts by black and south Asian immigrants such as Equiano, Seacole, and Malabari. Here V.S. Naipaul is perhaps the preeminent example of a writer who alternates writing about his encounters with other cultures and places with the search for location within England and Englishness, culminating most powerfully and complexly in *The Enigma of Arrival* (1987). Naipaul described his return to and turn away from the Caribbean in *The Middle Passage* (1962), contentiously (and in contrast to C.L.R. James) pronouncing that 'History is built around achievement and creation; and nothing was created in the Caribbean.'[8] The incisive detail of Naipaul's descriptions led reviewers to compare him to D.H. Lawrence as a travel writer, and encouraged commissions for later works, such as *An Area of Darkness* (1964), which traverses India and finds there a static and sterile culture, *A Congo Diary* (1980), and *Among the Believers: An Islamic Journey* (1981). Naipaul's later novels often incorporate and build on the places and cultures described in the travel books, and simultaneously allude to earlier novelists and travellers such as Conrad. Thus, *A Bend in the River* (1979) draws on his earlier 'Congo Diary' and essay on Conrad to create a contemporary version of Conrad's *Heart of Darkness*, while *Guerillas* (1975) fictionalises his series of essays on Michael X while also alluding to both *Wuthering Heights* and *Jane Eyre*. One of the main protagonists, a South African journalist, is named Rochester, while the Michael X figure sees himself as a kind of Heathcliff.

Whereas earlier British novels have tended to separate the genres of adventure/travel/quest and domestic/romance fiction, one of the distinctive and intriguing features of these novels by Naipaul is the creation of a hybrid fiction combining the quest and the domestic genres. Naipaul has generally focussed on contemporary settings, but a later generation of black and Asian British novelists have begun to combine the exploration of place with the exploration and reappraisal of history, resulting in a remapping and revisioning of both. Thus Caryl Phillips has published trenchant travel writing, most notably *The European Tribe* (1987), where he echoes in his description of himself as both of, and not of, Europe C.L.R. James' more optimistic vision of a new generation of black Britons. But his fiction also moves across time and location. *Cambridge* (1991) alludes to both Equiano and the Brontës through its linguistic mimicry and its two main protagonists. One is a deeply religious slave named sequentially Olumide, David Henderson, and Cambridge; the other is Emily Cartwright, whose diaries express a romanticized and evasive picture of the Caribbean plantation she visits and the slaves who work on it. In this novel, Phillips also alludes to yet another predecessor, the white Caribbean novelist, Jean Rhys, and her rewriting of *Jane Eyre* in *The Wide Sargasso Sea* (1966). The name and character of Cambridge's common law wife, Christiana, echoes the name of the formidable black servant and supposed 'obeah woman', Christophine, in Rhys' novel. In his 1989 novel *The Higher Ground*, Phillips links the story of an eighteenth-century African with those of a twentieth-century African American prisoner and a Jewish woman whose family died in the concentration camps in Poland.

Like Naipaul, the novelists David Dabydeen and Abdulrazak Gurnah have also drawn on Conrad's *Heart of Darkness* as a textual background and map against which to ground a new vision of African or black identities and terrains. Dabydeen's *The Intended* (1991) provides a sharp and witty rereading of Conrad through its relocation and 'filming' in the heart of London by a group of schoolboys of Asian, Caribbean, and African descent. Gurnah's *Paradise* is set in East Africa, and takes its young Arab-African protagonist on a journey into the heartland to rediscover a terrain which becomes hauntingly vivid in its detail and its characters. The impenetrable mists and inscrutable crowds and sounds which bewilder Marlowe, are here scrutinized and given a reality, a context, and a poignancy which challenge the representations offered by both Conrad and Naipaul.

Like Phillips, Dabydeen has also turned to the eighteenth century and the history of slavery as a means of bringing to life a suppressed history. *Slave Song* (1984), *Coolie Odyssey* (1988), and *Turner* (1994) are long poems or poetic sequences giving voice, sometimes in the creolized and vivid language of Guyanese 'coolies' and slaves, to the experience of plantation life and immigration from India to Guyana and Britain. *Turner* takes as its starting point J.M.W. Turner's painting, *Slavers Throwing Overboard the Dead and Dying*, with both the picture and the poem recreating the 1783 *Zong* case which Equiano had been instrumental in publicizing and contesting. In almost all his works, Dabydeen sets up a linguistic and aesthetic struggle between the cultural traditions and experiences framed by the Western canon and histories and experiences which he as the descendant of a Guyanan plantation worker seeks to express.

The *Zong* case is also taken as the inspiration for Fred D'Aguiar's novel, *Feeding the Ghosts*, which writes back to Dabydeen, Turner, and the early slave narrators in its recreation of the consciousness and voice of an imagined survivor, Mintah, an enslaved woman. Mintah's memories, dreams, and visions as she floats in the sea encapsulate the struggle between a destructive history and the potentially redemptive powers of imagination. As members of that younger generation which was educated in Britain in the 1970s both Dabydeen and D'Aguiar offer in their poetry and fiction a confident response not only to a specifically canonical English literary tradition, but also to a tradition of black and Asian writing within and without Britain. For Dabydeen and D'Aguiar that tradition includes a distinctively Guyanan one, featuring the powerful visionary and anti-realist fiction of Wilson Harris, and later Pauline Melville, as well as other poets such as John Agard and Grace Nichols.

This later generation of writers (including Rushdie, Gurnah and Phillips) responds implicitly or explicitly to the experience of living in a Britain which heard outbursts of racist and anti-immigration rhetoric from Enoch Powell, Margaret Thatcher, and other prominent members of the establishment. It also witnessed riots in many British cities, and a concerned response by liberal institutions and members of the public to these. Schools and some universities in Britain in the late 1970s and 1980s sought to revise the literary curriculums to include works by African, Asian, African American, and black British writers such as Chinua Achebe, Anita Desai, Ralph Ellison, Toni Morrison, and Furrukh Dhondy. Organizations such as the Inner London Education Authority (ILEA) and the Association for Teaching Caribbean and African Literature (ATCAL) brought together teachers and writers from educational institutions and community organizations through the country to discuss texts, curriculum, and to disseminate information about black and Asian writing. ATCAL was responsible for inaugurating in 1984 the still-flourishing journal of African, Caribbean, Asian and associated literatures, *Wasafiri*. Under the editorship of Susheila Nasta, *Wasafiri* has continued to fulfil its original aim of creating an accessible forum for multicultural debates and to promote and give space to new creative writing. As a focus for postcolonial writing both inside and outside Britain, *Wasafiri* remains unique, although its presence has had a considerable influence on other journals and publishers in encouraging them to include within their brief Anglophone writing from a wider spectrum of writers and cultural traditions. But perhaps most importantly for this discussion, it has helped reinforce that sense of a wider cultural community, a multicultural audience, which is responsive to black and Asian British writers.

Such a sense of a diverse and multicultural audience has in turn encouraged a greater diversity of writing which paradoxically often rests upon a sense of solidarity among black and Asian Britons in the face of the 'little England' mentality expressed by Margaret Thatcher, some members of her cabinet, and some newspapers. In the 1980s, Salman Rushdie celebrated the 'hybridity' of his culture and identity, and 'hybridity' has become a term proclaimed by many later writers and critics, including pre-eminently Homi Bhabha. In a 1997 manifesto, 'Re-Inventing Britain', Bhabha advocated a move away from 'the multiculturalist thinking of the eighties', which in his view 'sought to revise the homogenous notion of national culture by emphasising the multiple identities of race/class/gender' and thus reinforced the notion of national or ethnic identities as given. For Bhabha, multiculturalist thinking obscures 'the hybrid cosmopolitanism of contemporary metropolitan life', a hybridity which is constantly in process and transformation.[9] Like Rushdie, he draws attention to the transformational powers of a cosmopolitan migrant culture, for not only do migrants reimagine their 'homelands', their places of ancestral origin, they also 'impose their needs on their new earth, bringing their own coherence to the new-found land, imagining it afresh'.[10] Commenting on Bhabha's manifesto, Stuart Hall perhaps reflects his experience as a Jamaican who came to England in the fifties, and his academic grounding as an eminent sociologist, when he expresses some scepticism about the view that globalization 'has completely evaporated the space of national culture'.[11] Indeed, he sees in many cases a hardening of cultural nationalism in the face of dislocation and globalization, although he too, in an earlier essay quoted in Chapter Two of this book, has also advocated a move away from fixed identities to an acceptance of the 'positionality' of identity.

Salman Rushdie's own fiction is perhaps the most widely recognized example of writing which reinvents histories and identities, and celebrates hybridity, not only in terms of cultures but also genres. Variously described by critics as magic realist, postmodern, and postcolonial, his novels draw on traditional Indian oral and written narrative forms, popular Indian film and theatre, as well as shifting and often disconcerting perspectives embraced by writers such as Gabriel Marcia Marquez. Remarkable for their energy, linguistic playfulness, and exuberance, his novels are also sharply satiric regarding the politics of India, Pakistan, and contemporary Britain. *Midnight's Children*, a surreal retelling of India's history since 1947, won the Booker Prize in 1981, and subsequently was awarded the 'Best of the Bookers' in twenty-five years of the award. Paradoxically *Satanic Verses*, the only one of Rushdie's novels which is mainly placed (if not grounded) in Britain, is also the one which has received the most virulent attacks from abroad, and resulted in a sentence of death (*fatwa*) by the Ayatollah Khomeini in Iran, as well as bannings, book-burnings, and death threats elsewhere.

Sharply critical of conservative British nationalism (as well as other nationalisms), *Satanic Verses* revisits British history and migrancy through the scenes set in the Hot Wax Club, an alternative version to that established by the iconic figures in Madame Tussaud's museum. Here the wax figures include Ignatius Sancho, Mary Seacole 'who did as much in the Crimea as another magic-lamping Lady, but, being dark, could scarce be seen for the flame of Florence's candle',[12] Abdul Karim, Grace Jones, Septimus Severus, and Ukawsaw Gronniosaw. Its episodic structure, its linguistic and generic transformations, and its character as a kind of Bildungsroman, also recall G.V. Desani's *All About H. Hatterr*, whose influence Rushdie has acknowledged. But as Leela Gandhi points out, the historical icons of an immigrant history in Britain are deployed by the Hot Wax Club's deejay, Pinkawalla, to 'lay claims to the nation's present'.[13] And, in a mode reminiscent of the poet Linton Kwesi Johnson (the novel also playfully refers to a character named Hanif Johnson, presumably an amalgamated allusion to Hanif Kureishi and Linton Kwesi Johnson), the deejay chants: '*Now-mi-feel-indignation-when-dem-talk-immigration-when-dem-make-insinuation-we-no-part-o-de-nation-an-mi-make-proclamation-a-de-true-situation-how-we-make-contribution-since-de-Rome-occupation.*'[14] The deejay, Pinkawalla, is described as a remarkably hybrid character, 'a seven-foot albino, his hair the palest rose, the whites of his eyes likewise, his features unmistakably Indian, the haughty nose, long thin lips, a face from *Hamza-nama* cloth. An Indian who has never seen India, East-India-man from the West Indies, white black man. A star.'[15] As an albino Indian and a singer, Pinkawalla recalls the albino child in Cornelia Sorabji's story, 'The Feast of Lights', but the difference between her shrill mimicry of Englishness and Pinkawalla's confidently hybrid mingling of cultures and linguistic forms also marks the historical change that has taken place in the movement from a bicultural identity, opposing two established traditions and homelands, to the fluidly communal and immigrant-inflected cosmopolitan culture that Rushdie celebrates.

In the 1990s and first years of the twenty-first century new realist fiction and drama continues to make an impact, for instance in the prize-winning *White Teeth* by Zadie Smith, which gives voice to West Indian, Asian, and Anglo-Saxon families in a grounded London setting, or the 'yardie' novels of Courttia Newland, or the historical revisiting of the eighteenth-century black British community in S.I. Martin's *Incomparable Worlds*, or the Bildungsromans by Andrea Levy of young West Indian women rediscovering their family histories. But the last decade of the century has also produced some striking experimental fiction and poetry, which sidesteps the powerful models provided by Rushdie by drawing on African and Amerindian traditions which in turn transform canonical English and European literary icons. Ben Okri's *The Famished Road*, awarded the Booker Prize in 1991, takes the traditional Yoruba (and Igbo) figure of the *abiku* (a child returned from the dead) to portray a hauntingly surreal picture of urban Nigeria and its thoroughly hybrid culture. Pauline Melville links Dante, Amerindian legend, and clever mimicry of Evelyn Waugh and Claude Levi-Strauss to revisit Guyana in the *Ventriloquist's Tale*. Bernardine Evaristo's *Lara* (1997) combines verse and prose in a richly evocative traversing of Brazilian, Nigerian, and British/Irish traditions and communities. Evaristo is also a witty and unusual poet, whose most recent verse novel, *The Emperor's Babe* (2001), recreates the world of a young girl of Sudanese parentage who grows up in Roman London eighteen hundred years ago. Jackie Kay's poetry draws on the distinctively Scottish female tradition represented by Liz Lochhead in Kay's autobiographical *The Adoption Papers* (1991), a set of poems which interweave the voices of natural and adoptive mothers with that of their Scottish-Nigerian child. Kay's recent novel, *Trumpet* (1998), tells the story of the love between a Scottish woman, a black trumpeter who 'passes' as a man, and their adopted mixed-race son. It is a story which recalls the narrative told by William Craft, with its clear understanding that racial and gendered identities are constructed and performed, and where the hybrid forms match the themes. Like so much of the writing by black and Asian people in Britain throughout the previous two centuries, it allows the reader to understand the extent to which individual selves as well as visions of Britain may be continually invented and reinvented. Indeed they *must* be reinvented in resistance to the persistently experienced pressure to confine peoples and communities within rigid categories.

Notes

INTRODUCTION

1. Richard Wright, *White Man Listen* (New York: Doubleday Anchor, 1964), p. xvii.
2. C.L.R. James, *Beyond a Boundary* (London: Serpent's Tail, 1983), p. xxi. (First published London: Stanley Paul/Hutchinson, 1963.)
3. C.L.R. James, 'Africans and Afro-Caribbeans: A Personal View', *Ten* 8, no.16 (1984). Reprinted in *Writing Black Britain 1948–1998*, ed. James Procter (Manchester University Press, 2000), pp. 60–3.
4. See for example, Procter, *Writing Black Britain*; special issues of *Wasafiri* (no.29, Spring 1999) and *Kunapipi* (21, no.2, 1999) on 'Black Writing in Britain' and 'Postcolonial London' respectively; Susheila Nasta, *Home Truths: Fictions of the South Asian Diaspora in Britain* (Basingstoke: Palgrave, 2001); Kwesi Owusu, ed. *Black British Culture and Society* (London: Routledge, 2000).
5. Peter Fryer, *Staying Power: The History of Black People in Britain* (London: Pluto Press, 1984); Rozina Visram, *Ayahs, Lascars, and Princes: The Story of Indians in Britain 1700–1947* (London: Pluto Press, 1986).

1 FIRST ENCOUNTERS: THE HISTORICAL CONTEXT

1. Fryer, *Staying Power*, pp. 3–4.
2. *The Poems of William Dunbar*, ed. W. Mackay Mackenzie (London: Faber and Faber, 1970), p. 66.
3. *Ibid.*, pp. 211–12. See also Fryer, *Staying Power*, p. 3.
4. Fryer, *Staying Power*, pp. 4–5.
5. *William Shakespeare, Othello*, Act 1, Sc.3, ll.133–44, in *The Norton Shakespeare* (New York: W.W. Norton, 1997), p. 2110.
6. Fryer, *Staying Power*, p. 8. 'A demi-Moor proper' indicated a half-length figure in natural colouring.
7. Ben Jonson, *The Masque of Blackness*, reprinted in *Court Masques. 1605–1640*, ed. David Lindley (Oxford University Press, 1995), pp. 1–9. This elaborately costumed and designed masque portrays the meeting of the River Niger and his daughters (the Niger being deemed the territory of the 'blackest nation of the world'), and the sons and daughters of Oceanus. The Niger

and his progeny are represented as figures of elegance and dignity, seeking to encounter the rumoured glories of Britannia.

8. Fryer, *Staying Power*, p. 11.
9. *Ibid.*, p. 12.
10. Visram, *Ayars, Lascars, and Princes*, p. 3.
11. Dale H. Porter, *The Abolition of the Slave Trade in England, 1784–1807* (Hamden, Conn.: Archon Books, 1970), pp. 1–5.
12. Quoted by Fryer, *Staying Power*, pp. 16–17. See also similar statements from eighteenth-century merchants and politicians quoted by Fryer, pp. 17–18.
13. David Dabydeen, *Hogarth's Blacks: Images of Blacks in Eighteenth-Century English Art* (Kingston-upon-Thames: Dangaroo Press, 1985), pp. 19–20.
14. *Ibid.*, pp. 32–6.
15. *Ibid.*, pp. 35–6.
16. Visram, *Ayahs, Lascars, and Princes*, p. 11.
17. *Ibid.*, p. 38.
18. Quoted by Dabydeen, *Hogarth's Blacks*, p. 18.
19. William Wordsworth, *The Prelude*, Book 7, in *Wordsworth: Poetical Works*, ed. Thomas Hutchinson (Oxford University Press, 1969), p. 540.
20. James Walvin, *England, Slaves and Freedom, 1776–1838* (Basingstoke: Macmillan, 1986), p. 21.
21. Fryer, *Staying Power*, p. 114.
22. *Ibid.*, pp. 124–6.
23. *Ibid.*, p. 128.
24. *Ibid.*, p. 130.
25. For a fuller discussion of the commodification of goods and peoples from the empire, see Laura Brown, 'The Romance of Empire: *Oroonoko* and the Trade in Slaves', in *The New Eighteenth Century: Theory, Politics, Literature*, ed. F. Nussbaum and L. Brown (New York and London: Methuen, 1987), pp. 41–61.
26. Cited by Pat Rogers, Introduction, *The Context of English Literature: The Eighteenth Century* (London: Methuen, 1978), p. 70.
27. Cited by Frances Smith Foster, *Witnessing Slavery: The Development of Ante-Bellum Slave Narratives* (Greenport, Conn.: Greenwood Press, 1979), pp. 33–5.
28. Cited by Vincent Carretta, ed. *The Letters of the Late Ignatius Sancho, An African* (Harmondsworth: Penguin, 1998), p. xxix.
29. *Othello*, Act 5, Sc.2, l.342. In a footnote appended by Olaudah Equiano, *The Interesting Narrative of the Life of Olaudah Equiano, or Gustavus Vassa, the African, Written by Himself, and other Writings*, ed. Vincent Carretta (Harmondsworth: Penguin, 1995), p. 238.
30. *The English Review* 11 (1788), p. 277. Cited by J.R. Oldfield, *Popular Politics and British Anti-Slavery 1787–1807* (Manchester University Press, 1995), p. 22.
31. Cited by S.E. Ogude, *Genius in Bondage: A Study of the Origins of African Literature in English* (University of Ife Press, 1983), p. 95. (From *The Philosophical Works of David Hume*, ed. T.H. Green and T.H. Grose–London, 1875, III, p. 390, n.2.)

2 EIGHTEENTH-CENTURY LETTERS AND NARRATIVES: IGNATIUS SANCHO, OLAUDAH EQUIANO, AND DEAN MAHOMED

1. Equiano, *Interesting Narrative*, pp. 93–4. Further quotations will be taken from this edition, which is based on the ninth and final edition (1794) which Equiano himself authorised before his death.
2. A *Narrative of the Remarkable Particulars in the Life of James Albert Ukawsaw Gronniosaw, An African Prince, related by himself* (Bath: W. Gye Printer, [1772?]). Reprinted in Vincent Carretta, ed. *Unchained Voices: An Anthology of Black Voices in the English-Speaking World of the Eighteenth Century* (Lexington: University Press of Kentucky, 1996), pp. 32–58. Page references to Gronniosaw's *Narrative* are to the 1772 first edition and will be included in the main text.
3. Quobna Ottobah Cugoano, *Thoughts and Sentiments on the Evil and Wicked Traffic of the Slavery and Commerce of the Human Species* . . . . London: T. Becket, 1787. Facsimile edition reprinted and edited by Paul Edwards (London: Dawson, 1968). This edition is reprinted with introduction and notes by Vincent Carretta (Harmondsworth: Penguin, 1999).
4. Carretta, *Unchained Voices*, p. 4, n.54.
5. *A Narrative of the Lord's Wonderful Dealings with John Marrant, A Black* (London: Gilbert and Plummer, 1785), 'Taken down from his own narration, arranged, corrected and published By the Rev Mr Aldridge'. Aldridge notes: 'I have always preserved Mr Marrant's ideas, tho' I could not his language; no more alterations, however, have been made than were thought necessary'; in Carretta, *Unchained Voices*, pp. 110–33; pp. 110–11.
6. *Poems on Various Subjects, Religious and Moral. By Phyllis Wheatley, Negro Servant to Mr John Wheatley, of Boston, in New England* (London: A. Bell; Boston: Cox and Berry, 1773).
7. Carretta, ed. Introduction, in Cugoano, *Thoughts and Sentiments*, pp. xxiii–xxv.
8. Cugoana, *Thoughts and Sentiments*, ed. Carretta, pp. 89–90.
9. *Ibid.*, p. 110.
10. *Ibid.*, pp. 110–11.
11. *The Letters of Ignatius Sancho*, ed. Paul Edwards and Polly Rewt (Edinburgh University Press, 1994), p. 22. Further page reference to this edition will be included in the main text.
12. Edwards and Rewt, eds. *Letters of Ignatius Sancho*, p. 48 identify the reference here as to Pope's *Eloisa and Abelard*, but Vincent Carretta's view that the reference is more probably to the currently widely read novel by Rousseau is persuasive. See Carretta, ed. *Letters of the Late Ignatius Sancho*, p. 265, n.5.
13. Jekyll, 'Life of Ignatius Sancho', in *Letters of the Late Ignatius Sancho*, ed. Carretta, pp. 6–7.
14. Edwards and Rewt, eds. *Letters of Ignatius Sancho*, pp. 25–9.
15. Cited by Carretta, *Letters of the Late Ignatius Sancho*, p. xv, from the *Gentleman's Magazine* (September 1782). However Carretta also cites a more liberal and

less racially focussed pronouncement from *The European Magazine and London Review* (September, 1782), *Letters*, p. xvi.

16. Carretta, *Letters of the Late Ignatius Sancho*, p. xvi.
17. *Ibid.*, p. xx.
18. Abbé H.B. Grégoire, *De la Littérature des Nègres* (Paris: n.p., 1808), pp. 252–60.
19. Norma Myers, *Reconstructing the Black Past, Blacks in Britain 1780–1830* (London: Frank Cass, 1996), p. 133.
20. James Walvin, *Black and White: The Negro and English Society, 1555–1945* (Harmondsworth: Penguin, 1973), p. 61.
21. Paul Edwards, ed. *Letters of the Late Ignatius Sancho, An African* (London: Dawson, 1968), p. xv.
22. Folarin Shyllon, *Black People in Britain, 1555–1833* (London: Oxford University Press for the Institute of Race Relations, 1977), p. 193. See also p. 202, n.26.
23. Ogude, *Genius in Bondage*, p. 101.
24. *Ibid.*, p. 116.
25. Keith A. Sandiford, *Measuring the Moment: Strategies of Protest in Eighteenth-Century Afro-English Writing* (Susquhanna University Press, 1988), p. 150.
26. S.S. Sandhu, 'Ignatius Sancho and Laurence Sterne', *Research in African Literatures* 29, no.4 (Winter 1998), pp. 88–105; p. 89.
27. *Ibid.*, pp. 92–3.
28. *Ibid.*, p. 94. See also Edwards and Rewt, eds. *Letters of Ignatius Sancho*, p. 112.
29. Stuart Hall, 'Cultural Identity and Diaspora', in Patrick Williams and Laura Chrisman, eds. *Colonial Discourse and Post-Colonial Theory: A Reader* (Hemel Hempstead: Harvester Wheatsheaf, 1993), pp. 392–403; p. 395.
30. *Ibid.*, pp. 396–7.
31. Jenny Uglow, *Hogarth: A Life and a World* (London: Faber and Faber, 1997), pp. 159–60.
32. The question of Equiano's place and date of birth is far from settled. Vincent Carretta has discovered information that suggests that Gustavus Vassa may have been a native of South Carolina and later assumed the name Olaudah Equiano and an African identity, or at least may have left Africa at a much younger age than twelve or eleven as his *Narrative* asserts. See Vincent Carretta, 'Olaudah Equiano or Gustavus Vassa? New Light on an Eighteenth-century Question of Identity', *Slavery and Abolition* 20, no.3 (December 1999), pp. 96–105.
33. Chinua Achebe, 'Work and Play in Tutuola's *The Palm-wine Drinkard*', *Okike* 14 (September 1978), pp. 25–33; p. 32.
34. Catherine Acholonu, 'The Home of Olaudah Equiano – a Linguistic and Anthropological Survey', *Journal of Commonwealth Literature* 22 (1987), pp. 5–16.
35. Ogude, *Genius in Bondage*, p. 137.
36. Equiano, *Narrative*, p. 7.
37. *Ibid.*, p. 32.
38. Quoted by Carretta, *ibid.*, pp. 242–3, n.57.

39. For further discussion of Equiano's combining of the personal and the public, see Sonia Hofkosh, 'Tradition and *The Interesting Narrative*,' in Alan Richardson and Sonia Hofkosh, eds. *Romanticism, Race, and Imperial Culture, 1780–1834* (Bloomington: Indiana University Press, 1996), pp. 330–44.

40. Olaudah Equiano, *The Interesting Narrative* (Leeds: James Nichols, 1914) in Henry Louis Gates, Jr, ed. *The Classic Slave Narratives* (New York: New American Library, 1987), p. 5.

41. Hofkosh, 'Tradition and *The Interesting Narrative*', pp. 334–5.

42. During the second half of his life, Sake Dean consistently spelled his name 'Mahomed,' although 'Mahomet' is used for the publication of the *Travels*. The spelling 'Mahomed' will be used in this book, except when directly quoting from the *Travels* or contemporary commentators.

43. Michael H. Fisher, *The First Indian Author in English: Dean Mahomed (1759–1851) in India, Ireland, and England* (New Delhi: Oxford University Press, 1996), pp. 226–32.

44. Cited by Balachandra Rajan, 'Feminising the Feminine: Early Women Writers in India', in Richardson and Hofkosh, *Romanticism, Race, and Imperial Culture*, pp. 149–72; p. 153. *Hartley House, Calcutta* (Anon, London: n.p., 1789) is an epistolary novel in the form of letters from Sophia Goldborne to a close friend in London. A pirated edition was published in Dublin in the same year. This novel may have inspired or set the context for Elizabeth Hamilton's *Translations of the Letters of a Hindu Rajah* (London: G. and J. Hamilton, 1796), with five editions between then and 1811.

45. Michael H. Fisher, ed. *The Travels of Dean Mahomet: An Eighteenth-Century Journey through India* (Berkeley: University of California Press, 1997), pp. 34–5. All further references will be to this edition of the text, which reproduces the text first published in Cork in 1794.

46. 'Seapoys' (or sepoys) were Indian soldiers enlisted to serve the East India Company army and given Europeanized uniforms.

47. The description of efforts by these administrators and rulers to give relief to the many dying of starvation during the drought and famine of 1769/70 is also echoed by similar descriptions by members of the Anglo-Irish ascendancy class (for example Somerville and Ross) of attempts to give assistance during the Famine of the 1840s.

48. Kate Teltscher, 'The Shampooing Surgeon and the Persian Prince: Two Indians in Early Nineteenth-century Britain', *Interventions* 2, no.3 (2000), pp. 409–23; p. 413.

49. For a detailed comparison of passages from Grose and Kindersley, see Fisher, *The First Indian Author in English*, pp. 227–33. The citations are from Jemima Kindersley, *Letters from the Island of Teneriffe, Brazil, the Cape of Good Hope, and the East Indies* (London: Norse, 1777) and John Henry Grose, *A Voyage to the East Indies with Observations* (London: S. Hooper and A. Morley, 1766).

50. Mary Louise Pratt, *Imperial Eyes: Travel Writing and Transculturation* (London: Routledge, 1992), p. 7 (her italics).

51. Michael Fisher points out that Hastings had considerably increased the amount of revenue originally agreed in the treaty between the East India Company and the Raja. Chayt Singh argued 'that these enhanced demands exceeded what the extant treaties required, and that he could not afford to meet them in any case'. *Travels of Dean Mahomet*, p. 24.

52. See *Travels of Mirza Abu Taleb Khan in Asia, Africa, and Europe, During the Years 1799, 1800, 1801, 1802, and 1803, and written by Himself in the Persian Language*. Trans. Charles Stewart (London: Longman, 1814), I, pp. 124–5.

3 SPEAKING TRUTH FOR FREEDOM AND JUSTICE: ROBERT WEDDERBURN AND MARY PRINCE

1. *Black Writers in Britain, 1760–1890*, ed. Paul Edwards and David Dabydeen (Edinburgh University Press, 1995), pp. 127–8. For further information about these groups see Iain McCalman, *Radical Underworld: Prophets, Revolutionaries and Pornographers in London, 1795–1840* (Cambridge University Press, 1988).

2. McCalman, *Radical Underworld*, pp. 53 and 147.

3. Edwards and Dabydeen, *Black Writers in Britain*, p. 129.

4. In T.B. Howell, *State Trials*, 33 vols. + index (London: Longman, 1826), XXXIII, pp. 1498–1566.

5. *'The Horrors of Slavery' and Other Writings by Robert Wedderburn*, ed. Iain McCalman (Cambridge University Press, 1991), p. 43. Further references to this edition will be included in the main text.

6. Reprinted in *ibid.*, pp. 65–77.

7. Paul Gilroy, *The Black Atlantic: Modernity and Double Consciousness* (Cambridge, Mass.: Harvard University Press, 1993), p. 12.

8. See McCalman's introduction to *'The Horrors of Slavery'*, pp. 12ff. See also McCalman's chapters on Spence and Wedderburn in *Radical Underworld*.

9. McCalman, introduction to *'The Horrors of Slavery'*, p. 18.

10. *The History of Mary Prince, A West Indian Slave*, ed. Sara Salih (Harmondsworth: Penguin, 2000), p. 42. Subsequent references to this edition, which also contains Pringle's preface and supplementary material relating to her court case, will be included in the text.

11. Thomas Pringle was at the time secretary of the Anti-Slavery Society. He is known today as one of South Africa's pioneer poets.

12. *Mary Prince*, p. 44.

13. *The History of Mary Prince* and another narrative of slavery (the *Narrative of Ashton Warner*) are actually ascribed to Susanna Moodie by some critics. See, for example, Misao Dean's entry on Moodie in *The Encyclopedia of Post-Colonial Literatures in English*, ed. E. Benson and L.W. Conolly (London: Routledge, 1994), p. 1037. Such an unqualified ascription is puzzling, given that Susanna Strickland's name (as she was then) appears nowhere in the material accompanying the *History*, and given the emphasis on the words being Mary Prince's own. On the other hand, one might speculate that

Susanna Moodie's involvement in transcribing this history might well have suggested the autobiographical works she wrote later, works which at times shocked Victorian sensibilities with their descriptions of the 'unfeminine' field work she participated in as a pioneer 'roughing it in the bush' (to use the title of her first major autobiographical work).

14. Quoted by Gillian Whitlock, *The Intimate Empire: Reading Women's Autobiography* (London: Cassell, 2000), p. 18.
15. *Ibid.*, p. 19.
16. Moira Ferguson, *Subject to Others: British Women Writers and Colonial Slavery, 1670–1834* (London: Routledge, 1992), p. 296.
17. Ferguson is here quoting from Karl Marx, *The Eighteenth Brumaire of Louis Bonaparte.*
18. Ferguson, *Subject to Others*, p. 282.
19. Harriet Jacobs, *Incidents in the Life of a Slave Girl, Written by Herself*, ed. Jean Fagan Yellin (Cambridge, Mass.: Harvard University Press, 1985), p. 5.
20. 'Osnaburgs' refer to a rough linen cloth originally made in the town of Osnabruck in Germany, and used to make clothing for servants and slaves.
21. Willie Lee Rose, *Slavery and Freedom* (New York: Oxford University Press, 1982), p. 21. For further discussion of the discourse of domesticity and its refutation in the autobiographies of Frederick Douglass and Harriet Jacobs, see Donald B. Gibson, 'Harriet Jacobs, Frederick Douglass, and the Slavery Debate: Bondage, Family, and the Discourses of Domesticity', in *Harriet Jacobs and 'Incidents in the Life of a Slave Girl'*, ed. Deborah M. Garfield and Rafia Zafar. (Cambridge University Press, 1996), pp. 156–78.
22. Pringle in this same passage emphasizes Mary Prince's 'decency and propriety of conduct' and her 'delicacy' in relationships with others. As Sara Salih points out in the introduction to her edition of *The History of Mary Prince*, details which might have led contemporary readers to judge Mary Prince as less than decent or proper were suppressed by Susanna Strickland, including her seven-year liaison with a Captain Abbot. During a libel trial brought by John Wood against Pringle, Prince spoke frankly about this relationship and affirmed that she had also reported it to Strickland as part of her narrative (*Mary Prince*, p. xxix).
23. Ferguson, *Subject to Others*, p. 284.
24. Pringle does not himself escape the discourse of race, although he seeks to refute it. For example, 'We consider her on the whole as respectable and well-behaved a person in her station, as any domestic, white or black (and we have had ample experience of both colours,) that we have ever had in our service' (p. 55).
25. Pringle's appendix also mentions a possible liaison with a white captain and expresses the view that such relations are condoned in the West Indies as 'normal', and that slave women have no other possibility since they are denied marriage. There is no mention of such a relationship in Prince's *History*, although one might speculate that Mary's reference to being too

ashamed to speak of her sins and crying all night for forgiveness after her visit to a Methodist prayer meeting one Christmas may have been to do with the alleged liaison.

4 THE IMPERIAL CENTURY

1. Shyllon, *Black People in Britain*, p. 159. Of course, others such as the descendants of Sake Dean Mohamed remained aware of their ancestry, although their names were often Anglicized.
2. *Ibid.*, p. 161.
3. McCalman, *Radical Underworld*, p. 54.
4. For more details about Davidson and Wedderburn, see Chapter Three. For an account of this group as a whole, sometimes referred to as 'the blackbirds', see McCalman, *Radical Underworld*. They are the subject of S.I. Martin's 1996 novel, *Incomparable World* (London: Quartet Books), although Martin portrays them more as beggars, prophets, and pornographers than as revolutionaries.
5. For a full discussion of the British anti-slavery movement, see Christine Bolt, *The Anti-Slavery Movement and Reconstruction: A Study of Anglo-American Cooperation, 1833–1877* (London: Oxford University Press, 1969). See also Howard Temperley, *British Anti-Slavery, 1833–1870* (London: Longman, 1972). In their focus on the activities of white Britons to abolish slavery, neither author gives more than a passing mention to the ex-slaves and others of African descent whose writing and lecturing helped fuel the anti-slavery crusades.
6. Jennifer DeVere Brody, *Impossible Purities: Blackness, Femininity, and Victorian Culture* (Durham, N.C.: Duke University Press, 1998), p. 75. See also Audrey Fisch, *American Slaves in Victorian England: Abolitionist Politics in Popular Literature and Culture* (Cambridge University Press, 2000).
7. Brody, *Impossible Purities*, pp. 131–2.
8. Cited by Fryer, *Staying Power*, p. 242.
9. See especially Ronald Hyam, *Britain's Imperial Century, 1815–1914* (Basingstoke: Macmillan, 1993).
10. Eric Stokes, *The English Utilitarians and India* (Oxford University Press, 1959), p. 147.
11. Cited by Thomas R. Metcalf, *Ideologies of the Raj* (Cambridge University Press, 1994), p. 34.
12. Cited by Simon C. Smith, *British Imperialism, 1750–1970* (Cambridge University Press, 1998), p. 51.
13. Edward A. Freeman, *A History of the Norman Conquest*, 6 vols. (Oxford: Clarendon Press, 1870–9), v, p. 554. Cited by Brody, *Impossible Purities*, p. 141.
14. Matthew Arnold, *On the Study of Celtic Literature* (London: Smith, Elder and Co., 1867).
15. Charles Darwin, *The Variation of Animals and Plants under Domestication* (London: John Murray, 1868); quoted by Brody, *Impossible Purities*, p. 137.

16. Robert J.C. Young, *Colonial Desire: Hybridity in Theory, Culture and Race* (London: Routledge, 1995), Chapter One.

17. See for example V.D. Savarkar, *The Indian War of Independence of 1857* (London: n.p., 1909).

18. Cited by Smith, *British Imperialism*, p. 54.

19. Quoted by Christine Bolt, *Victorian Attitudes to Race* (London: Routledge, 1971), p. 162.

20. *Ibid.*, p. 162.

21. Gayatri Chakravorty Spivak, 'Can the Subaltern Speak', in C. Nelson and L. Grossberg, eds. *Marxism and the Interpretation of Culture* (Basingstoke: Macmillan, 1988), pp. 271–313.

22. Jennifer Sharpe, 'The Unspeakable Limits of Rape: Colonial Violence and Counter-Insurgency', *Genders* 10 (Spring 1991), pp. 25–46.

23. Quoted by Catherine Hall, *White, Male, and Middle Class: Explorations in Feminism and History* (Cambridge: Polity Press, 1992), p. 284.

24. *Ibid.*, pp. 284–5.

25. Bolt, *Victorian Attitudes to Race*, pp. 81–3.

26. *The Bee Hive*, 9 December 1865. Quoted by Bolt, *Victorian Attitudes to Race*, p. 84.

27. Bolt, *Victorian Attitudes to Race*, pp. 83ff.

28. Simon Gikandi, *Maps of Englishness: Writing Identity in the Culture of Colonialism* (New York: Columbia University Press, 1996), pp. 50–69. Gikandi goes on to analyse the continuities between mid nineteenth- and mid twentieth-century constructions of Englishness through the invocation of racial difference in the speeches of Enoch Powell.

29. *Ibid.*, p. 66.

30. Gikandi, *Maps of Englishness*, p. xix.

31. Jennifer DeVere Brody provides in *Impossible Purities* a detailed analysis of the role of Rhoda Swartz in the novel and in the context of Victorian anxieties about race and hybridity.

32. Charles Reade, *Peg Woffington* (London: Bradbury, Evans, and Co., 1868), p. 46.

33. *Charles Kingsley, His Letters and Memories of His Life*, Edited by his Wife, 2 vols. (London: H.S. King and Co., 1877), II, p. 107.

34. Cited by Fryer, *Staying Power*, pp. 253–5.

35. Smith, *British Imperialism*, p. 56.

36. H.G. Wells, *Anticipations of the Reaction of Mechanical and Scientific Progress Upon Human Life and Thought* (London: Chapman and Hall, 1901), p. 317.

5 QUERYING RACE, GENDER, AND GENRE: NINETEENTH-CENTURY NARRATIVES OF ESCAPE

1. C. Peter Ripley, ed. *The Black Abolitionist Papers, Vol.1: The British Isles, 1835–65* (Chapel Hill: University of North Carolina Press, 1985), p. 62.

2. Fryer, *Staying Power*, p. 432.

3. Moses Roper, *A Narrative of the Adventures and Escape of Moses Roper from American Slavery*. With a Preface by the Rev. T. Price. (London: Darton, Harvey, and Darton, 1837), p. 78. Further page references to this narrative will be included in the main text.

4. Published as L.A. Chamerovzow, ed. *Slave Life in Georgia: A Narrative of the Life, Suffering, and Escape of John Brown, Fugitive Slave, Now in England* (London, L.A. Chamerovzow, 1855). Reprinted: F.N. Boney, ed. *Slave Life in Georgia: A Narrative of the Life, Suffering, and Escape of John Brown, Fugitive Slave* (Beehive Press: Library of Georgia, Savannah, 1991). All page references are to this later reprint and will be included in the main text.

5. Louis Alexis Chamerovzow succeeded J. Scoble as secretary in 1851, when Scoble went to Canada to set up the Dawes institute for Negro Fugitives. Brown's narrative suggests some reservations about this institute and its management. Chamerovzow remained secretary of the society until 1869. The very literary style of Chapters Four ('The Story of John Glasgow'), Eighteen ('The Cultivation of Cotton, Tobacco, and Rice'), and Twenty-One ('The Underground Railroad'), as well as their content, suggest that they are mainly the work of Chamerovzow rather than Brown.

6. *Slave Life in Georgia*, p. 5. F. Boney suggests that Brown must have been older than this, but there are no extant records of his birth or age (p. 5, n.1).

7. Brown speaks thus of his work in the saw-mills in the Dawes Institute (set up to provide training for fugitive slaves) in Canada, where Josiah Henson (who later toured England as 'the real Uncle Tom') also worked: 'I helped to saw the walnut timber which was sent to the Great Exhibition in Hyde Park in 1851 and exhibited in the Canadian Department, where I afterwards saw it again; and I also constructed a floating self-acting car-way, designed to draw timber from the water to the saw, which answered very well, and for which I was praised' (p. 140).

8. Francis Fedric, *Life and Sufferings of Francis Fedric, While in Slavery, An Escaped Slave After Fifty Years of Bondage* (Birmingham: Thomas and Jones, 1859); Francis Fedric, *Slave Life in Virginia and Kentucky, or Fifty Years of Slavery in the Southern States of America* (London: Wertheim, Macintosh and Hunt, 1863).

9. Fedric, *Slave Life*, p. 110.

10. Fedric, *Life and Sufferings*, p. 12.

11. Reverend Charles Lee, Preface, in Fedric, *Slave Life*, p. iv.

12. Title page, Fedric, *Life and Sufferings*. Future page references to this pamphlet will be included in the main text.

13. Reverend Charles Lee, Preface, in Fedric, *Slave Life*, p. iv. Future page references to this narrative will be included in the main text.

14. Compare in the second chapter, the vivid and 'sublime' description of the 'wild and hard' Kentucky landscape, with its mountains, towering rocks, and waterfalls, where the screeching of 'blackbirds' – not like the 'beautiful note' of the 'English bird of this name' – the howling of wolves, and other wild animals' break 'the solemn stillness which reigned widely around us' (Fedric, *Slave Life*, p. 17).

15. *Running a Thousand Miles for Freedom: Or The Escape of William and Ellen Craft from Slavery*. First published 1860. Reprinted in *Great Slave Narratives*, ed. Arna Bontemps (Boston: Beacon Press, 1969), pp. 269–331. Reprinted most recently with a foreword and biographical essay by R.J.M. Blackett (Baton Ronge: Louisiana State University Press, 1999). Page references are to this latest edition unless otherwise indicated.
16. Bontemps, *Great Slave Narratives*, p. 269.
17. *Ibid.*, p. 269.
18. Bontemps in his preface incorrectly names James Polk as the President who vowed to recapture the couple after the passing of the Fugitive Slave Act threatened their safety in Boston.
19. Benjamin Quarles, *Black Abolitionists* (New York: Oxford University Press, 1969), pp. 62–3. John Brown takes for granted his audience's knowledge of their story and appearance when he compares one of the female slaves on his plantation to Ellen Craft. 'One of these women I well remember. She was as white as Ellen Craft: that is, she might have passed for a white person without much fear of detection' (*Slave Life in Georgia*, p. 112).
20. Cited by Quarles, *Black Abolitionists*, p. 137.
21. Craft states his aim in writing the narrative thus, 'My story is intended not as a full history of the life of my wife, nor of myself; but merely as an account of our escape; together with other matter which I hope may be the means of creating in some minds a deeper abhorrence of the sinful and abominable practice of enslaving and brutifying our fellow-creatures' (*Running a Thousand Miles*, p. 1).
22. *Ibid.*, p. 298.
23. *The American Prejudice Against Color: An Authentic Narrative, Showing how Easily the Nation Got into an Uproar. By William G. Allen, A refugee from American Despotism* (London: W. and F.G. Cash, 1853). Reprint edition 1969 by New York: Arno Press, Inc. (Reprinted from a copy in Cornell University Library).
24. *Ibid.*, pp. 3–4. Further page references from the 1969 reprint edition will be included in the main text.
25. Quarles, *Black Abolitionists*, p. 35.
26. *Ibid.*, p. 358, n.1.
27. William Allen, *A Short Personal Narrative* (Dublin: William Curry and Co., 1860).
28. Cited by Fryer, *Staying Power*, p. 434.
29. In this aspect it has something in common with Harriet Wilson's autobiographical novel, *Our Nig*, subtitled 'Sketches from the Life of a Free Black, in a Two-Story White House North, Showing that Slavery's Shadows Fall Even There' (London: Alison and Busby, 1984). First published Boston: George C. Rand and Avery Co., 1859.
30. Cited by Quarles from a letter to Douglass in *Douglass's Paper* (20 May 1852), *Black Abolitionists*, p. 221.
31. Quarles, *Black Abolitionists*, p. 138.
32. Quoted by Quarles, *ibid.*, p. 225. No footnote or reference is given and I have not been able to trace the poem.

33. For description and discussion of such shows, see Hazel Waters, 'Putting on "Uncle Tom" on the Victorian Stage', *Race and Class* 42, no.3 (January–March 2001), pp. 29–48.
34. *From Bondage to Liberty* (London: Smethwick, 1889), p. 1. Future page references to this work will be included in the main text.
35. I have no idea whether the translations are at all accurate and how well they correspond to any actual native American speech. I quote here just one stanza, the first, from his version of 'In the Sweet By and By':

> Wh tawh uh kih ail wee kih jib w'eikh,
> Kih jee tay hye yain gwagh om k'nam nan,
> K'sau kee koon nuh kooch nuh a puh yainqk,
> Fatie sillaif can war ix awrt lj ll ay seeck,
> Weeg eel laiwh aish kih louy,
> K'naiwh tih noj weeng auwh zoowh wau kun ing.

36. Thomas L. Johnson, *Twenty-Eight Years a Slave, or the Story of My Life in Three Continents*. Subtitled 'Twenty-eight years a Slave in Virginia, afterwards, at Forty years of age, a Student in Spurgeon's College, Missionary in Africa, Evangelist in England (Bournemouth: W. Mate and Sons, 1909). Note: This is the seventh edition, with a preface dated 1908 (first edition, London: Yates Alexander and Shepheard, 1882). Page references to the 1909 edition will be included in the main text.
37. The original oil painting by Thomas Jones Barker, showed Queen Victoria presenting a Bible in the audience chamber at Windsor (c.1861). It is titled *The Secret of England's Greatness*, and now hangs in the National Portrait Gallery, London.

6 TRAVELLERS AND REFORMERS: MARY SEACOLE AND B.M. MALABARI

1. John Emmanuel Ocansey, *African Trading; or the Trials of William Narh Ocansey* (Liverpool: n.p., 1881. Extracts are printed in Edwards and Dabydeen, *Black Writers in Britain*, pp. 196–207. Ocansey and his letters also feature in Caryll Phillips, *The Atlantic Sound* (London: Faber and Faber, 2000).
2. Behramji M. Malabari, *The Indian Eye on English Life; or Rambles of a Pilgrim Reformer* (Westminster: Archibald Constable, 1893) (also published the same year in Bombay).
3. *The Wonderful Adventures of Mrs Seacole in Many Lands* (London: James Blackwood, 1857).
4. Mary Seacole, *The Wonderful Adventures of Mrs Seacole in Many Lands*, ed. Ziggy Alexander and Audrey Dewjee (Bristol: Falling Wall Press, 1984), p. 49. Future references to this edition will be included in the main text.
5. From 'A Stir for Seacole', *Punch*, 6 December 1856. Also published as an appendix to *The Wonderful Adventures of Mary Seacole in Many Lands*, ed. Alexander and Dewjee.

6. Count Gleichen, a nephew of Queen Victoria, who was later to carve a bust of Mrs Seacole, greeted her as 'Mami' when he met her in the Crimea. Seacole explains that 'he had been in the West Indies, and so called me by the familiar term used by the Creole children' (p. 201).

7. Whitlock, *The Intimate Empire*, pp. 90–1.

8. *Ibid.*, p. 92.

9. Pratt, *Imperial Eyes*, pp. 6–7; Whitlock, *The Intimate Empire*, p. 91.

10. Mary Poovey, *Uneven Developments: The Ideological Work of Gender in Mid-Victorian England* (London: Virago, 1989), p. 164.

11. Of her reaction to her husband's death she writes:

    This was my first great trouble, and I felt it bitterly. For days I never stirred – lost to all that passed around me in a dull stupor of despair. If you had told me the day would soon come when I would remember this sorrow calmly, I should not have believed it possible; and yet it was so. I do not think that we hot-blooded Creoles sorrow less for showing it impetuously; but I do think that the sharp edge of our grief wears down sooner than theirs who preserve an outward demeanour of calmness, and nurse their woe secretly in their hearts. (pp. 59–60)

12. Cited by Alexander and Dewjee, *Wonderful Adventures*, p. 31.

13. *Times*, 28 July 1857. Cited by Alexander and Dewjee, *Wonderful Adventures*, pp. 32–3.

14. See Illustration 15, Alexander and Dewjee, *Wonderful Adventures*, between pp. 120–1.

15. *Punch*, January 1867. Advertisement reprinted in Alexander and Dewjee, *Wonderful Adventures*, p. 237.

16. Alexander and Dewjee, *Wonderful Adventures*, p. 38.

17. Poovey, *Uneven Developments*, pp. 164–5.

18. *Ibid.*, p. 169.

19. Cited by Poovey, *Uneven Developments*, p. 182, from Nightingale, *Sanitary Nursing*, ed. L.R. Semer, p. 37.

20. Gikandi, *Maps of Englishness*, p. 130.

21. B.M. Malabari, *The Indian Muse in English Garb* (Bombay: The Reporters' Press, 1876).

22. Cited by Dayarum Gidumal, *Behramji M. Malabari: A Biographical Sketch* (London: T. Fisher Unwin, 1892), p. 127. Florence Nightingale provides a short introduction to the biography.

23. B.M. Malabari, *Infant Marriage and Enforced Widowhood in India ...* (Bombay: Voice of India Printing Press, 1887).

24. Cited by Antoinette Burton, *At the Heart of Empire: Indians and the Colonial Encounter in Late Victorian Britain* (Berkeley: University of California Press, 1998), p. 163; from Dayaram Gidumal, *The Life and Work of Behramji M. Malabari* (Byculla: Bombay Education Society Press, 1888), p. 206.

25. Quoted by Burton, *At the Heart of Empire*, p. 163; from Malabari's essay 'Some Results of Infant Marriage', cited in Gidumal's *Life*, p. 201.

26. B.M. Malabari, *An Appeal from the Daughters of India* (London: Farmer and Sons, 1890).

27. Burton, *At the Heart of Empire*, p. 166.
28. Malabari, *The Indian Eye*, p. 40.
29. *Ibid.*, p. 192.

7 CONNECTING CULTURES: CORNELIA AND ALICE SORABJI

1. *India Calling: The Memories of Cornelia Sorabji* (London: Nisbet and Co., 1934), p. 1.
2. *Ibid.*, p. 4.
3. *Ibid.*, p. 7.
4. George Valentine had been her father's tutor; Cornelia Ford (Lady Ford) was her mother's adoptive mother, to whom she owed 'her education and ideals'. Sorabji describes in much greater detail her parents' ideals and practice embracing respect for all customs and religions as well as the influence of George Valentine and Cornelia Ford, in her memoir of her parents, *'Therefore': An Impression of Sorabji Kharsedji Langana and his Wife Franscina* (London: Oxford University Press, 1924). This volume does not carry her name (or anyone else's) as author, but she acknowledges it in a footnote in *India Calling*.
5. C. Sorabji, *India Calling*, p. 8. Future page references for this autobiography will be included in the main text.
6. Cornelia Sorabji, *Susie Sorabji, Christian-Parsee Educationist of Western India; A Memoir by Her Sister* (London: Oxford University Press, 1932).
7. Cited by Visram, *Ayars, Lascars, and Princes*, p. 188.
8. Both when it came to persuading the authorities to let her study law and persuading them to let her sit the examinations with the other (male) students, Sorabji tells us that they yielded when she had explained why she was so keen to do so. One suspects that the authorities relented because she was seen as a special case, an Indian woman desiring to practise law in the service of Indian women and not in England alongside Englishmen. In endorsing her cause they were also endorsing one British rationale for governing India, the protection of Indian women from customs which were seen to put them at the mercy of 'brown men'.
9. Gopal Krishna Gokhale (1866–1915) was a political advisor to Gandhi. He was the leader of the Moderate group in the Indian National Congress. In her memoir of her sister, Sorabji comments that 'in the political crisis in India she early realized the danger of Ghandhi's appeal to the young and to those immature in judgement. She knew India, and that the call to sacrifice themselves for their country stirred in the blood of Hindu women the same impulse which had resulted in Suttee' (*Susie Sorabji*, p. 34). Sorabji goes on to record how her sister personally appealed to Ghandhi to put an end to violence and terrorism in 1930, and even sought to convert him to Christianity.
10. Cornelia Sorabji, *The Purdahnashin*, with a foreword by the Countess of Minto (Calcutta: Thacker, Spink, and Co., 1917).

11. *Ibid.*, p. ix.
12. *Ibid.*, p. 35.
13. *Ibid.*, p. 43.
14. *Ibid.*, p. 37.
15. *Ibid.*, p. 39.
16. *Ibid.*, p. 79.
17. Visram, *Ayars, Lascars, and Princes*, mentions five books, but Prabhu Guptara in his *Black British Literature: An Annotated Bibliography* (Sydney: Dangaroo Press, 1986) lists thirteen, of which three were published in India and so far I have not been able to locate all of them. Guptara's list does not include her biography of her parents, '*Therefore*', but does include *Queen Mary's Book of India*, which although it does not include her name, resulted from letters written by Sorabji to various eminent writers, letters which can be found in the files of her own correspondence and, for example, in the papers of T.S. Eliot.
18. Cornelia Sorabji, *Love and Life Behind the Purdah* (London: Fremantle and Co., 1901). 'Achtar: The Story of a Queen', which appears to be her first publication in England, was published in the *Nineteenth Century* 39 (June 1896), pp. 1006–11. 'Behind the Purdah' was first published in *Macmillan's Magazine* 82 (May–October 1900), pp. 193–200. The version here is almost identical with the one printed in the anthology, except that the term 'Purdah' is footnoted and explained, and the term for the old queen is spelled 'Thekrani' rather than 'Tharkani'. The same volume of *Macmillan's Magazine* includes an anonymous tale set in India, 'The Rani and the Fortune Teller', (pp. 463–7) which tells of the murder of the young Rani after she attempts to win back her prince's love with a potion. She suspects the white women of stealing his heart, and resents his obsession with 'angresi logue' (English folk) and his taking up their ways.
19. C. Sorabji, *Love and Life*, pp. xi–xii.
20. *Ibid.*, p. xii.
21. Cornelia Sorabji, 'An Indian Plague Story', *Nineteenth Century* 46, no.71 (September 1899), pp. 410–31. The story is placed between an article on 'The Craig Brook Salmon Hatchery' and a review essay on an edition of Cicero's letters. This particular issue also continues the debate begun in earlier numbers about the International Women's Congress held the previous year. The articles and the contributors reveal the journal's diverse interests and international readership. Sorabji also published essays and reports in the *Nineteenth Century*, including an essay on 'The Legal Status of Women in India' 44 (1898), pp. 854–66, which emphasizes that contrary to British assumptions, Indian women are not regarded as chattels and do have rights, but often do not have access to the law which upholds their rights. She asserts:

English law before the Married Woman's Property Act of 1882, as everyone knows, in dealing with a married woman made her identity merge in that of her husband; i.e., there was an absolute community of interest. In Muhammadan Law we find an absolute diversity of interests between husband and wife. In Hindu law we find the mean between the two – a community as regards some things, a diversity as regards others. (p. 858)

A subsequent issue of the journal has an article by the Hon. Justice Ameer Ali on 'The Influence of Women in Islam' (Volume 45, pp. 755–74), which to some extent responds to Sorabji's rather more pro-Hindu view that the restrictions of Indian women's roles began in part with Islamic influence. He offers a survey of distinguished and influential women in Arabic and Indian Muslim cultures, for example Nawab Sikandra Begum of Bophal who prevented her own troops from joining in the mutiny. He argues for stronger influence from Muslim communities to assist Hindu women: 'If the Mussulmans [sic] of India desire to raise themselves, they should restore women to the pedestal they occupied in the early centuries of Islam' (p. 77). Volume 50 (June–December 1901) includes another report by Cornelia Sorabji, 'Concerning an Imprisoned Rani' (pp. 623–38).

Other articles in volume 50 include 'The Irish Nuisance and How to Abate It' by Edward Dicey, descriptions of rural Irish customs and characters by Martin MacDonough, and an essay titled 'The White Peril' by George Macaulay Trevelyan, deploring the vulgarity and materialism, and the loss of imperial spirit, ideals, and religion, all a much greater danger to England and the white race than 'the Yellow Peril' (p. 1054).

22. C. Sorabji, *Love and Life*, p. 21. Future page references to this volume will be included in the main text.

23. For information on British literary representations of India and Indians, see Alan J. Greenberger, *The British Image of India* (London: Oxford University Press, 1969); Bhupal Singh, *A Survey of Anglo-Indian Fiction* (London: Oxford University Press, 1934); and Rashna Singh, *Imperishable Empire; a Study of British Fiction on India* (Pueblo, Colo.: Passeggiata Press, 1988).

24. For comparable examples of educated African 'natives' who regress, see Joyce Cary's *Aissa Saved* (London: Ernest Benn, 1932) and *The African Witch* (London: Victor Gollancz, 1936).

25. Rudyard Kipling, *Kim* (Basingstoke: Macmillan, 1963), pp. 99–100.

26. Other contributors to *Macmillan's Magazine* during the last decade of the nineteenth century include Henry James, Walter Pater, George Saintsbury, Arthur Symons, Ernest Rhys, Bret Harte, and Mrs Oliphant. Novels by James, Harte, and Oliphant were serialized in the journal. The contents of the journal convey the multiplicity of aesthetic and political concerns and attitudes extant during that decade. The preoccupation with the colonies, with colonial rule, and the future of various 'races' within the colonies is evident in the many contributions addressing or representing these areas.

27. These Kipling ballads all appear in *Macmillan's Magazine* 61 (November 1889–April 1890), and so were published during the first year Sorabji was a student at Oxford.

28. Cornelia Sorabji, *Sun-Babies: Studies in the Child-Life of India* (London: John Murray 1904).

29. 'The Feast of Lights', in C. Sorabji, *Sun-Babies* (1904), p. 134.
30. Cornelia Sorabji, *Between the Twilights: Being Studies of Indian Women by One of Themselves* (London: Harper and Brothers, 1908). The cover and endpaper for this book was designed by J. Lockwood Kipling.
31. 'Portraits of Some Indian Women', in C. Sorabji, *Between the Twilights*, p. 129.
32. *Ibid.*, p. 148.
33. *Ibid.*, p. 149.
34. Preface, C. Sorabji, *Between the Twilights*, p. ix.
35. Cornelia Sorabji, *Indian Tales of the Great Ones Among Men, Women, and Bird-People* (London: Blackie and Son, 1916).
36. C. Sorabji, *Sun-Babies* (London: Blackie and Son: 1920).
37. *Ibid.*, p. 9.
38. *Ibid.*, p. 45.
39. *Gold Mohur Time: 'To Remember'* (London: Alexander Moring, 1930).
40. *Ibid.*, p. 3.
41. *Ibid.*, p. 15.
42. Alice M. Sorabji Pennell, *Pennell of the Afghan Frontier: The Life of Theodore Leighton Pennell* (London: Seeley, Service, and Co., 1914).
43. *Ibid.*, p. 298. Pennell was touring India with a school football team from Bannu.
44. Alice M. Pennell, *A Hero of the Afghan Frontier: The Splendid Life Story of T.L. Pennell, M.D., B.Sc., F.R.C.S. (Kaisir-I-Hind Gold Medal for Public Service in India)* (Seeley, Service, and Co. Ltd: London, 1915).
45. *Ibid.*, p. 32.
46. *Ibid.*, pp. 33–4.
47. Mrs Theodore Pennell, *Children of the Border* (London: John Murray, 1926).
48. *Ibid.*, pp. 149 and 50. Changes are made in the anecdotes, however, for whereas in the novel the wife dies of cancer and the husband undergoes his operation and survives, in the biography version the wife survives her ordeal, whereas the warrior refuses the amputation, is carried back to his village, and dies. In the biography, the two characters are unrelated.
49. The advertisement is included opposite the title page of Alice Pennell's second novel, *The Begum's Son* (London: John Murray, 1928).
50. Pennell, *Children of the Border*, pp. 8–9.
51. *Ibid.*, p. 10.
52. *Ibid.*, p. 15.
53. *Ibid.*, pp. 18–25.
54. *Ibid.*, p. 21. The opposition made here compares interestingly with the oppositions set up by Chinua Achebe's hero, Okonkwo, in *Things Fall Apart* (1958) between the masculine values of a traditional warrior society and what are perceived as the effeminate values of the Christian missionaries and their followers. In Pennell's novel, however, the oppositions are rarely seen also as internal to the society, nor are they so successfully woven into the tragic history of the clan.

55. Pennell, *Children of the Border*, p. 170.
56. *Ibid.*, p. 179.
57. Pennell, *The Begum's Son*, p. 320.
58. *Ibid.*, p. 322.
59. *Ibid.*, p. 320.
60. *Ibid.*, p. 322.
61. Mrs Theodore Pennell, *Doorways of the East: An Indian Novel* (John Murray: London, 1931). The title is a reference to the poem by Francis Thompson, 'The Night of Forebeing', and gives these lines from the poem as its epigraph: 'Cast wide the folding doorways of the East / For now is light increased!'
62. Pennell, *Doorways of the East*, p. 11. Future page references to this novel will be included in the main text.
63. Other less appealing aspects of the British imperial exercise, including robbery and rape, are referred to however, as Mathaji recalls the tales she had been told of the *Feringhi*, tales in which they feature as red-faced, yellow-haired looters who, 'with a single glance [were able to] make a maiden lose her beauty, and become old and withered!', so that all the young girls hid from the English soldiers as they marched through Lahore (Pennell, *Doorways of the East*, p. 14).
64. Devi and Kamala together form a kind of amalgam of the well-known radical, Madame Cama, who organized nationalist activity in Paris and other European cities. The daughter of Sorabji Patel and brought up in Bombay, she married the Parsi reformer Rustum Cama. The British authorities referred to her programme as 'frankly revolutionary and murderous' (Visram, *Ayars, Lascars, and Princes*, p. 254, n.144).
65. The comparison between Indian and Irish sensibilities is made on other occasions in the novel. Thus, Theodora Marchmont, a professor at an Indian College for Women, 'thanks the gods that had given her a dash of Irish blood in her veins' and so made it possible for her to make friends easily with Indian women (Pennell, *Doorways of the East*, p. 78).
66. The gullibility of Western audiences and the consequent distortions of 'oriental art' presented to them, is also addressed by the figure of Dilkhush. This very 'modern' dancer, part English, part Indian, had acquired a name as an exponent of Oriental dancing. Pennell describes 'her conceit, vulgar posters advertising her performance', and her dance 'too horrible for words. It was the suggestive dance of the nautch-girl, intensified and made worse by an admixture of the modern western dances imported from Africa' (*ibid.*, p. 217).

8 ENDING EMPIRE

1. W.E.B. DuBois, *The Crisis*, August 1911.
2. Edward Saïd notes that in 1914 'Europe held a grand total of roughly 85% of the Earth as colonies, protectorates, dependencies, dominions, and

commonwealths', with England and France as the main imperial powers (*Culture and Imperialism* (London: Chatto and Windus, 1993), p. 6).

3. Extract from J.E. Casely Hayford, *Ethiopia Unbound*, in *Empire Writing*, ed. Elleke Boehmer (Oxford University Press, 1998), pp. 361–8; pp. 367–8.

4. Quoted by Visram, *Ayahs, Lascars, and Princes*, p. 83. For further information about Naoroji and the text of his address to his electorate in 1895, see Visram, pp. 77–92.

5. Quoted by Visram, *Ayahs, Lascars, and Princes*, p. 85. Naoroji had by this date lived for over thirty years in England. The irony of the comparison between Parsis and English rulers in India seems to have escaped Sir Lepel.

6. *Ibid.*, p. 87.

7. *Ibid.*, p. 88.

8. Dadabhai Naoroji, *Poverty and Un-British Rule in India* (London: Swan Sonnenschein, 1901).

9. Fryer, *Staying Power*, p. 265.

10. Visram, *Ayahs, Lascars, and Princes*, pp. 93–4.

11. *Ibid.*, p. 95.

12. Bhownaggree remained in Britain until his death in 1933 at the age of eighty-two. The Bhownaggree gallery in the Commonwealth Institute building in Kensington High Street is named after him. For further information about his life and work, see *ibid.*, pp. 92–7.

13. *Times*, 4 August 1928. Quoted by Visram, *Ayahs, Lascars, and Princes*, pp. 101–2. Syed Ameer Ali was a regular contributor to the *Nineteenth Century* and to the *Times*. His publications include *Memoirs and other Writings of Syed Ameer Ali*; *The Spirit of Islam*; *A Critical Examination of the Life and Teachings of Muhammad*; *Woman in Islam*; *Muhammadan Law*; *Islam*; *A Short History of the Saracens*; *The Legal Position of Women in Islam*. He had married Isabella Ida Konstan in London in 1884, and in 1904 settled permanently in England.

14. For further information on Krishnavarma and *The Indian Sociologist*, see Chapter Nine.

15. Visram, *Ayahs, Lascars, and Princes*, pp. 105–7.

16. Quoted by Fryer, *Staying Power*, p. 269.

17. Ron Ramdin, *Reimaging Britain: 500 Years of Black and Asian History* (London: Pluto Press, 1999), p. 86.

18. Designed as a monthly journal, the first issue of *Pan African* appeared in October 1901, but folded after six issues (Ramdin, *Reimaging Britain*, p. 87).

19. Horton's major work, published in 1868, was *West African Countries and Peoples*. He died in 1883 at the early age of forty-eight, and is now recognized as 'the father of modern African political thought' (Fryer, *Staying Power*, pp. 276–7).

20. Samuel Jules Celestine Edwards was born on Dominica in the Caribbean in 1858. He settled in Britain in the 1870s and travelled throughout Britain speaking on behalf of the temperance movement, religion and the plight of black people throughout the Caribbean, the United States and the African continent. He died in 1894.

21. For information about Celestine Edwards see Fryer, *Staying Power*, pp. 277–9.
22. *Ibid*., pp. 281–2.
23. Quoted by Fryer, *ibid*., p. 286, from Owen Mathurin's biography of Sylvester Williams, *Henry Sylvester Williams and the origins of the Pan-African Movement, 1869–1911*, Contributions in Afro-American and African Studies, no.21 (London, Greenwood Press, 1976), pp. 49–50.
24. Quoted by Fryer, *Staying Power*, p. 282.
25. *Ibid*., pp. 284–5.
26. The son of a Barbadan ship's steward and an Irish woman, John Richard Archer was born in Liverpool in 1863. Archer and his black Canadian wife moved to London in the last decade of the nineteenth century and he set up a successful business as a photographer. Peter Fryer notes that his photographs won many prizes. He was elected to the Batttersea Borough Council in 1906, and Mayor of Battersea in 1911. As a member of the Labour party, he campaigned on behalf of Charlotte Despard and succeeded in getting Shapurji Saklatvala, although a Communist, elected as Labour candidate for North Battersea in 1922. Until his death in 1932, Archer was active in both Labour and Pan-Africanist politics, and was elected president of the African Progress Union in 1918, an organization also supported by Duse Mohamed Ali (see Chapter Nine). For further information about Archer see Fryer, *Staying Power*, pp. 290–4. Fryer prints as an appendix to his book, the text of Archer's address to the African Progress Union at its inaugural meeting (Appendix E, pp. 410–16).
27. Quoted by Fryer, *Staying Power*, p. 94.
28. *Ibid*., p. 296.
29. *Ibid*., p. 301.
30. For example, an editorial headed 'Black and White' in the *Liverpool Courier* declared: 'One of the chief reasons of popular anger behind the present disturbance lies in the fact that the average negro is nearer the animal than is the average white man, and that there are women in Liverpool who have no self-respect...The white man...regards [the black man] as part child, part animal, and part savage' (cited by Fryer, *Staying Power*, p. 302). A letter to the London *Times* from Sir Ralph Williams, Governor of the Windward Islands from 1906–9, remarked that his observations from work and travel led him to the inevitable conclusion that 'to almost every white man and woman who has lived a life among coloured races, intimate association between black or coloured men and white women is a thing of horror...It is an instinctive certainty that sexual relations between white women and coloured men revolt our very nature...What blame...to those white men who, seeing these conditions and loathing them, resort to violence?' (quoted by Fryer, *Staying Power*, p. 311, from the *Times* no.42, 126 (14 June 1919), p. 8).
31. See details in Chapter Nine.
32. Quoted by Fryer, *Staying Power*, p. 311, from the *Times* no.42, 130 (19 June 1919), p. 8.

33. The *African Telegraph* was financed by John Eldred Taylor, the Sierra Leonean businessman who had earlier provided financial support for the *African Times and Orient Review*, with Duse Mohamed Ali as editor.

34. Quoted by Fryer, *Staying Power*, p. 316, from the *African Telegraph* 1, no.13 (July–August 1919), p. 253.

35. For a detailed history of Pan-Africanism and its interrelationships with Socialist ideologies, see Robert J.C. Young, *Postcolonialism: An Historical Introduction* (Oxford: Blackwell, 2001), Chapters Seventeen and Eighteen. Young gives an analysis of the contributions of, among others, James and Padmore, and also discusses their differences.

36. Quoted by Fryer, *Staying Power*, p. 344.

37. Ras Makonnen, *Pan-Africanism from Within*, ed. Kenneth King (Nairobi: Oxford University Press, 1973), quoted by Fryer, *Staying Power*, p. 347.

38. Makonnen, *Pan-Africanism*, p. 164. Quoted by Fryer, *Staying Power*, pp. 347–8.

39. Fryer, *Staying Power*, p. 350.

40. *Ibid.*, pp. 350–1.

41. Quoted by James Longenbach, *Stone Cottage: Pound, Yeats, and Modernism* (Oxford University Press, 1994), p. 23.

42. *Ibid.*

43. W.B. Yeats, Introduction to Rabindranath Tagore, *Gitanjali* (Macmillan: London, 1912), p. xii.

44. Longenbach, *Stone Cottage*, pp. 24–5.

45. Visram, *Ayahs, Lascars, and Princes*, p. 160.

46. For further details see Fryer, *Staying Power*, pp. 367–71.

47. For details of West Indian writers and artists who arrived in Britain in the late 1940s and the 1950s see Anne Walmsley, *The Caribbean Artists Movement, 1966–1972* (London: New Beacon Books, 1992), pp. 4–32.

48. For examples of incidents leading to and during the riots, and reporting of them, see Fryer, *Staying Power*, pp. 376–381.

9 DUSE MOHAMED ALI, ANTI-IMPERIAL JOURNALS, AND BLACK AND ASIAN PUBLISHING

1. Ian Duffield, 'Duse Mohamed Ali: His Purpose and His Public', in *The Commonwealth Writer Overseas*, ed. Alastair Niven (Brussels: Librairie Marcel Didier, 1976), pp. 151–73; pp. 155–6. Duffield expresses some scepticism about Duse Mohamed Ali's claims, as his story is not entirely consistent; he gave different names for his father and for himself, and he spoke no Arabic.

2. *Ibid.*, p. 156. Duffield lists many of Duse Mohamed Ali's publications in an appendix to his article.

3. Ian Duffield, 'Duse Mohamed Ali and the Development of Pan-Africanism, 1866–1945' (Ph.D. dissertation, Edinburgh University, October 1971). Duffield cites two autobiographical works – a brief sketch in the *Hull Lady* (June 1902, p. 43), a journal to which he was a regular contributor; and his weekly column, 'Leaves from an Active Life', published from June 1937

until March 1938 in the Lagos (Nigeria) *Comet*. There are also references to Duse Mohamed Ali in Wilfred Scawen Blunt's *My Diaries* (London: Martin Secker, 1919), p. 759. Given the recent revelation that many of Blunt's sonnets were in fact written by Lady Gregory, his dismay concerning Duse Mohamed's plagiarisms of his work is somewhat ironic. Duffield's work on Duse Mohamed Ali is a goldmine of information about both the man and his times, and it is a shame that only small portions of it have been published in now out-of-print collections of essays.

4. Duffield, 'Duse Mohamed Ali and . . . Pan-Africanism', p. 24.
5. *Ibid*., p. 25.
6. *Ibid*., pp. 32 and 33.
7. *Ibid*., pp. 33 and 73.
8. Cited by Duffield, *ibid*., p. 70, from *The Stage* (June 1903, p. 13).
9. Cited by Duffield, 'Duse Mohamed Ali and . . . Pan-Africanism', p. 66, from Act 1, Sc.3, l.61 (p. 2). Duffield points out that this play was particularly popular in the context of press reporting and other writing about events in the Sudan. Compare McGonagall's poems on the Sudan, and A.V. Mason's very popular novel *The Four Feathers* (London: Smith, Elder and Co., 1902). Such jingoist publications and plays were criticised by J.A. Hobson in *The Psychology of Jingoism* (London: Grant Richards, 1901) for their encouragement of 'ignorant contempt of foreigners' and 'generation of military passion' (p. 3).
10. Duffield, 'Duse Mohamed Ali and . . . Pan-Africanism', p. 54.
11. He wrote at least three pieces for the *Hull Lady*: an autobiographical account in 1, no.5 (May 1902, pp. 38–9); 'Hull's Coronation Ode' (June 1902, pp. 3–5); and 'The Foiling of the King' in 1, no.7 (1902, pp. 23–8).
12. *Hull Lady* (June 1902), p. 4.
13. Duffield, 'Duse Mohamed Ali and . . . Pan-Africanism', p. 80.
14. The libretto and music exist only in an unpublished manuscript. According to Ian Duffield, the work, which received dismissive reviews, was banal and overcomplicated, with uninspired music (*ibid*., p. 86).
15. Altogether, Duse Mohamed published eleven pieces in the *New Age* between January 1909 and April 1911. These are: 'White Women and Coloured Men. The Other Side of the Picture' (21 January 1909, pp. 262–3); 'Western Civilisation through Eastern Spectacles' (4 February 1909, p. 301; 18 February 1909, pp. 341–2; 4 March 1909, p. 381; 25 March 1909, p. 443; 22 April 1909, p. 51); 'The Situation in Egypt' (16 June 1910, pp. 148–50); 'France and the Egyptian Nationalists' (29 September 1910, pp. 509–10); 'Egypt's Ruin', (review article) (22 December 1910, pp. 110–74); 'Quo Vadis' (23 February 1911, pp. 387–90); 'The Good Friday Procession. An Impression' (27 April 1911, pp. 606–7).
16. Duse Mohamed, 'Western Civilisation through Eastern Spectacles', p. 301.
17. 'Egypt's Case Stated', *T.P.'s Magazine* (November 1910), pp. 189–94. T.P. Connor was later to become an Irish nationalist MP.

18. Cited by Duffield, 'Duse Mohamed Ali and the Development of Pan-Africanism', p. 118.
19. 'Quo Vadis', pp. 387–90; 'The Coloured Man in Art and Letters', *T.P.'s Magazine* (June 1911), pp. 399–407.
20. Duse Mohamed Ali, *In the Land of the Pharaohs: A Short History from the Fall of Ismail to the Assassination of Boutros Pasha* (London: Stanley Paul, 1911), pp. 1–2. Future page references for this work will be included in the main text.
21. Similar rhetorical appeals are made by other nationalist writers of this period, for example Naoroji, *Poverty and Un-British Rule in India* and J.E. Casely Hayford, *Gold Coast Native Institutions* (London: Sweet and Maxwell, 1903); and his later *Ethiopia Unbound*.
22. Ian Duffield lists a series of passages lifted from Theodore Rothstein's *Egypt's Ruins* (which Duse Mohamed had reviewed for the *New Age*), from William Scawen Blunt's *Secret History*, and from Evelyn Baring, Earl of Cromer's *Modern Egypt* ('Duse Mohamed Ali and the Development of Pan-Africanism', p. 121). Although Blunt seemed relatively untroubled by the plagiarisms (Duse Mohamed recounts a subsequent visit to Blunt's house as overnight guest, and observes the irony that while Blunt had dressed for dinner in Oriental clothes, Duse himself wore a western suit). Rothstein, however, was furious about the extensive and unacknowledged borrowing and demanded the book either be withdrawn or an apology included. His protest immediately precedes Duse Mohamed's last publication in the *New Age*, and may account for a breaking off of relations with A.R. Orage.
23. Cited by Duffield, 'Duse Mohamed Ali and the Development of Pan-Africanism', p. 172.
24. Concerning his role in founding the *Review*, Duse Mohamed was later to write, 'To an Egyptian, resident for many years in London, and married to an English lady, came the happy inspiration to found a paper that should form a link between all peoples of the darker races who use the English language', *African Times and Orient Review* 6, no.1 (July 1918), p. 8. Henceforth abbreviated as *ATOR*.
25. *ATOR* 1, no.1 (July 1912), p. 10.
26. *Ibid.*, p. 1.
27. It was after this first issue that Taylor was ousted, and Casely Hayford and others formed a new board of directors (Duffield, 'Duse Mohamed Ali and the Development of Pan-Africanism', p. 259).
28. *ATOR* 1, no.1 (July 1912), p. 14.
29. I have not been able to trace this book or any further reference to it.
30. The 'International Conference of the Negro', was held at Tuskegee Institute, Alabama, 17–19 April 1912, and hosted by the institute's principal, Booker T. Washington.
31. *ATOR* 1, no.1 (July 1912), p. 25. Later 'National Rhymes' in the same style include 'At the Feet of the Sphinx', in 1, no.4.

32. *ATOR* 1, no.1 (July 1912), p. 33.
33. *Ibid.*, p. 33.
34. Duffield, 'Duse Mohamed Ali and the Development of Pan-Africanism', p. 205. Garvey's article, 'The British West Indies in the Mirror of Civilisation. History Making by Colonial Negroes', appeared in the October 1913 issue of *ATOR* 2, no.14, pp. 158–60.
35. *ATOR* 1, no.2 (August 1912).
36. *ATOR* 1, no.3 (September 1912).
37. *ATOR* 1, no.3 (September 1912), p. 92.
38. *ATOR* 1, no.5 (November 1912), p. 152. The poem is by Charles B. White.
39. *ATOR* 2, nos. 17–18 (Christmas 1913).
40. 'Katabet the Priestess', *ATOR* 2, nos. 17–18 (Christmas 1913), pp. 3–7.
41. Duffield, 'Duse Mohamed Ali and the Development of Pan-Africanism', p. 201.
42. See especially Shaikh M.H. Kidwai, 'Is India Unfit for Self-Government, or Is England?', *ATOR* 4, no.1 (November 1917), pp. 96–8.
43. *ATOR* 4, no.1 (November 1917), p. 2.
44. Ian Duffield cites Duse Mohamed's exchange of letters with the War Office seeking permission to send Hutchinson as war correspondent. One letter notes the significant role played by 'coloured people of the world' both as combatants and industrially. His request was treated dismissively by Aubrey Herbert MP, and inter-departmental correspondence refers to Duse Mohamed as 'the nigger editor'. However, the War Office finally agreed to supply information to Hutchinson and the *African Times and Orient Review* on the grounds that 'it may serve to encourage the coloured press in the United States and the Allied Niggers generally' ('Duse Mohamed Ali and the Development of Pan-Africanism', pp. 315–17).
45. *Africa and Orient Review* 1, no.1 (January 1920), pp. 10–11.
46. *Ibid.*, p. 11.
47. These later autobiographical series were published in serialized form as 'Leaves from an Active Life' in *Comet* (Nigeria) (12 June 1937–5 March 1938).
48. Duffield, 'Duse Mohamed Ali and the Development of Pan-Africanism', pp. 211–20.
49. Cited by Visram, *Ayahs, Lascars, and Princes*, p. 103. For further details about Krishnavarma's life and activities see Visram, pp. 97–105.
50. *Ibid.*, p. 103.
51. Quoted by Visram, *ibid.*, p. 253, n.141, from the *Indian Sociologist* 2, no.12.
52. For further information about the *Negro Worker* and its contributors see Roderick J. Macdonald, ' "The Wisers Who Are Far Away": The Role of London's Black Press in the 1930s and 1940s', in *Essays on the History of Blacks in Britain*, ed. Jagdish S. Gundara and Ian Duffield (Aldershot: Avebury, 1992), pp. 150–68; pp. 153–4.
53. Macdonald, ' "The Wisers who are Far Away" ', p. 152.

54. 'Afro-Americans and West Africans: A New Understanding', *WASU* (1929), cited by Macdonald, '"The Wisers who are Far Away"', p. 153.
55. *Ibid.*, p. 153.
56. Essays listed by Macdonald, *ibid.*, pp. 157–8. Eric Walrond was born in Georgetown, in then British Guiana, in 1898. He went to New York in 1918 to study at City University and Columbia University. In New York he was an associate editor for Marcus Garvey's *Negro World*, and also worked for other black journals. In 1926, his sole book, *Tropic Death*, a collection of short stories set in the Caribbean, was published to considerable acclaim. Walrond died in England in 1966. For a complete collection of *The Black Man*, see Robert A. Hill, ed. *The Black Man. A Monthly Magazine of Negro Thought and Opinion* (Millwood, N.Y.: Kraus Thompson Reprints, 1975).
57. Born in Kingston, Jamaica, in 1882, Harold Arundel Moody came to London in 1904 to train and qualify as a doctor at King's College, London. He was president of the League of Coloured Peoples until his death in 1947. He was the older brother of the distinguished sculptor, Ronald Moody.
58. Quoted by Fryer, *Staying Power*, p. 327.
59. *The Keys* can be read in a reprint collection edited by Roderick J. MacDonald: *The Keys. The Official Journal of the League of Coloured Peoples* (Millwood, N.Y.: Kraus Thompson Reprints, 1976).
60. For more detailed information about these contributions see Roderick Macdonald, '"The Wisers who are Far Away"', pp. 162–3.
61. These reasons for the journal's short life were given by George Padmore. Roderick J. Macdonald sees them as perhaps contributing causes, but speculates that the reasons were mainly financial, as the journal was expensive to produce (*ibid.*, p. 165).

10 SUBALTERN VOICES AND THE CONSTRUCTION OF A GLOBAL VISION

1. James, 'Africans and Afro-Caribbeans: A Personal View', p. 63.
2. C.L.R. James, 'Discovering Literature in Trinidad: The 1930s', in *Spheres of Existence: Selected Writings* (London: Allison and Busby, 1980), pp. 237–44; p. 237. The essay was first published in the *Journal of Commonwealth Literature* (July 1969).
3. James, 'Discovering Literature in Trinidad: The 1930s', p. 244.
4. C.L.R. James, *The Life of Captain Cipriani* (Nelson, Lancs.: Coulton and Co., 1932). Later condensed and reprinted as *The Case for West Indian Self-Government*, published by L. and V. Woolf, Day to Day Pamphlets no.16 (Hogarth Press: London, 1933).
5. James, *The Life of Captain Cipriani*, p. 1.
6. C.L.R. James, *Minty Alley* (New Beacon Books: London, 1971). First published by Secker and Warburg, London, 1936.

7. Cited by Louis James, *Caribbean Literature in English* (Longman: London, 1999), p. 65.

8. One might see also an analogy with Synge's play in the rivalry between younger and older women over 'possession' of the young outsider, culminating in James' novel with a furious and mud-spattered battle between Maisie and Mrs Rouse. It is interesting also to compare James' protagonist Haynes with the character of Haines in Joyce's *Ulysses*, for he too is an outsider, thoroughly immersed in English culture and assumptions, who has come to observe the natives, and who listens rather than takes part. Both Synge and Joyce are acknowledged influences for Derek Walcott, and it is likely that James was also aware of their work.

9. Kenneth Ramchand, *The West Indian Novel and Its Background* (London: Faber and Faber, 1972), p. 70.

10. Published as *The Black Jacobins*, in *A Time and a Season: 8 Caribbean Plays*, ed. Errol Hill (Trinidad: Extramural Studies Unit, University of the West Indies, 1976), pp. 355–420. The earlier version of the play titled *Toussaint L'Ouverture* was rewritten by James and retitled for a 1967 production in Ibadan, Nigeria, during the Nigerian Civil War. In a programme note for the Nigerian production, James states, 'Every major episode in the play is historically grounded, none more so than the hair-raising contribution of Cathcart, the English agent, to the ultimate deterioration of the condition of Haiti'. Quoted by Errol Hill in the introduction to *A Time and a Season: 8 Caribbean Plays*, p. xiv.

11. C.L.R. James, 'Paul Robeson: Black Star', in *Spheres of Existence*, pp. 256–9.

12. Quoted by James from the *Times*, 22 March 1936, and the *Observer*, 22 March 1936, in *Spheres of Existence*, pp. 258–9.

13. James, *The Black Jacobins*, Act 2, Sc.3, p. 392.

14. *Ibid.*, Act 3, Sc.1, p. 413.

15. C.L.R. James, *The Black Jacobins: Toussaint L'Ouverture and the San Domingo Revolution* (London: Allison and Busby, 1994). This edition, first published in 1980, includes a forward by James commenting on the impact of the work, and a remarkable appendix, 'From Toussaint L'Ouverture to Fidel Castro', which gives a succinct survey of Caribbean history from the end of the San Domingo Revolution until 1980, and draws on Francophone, Hispanic, and Anglophone Caribbean writers (along with T.S. Eliot) to illustrate the new and productive West Indian perspective which starts from a local rather than externally stimulated vision. *Black Jacobins* was first published in 1938 by Secker and Warburg.

16. Paul Buhle, *C.L.R. James: The Artist as Revolutionary* (London: Verso, 1988), p. 59.

17. James, *The Black Jacobins: Toussaint L'Ouverture*, p. 25.

18. *Ibid.*, p. 51.

19. Young, *Postcolonialism*, p. 224.

20. James, *The Black Jacobins: Toussaint L'Ouverture*, p. 82.

21. *Ibid.*, p. 283.

22. C.L.R. James, *Mariners, Renegades, and Castaways: The Story of Herman Melville and the World We Live In* (London: Allison and Busby, 1985). First published New York: The Author, 1953 James states his admiration for Melville, and exalts him as the writer of 'the greatest of American novels' in a number of essays and lectures. See, for example, 'Two Young American Writers', in *Spheres of Influence*, pp. 106–12; p. 106.

23. A fuller discussion of this work lies beyond the chronological boundaries of this study. For two excellent discussions of *Beyond a Boundary*, see Sylvia Wynter, 'In Quest of Matthew Bondman: Some Cultural Notes on the Jamesian Journey', in *C.L.R. James: His Life and Work*, ed. Paul Buhle (London: Allison and Busby, 1986), pp. 131–45; and Neil Lazarus, *Nationalism and Cultural Practice in the Postcolonial World* (Cambridge University Press, 1999), Chapter 3.

24. James, *Beyond a Boundary*, p. xxi.

25. *Ibid.*, p. xxi.

26. Jomo Kenyatta, *Facing Mount Kenya* (London: Heinemann Educational Books, 1979). First published London: Secker and Warburg, 1938. Kenyatta firmly insists on the spelling 'Gikuyu' rather than 'Kikuyu' when referring to the people and their language.

27. *Ibid.*, p. xv.

28. Chinua Achebe, 'The Role of the Writer in the New Nation', *Nigeria Magazine* 81 (1964), pp. 157–60; p. 157.

29. James, *Facing Mount Kenya*, p. xv.

30. For details of Una Marson's childhood and education at Hampton High in Jamaica, see Delia Jarrett-Macauley, *The Life of Una Marson 1905–1965* (Manchester University Press, 1998), pp. 16–22.

31. Quoted by Jarrett-Macauley, *Life of Una Marson*, p. 30.

32. *Ibid.*, p. 37.

33. *At What a Price* was first produced at Kingston's Ward Theatre in June 1932, receiving generally favourable reviews. The two volumes of poetry show considerable competence as a poet, but little sense of an individual voice.

34. For further information on Moody and the League of Coloured Peoples, see Chapters Eight and Nine. See also Walmsley, *Caribbean Artists Movement*, Chapter One.

35. Quoted by Jarrett-Macauley, *Life of Una Marson*, p. 53.

36. *Ibid.*, p. 54.

37. Rhonda Cobham and Merle Collins, eds. *Watchers and Seekers: Creative Writing by Black Women* (London: The Women's Press, 1987), p. 4.

38. Una Marson, *The Moth and the Star* (Kingston, Jamaica: The Author, 1937), p. 13.

39. *Ibid.*, p. 93.

40. *Ibid.*, p. 91.

41. 'Gettin' de Spirit', in Marson, *The Moth and the Star*, p. 76.

42. Marson, *The Moth and the Star*, p. 70.

43. Jarrett-Macauley, *Life of Una Marson*, p. 55. There does not appear to be any manuscript or published version of this play extant.

44. *Ibid.*, p. 74. Jarrett-Macauley notes how this phrase, from the British Commonwealth League Constitution, betrays 'the double-edged experience' Una Marson was to have in relation to the league.

45. *Ibid.*, pp. 76–8. Marson also wrote a poem about Holtby, mourning her death ('Winifred Holtby', *The Moth and the Star*, p. 79).

46. Quoted in Jarrett-Macauley, *Life of Una Marson*, p. 90.

47. Walmsley, *Caribbean Artists Movement*, p. 6. For a fuller account of the programme which became *Caribbean Voices* and its influence, see Rhondha Cobham, 'The *Caribbean Voices* Programme and the Development of West Indian Short Fiction: 1945–1958', in *The Story Must be Told: Short Narrative Prose in the New English Literatures*, ed. Peter O. Stummer (Bayreuth: Koningshausen/Newman, 1986), pp. 146ff.

48. Quoted in Jarrett-Macauley, *Life of Una Marson*, p. 157.

49. Una Marson, *Towards the Stars* (University of London Press, 1945), p. 5.

50. *Ibid.*, p. 40.

51. Quoted by Jarrett-Macauley, *Life of Una Marson*, p. 162.

52. Marson, *Towards the Stars*, p. 3.

53. *Ibid.*, p. 4.

54. *Ibid.*, p. 44.

55. 'There Will Come a Time', in Marson, *Towards the Stars*, pp. 62–3.

56. Quoted by Jarrett-Macauley, *Life of Una Marson*, p. 175.

57. For further information about *Caribbean Voices* see Walmsley, *Caribbean Artists Movement*, pp. 5–7 and 9–13.

58. Mulk Raj Anand, *Apology for Heroism: A Brief Autobiography of Ideas* (Bombay: Kutub-Popular, 1957), p. 51. First published London: Hutchinson, 1945.

59. *Ibid.*, p. 52.

60. Quoted by Margaret Berry, *Mulk Raj Anand, the Man and the Novelist* (Amsterdam: Oriental Press, 1971), p. 14.

61. Mulk Raj Anand interview with Jane Williams, 'Talking of Tambi: The Dilemma of the Asian Intellectual', in *Tambimuttu: The Bridge Between Two Worlds*, ed. Jane Williams (London: Peter Owen, 1989), pp. 191–201; p. 197.

62. *Ibid.*, p. 99, n.26.

63. E.M. Forster, Preface in Mulk Raj Anand, *Untouchable* (Bombay: Kutub Popular Books, n.d.), p. v. First published London, Laurence Wishart, 1935 Forster also cites the discovery of a second-hand copy of his own *Passage to India* on the front page of which 'an indignant colonel' had written 'burn when done' and 'has a dirty mind, see p. 215'. The page in question refers to a strike by sweepers, leaving 'half the commodes of Chandrapore… desolate in consequence'.

64. *Ibid.*, p. 126.

65. *Ibid.*, p. 127.

66. Mulk Raj Anand, *The Golden Breath: Studies in Five Poets of the New India* (London: John Murray, 1933). The other four poets included in this study

were Rabindranath Tagore, Puran Singh, Sarojini Naidu, and Harindra Nath Chattopadhyaya.

67. Anand, *Untouchable*, p. 134.
68. In addition to *Untouchable*, these early novels include *The Coolie* (London: Laurence Wishart, 1936); *Two Leaves and a Bud* (London: Laurence Wishart, 1937); *The Village* (London: Hutchinson, 1939); *Lament for the Death of a Master of Arts* (Lucknow: Naya Sansar, 1939); and *Across the Black Waters* (Bombay: Kutub Publishers, 1955. First published London: Laurence Wishart, 1940).
69. Quoted by Berry, *Mulk Raj Anand*, pp. 29–30.
70. *Ibid.*, p. 30.
71. *Ibid.*, p. 15.
72. M.K. Naik, 'Mulk Raj Anand', in *Encyclopedia of Postcolonial Literatures in English*, ed. Eugene Benson and L.W. Conolly (London: Routledge, 1994), p. 38.
73. Anand, *Across the Black Waters* (1955), p. 9.
74. Mulk Raj Anand, *Asiatic Review*, N.S. 39 (July 1941), p. 248. Quoted by Berry, *Mulk Raj Anand*, p. 32.
75. Quoted by Berry, *Mulk Raj Anand*, p. 81.
76. *Ibid.*
77. Quoted by Berry, *ibid.*, p. 84, from Jack Lindsay, *Mulk Raj Anand: A Critical Essay* (Bombay: Hind-Kitabs, 1948), p. 26.
78. Anand, *Apology for Heroism*, pp. 79–80.
79. Anand, 'Talking of Tambi', pp. 191–201.
80. *Ibid.*, p. 193.
81. Opening manifesto, *Poetry London*, no.1 (February 1939), p. 3.
82. M.J. Tambimuttu, ed. *Poetry in Wartime* (London: Faber and Faber, 1942).
83. M.J. Tambimuttu, *Out of This War* (London: The Fortune Press, 1941). The poem is dated October 1940.
84. *Ibid.*, p. 9.
85. *Ibid.*
86. *Ibid.*, p. 14.
87. *Ibid.*, p. 19.
88. *Ibid.*, p. 21.
89. M.J. Tambimuttu, *Natarajah: A poem for Mr T.S. Eliot's Sixtieth Birthday*. Poetry London Pamphlet no.6 (Editions Poetry London, 1948).
90. *Ibid.*, p. 1.
91. *Ibid.*, p. 2.
92. Aubrey Menen, *The Prevalence of Witches* (London: Chatto and Windus, 1947).
93. *Ibid.*, p. 66.
94. *Ibid.*, pp. 270–1 (ellipsis in original).
95. G.V. Desani, *All About H. Hatterr* (New Delhi: Penguin Books India 1998) (uses plates from McPherson edition, with added notes by author). First published 1948, by Francis Aldor, London. Reissued by Saturn Books, London, 1949. Since its first publication, the 'novel' has been revised many times by the author.
96. *Ibid.*, p. 1.

97. *Ibid.*, p. 33.
98. Statement by Desani about the novel on the back cover of the first edition of *Hali* (London: Saturn Books, 1949). This statement sheds interesting light on Desani's own view of the book, and his response to the kind of praise it received.
99. See preceding footnote.
100. *Ibid.*
101. G.V. Desani, *Hali* (London: Saturn Press, 1949). This first edition carries a portrait of the author 'in Indian costume' on the front cover. The forewords by Eliot and Forster read thus:

> I consider Mr Desani's Hali a striking and unusual piece of work. It is a completely different sort of thing from his Hatterr, and often the imagery is terrifyingly effective. It is, of course, as poetry that I take Hali.
> Hali is not likely to appeal quickly to the taste of many readers and yet, in general, I find myself in agreement with what Mr Forster Says. (T.S. Eliot (complete quote))

> I have no inner knowledge of poetry, and so am diffident of my judgements on it, but Hali does strike me as genuine, personal and passionate. I get a view through it, though I should find difficulty in describing what I see. It seems to treat life as if life were what death might be – perhaps that is the method of its wild pilgrimage, and why it keeps evoking heights above the 'summit-City' of normal achievement. It depends upon a private mythology – a dangerous device. Yet is succeeds in being emotionally intelligible and in creating overtones. (E.M. Forster (complete quote))

102. Salman Rushdie, *Midnight's Children* (London: Jonathan Cape, 1981), p. 47.

11 EPILOGUE

1. Samuel Selvon, *The Lonely Londoners* (London: Longman, 1956).
2. George Lamming, *In the Castle of My Skin* (London: Longman, 1953).
3. George Lamming, *The Pleasures of Exile* (London: Michael Joseph, 1960).
4. For a fully documented study of the Caribbean Artists Movement and its influence, see Walmsley, *Caribbean Artists Movement*.
5. James Berry, *Lucy's Letters and Loving* (London and Port of Spain: New Beacon Press, 1982).
6. Wilson Harris, 'Tradition and the West Indian Novel', in *Tradition, the Writer, and Society: Critical Essays* (London: New Beacon Press, 1967), pp. 28–47. Harris' lecture, first delivered to the West Indian Student Society in 1965, has remained an influential touchstone for later evaluation of West Indian fiction.
7. Susheila Nasta, 'Setting up Home in a City of Words: Sam Selvon's London Novels', in *Other Britain, Other British*, ed. A. Robert Lee (London: Pluto, 1995), pp. 48–68; pp. 51–2.
8. V.S. Naipaul, *The Middle Passage: The Caribbean Revisited* (Harmondsworth: Penguin, 1969), p. 29.

9. Homi Bhabha, 'Re-Inventing Britain: A Manifesto', in *British Studies Now (Re-Inventing Britain: Identity, Transnationalism, and the Arts)* no.9 (April 1997) (London: the British Council, 1997), p. 9. Reprinted, together with an interview with Homi Bhabha and comments by Stuart Hall, in *Wasafiri* no.29 (Spring 1999), pp. 38–43.
10. Salman Rushdie, *The Satanic Verses* (London: Viking, 1988).
11. *Wasafiri* no.29 (Spring 1999), p. 43.
12. Rushdie, *Satanic Verses*, p. 292.
13. Leela Gandhi, ' "Ellowen, Deeowen": Salman Rushdie and the Migrant's Desire', in Ann Blake, Leela Gandhi, and Sue Thomas, *England Through Colonial Eyes in Twentieth-Century Fiction* (Basingstoke: Palgrave: 2001), pp. 157–70; p. 160.
14. Rushdie, *Satanic Verses*, p. 292.
15. *Ibid*.

Notes on writers
(Compiled by Mark Stein)

William G. Allen (c.1820–?) co-edited a short-lived newspaper in Troy, USA, and later took up a professorship in Classics and Belles-Lettres at New York Central College, McGrawville. His marriage to a white woman led to violent protests and the couple was forced to leave the United States for England in 1853. While in London he gave anti-slavery lectures and wrote *The American Prejudice Against Color*. After several years in Dublin teaching elocution, Allen and his wife opened a school in Islington, London in 1864.

Bibliography: *The American Prejudice Against Color: An Authentic Narrative, Showing How Easily the Nation Got into an Uproar* (London: W. and F.G. Cash, 1853). Reprint edition New York: Arno Press, Inc., 1969 (Reprinted from a copy in Cornell University Library). Also *A Short Personal Narrative* (Dublin: William Curry & Co., 1860).

Mulk Raj Anand (1905–) was born in Peshawar (now Pakistan) and studied philosophy at the Universities of Punjab (India) and London (England). During the Spanish Civil War he joined the International Brigade. In the 1930s he spent time both in India and England, settling permanently in India from 1945. Anand founded the journal *Marg* in 1946 which he edited for over thirty years, and among other appointments was Professor of Art and Literature at Punjab University.

Bibliography: In addition to his many novels and short stories, he has published several volumes of literary criticism, art criticism, and letters. These include: *The Coolie* (London: Laurence Wishart, 1936); *Two Leaves and a Bud* (London: Laurence Wishart, 1937); *Lament for the Death of a Master of Arts* (Lucknow: Naya Sansar, 1939); *The Village* (London: Hutchinson, 1939); *Across the Black Waters* (London: Laurence Wishart, 1940); *The Sword and the Sickle* (Bombay: Kutub Publishers, 1942); *Seven Summers* (London: Hutchinson, 1951); *The Private Life of an Indian Prince* (London: Hutchinson, 1953); *Morning Face* (Bombay: Kutub Publishers, 1968); *Confession of a Lover* (New Delhi: Arnold Heinemann, 1976); *Conversations in Bloomsbury* (London: Wildwood House, 1981); *The Bubble* (New Delhi: Arnold Heinemann, 1984); *Little Plays of Mahatma Gandhi* (New Delhi: Arnold Heinemann, 1991); *Selected Short Stories of Mulk Raj Anand*, ed. M.K. Naik (New Delhi: Arnold Heinemann, 1977).

John Brown (1815–76) was born in Southampton County, Virginia, to slave parents owned by different masters. He worked for various owners in Virginia and Georgia before painful medical experiments and punishments drove him to escape in 1847. From New Orleans he had himself 'sold' to a Mississippi planter whom he left after three months for his freedom in St Louis, and then Detroit and Canada. In 1850 Brown went to England, settling in Bristol. Later he began to travel in England, giving anti-slavery lectures to earn a living. In 1855, aided by the secretary of the British and Foreign Anti-Slavery Society, Louis Alexis Chamerovzow, he finished his *Slave Life in Georgia* which went through two editions.
Bibliography: *Slave Life in Georgia: A Narrative of the Life, Suffering, and Escape of John Brown, Fugitive Slave, Now in England*, ed. L.A. Chamerovzow (London, L.A. Chamerovzow, 1855); *Slave Life in Georgia: A Narrative of the Life, Suffering, and Escape of John Brown, Fugitive Slave*, ed. F.N. Boney (Savannah, Ga.: Beehive Press, 1991).

William Craft (c.1822–1900) and his wife Ellen (1826–91) escaped from their owners in Macon, Georgia, in 1848. While the light-skinned Ellen disguised herself as a white southern gentleman, her darker husband acted as her slave. The public took great interest in their adventure and they spoke at numerous anti-slavery meetings in north America, before the passing of the Fugitive Slave Act in 1851 impelled them to seek refuge in England. They were supported by Harriet Martineau, Lady Byron, and others, and received an education at a progressive agricultural school in Ockham, Surrey. They also appeared at abolitionist rallies and gave lectures throughout England and Scotland, at which sketches of Ellen dressed as a white gentleman sold very well, and were founders of the London Emancipation Committee. In 1860 William Craft published their story in *Running a Thousand Miles for Freedom*. William Craft twice visited Dahomey, seeking to establish free labour cotton plantations, trade agreements, and a school there. He urged reform both in Dahomey and in European attitudes and responses to practices there. In 1869 Ellen and William returned to the United States to found a plantation and educational institution in Woodville near Savannah, Georgia.
Bibliography: *Running a Thousand Miles for Freedom: Or The Escape of William and Ellen Craft from Slavery* (London: William Tweedie, 1860). Reprinted in Arna Bontemps, ed. *Great Slave Narratives* (Boston: Beacon Press, 1969), pp. 269–331. Reprinted with foreword and biographical essay in R.J.M. Blackett, ed. *Running a Thousand Miles for Freedom: The Escape of William and Ellen Craft from Slavery* (Baton Rouge: Louisiana State University Press, 1999).

Quobna Ottobah Cugoano (c.1757–c.92), baptized John Stuart, was born in Agimaque or Ajumako, now Ghana. He was kidnapped and enslaved when aged about thirteen and taken to Grenada. His owner Alexander Campbell took him to England in late 1772. By 1788 he was a freeman, a personal servant to Richard Cosway. He became one of the leaders of the black community and may have known Gronniosaw. He was devoted to the cause of emancipation and his views were more radical than those of many of his contemporaries such as Hammon, Gronniosaw and Sancho. He was a friend of Equiano who may have edited his book. He also published co-signed letters in London newspapers between 1787–9.

Bibliography: *Thoughts and Sentiments on the Evil and Wicked Traffic of the Slavery and Commerce of the Human Species, Humbly Submitted to The Inhabitants of Great Britain, by Ottobah Cugoano, A Native of Africa* (London: T. Becket, 1787; at least three issues in 1787). Facsimile of the first edition, with notes and introduction, by Paul Edwards (London: Dawsons, 1968). A French edition was published in 1788. First edition reprinted and edited with notes and introduction by Vincent Carretta (Harmondsworth: Penguin, 1999). Abridged from the 1787 edition: *Thoughts and Sentiments on the Evil of Slavery; or, the Nature of Servitude as Admitted by the Law of God, Compared to the Modern Slavery of the Africans in the West-Indies; In an Answer to the Advocates for Slavery and Oppression. Addressed to the Sons of Africa, by a Native* (London: The Author, 1791).

Govindas Vishnoodas Desani (1909–2000) was born and grew up in Nairobi, Kenya. He visited England from 1926 till 1928, working as a film actor, and returned again in 1939, remaining there for thirteen years. During these years he wrote the first version of *All About H. Hatterr* and the poetic play, *Hali*. He worked as a journalist, in broadcasting (BBC World Service), and as a lecturer on Indian affairs, and in 1968 was appointed professor of philosophy at the University of Texas, Austin, USA. Desani is probably best-known for *All About H. Hatterr*, which has undergone revisions and many republications, but he has also published drama, sketches, parodies, short fiction, and essays.

Bibliography: *All About Mr Hatterr, A Gesture* (London: Francis Aldor, 1948). Reprinted London: Saturn, 1949. New rev. ed.: *All About H. Hatterr* (London: Bodley Head, 1970); *Hali: A Poetic Play* (London: Saturn Press, 1950); *Hali and Collected Stories* (Kingston, N.Y.: McPherson and Co., 1991).

Duse Mohamed Ali (1866–1945). Born Mohamed Ali in Alexandria, he later took the name Duse Mohamed in honour of one of his guardians. It is not entirely clear at what stage he came to England, but according to his *In the Land of the Pharaohs* he was educated in Britain from 1876, and resided there from 1884 to 1923. He had an acting career and wrote a history, a novel, playlets, a musical comedy script, a full-length autobiography, and many journalistic pieces. From the 1890s he worked as a journalist and editor. He was founding editor of the *African Times and Orient Review*, a monthly 'devoted to the interests of the coloured Races of the World' which first appeared in July 1912. Despite financial difficulty the journal appeared (irregularly) until 1920 (by then re-titled the *Africa and Orient Review*). Duse Mohamed emigrated to Nigeria in 1923, continuing his journalistic career there. He became managing editor of the Lagos *Times* and from 1933 until his death in 1945, of the *Comet* (later the *Daily Comet*).

Bibliography: Duse Mohamed wrote prolifically but is best known for: *In the Land of the Pharaohs: A Short History from the Fall of Ismail to the Assassination of Boutros*

Pasha (London: Stanley Paul, 1911). Reprinted with an introduction by Khalil Mahmud (London: Frank Cass, 1968). See the main Bibliography for a list of other publications and manuscripts, including numerous articles in the *African Times and Orient Review*.

Olaudah Equiano (c.1745–97) according to his autobiography, Equiano was born in what is today south-east Nigeria. Kidnapped at the age of eleven or twelve, he was taken to the West Indies and on to Virginia where he was sold to a planter. This information has sometimes been questioned since its first publication, and a recent article by Vincent Carretta has renewed speculation that Equiano may have been born in South Carolina, not Africa. He was then resold, taken to London, and renamed Gustavus Vassa, the name he came to use himself. After buying his freedom, he served in the Royal Navy as a seaman, explored the Arctic, and acted as a buyer and overseer of slaves. When he resigned from this position, he began to lobby for the abolition of the slave-trade and was involved in the Sierra Leone resettlement scheme. He published the first edition of *The Interesting Narrative of the Life of Olaudah Equiano, or Gustavus Vassa, the African. Written by Himself* in 1789 which sold very well; the ninth edition, the last to be published during Equiano's lifetime, appeared in 1794. The text was translated into Dutch (1790), German (1792), and Russian (1794).
Bibliography: There have been numerous editions of Equiano's autobiography, and only a few of the most significant or accessible ones are mentioned below: Paul Edwards, ed. and introduction, *The Interesting Narrative of the Life of Olaudah Equiano, or Gustavus Vassa, the African. Written by Himself.* Facsimile of the first edition (London: Dawson, 1968); Vincent Carretta, ed. *The Interesting Narrative of the Life of Olaudah Equiano, or Gustavus Vassa, the African. Written by Himself* (Harmondsworth: Penguin, 1995) is based on the ninth edition, and the last that Equiano published in his lifetime. Werner Sollors, ed. *The Interesting Narrative of the Life of Olaudah Equiano, or Gustavus Vassa, the African, Written by Himself* (New York: Norton, 2000); Heinemann African Writers Series, abridged ed. (Oxford: Heinemann, 1996).

Francis Fedric (c.?1804–18??) was born a slave in Virginia and taken to a tobacco plantation in Kentucky when aged about fourteen. Several attempts to escape were unsuccessful until he escaped to Canada through the underground railway. There he married an English woman and emigrated to England in 1857, establishing a lodging-house in Manchester. He continued his work as an anti-slavery speaker which he had begun in Toronto.
Bibliography: Fedric published two autobiographical works: *Life and Sufferings of Francis Fedric: While in Slavery, An Escaped Slave After Fifty Years of Bondage* (Birmingham: Thomas and Jones, 1859), [12 pp.]; *Slave Life in Virginia and Kentucky, or Fifty Years of Slavery in the Southern States of America* (London: Wertheim, Macintosh and Hunt, 1863), [c.110 pp.].

Ukawsaw Gronniosaw (1710–?), also known as James Albert, was born in Borno, kidnapped as a teenager and taken to America, where he worked as a house slave. After manumission he went to sea on a privateer. He signed up with Admiral Pocock's fleet and came to England. There he married a white woman and they and their children often lived in poverty.

Bibliography: His book, *A Narrative of the Remarkable Particulars in the Life of James Albert Ukawsaw Gronniosaw, An African Prince, related by himself* (Bath: W. Gye Printer, [1772]; various editions) was recorded for him by Hannah More. 1840 edition, reprinted by Kraus Reprints: Nendeln, 1972.

C.L.R. [Cyril Lionel Robert] James (1901–89) was a writer, theorist, and activist. He was born in Tunapuna, Trinidad. He lectured at Queen's Royal College and the Teacher's Training College in Port of Spain. In 1932 he went to London and involved himself in Pan-African politics. He worked as a cricket columnist for the *Manchester Guardian* from 1933 onwards. From 1938 he lived in the United States and was involved in the American Trotskyite movement. He was interned, expelled, and deported to Britain in 1953. In 1958 he returned to Trinidad, leaving for England in 1962, but again returned to Trinidad as a cricket journalist in 1965. Although placed under house arrest, he formed the Workers and Farmers Party which was unsuccessful in the 1966 elections in Trinidad. During 1967–8 he lectured in East and West Africa. Between 1968 and 1980 he was permitted to re-enter the United States for various university appointments, but was mainly based in England. In 1981 he settled in Brixton, London, where he died in 1989.

Bibliography: James published short stories in Trinidad in *The Beacon* magazine, and his novel in England, *Minty Alley* (London: Secker and Warburg, 1936). A prolific writer, some of his most important publications include: *The Life of Captain Ciprian*: (Nelson, Lancs.: Coulton and Co., 1932). Condensed and reprinted as *The Case for West Indian Self-Government* published by L. and V. Woolf, Day to Day Pamphlets, no.16 (London: Hogarth Press, 1933); *The Black Jacobins: Toussaint L'Ouverture and the San Domingo Revolution* (London: Secker and Warburg, 1938). Reprinted (London: Allison and Busby, 1980); *Mariners, Renegades, and Castaways: The Story of Herman Melville and the World We Live In* (New York: The Author, 1953); (London: Allison and Busby, 1985); *Beyond a Boundary* (London: Stanley Paul Hutchinson, 1963). Reprinted (New York: Pantheon, 1983), (London: Serpent's Tail, 1994); *The Future of the Present. Selected Writings* (London: Allison and Busby, 1977); *Spheres of Existence: Selected Writings* (London: Allison and Busby, 1980); *At the Rendezvous of Victory. Selected Writings* (London: Allison and Busby, 1984); *World Revolution* (London: Secker and Warburg, 1937, 1971); *A History of the Pan African Revolt* (London: The Author, 1938, 1986); *Notes on Dialectics: Hegel, Marx, Lenin* (1948 private circulation; 1965 mimeographed; 1980); *Facing Reality* (Port of Spain: PNM, 1960, [1973]); *Modern Politics* (Port of Spain: PNM, 1960, 1973).

Thomas Lewis Johnson (1836–c.1910) was born in Virginia to a freeman and an enslaved mother. He and his wife Henrietta were liberated in 1865 when northern troops took Richmond. Johnson and his wife went to New York and in 1876 they sailed for England where Johnson studied before going to Africa as a Baptist missionary.

Bibliography: *Africa for Christ. Twenty-Eight Years a Slave* (London: Yates Alexander and Shepheard [sic], 1882); *Twenty-Eight Years a Slave, or the Story of My Life in Three Continents* (Twenty-eight years a Slave in Virginia, afterwards, at Forty years of age, a Student in Spurgeon's College, Missionary in Africa, Evangelist in England), seventh edition (Bournemouth: W. Mate and Sons, 1909).

Sake Dean Mahome[d/t] (1759[or 1749]–1851) was born in Patna, Bihar to a family with a tradition of serving the Moghul empire. At an early age, from 1769 to 1784 he worked for the East India Company's army for Captain Baker, finally rising to Subidar (captain) rank. In 1784, when Baker returned to Britain, Dean Mahomed resigned from his position to accompany him. He first settled in Cork, married and published his first book, *The Travels of Dean Mahomet.* He moved to London in c.1807, where he worked as a medical practitioner and then as the owner of an Indian 'coffeehouse', before settling in Brighton in 1812. When he arrived in Brighton it was a growing health resort. Dean Mahomed introduced an Indian vapour baths and shampooing firm and went on to cure ailments – and to make a name for himself. He was appointed 'the Shampooing Surgeon to George IV' and became superintendent of the Royal Baths at the Brighton Pavilion. Dean Mahomed's second book, *Shampooing*, described the cases he cured.

Bibliography: *Shampooing; or Benefits Resulting from the Use of the Indian Medicated Vapour Bath...* (Brighton: The Author, 1822; second edition 1826; third edition, 1832); *The Travels of Dean Mahomet, a native of Patna in Bengal, through several parts of India, while in the service of the Honourable East India Company. Written by himself, in a series of letters to a friend,* 2 vols. (Cork, 1794). Michael H. Fisher, *The first Indian Author in English, Dean Mahomed (1759–1851) in India, Ireland and England* (Delhi: Oxford University Press, 1996), includes a complete reprint of the travels; Michael H. Fisher, ed. *The Travels of Dean Mahomet: An Eighteenth-Century Journey through India* (Berkeley: University of California Press, 1997).

Behramji Merwanji Malabari (1853–1912), a Parsi from Bombay, arrived in London in 1890 as an established poet and journalist, writing in Gujarati as well as English. He came to lobby support from English reformers and politicians for a reform of Hindu marriage customs. He wrote about his experiences in London in *The Indian Eye on English Life* (1893).

Bibliography: *The Indian Muse in English Garb* (Bombay: The Reporters' Press, 1876), [collection of poems in English]. Reprinted (Bombay: The Reporters' Press, 1877); *Infant Marriage and Enforced Widowhood in India: Being a Collection of Opinions for and Against Received by B.M. Malabari from Representative Hindu Gentlemen and Officials and Other Authorities* (Bombay: Voice of India Printing Press, 1887); *An Appeal from the Daughters of India* (London: Farmer and Sons, 1890); *The Indian Eye on English Life; or, Rambles of a Pilgrim Reformer* (Westminster: Archibald Constable, 1893) (also published the same year in Bombay).

Una Marson (1905–65) was born and educated in Jamaica, where she founded and edited the first Caribbean women's magazine, *Cosmopolitan*. She travelled to England in 1932, and there worked for The League of Coloured Peoples as secretary and as editor of its magazine, *The Keys*. She also worked for the Emperor Haile Selassie, and spoke as a delegate in international women's conventions. Marson published four volumes of poetry, wrote at least two plays, and produced the BBC series *Calling the West Indies* and contributed to the BBC programme *Voice*.

Bibliography: *Tropic Reveries* (Kingston, Jamaica: Gleaner 1930); *Heights and Depths* (Kingston, Jamaica: The author, 1931); 'At What a Price' (unpublished playscript, 1932, British Library); *The Moth and the Star* (Kingston, Jamaica: Gleaner 1937. publ. by the author); 'Pocomania. A New Three Act Play', in *Anglophone Karibik-USA. Gulliver* 30 (1991) ed. Michael Hoenisch and Remco van Capelleveen, pp. 117–147; *Towards the Stars* (University of London Press, 1945). Short Stories: 'Sojourn', *Cosmopolitan* (February 1931); 'Christmas on Poinsettia Island', *American Junior Red Cross News* 42, 3 (1960). Delia Jarrett-Macaulay, *The Life of Una Marson, 1905–1965* (Manchester University Press, 1998); Erica Smilowitz, 'Marson, Rhys, and Mansfield' (Ph.D. thesis, University of New Mexico, 1984).

Aubrey Menen (1912–89) was born and educated in London, the son of an Indian businessman and an Irish woman. After obtaining his degree from the University of London, he worked in India for some years as an education officer, returning to England in 1947. In 1948 he moved to Italy, where he lived and wrote for some thirty years. He died in Trivandrum, Kerala where he spent the last eight years of his life. He was a prolific writer of novels, travel books, and biographical works. He also published an adapted version of the *Ramayana*, which was banned in India because it was considered irreverent.

Bibliography: Autobiographies: *Dead Man in the Silver Market* (London: Chatto and Windus, 1954); *Space Within the Heart* (London: Chatto and Windus, 1970). Novels: *The Prevalence of Witches* (London: Chatto and Windus, 1947); *The Stumbling Stone* (London: Chatto and Windus, 1949); *The Backward Bride* (London: Chatto and Windus, 1950); *The Duke of Galladoro* (London: Chatto and Windus, 1952); *The Abode of Love* (London: Chatto and Windus, 1957); *The Fig Tree* (London: Chatto and Windus, 1959); *SheLa: A Satire* (London: Hamish Hamilton, 1964); *A Conspiracy of Women* (London: Hamish Hamilton, 1966); *Fonthill* (London: Hamish Hamilton, 1974); *Four Days of Naples* (London: Hamish Hamilton, 1979). Travel books and cultural studies: *The Ramayana as Told by Aubrey Menen* (London: Chatto and Windus, 1954); *Rome for Ourselves* (London: Thames and Hudson, 1960); *Speaking the Language Like a Native: Aubrey Menen on Italy* (London: Hamish Hamilton, 1962); *Cities in the Sand* (London: Thames and Hudson, 1973); *The New Mystics and the True Indian Tradition* (London: Thames and Hudson, 1974); *London* (Amsterdam: Time-Life Books, 1976); *Venice* (Amsterdam: Time-Life Books, 1977).

John E. Ocansey (?–1889) was enslaved as a child by the prosperous merchant William Narh Ocansey in Addah/Ada, Gold Coast (today's Ghana). He was subsequently adopted by Ocansey and later married his daughter. In 1880 he was sent on the first of two visits to Liverpool and London to observe a lawsuit for the family. His book *African Trading* describes the author's encounters with Victorian England.
Bibliography: *African Trading; or the Trials of William Narh Ocansey* (Liverpool, 1881).

Alice M. Sorabji Pennell (c.1870–1951), Cornelia Sorabji's youngest sister, trained as a doctor, and worked on the North-West Frontier with her husband, Theodore Leighton Pennell. After his death in 1912, she and her young son moved to England, where she died in 1951. She is the author of three novels, and also wrote two biographies of her husband, also published under the names of Alice M. Pennell or Mrs Theodore Pennell.
Bibliography: As Alice M. Pennell, *Pennell of the Afghan Frontier, the Life of Theodore Leighton Pennell* (London: Seeley, Service, and Co., 1914); *A Hero of the Afghan Frontier: The Splendid Life Story of T.L. Pennell* ... (London: Seeley, Service, and Co., 1915). As Mrs Theodore Pennell: *Children of the Border* (London: John Murray, 1926); *The Begum's Son* (London: John Murray, 1928); *Doorways of the East: An Indian Novel* (John Murray: London, 1931).

Mary Prince (c.1788–?) was born a slave in Bermuda. She laboured in a number of Caribbean islands, was baptized in 1817, married in 1826, and was taken to London by her owners in 1828. Missionaries of the Moravian church offered support and the Anti-Slavery Society took up her case. Thomas Pringle employed her as a domestic and attempted to buy her freedom, but her owners refused. Prince was therefore unable to rejoin her husband in the West Indies, stayed in England and fought her case. Her autobiography *The History of Mary Prince*, the first such account by a back female slave, was very popular and achieved three editions in 1831, the first year of publication. Her narrative was dictated to Susanna Strickland of the Anti-Slavery Society and edited by its secretary, Thomas Pringle. The book entailed a widespread public debate on slavery but Prince legally remained a slave until 1833/4 when slavery was abolished in the British colonies.
Bibliography: *The History of Mary Prince, A West Indian Slave. Related by Herself* (London, 1831 [three editions, second edition lost]). Reprinted in H.L. Gates Jr, ed. *Six Women's Slave Narratives* (Oxford University Press, 1988); Moira Ferguson, ed. *The History of Mary Prince* (Ann Arbor: University of Michigan Press, 1993); Sara Salih, ed. *The History of Mary Prince* (Harmondsworth: Penguin, 2000).

Moses Roper (c.1810–18??), born in North Carolina, was the son of his master, Henry Roper. The light-skinned son and mother were sold shortly after Moses' birth. After many unsuccessful attempts to escape, Roper finally

obtained a forged pass and worked as a steward on a ship sailing to New York
from Savannah. Fearing recapture (when seeing advertisements for him in local
newspapers) Roper left for England, arriving in Liverpool in 1835. Assisted by
many prominent abolitionists, he received a university education in London.
He gave 'upward of 2,000 lectures' to reform and abolitionist societies, and sold
25,000 copies of his book in English, and another 5,000 in Welsh translation.
After nine years in Britain he emigrated to Canada.

Bibliography: *A Narrative of the Adventures and Escape of Moses Roper from American
Slavery. With a Preface by the Rev. T. Price* (London: Darton, Harvey, and Darton,
1837).

Ignatius Sancho (1729–80) was a one of the spokesmen for the black community of his time. He was born on a slave-ship, separated from his parents in
infancy and then sold to three women in Greenwich, who denied him education. In his teenage years Sancho became the protégé of the Duke of Montagu
[sic] and he later ran away (c.1749 or 50), seeking the protection of the Montagu household, where he met the novelist Sterne and the actor David Garrick.
He developed an interest in painting, the theatre, and composed music. Joseph
Jekyll's memoir, prefixed to the letters, suggests that Sancho also gambled in
middle life. He married and his wife Anne gave birth to six children. When
too ill to work as household servant, Sancho and his wife set up a grocery shop
in Mayfair. Sancho's two-volume *Letters of the late Ignatius Sancho, an African* were
published posthumously in London in 1782. Jekyll mentions two plays which are
now lost and also a 'Theory of Music'. He also published essays in newspapers,
and a collection of his musical compositions.

Bibliography: *Letters of the late Ignatius Sancho, an African. In two volumes. To which
are prefixed, memoirs of his life* (London: J. Nichols, 1782; second ed. London: J.
Nichols, 1783; third ed. Dublin, 1784 and London, 1784; fifth ed. London:
William Sancho, 1802/3). Edwards, Paul, ed. facsimile of fifth edition, with an
introduction and notes by Paul Edwards (London: Dawson, 1968); Edwards,
Paul and Polly Rewt, eds. *The Letters of Ignatius Sancho.* (Edinburgh University
Press, 1994, based on the fifth ed., 1802/3); Carretta, Vincent, ed. *Letters of the
late Ignatius Sancho, An African*, introduction and notes by Carretta (London and
New York: Penguin 1998). Wright, Josephine R.B. ed. *Ignatius Sancho (1729–
1780), An Early African Composer in England: The Collected Editions of His Music in
Facsimile* (New York: Garland, 1981).

Mary Seacole (1805–84), daughter of a Scottish army officer and free black
woman, was born a free woman in Jamaica. She practised as a doctor and nurse
and also as a hotelier in Jamaica, Panama, and Columbia. During the Crimean
War she worked as a nurse and was recognized alongside Florence Nightingale.
She published her autobiography in 1857.

Bibliography: *The Wonderful Adventures of Mrs Seacole in Many Lands* (London:
James Blackwood, 1857). Reprinted: Henry L. Gates, ed. with introduction
by William Andrews (Oxford University Press, 1988); Z. Alexander and Audrey

Dewjee, eds., *The Wonderful Adventures of Mary Seacole in Many Lands* (Bristol: Falling Wall Press, 1984).

Cornelia Sorabji (1866–1954) was born a Parsi in Nasik, India. She studied in Poona and won an award to study in Britain which, because she was a woman, was not awarded to her. Instead she taught English in Ahmedabad until her savings and a scholarship enabled her to study at Somerville Hall, Oxford from 1889. She read law, wishing to help women in *purdah*. A degree was awarded her, but women remained barred from the legal profession until 1919. She became a member of Lincoln's Inn in 1922. From 1894 she practised legal and welfare work in India for almost thirty years; she retired in 1929 and settled in England. Between 1901 and 1934 she published at least thirteen books and pamphlets, including autobiography, biography, short stories, and drama. She was also an organizer and editor for an anthology entitled *Queen Mary's Book of India* (Harrap: London, 1943).
Bibliography: A list of Cornelia Sorabji's publications are included in the main Bibliography, including *Love and Life Behind the Purdah* (London: Fremantle and Co., 1901); *The Purdahnashin* (Calcutta: Thacker, Spink, and Co., 1917), with a foreword by the Countess of Minto; *India Calling: The Memories of Cornelia Sorabji* (London: Nisbet and Co., 1934; *India Recalled* (London: Nisbet and Co, 1936).

P.T. Stanford (c.1859–19??) was born a slave and separated from his mother at the age of three. He was kidnapped by Indians and lived with them for over two years during the Civil War. Being adopted by Mr Perry Stanford of Boston he was named after him. After running away he lived in the streets with other children and started earning money as a shoeblack at the age of twelve. He was later baptized, sought to become a minister, and obtained a licence to preach as a member of Bereas Baptist Church. He worked his way through Suffield College, graduated in 1881 and took up a position as missionary to coloured people in Hartford, Connecticut. He arrived in Liverpool in 1883 where he pleaded the cause of coloured people in Canada. However, robbed of his money on the voyage and not being helped by his contacts he faced continued hardship and some opposition from his congregations. He wrote and published his autobiography.
Bibliography: Rev. P.T. Stanford, *From Bondage to Liberty: Being the Life Story of the Rev P.T. Stanford who was Once a Slave! and is Now the Recognised Pastor of an English Baptist Church* (London: Smethwick, 1889). First edition 65 pp. He also refers to a publication by himself titled 'Cry of Ex-Slaves'.

Robert Wedderburn (c.1761–c.1835) was born in Jamaica and died in London. The wealthy Scottish Jamaican, James Wedderburn, and one of his slaves, were Robert's parents. In 1778 he came to England, working in the navy and as a privateer. He then worked as a tailor before becoming a Unitarian preacher, founding a sect he called 'Christian Diabolists or Devil Worshippers'. He also kept a brothel and published a radical newsletter, *Axe to the Root*. He was imprisoned for blasphemy in 1820, and in 1831 received a two-year sentence of hard labour for operating a bawdy house.

Bibliography: *Truth, Self-supported: Or, A Refutation of Certain Doctrinal Errors Generally Adopted in the Christian Church*, by Robert Wedderburn, (a Creole from Jamaica) (London: Printed the Author, by W. Glindon; and sold by G. Riebau, [1795?]); *'The Horrors of Slavery' and Other Writings*, ed. with introduction by Ian McCalman (Cambridge University Press, 1991); Iain McCalman, *Radical Underworld: Prophets, Revolutionaries and Pornographers in London, 1795–1840* (Cambridge University Press, 1988).

Bibliography

Achebe, Chinua. 'The Role of the Writer in the New Nation', *Nigeria Magazine* 81 (1964), pp. 157–60.
'Work and Play in Tutuola's *The Palm-wine Drinkard*', *Okike* 14 (September 1978), pp. 25–33.
Acholonu, Catherine. 'The Home of Olaudah Equiano – a Linguistic and Anthropological Survey', *Journal of Commonwealth Literature* 22 (1987), pp. 5–16.
Ali, Duse Mohamed. See Duse, Mohamed Ali.
Allen, W.G. *The American Prejudice Against Color: An Authentic Narrative, Showing how Easily the Nation Got into an Uproar*. London: W. and F.G. Cash, 1853. Reprinted by New York, Arno Press, Inc., 1969.
A Short Personal Narrative. Dublin: William Curry and Co., 1860.
Anand, Mulk Raj. *The Golden Breath: Studies in Five Poets of the New India*. London: John Murray, 1933.
Untouchable. Bombay: Kutub Popular Books, nd. First published London: Laurence Wishart, 1935.
The Coolie. London: Laurence Wishart, 1936.
Two Leaves and a Bud. London: Laurence Wishart, 1937.
The Village. London: Hutchinson, 1939.
Across the Black Waters. Bombay: Kutub Publishers, 1955. First published London: Laurence Wishart, 1940.
Apology for Heroism: A Brief Autobiography of Ideas. Bombay: Kutub-Popular, 1957. First published London: Hutchinson, 1945.
Conversations in Bloomsbury. London: Wildwood House, 1981.
'Talking of Tambi: The Dilemma of the Asian Intellectual', in *Tambimuttu: The Bridge Between Two Worlds*. Ed. Jane Williams. London: Peter Owen, 1989, pp. 191–201.
Anon. *Hartley House, Calcutta*. London: n.p., 1789.
Arnold, Matthew. *On the Study of Celtic Literature*. London: Smith, Elder and Co., 1867.
Barker, Francis, Hulme, Peter, and Iversen, Margaret. *Colonial Discourse/Post-colonial Theory*. Manchester University Press, 1994.
Barrell, John. *English Literature in History, 1730–80*. London: Hutchinson, 1983.

Behn, Aphra. *Oroonoko*. Ed. Joanna Lipking. New York: W.W. Norton, 1997.

Benson, E. and Conolly, L.W. *The Encyclopedia of Post-Colonial Literatures in English*. London: Routledge, 1994.

Berry, James. *Lucy's Letters and Loving*. London and Port of Spain: New Beacon, 1982.

Berry, James. ed. *Bluefoot Traveller: Poetry by West-Indians in Britain*. London: Limestone Publications, 1964; revised edition Harrap, 1981; Nelson, 1985.

  Chain of Days. London: Oxford University Press, 1985.

  News for Babylon: The Chatto Book of West Indian-British Poetry. London: Chatto and Windus, 1984.

Berry, Margaret. *Mulk Raj Anand, the Man and the Novelist*. Amsterdam: Oriental Press, 1971.

Bhabha, Homi. 'Re-Inventing Britain: A Manifesto', in *British Studies Now (Re-Inventing Britain: Identity, Transnationalism, and the Arts)*, no.9 (April 1997). London: The British Council, 1997. Reprinted in *Wasafiri*, no.29 (Spring 1999), pp. 38–43.

Blake, Ann, Gandhi, Leela, and Thomas, Sue. *England Through Colonial Eyes in Twentieth-Century Fiction*. Basingstoke: Palgrave, 2001.

Bland, Sterling Decatur. *Voices of the Fugitives: Runaway Slave Stories and Their Fictions of Self-Creation*. Westport, Conn.: Greenwood Press, 2000.

Blunt, William Scawen. *My Diaries*. London: Martin Secker, 1919.

Boehmer, Elleke, ed. *Empire Writing*. Oxford University Press, 1998.

Bolt, Christine. *The Anti-Slavery Movement and Reconstruction: A Study of Anglo-American Cooperation, 1833–1877*. London: Oxford University Press, 1969.

  Victorian Attitudes to Race. London: Routledge, 1971.

Bontemps, Arna, ed. *Great Slave Narratives*. Boston: Beacon Press, 1969.

Brewer, John. *Party Ideology and Popular Politics at the Accession of George III*. Cambridge University Press, 1976.

Brody, Jennifer DeVere. *Impossible Purities: Blackness, Femininity, and Victorian Culture*. Durham, N.C.: Duke University Press, 1998.

Brown, John. *Slave Life in Georgia: A Narrative of the Life, Suffering, and Escape of John Brown, Fugitive Slave, Now in England*. Ed. L.A. Chamerovzow. London: L.A. Chamerovzow, 1855.

  Slave Life in Georgia: A Narrative of the Life, Suffering, and Escape of John Brown, Fugitive Slave. Ed. F.N. Boney. Savannah, Ga.: Beehive Press: Library of Georgia, Savannah, 1991.

Brown, Laura. 'The Romance of Empire: *Oroonoko* and the Trade in Slaves,' in *The New Eighteenth Century: Theory, Politics, Literature*. Ed. F. Nussbaum and L. Brown. New York and London: Methuen, 1987, pp. 41–61.

Buhle, Paul, ed. *C.L.R. James: His Life and Work*. London: Allison and Busby, 1986.

  C.L.R. James: The Artist as Revolutionary. London: Verso, 1988.

Burton, Antoinette. *At the Heart of the Empire: Indians and the Colonial Encounter in Late-Victorian Britain*. Berkeley: University of California Press, 1998.

Carretta, Vincent. 'Olaudah Equiano or Gustavus Vassa? New Light on an Eighteenth-Century Question of Identity', *Slavery and Abolition* 20, no.3 (December 1999), pp. 96–105.

Carretta, Vincent, ed. *Olaudah Equiano: The Interesting Narrative and Other Writings*. Harmondsworth: Penguin, 1995.

Unchained Voices: An Anthology of Black Voices in the English-Speaking World of the Eighteenth Century. Lexington: University Press of Kentucky, 1996.

The Letters of the Late Ignatius Sancho, An African. Harmondsworth: Penguin, 1998.

Casely Hayford, J.E. *Gold Coast Native Institutions*. London: Sweet and Maxwell, 1903.

Ethiopia Unbound. London: C.M. Phillips, 1911. Extract reprinted in Elleke Boehmer, ed. *Empire Writing*. Oxford University Press, pp. 361–68.

Cirker, Blanche, ed. *1800 Woodcuts by Thomas Bewick and His School*. New York: Dover, 1962.

Clarkson, Thomas. *An Essay on the Slavery and Commerce of the Human Species, particularly the African*. London: J. Phillips, 1786.

Cobham, Rhonda. 'The *Caribbean Voices* Programme and the Development of West Indian Short Fiction: 1945–1958', in *The Story Must be Told: Short Narrative Prose in the New English Literatures*. Ed. Peter O. Stummer. Bayreuth: Koningshausen/Newman, 1986.

Cobham, Rhonda and Collins, Merle, eds. *Watchers and Seekers: Creative Writing by Black Women*. London: The Women's Press, 1987.

Colley, Linda. *Britons: Forging the Nation 1707–1837*. London: Pimlico, 1994.

Cowper, William. *Poetical Works*. Ed. H.S. Milford. London: Oxford University Press, 1967.

Craft, William. *Running a Thousand Miles for Freedom: Or The Escape of William and Ellen Craft from Slavery*. London: William Tweedie, 1860. Reprinted in Arna Bontemps, ed. *Great Slave Narratives*. Boston: Beacon Press, 1969, pp. 269–331. Reprinted with a foreword and biographical essay by R.J.M. Blackett. Baton Rouge: Louisiana State University Press, 1999.

Cugoano, Quobna Ottobah. *Thoughts and Sentiments on the Evil and Wicked Traffic of Slavery and Commerce of the Human Species, Humbly Submitted to the Inhabitants of Great Britain, by Ottobah Cugoano, A Native of Africa*. London: T. Becket, 1787. Facsimile edition reprinted and edited by Paul Edwards. London: Dawson, 1968.

Thoughts and Sentiments on the Evil of Slavery; or the Nature of Servitude as Admitted by the Law of God, Compared to the Modern Slavery of the Africans in the West-Indies; In an Answer to the Advocates for Slavery and Oppression. Addressed to the Sons of Africa, by a Native. London: The Author, 1791.

Thoughts and Sentiments on the Evils of Slavery. Ed. Vincent Carretta. Harmondsworth: Penguin, 1999.

Curtin, Philip D., ed. *Africa Remembered: Narratives by West Africans from the Era of the Slave Trade*. University of Wisconsin Press, 1967.

Curtis, Lewis Perry, ed. *Letters of Laurence Sterne*. Oxford University Press, 1965.

Dabydeen, David. *Slave Song*. Sydney: Dangaroo Press, 1984.
  Hogarth's Blacks: Images of Blacks in Eighteenth-Century English Art. Kingston-upon-
    Thames: Dangaroo Press, 1985.
  Coolie Odyssey. London: Hansib, 1988.
  The Intended. London: Secker and Warburg, 1991.
  Turner: New and Selected Poems. Chatto and Windus, 1994.
Dabydeen, David, ed. *The Black Presence in English Literature*. Manchester Univer-
    sity Press, 1985.
D'Aguiar, Fred. *Mama Dot*. London: Chatto and Windus, 1985.
  Airy Hall. London: Chatto and Windus, 1989.
  Feeding the Ghosts. London: Vintage, 1998.
Darwin, Charles. *The Variation of Animals and Plants under Domestication*. London:
    John Murray, 1868.
Davis, David Brion. *The Problem of Slavery in Western Culture*. Ithaca, N.Y.: Cornell
    University Press, 1975.
Desani, G.V. *All About H. Hatterr*. New Delhi: Penguin Books India, 1998.
    First published (as *All About Mr Hatterr, A Gesture*). London: Francis Aldor,
    1948.
  Hali: A Poetic Play. Calcutta: Writers' Workshop, 1967. First published London:
    Saturn Press, 1950.
  Hali and Collected Stories. Kingston, N.Y.: McPherson and Co., 1991.
Donnell, Alison and Welsh, Sarah Lawson, eds. *The Routledge Reader in Caribbean
    Literature*. London: Routledge, 1996.
Duffield, Ian. 'John Eldred Taylor and West African Opposition to Indirect
    Rule in Nigeria,' *African Affairs* 70 (1971), pp. 252–68.
  'Duse Mohamed Ali and the Development of Pan-Africanism, 1866–1945.'
    Ph.D. dissertation, Edinburgh University, October 1972.
  'Duse Mohamed Ali: His Purpose and His Public,' in *The Commonwealth
    Writer Overseas*. Ed. Alastair Niven. Brussels: Librairie Marcel Didier, 1976,
    pp. 151–73.
Dunbar, William. *The Poems of William Dunbar*. Ed. W. Mackay Mackenzie.
    London: Faber and Faber, 1970.
Duse, Mohamed Ali. 'White Women and Coloured Men. The Other Side of
    the Picture', *New Age* (21 January 1909), pp. 262–3.
  'Western Civilisation through Eastern Spectacles', *New Age* (4 February 1909),
    p. 301; (18 February 1909), pp. 341–2; (4 March 1909), p. 381; (25 March
    1909), p. 443 and (22 April 1909), p. 519.
  'The Situation in Egypt', *New Age* (16 June 1910), pp. 148–50.
  'France and the Egyptian Nationalists', *New Age* (29 September 1910),
    pp. 509–10.
  'Egypt's Case Stated', *T.P.'s Magazine* (November 1910), pp. 189–94.
  'Egypt's Ruin' (review article), *New Age* (22 December 1910), pp. 110–74.
  'Quo Vadis', *New Age* (23 February 1911), pp. 387–90.
  'The Good Friday Procession. An Impression', *New Age* (27 April 1911),
    pp. 606–7.

'The Coloured Man in Art and Letters', *T.P.'s Magazine* (June 1911), pp. 399–407.

In the Land of the Pharaohs: A Short History from the Fall of Ismail to the Assassination of Boutros Pasha. London: Stanley Paul, 1911.

Duse, Mohamed Ali, ed. *The African Times and Orient Review.* London, 1912–18.

Duse, Mohamed Ali, ed. *The Africa and Orient Review.* London, 1920.

Edwards, Paul and Dabydeen, David, eds. *Black Writers in Britain, 1760–1890.* Edinburgh University Press, 1995.

Emecheta, Buchi. *In the Ditch.* London: Allison and Busby, 1975.

Second Class Citizen. London: Fontana/Collins, 1977.

Equiano, Olaudah. *The Interesting Narrative of the Life of Olaudah Equiano, or Gustavus Vassa, the African Written by Himself, and Other Writings.* Ed. Vincent Carretta. Harmondsworth: Penguin, 1995.

Evaristo, Bernardine. *Lara.* Tunbridge Wells: Angela Royal Publishing, 1997.

The Emperor's Babe. London: Hamish Hamilton, 2001.

Fedric, Francis. *Life and Sufferings of Francis Fedric, While in Slavery, An Escaped Slave After Fifty Years of Bondage.* Birmingham: Thomas and Jones, 1859.

Slave Life in Virginia and Kentucky, or Fifty Years of Slavery in the Southern States of America. London: Wertheim, Macintosh and Hunt, 1863.

Ferguson, Moira. *Subject to Others: British Women Writers and Colonial Slavery, 1670–1834.* London: Routledge, 1992.

Fisch, Audrey. *American Slaves in Victorian England: Abolitionist Politics in Popular Literature and Culture.* Cambridge University Press, 2000.

Fisher, Michael H. *The First Indian Author in English: Dean Mahomed (1759–1851) in India, Ireland, and England.* New Delhi: Oxford University Press, 1996.

Fladeland, B. *Men and Brothers.* Urbana: University of Illinois Press, 1972.

Foster, Frances Smith. *Witnessing Slavery: The Development of Ante-Bellum Slave Narratives.* Greenport, Conn.: Greenwood Press, 1979.

Fryer, Peter. *Staying Power: The History of Black People in Britain.* London: Pluto Press, 1984.

Black People in the British Empire: An Introduction. London: Pluto Press, 1988.

Fulford, Tim and Kitson Peter, eds. *Romanticism and Colonialism: Writing and Empire, 1780–1830.* Cambridge University Press, 1998.

Gandhi, Leela. ' "Ellowen, Deeowen": Salman Rushdie and the Migrant's Desire', in Ann Blake, Leela Gandhi, and Sue Thomas, *England Through Colonial Eyes in Twentieth-Century Fiction.* Basingstoke: Palgrave, 2001, pp. 157–70.

Garfield, Deborah M. and Zafar, Rafia, eds. *Harriet Jacobs and 'Incidents in the Life of a Slave Girl'.* Cambridge University Press, 1996.

Gates, Henry Louis Jr, ed. *The Classic Slave Narratives.* New York: New American Library, 1987.

Six Women's Slave Narratives. Oxford University Press, 1988.

Signifying Monkey: A Theory of African-American Literary Criticism. Oxford University Press, 1988.

George, M. Dorothy. *Catalogue of Political and Personal Satires Preserved in the Department of Prints and Drawings in the British Museum*. London: The British Museum, 1978.

Gerzina, Gretchen. *Black England: Life before Emancipation*. London: John Murray, 1995.

Gibson, Donald B. 'Harriet Jacobs, Frederick Douglass, and the Slavery Debate: Bondage, Family, and the Discourses of Domesticity', in *Harriet Jacobs and 'Incidents in the Life of a Slave Girl'*. Ed. Deborah M. Garfield and Rafia Zafar. Cambridge University Press, 1996, pp. 156–78.

Gidumal, Dayarum. *The Life and Work of Behramji M. Malabari*. Byculla: Bombay Education Society Press, 1888.

    Behramji M. Malabari: A Biographical Sketch. London: T. Fisher Unwin, 1892.

Gikandi, Simon. *Maps of Englishness: Writing Identity in the Culture of Colonialism*. New York: Columbia University Press, 1996.

Gilroy, Beryl. *Black Teacher*. London: Cassell, 1976.

Gilroy, Paul. *The Black Atlantic: Modernity and Double Consciousness*. Cambridge, Mass.: Harvard University Press, 1993.

Greenberger, Alan J. *The British Image of India*. London: Oxford University Press, 1969.

Grégoire, Abbé H.B. *De la Littérature des Nègres*. Paris: n.p., 1808.

Griggs, Earl Leslie. *Thomas Clarkson, the Friend of Slaves*. London: George Allen and Unwin, 1936.

Gronniosaw, James Albert Ukawsaw. *A Narrative of the Remarkable Particulars in the Life of James Albert Ukawsaw Gronniosaw, An African Prince, related by himself*. Bath: W. Gye Printer, [1772].

Gunesekera, Romesh. *Monkfish Moon*. London: Granta, 1992.

    The Reef. London: Granta, 1994.

Guptara, Prabhu. *Black British Literature: An Annotated Bibliography*. Sydney: Dangaroo Press, 1986.

Gurnah, Abdulrazak. *Pilgrim's Way*. London: Jonathan Cape, 1983.

    Dottie. London: Jonathan Cape, 1989.

    Paradise. London: Hamish Hamilton, 1994.

Hall, Catherine. *White, Male, and Middle Class: Explorations in Feminism and History*. Cambridge: Polity Press, 1992.

Hall, Stuart. 'Cultural Identity and Diaspora', in *Colonial Discourse and Post-Colonial Theory: A Reader*. Ed. Patrick Williams and Laura Chrisman. Hemel Hempstead: Harvester Wheatsheaf, 1993, pp. 392–403.

Hamilton, Elizabeth. *Translations of the Letters of a Hindu Rajah*. London: G. and J. Robinson, 1796.

Harris, Wilson. *Palace of the Peacock*. London: Faber and Faber, 1960.

    Tradition, the Writer and Society: Critical Essays. London: New Beacon Press, 1967.

    Black Marsden. London: Faber and Faber, 1972.

Hill, Robert A., ed. *The Black Man: A Monthly Magazine of Negro Thought and Opinion*. Millwood, N.Y.: Kraus Thompson Reprints, 1975.

Hiro, Dilip. *A Triangular View*. London: Dennis Dobson, 1969.

Hobson, J.A. *The Psychology of Jingoism*. London: Grant Richards, 1901.

Hofkosh, Sonia. 'Tradition and *The Interesting Narrative*', in *Romanticism, Race, and Imperial Culture, 1780–1834*. Ed. Alan Richardson and Sonia Hofkosh. Bloomington: Indiana University Press, 1996, pp. 330–44.

Howell, T.B. *State Trials*. 33 vols. + index. London: Longman, 1826.

Hyam, Ronald. *Britain's Imperial Century, 1815–1914*. Basingstoke: Macmillan, 1993.

Jacobs, Harriet. *Incidents in the Life of a Slave Girl, Written by Herself*. Ed. Jean Fagan Yellin. Cambridge, Mass.: Harvard University Press, 1985.

James, C.L.R. *The Life of Captain Cipriani*. Nelson, Lancs.: Coulton and Co., 1932. Condensed and reprinted as *The Case for West Indian Self-Government*, published by L. and V. Woolf, Day to Day Pamphlets no.16. London: Hogarth Press, 1933.

Minty Alley. London: New Beacon Books, 1971. First published London: Secker and Warburg, 1936.

The Black Jacobins: Toussaint L'Ouverture and the San Domingo Revolution. London: Allison and Busby, 1994. First published London: Secker and Warburg, 1938.

Mariners, Renegades, and Castaways: The Story of Herman Melville and the World We Live In. London: Allison and Busby, 1985. First published New York: The Author, 1953.

Beyond a Boundary. New York: Pantheon, 1983. First published London: Stanley Paul/Hutchinson, 1963.

Toussaint L'Ouverture. Published as *The Black Jacobins*, in *A Time and a Season: 8 Caribbean Plays*. Ed. Errol Hill. Trinidad: University of the West Indies Extra Mural Studies Unit, 1976, pp. 355–420.

Spheres of Existence: Selected Writings. London: Allison and Busby, 1980.

'Discovering Literature in Trinidad: The 1930s', in *Spheres of Existence: Selected Writings*. London: Allison and Busby, 1980, pp. 237–44.

'Africans and Afro-Caribbeans: a Personal View', *Ten* 8, no.16 (1984). Reprinted in James Procter, ed. *Writing Black Britain 1948–1998*. Manchester University Press, 2000, pp. 60–3.

James, Louis. *Caribbean Literature in English*. London: Longman, 1999.

Jarrett-Macaulay, Delia. *The Life of Una Marson 1905–1965*. Manchester University Press, 1998.

Johnson, Linton Kwesi. *Dread Beat and Blood*. London: Bogle L'Ouverture Press, 1975.

Johnson, Thomas L. *Twenty-Eight Years a Slave, or the Story of My Life in Three Continents*. Bournemouth: W. Mate and Sons, 1909. (Shorter version first published 1882.)

Jonson, Ben. *The Masque of Blackness*, in *Court Masques, 1605–1640*. Ed. David Lindley. Oxford University Press, 1995, pp. 1–9.

Kaplan, Cora. 'Black Heroes/White Writers: Toussaint L'Ouverture and the Literary Imagination', *History, Workshop Journal* 46 (Autumn 1998), pp. 33–62.

Kay, Jackie. *The Adoption Papers*. Newcastle-upon-Tyne: Bloodaxe Books, 1991.
Trumpet. Basingstoke: Picador, 1998.

Kenyatta, Jomo. *Facing Mount Kenya*. London: Heinemann Educational Books, 1979. First published London: Secker and Warburg, 1938.

Khan, Mirza Abu Taleb. *Travels of Mirza Abu Taleb Khan in Asia, Africa, and Europe, During the Years, 1799, 1800, 1801, 1802, and 1803, and written by Himself in the Persian Language*. Trans. Charles Stewart. London: Longman, 1814.

Kingsley, Charles. *Charles Kingsley, His Letters and Memories of His Life*. Edited by his Wife. 2 vols. London: H.S. King and Co., 1877.

Kipling, Rudyard. *Kim*. Basingstoke: Macmillan, 1963.

Kitson, Peter J. '"Bales of Living Anguish": Representations of Race and the Slave in Romantic Writing', *ELH* 67, no.2 (Summer 2000), pp. 515–37.

Kunapipi 21, no.2 (1999).

Kureishi, Hanif. *My Beautiful Laundrette and Other Writings*. London: Faber and Faber, 1986.
The Buddha of Suburbia. London: Faber and Faber, 1990.

Lamming, George. *In the Castle of My Skin*. London: Longman, 1953.
The Pleasures of Exile. London: Michael Joseph, 1960.

Lazarus, Neil. *Nationalism and Cultural Practice in the Postcolonial World*. Cambridge University Press, 1999.

Lee, A.R.L., ed. *Other Britain, Other British*. London: Pluto Press, 1995.

Lindsay, Jack. *Mulk Raj Anand: A Critical Essay*. Bombay: Hind-Kitabs, 1948.

Longenbach, James. *Stone Cottage: Pound, Yeats, and Modernism*. Oxford University Press, 1994.

Lorimer, Douglas A. *Colour, Class and the Victorians: English Attitudes to the Negro in the Mid-Nineteenth Century*. Leicester University Press, 1978.

McCalman, Iain. *Radical Underworld: Prophets, Revolutionaries and Pornographers in London, 1795–1840*. Cambridge University Press, 1988.

MacDonald, Roderick J. '"The Wisers Who Are Far Away": The Role of London's Black Press in the 1930s and 1940s', in *Essays on the History of Blacks in Britain*. Ed. Jagdish S. Gundara and Ian Duffield. Aldershot: Avebury, 1992, pp. 150–68.

MacDonald, Roderick J., ed. *The Keys: The Official Journal of the League of Coloured Peoples*. Millwood, N.Y.: Kraus Thompson Reprints, 1976.

McKendrick, Neil, et al. *The Birth of a Consumer Society: The Commercialisation of Eighteenth Century England*. London: Hutchinson, 1982.

Mahomed, Sake Dean. *The Travels of Dean Mahomet, a native of Patna in Bengal, through several parts of India, while in the service of the Honourable East India Company. Written by himself, in a series of Letters to a friend*. 2 vols. Cork, 1794.
Shampooing; or Benefits Resulting from the Use of the Indian Medicated Vapour Bath as introduced into this Country by S.D. Mahomed. Brighton: The Author, 1826.
The Travels of Dean Mahomet: An Eighteenth-Century Journey through India. Ed. Michael H. Fisher. Berkeley: University of California Press, 1997.

Makonnen, Ras. *Pan-Africanism from Within*. Ed. Kenneth King. Nairobi, Oxford University Press, 1973.

Malabari, B.M. *The Indian Muse in English Garb*. Bombay: The Reporters' Press, 1876.

Infant Marriage and Enforced Widowhood in India: Being a Collection of Opinions for and Against Received by B.M. Malabari ... Bombay: Voice of India Press, 1887.

An Appeal from the Daughters of India. London: Farmer and Sons, 1890.

The Indian Eye on English Life; or Rambles of a Pilgrim Reformer. London: Constable, 1893.

Marrant, John. *A Narrative of the Lord's Wonderful Dealings with John Marrant, A Black*. London: Gilbert and Plummer, 1785. Reprinted in Vincent Carretta, ed. *Unchained Voices: An Anthology of Black Voices in the English Speaking World of the Eighteenth Century*. Lexington: University Press of Kentucky, 1996, pp. 110–33.

Marson, Una. *The Moth and the Star*. Kingston, Jamaica: The Author, 1937.

Towards the Stars. University of London Press, 1945.

Martin, S.I. *Incomparable World*. London: Quarter Books, 1996.

Mason, A.V. *The Four Feathers*. London: Smith, Elder, and Co., 1902.

Mathurin, Owen. *Henry Sylvester Williams and the Origins of the Pan-African Movement, 1869–1911* (Contributions in Afro-American and African Studies, no.21). London: Greenwood Press, 1976.

Menen, Aubrey. *The Prevalence of Witches*. London: Chatto and Windus, 1947.

Metcalf, Thomas R. *Ideologies of the Raj*. Cambridge University Press, 1994.

Midgley, Clare. *Women Against Slavery: The British Campaign, 1780–1870*. London: Routledge, 1992.

Mohamed, Duse. See Duse, Mohamed Ali.

Montgomery, James, Grahame, James, and Benger, E. *Poems on the Abolition of the Slave Trade*. Freeport, N.Y.: Books for Libraries Press, 1971.

More, Hannah. *Slavery: A Poem*. London: n.p., 1788.

Cheap Repository Tracts. London: J. Marshall, 1795.

Myers, Norma. *Reconstructing the Black Past: Blacks in Britain 1780–1830*. London: Frank Cass, 1996.

Naipaul, V.S. *The Mimic Men*. Harmondsworth: Penguin, 1967.

An Area of Darkness. Harmondsworth: Penguin, 1968.

The Middle Passage: The Caribbean Revisited. Harmondsworth: Penguin, 1969.

In a Free State. Harmondsworth: Penguin, 1973.

Guerrillas. Harmondsworth: Penguin, 1976.

A Bend in the River. Harmondsworth: Penguin, 1980.

A Congo Diary. Los Angeles: Sylvester and Orphanos, 1980.

Enigma of Arrival. London: Viking, 1987.

Naoroji, Dadabhai. *Poverty and Un-British Rule in India*. London: Swan Sonnenschein, 1901.

Nasta, Susheila. 'Setting up Home in a City of Words: Sam Selvon's London Novels', in A. Robert Lee, ed. *Other Britain, Other British*. London: Pluto, 1995, pp. 48–68.

Home Truths: Fictions of the South Asian Diaspora in Britain. Basingstoke: Palgrave, 2001.

Nasta, Susheila, ed. *Reading the New Literatures in a Postcolonial Era*. Cambridge: Boydell and Brewer, 2000.

Nichols, Grace. *I is a long memoried woman*. Sydney: Dangaroo Press, 1983.

The Fat Black Women and Other Poems. London: Virago, 1984.

Ocansey, John Emmanuel. *African Trading; or the Trials of William Narh Ocansey*. Liverpool: n.p., 1881.

Ogude, S.E. *Genius in Bondage: A Study of the Origins of African Literature in English*. University of Ife Press, 1983.

Okri, Ben. *The Famished Road*. London: Vintage, 1992.

Oldfield, J.R. *Popular Politics and British Anti-Slavery, 1787–1807*. Manchester University Press, 1995.

Owusu, Kwesi, ed. *Black British Culture and Society*. London: Routledge, 2000.

Pennell, Alice M. Sorabji. *Pennell of the Afghan Frontier: The Life of Theodore Leighton Pennell*. London: Seeley, Service and Co., 1914.

A Hero of the Afghan Frontier: The Splendid Life Story of T.L. Pennell, M.D. B.Sc., F.R.C.S. (Kaisir-I-Hind Medal for Public Service in India). London: Seeley, Service and Co., 1915.

The Begum's Son. London: John Murray, 1928.

Children of the Border. London: John Murray, 1926.

Doorways of the East: An Indian Novel. London: John Murray, 1931.

Phillips, Caryl. *The Final Passage*. London: Faber and Faber, 1985.

The European Tribe. London: Farrar Strauss, 1987.

The Higher Ground. Harmondsworth: Penguin, 1989.

Cambridge. London: Faber and Faber, 1991.

Extravagant Strangers. London: Faber and Faber, 1997.

The Atlantic Sound. London: Faber and Faber, 2000.

Plasa, Carl. *Textual Politics from Slavery to Postcolonialism: Race and Identification*. Basingstoke: Macmillan, 2000.

Poovey, Mary. *Uneven Developments: The Ideological Work of Gender in Mid-Victorian England*. London: Virago, 1989.

Porter, Dale H. *The Abolition of the Slave Trade in England, 1784–1807*. Hamden, Conn.: Archon Books, 1970.

Pratt, Mary Louise. *Imperial Eyes: Travel Writing and Transculturation*. London: Routledge, 1992.

Prince, Mary. *The History of Mary Prince, A West Indian Slave*. Ed. Sara Salih. Harmondsworth: Penguin, 2000.

Procter, James. *Writing Black Britain, 1948–1998*. Manchester University Press, 2000.

Quarles, Benjamin. *Black Abolitionists*. New York: Oxford University Press, 1969.

Rajan, Balachandra. 'Feminising the Feminine: Early Women Writers in India', in Alan Richardson and Sonia Hofkosh, eds. *Romanticism, Race, and Imperial Culture, 1780–1834*. Bloomington: Indiana University Press, 1996, pp. 149–72.

Ramchand, Kenneth. *The West Indian Novel and its Background*. London: Faber and Faber, 1972.

Ramdin, Ron. *Reimaging Britain: 500 Years of Black and Asian History*. London: Pluto Press, 1999.

Randhawa, Ravinder. *A Wicked old Woman*. London: The Women's Press, 1987.

Reade, Charles. *Peg Woffington*. London: Bradbury, Evans, and Co., 1868.

Rich, Paul B. *Race and Empire in British Politics*. Cambridge University Press, 1986.

Richards, David. *Masks of Difference: Cultural Representations in Literature, Anthropology and Art*. Cambridge University Press, 1994.

Richardson, Alan and Hofkosh, Sonia, eds. *Romanticism, Race, and Imperial Culture, 1780–1834*. Bloomington: Indiana University Press, 1996.

Richardson, Richard Kent. *Moral Imperium: Afro-Caribbeans and the Transformation of British Rule, 1776–1888*. Westport, Conn.: Greenwood Press, 1987.

Riley, Joan. *The Unbelonging*. London: The Women's Press, 1985.

Ripley, C. Peter, ed. *The Black Abolitionist Papers, Vol. I: The British Isles, 1830–1865*. Chapel Hill: University of North Carolina Press, 1985.

Robertson, Bruce Carlisle. *Raja Rammohan Roy: The Father of Modern India*. Delhi: Oxford University Press, 1995.

Rogers, Pat. *The Context of English Literature: The Eighteenth Century*. London: Methuen, 1978.

Roper, Moses. *A Narrative of the Adventures and Escape of Moses Roper from American Slavery*. With a preface by the Rev. T. Price. London: Darton, Harvey, and Darton, 1837.

Rose, Willie Lee. *Slavery and Freedom*. New York: Oxford University Press, 1982.

Rushdie, Salman. *Midnight's Children*. London: Jonathan Cape, 1981.

    The Satanic Verses. London: Viking Penguin, 1988.

    Imaginary Homelands: Essays and Criticism 1981–1991. London: Granta, 1991.

    East West. London: Vintage, 1995.

Saïd, Edward W. *Culture and Imperialism*. London: Chatto and Windus, 1993.

Salih, Sara, ed. *The History of Mary Prince*. Harmondsworth: Penguin, 2000.

Salkey, Andrew. *Escape to an Autumn Pavement*. London: Hutchinson, 1960.

    The Adventures of Catullus Kelly. London: Hutchinson, 1969.

    Come Home Malcolm Heartland. London: Hutchinson, 1976.

Sancho, Ignatius. *Letters of the Late Ignatius Sancho, An African*. Ed. Paul Edwards. London: Dawson, 1968.

    The Letters of Ignatius Sancho. Ed. Paul Edwards and Polly Rewt. Edinburgh University Press, 1994.

    Letters of the Late Ignatius Sancho, An African. Ed. Vincent Carretta. London and New York: Penguin, 1998.

Sandhu, S.S. 'Ignatius Sancho and Laurence Sterne', *Research in African Literatures* 29, no.4 (Winter 1998), pp. 88–105.

Sandhu, S.S. and Dabydeen, D., eds. *Slavery, Abolition, and Emancipation: Writings in the British Romantic Period, Vol. 1, Black Writers*. London: Pickering and Chatto, 1999.

Sandiford, Keith A. *Measuring the Moment: Strategies of Protest in Eighteenth-Century Afro-English Writing*. Susquhanna University Press, 1988.

Savarkar, V.D. *The Indian War of Independence of 1857*. London, 1909.

Seacole, Mary. *The Wonderful Adventures of Mrs Seacole in Many Lands*. Ed. Ziggy Alexander and Audrey Dewjee. Bristol: Falling Wall Press, 1984. First published London: James Blackwood, 1857.

Selvon, Samuel. *The Lonely Londoners*. London: Longman, 1956.

Moses Ascending. London: Longman, 1975.

Shakespeare, William. *The Norton Shakespeare*. New York: W.W. Norton, 1997.

Sharpe, Jennifer. 'The Unspeakable Limits of Rape: Colonial Violence and Counter-Insurgency', *Genders* 10 (Spring 1991), pp. 25–46. Reprinted in Williams, P. and Chrisman, L. eds. *Colonial Discourse and Postcolonial Theory, A Reader*. Hemel Hempstead: Harvester Wheatsheaf, 1993, pp. 221–43.

Shyllon, Folarin. *Black People in Britain, 1555–1833*. London: Oxford University Press for the Institute of Race Relations, 1977.

Singh, Bhupal. *A Survey of Anglo-Indian Fiction*. London: Oxford University Press, 1934.

Singh, Rashna. *Imperishable Empire; a Study of British Fiction on India*. Pueblo, Colo.: Passeggiata Press, 1988.

Smith, Simon C. *British Imperialism, 1750–1970*. Cambridge University Press, 1998.

Sorabji, Cornelia. 'Achtar: The Story of a Queen', *The Nineteenth Century* 39 (June 1896), pp. 1006–11 (reprinted in *Love and Life Behind the Purdah*).

'The Legal Status of Women in India', *The Nineteenth Century* 44 (1898), pp. 854–66.

'An Indian Plague Story', *The Nineteenth Century* 46 (September 1899), pp. 410–31 (reprinted in *Love and Life Behind the Purdah* as 'The Pestilence at Noonday').

'Behind the Purdah', *Macmillan's Magazine* 82 (May–October 1900), pp. 193–200 (reprinted in *Love and Life Behind the Purdah*).

Love and Life Behind the Purdah. London: Fremantle and Co., 1901.

'Concerning an Imprisoned Rani', *The Nineteenth Century* 50 (June–December 1901), pp. 623–38.

Sun-Babies: Studies in the Child-Life of India. London: John Murray, 1904.

Between the Twilights: Being Studies of Indian Women by One of Themselves. London: Harper and Brothers, 1908.

Social Relations: England and India. London: SPCK, 1908.

Indian Tales of the Great Ones Among Men, Women, and Bird-People. London: Blackie and Son, 1916.

The Purdahnashin. With a foreword by the Countess of Minto. Calcutta: Thacker, Spink and Co, 1917.

Shubala: A Child Mother. Calcutta: Baptist Mission Press, 1920.

Sun-Babies (second series). London: Blackie and Son, 1920.

'Therefore', *An Impression of Sorabji Kharsedji Langrana and his Wife Franscina*. London: Oxford University Press, 1924.

Gold Mohur Time: To 'Remember'. London: Alexander Moring, 1930.

Susie Sorabji, Christian-Parsee Educationist of Western India: A Memoir by Her Sister. London: Oxford University Press, 1932.

India Calling: The Memories of Cornelia Sorabji. London: Nisbet and Co., 1934.

India Recalled. London: Nisbet and Co., 1936.

Spivak, Gayatri Chakravorty, 'Can the Subaltern Speak?', in C. Nelson and L. Grossberg, eds. *Marxism and the Interpretation of Culture*. Basingstoke: Macmillan, 1988, pp. 271–313.

Stanford, Peter. *From Bondage to Liberty*... London: Smethwick, 1889.

Stein, Mark. 'The Black British Bildungsroman: Novels of Transformation.' Ph.D. dissertation. Johann Wolfgang Goethe University, Frankfurt, 2000.

Stokes, Eric. *The English Utilitarians and India*. Oxford University Press, 1959.

Syal, Meera. *Anita and Me*. London: Flamingo, 1997.

Tagore, Rabindranath. *Gitanjali* (with introduction by W.B. Yeats). London: Macmillan, 1912.

Tambimuttu, M.J. *Out of this War*. London: The Fortune Press. 1941.

Natarajah: A Poem for Mr T.S. Eliot's Sixtieth Birthday. Poetry London Pamphlet no.6. Editions Poetry London, 1948.

Tambimuttu, M.J., ed. *Poetry in Wartime*. London: Faber and Faber, 1942.

Tambimuttu, M.J. and March, Richard, eds. *T.S. Eliot*. London: Frank Cass and Co., 1948.

Teltscher, Kate. 'The Shampooing Surgeon and the Persian Prince: *Two Indians in Early Nineteenth-Century Britain*', *Interventions* 2, no.3 (2000), pp. 409–23.

Temperley, Howard. *British Anti-Slavery, 1833–1870*. London: Longman, 1972.

Thomas, Helen. *Romanticism and Slave Narratives*. Cambridge University Press, 2000.

Thomson, David. *Wild Excursions: The Life and Fiction of Laurence Sterne*. London: Weidenfeld and Nicolson, 1972.

Turley, David. *The Culture of English Anti-Slavery, 1780–1960*. London: Routledge, 1991.

Slavery. Oxford: Blackwell, 2000.

Uglow, Jenny. *Hogarth: A Life and a World*. London: Faber and Faber, 1997.

Visram, Rozina. *Ayars, Lascars, and Princes: The Story of Indians in Britain 1700–1947*. London: Pluto Press, 1986.

Asians in Britain. London: Pluto Press, 2001.

Walmsley, Anne. *The Caribbean Artists Movement, 1966–1972*. London: New Beacon Books, 1992.

Walvin, James. *The Black Presence: A Documentary History of the Negro in England, 1555–1860*. London: Orbach and Chambers, 1971.

Black and White: The Negro and English Society, 1555–1945. Harmondsworth: Penguin, 1973.

England, Slaves and Freedom, 1776–1838. Basingstoke: Macmillan, 1986.

Black Ivory: A History of British Slavery. London: Harper Collins, 1992.

Wasafiri, no.29 (Spring 1999).

Waters, Hazel. 'Putting on "Uncle Tom" on the Victorian Stage', *Race and Class* 42, no.3 (January–March 2001), pp. 29–48.

Wedderburn, Robert. *'The Horrors of Slavery' and Other Writings*. Ed. Iain McCalman. Cambridge University Press, 1991.

300   *Bibliography*

Wells, H.G. *Anticipations of the Reaction of Mechanical and Scientific Progress Upon Human Life and Thought*. London: Chapman and Hall, 1901.

West, Shearer, ed. *The Victorians and Race*. Aldershot: Scolar Press, 1996.

Wheatley, Phyllis. *Poems on Various Subjects, Religions and Moral. By Phyllis Wheatley, Negro Servant to Mr John Wheatley, of Boston, in New England*. London: A. Bell; Boston: Cox and Berry, 1773.

Whitlock, Gillian. *The Intimate Empire: Reading Women's Autobiography*. London: Cassell, 2000.

Wilson, Harriet. *Our Nig*. London: Allison and Busby, 1984. First published Boston: George C. Rand and Avery Co., 1859.

Wordsworth, William. *Poetical Works*. Ed. Thomas Hutchinson, Oxford University Press, 1969.

Wright, Richard. *White Man Listen*. New York: Doubleday Anchor, 1964.

Wynter, Sylvia. 'In Quest of Matthew Bondman: Some Cultural Notes on the Jamesian Journey', in *C.L.R. James: His Life and Work*. Ed. Paul Buhle. London: Allison and Busby, 1986, pp. 131–45.

Yeats, W.B. Introduction, in *Gitanjali* by Rabindranath Tagore. London: Macmillan, 1912.

Young, Arthur. *A Tour in Ireland*. Ed. Constantia Maxwell. Cambridge University Press, 1925.

Young Robert J.C. *Colonial Desire: Hybridity in Theory, Culture and Race*. London: Routledge, 1995.

  Postcolonialism: An Historical Introduction. Oxford: Blackwell, 2001.

Index